HEALTHY EATING

HEALTHY EATING

HEALTHY AND DELICIOUS RECIPES

bay books

CONTENTS

THE BENEFITS OF HEALTHY EATING

The food we eat does more than simply fill an empty stomach. Our physical and mental
health is directly affected by each and every morsel that passes our lips.

If you want to improve your health, both now and in the future, and the way you look and feel, a healthy lifestyle that includes regular exercise and a balanced diet is the key to achieving this goal. Your dietary habits have a direct effect on your physical and mental health. This isn't surprising when you consider that the foods and drinks you consume actually become part of your body—they are broken down by your digestive system and then absorbed into your cells to provide you with energy or materials for growth, repair and vital bodily processes. So it's true—you are what you eat. And if you don't feed your body all the elements it needs, you won't feel or perform as well as you could.

It's estimated that more than 50 per cent of people in industrialised countries die from nutrition-related diseases (heart disease, stroke, some cancers, diabetes) and many people are also overweight, which can further increase the risk of developing some diseases. This is a sad state of affairs when many of these early deaths could have been prevented by a healthy lifestyle.

Disease isn't only due to bad luck or genetics, it also depends on how well

you treat your body. Lifestyle factors play an important role in determining your state of health, which means you can actually play an active role in protecting yourself.

Many people complain of a lack of energy and vitality, and often feel tired and run-down. This is often due to poor dietary habits, which make it more difficult to cope with life's demands, and a stressful environment. By choosing the best foods for your body and by keeping active, you will feel more energetic and protect yourself against disease at the same time.

SOME BENEFITS OF A HEALTHY LIFESTYLE
- Better mental and physical performance
- A better-looking body
- A better self-image
- Higher energy levels
- A well-functioning immune system
- Lower blood cholesterol levels
- A reduced risk of many diseases
- Attaining a healthy weight without strict dieting.

Another good reason to look after your health as you grow older is that people in western societies have never had such a long life-expectancy and good quality of life to look forward to after they retire. Since the start of the 1900s, the average life-expectancy for men and women has increased by more than 20 years. From a relatively young age, we're encouraged to start saving for our retirement, but you should also be investing in your health. Like your income, your health also needs protection as you age, so that when you retire you'll be able to enjoy all the things you missed during full-time employment or parenthood. If you don't have a healthy lifestyle when you're young, you may have to spend more of your hard-earned retirement money on medication, doctors' fees and higher insurance premiums. Unlike investing in the stock market, there's no risk involved in looking after your health.

Although many people regularly take vitamin and mineral supplements, there's little evidence that they give you the same or as many health benefits as a balanced diet. Spend your money on a wide variety of good-quality fresh foods so that you don't need to take supplements, and make time to prepare some of the great-tasting recipes in this book. You'll soon see how easy it is to prepare healthy meals, and you'll wonder why anyone thinks healthy eating isn't enjoyable.

Often healthy, low-fat dishes use more flavoursome ingredients than their high-fat counterparts. Far from being boring or bland, healthy food can taste great.

WHY ALL THE CONFUSION ABOUT HEALTHY EATING?

Many people are confused about healthy eating because there is so much contradictory information published in newspapers, magazines, books and on the Internet. This information can be written by qualified health professionals and nutrition scientists, or by journalists and business people—who may not have the relevant qualifications.

Although food manufacturers are subject to strict laws preventing them from printing any misleading health claims on their products, other sources of nutrition information are not subject to the same laws, which is a constant source of frustration for health professionals. It is difficult for officials to regulate all the information that is published because there's simply too much information and advertising from so many different sources.

Some people also have a vested interest in telling you that particular diets or supplements produce certain effects because they are trying to sell you these products. Others simply don't know that they haven't researched their information thoroughly enough to be able to give you the whole story.

You need considerable training and background knowledge to be able to interpret the results from scientific studies, and also to decide whether or not the studies have used appropriate methods. Nutrition science is a young and dynamic science. As more research tools are being developed, we are learning more about the active chemicals in foods and how they affect our health. There are still many exciting new discoveries to be made.

But here's the good news—official science-based recommendations for healthy eating have changed very little over the last 20 years, despite all of the new research findings. For decades the recipe for health has been a diet based on low-fat grain products, legumes, fruits and vegetables, with moderate

amounts of lean meat and dairy products. And there's no indication that this message will change.

ABOUT THIS BOOK

The information in this book is based on current dietary recommendations from health authorities, which have been developed after careful consideration of the results from valid scientific studies.

This book is about healthy eating and the benefits you can expect from a healthy lifestyle. It is designed to provide you with accurate information about how nutrients and different foods can affect your health so you can make informed food choices that will last a lifetime. Good nutrition doesn't mean giving up all the foods you like—it means making smarter choices to help you select a diet that promotes health and provides enjoyment. If you're active and eat well most of the time, there's still room to enjoy your favourite indulgences in moderation. Better still, select a healthier version of your favourite treats. There are plenty of recipes in this book that show you how.

This book also contains practical tips for general healthy eating and cooking, as well as for weight loss and some medical conditions. If you have a medical condition, you should consult

your doctor before making any changes to your diet or exercise habits, in case they interfere with your condition or any medication you're taking. Your doctor can also refer you to a dietitian who can design a healthy diet plan that suits you. Pregnant women should also consult their doctor before making any dietary changes.

The healthy eating guidelines in this book are suitable for teenagers and children, in terms of the types of foods they should be eating most often. However, children and teenagers may need different quantities of certain foods to adults. In addition, low-fat diets are not suitable for children under five years of age, because they need more fat than adults while their bodies and brains are still developing. For more advice about the types and amounts of foods that are suitable for you and other family members, consult a qualified dietitian.

THE RECIPES

This book also contains a complete set of tested recipes that will provide you with a large range of delicious and nutritious soups, salads, main meals, desserts and snacks—plenty of ideas for everyday meals as well as special events. The recipes have been designed with three things in mind: they're easy to follow, they're healthy, and, most importantly, they're delicious. You'll find plenty of options that will suit everyone's tastes.

All of the recipes comply with the guidelines for a healthy diet, so it will be easy for you to make healthy eating part of your lifestyle. The nutrient content of an average portion is listed underneath each recipe so you can compare different foods and keep a check on your daily energy and fat intakes. There are low-fat alternatives for many popular dishes that are traditionally high in fat, as well as some totally new recipes. In many cases, the ingredients that have been used to lower the fat content of the dish have improved its nutritional quality, which means that you'll get less fat but more nutrients per mouthful. You'll also be able to taste the flavours of the low fat ingredients and seasonings used in the recipes, rather than the overriding creaminess of fat, and it's almost impossible to distinguish between reduced-fat and full-fat dairy ingredients in many of the recipes.

Fat is often used in cooking to add texture or crispness to foods, so extra ingredients have been added in place of fat in some of the recipes to maintain these qualities. This means that not all of the recipes are low in calories. Make sure that you eat normal-sized portions, so that you benefit from their low fat content.

DID YOU KNOW?

It's never too late to change your eating habits and start repairing any damage you have done to your body. The body has an amazing capacity to heal itself, especially when fed a nutritious diet. You can reduce your risk of some diseases even after only two weeks of healthy eating. Simple changes to your diet, such as eating less fat, eating fish two to three times a week, and eating fresh fruit and vegetables daily, can quickly reduce your risk of diabetes, heart attack and stroke. Health benefits are even greater if you also exercise regularly and you don't smoke. Even small changes can result in big improvements in your health and quality of life.

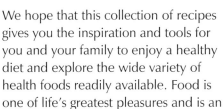

We hope that this collection of recipes gives you the inspiration and tools for you and your family to enjoy a healthy diet and explore the wide variety of health foods readily available. Food is one of life's greatest pleasures and is an important part of our culture. Sharing a meal with family or friends is an enjoyable way of nurturing important relationships. Taking the time to prepare healthy meals is a great way to care for your family

NUTRIENTS

Nutrients are the substances in foods that are used by the body to perform its essential functions.
There are seven main types of nutrients, none of which your body can live without.

WHAT ARE NUTRIENTS?

Nutrients are the substances in foods needed by the body for life, growth and repair. There are seven main types of nutrients needed by the human body, which must all be obtained from food and drink: carbohydrate, protein, fat, fibre, vitamins, minerals and water. An inadequate intake of just one type of nutrient can result in health problems either in the short or long term.

Carbohydrate, protein, fat, fibre and water are called macronutrients, because relatively large quantities of these nutrients are found in foods and they are needed in large amounts by the body. Vitamins and minerals are called micronutrients, because only small quantities of them are found in foods and they are needed in very small amounts by the body.

Scientists are still discovering more compounds in foods that have beneficial health effects, such as phytochemicals in soya beans and other plant foods, but more research is needed to determine how these nutrients work, how much we need to eat for health, and how many others exist that we don't yet know about. These unknown compounds aren't included in supplements, so a balanced diet is more likely to give you all the elements you need for good health.

WHAT DO NUTRIENTS DO?

Carbohydrate, protein and fat provide the body with the energy or fuel that it needs for life and activity.

Water, protein, fat and minerals are required to maintain the structure of cells and tissues, which form cell membranes, muscles, bones and teeth.

Water, protein, vitamins and minerals have important regulatory roles in the body. Water regulates the body's temperature. Protein is needed to make hormones and enzymes that regulate many biochemical processes. Vitamins and minerals are needed for the reactions that release the energy in carbohydrate, fat and protein; for the muscles, organs and brain to function; for bones to grow; and in the immune system to protect the body from disease.

WHAT IS ENERGY?

Most people measure their energy level by the way they feel, but nutritionists think of energy as the fuel that we obtain from the nutrients in food and drink. With the help of vitamins and minerals, the body can convert the carbohydrate, protein or fat in the food we eat into the energy that is needed to power bodily functions, such as breathing, pumping blood around the body, moving muscles and thinking.

The energy used by the body and the energy in foods is measured in kilojoules (kJ), the metric unit, or kilocalories (Cal), usually known as calories, the imperial unit. Kilojoules and kilocalories are simply two different units for measuring energy. One calorie is equal to approximately 4.2 kilojoules.

The energy value of a food depends on the amount of carbohydrate, protein, fat, fibre and alcohol it contains. Because these nutrients have different chemical structures, they provide different amounts of energy.

NUTRIENT	KILOJOULES PER GRAM	KILOCALORIES PER GRAM
Protein	17	4
Carbohydrate	16	4
Fat	37	9
Alcohol	29	7
Water	0	0

EXAMPLE: A 250 ml (1 cup) glass of full-cream milk contains 8 grams of protein, 12 grams of carbohydrate and 10 grams of fat. Energy content: (8 x 17) + (12 x 16) + (10 x 37) = 698 kJ (166 Cal).

HOW MUCH ENERGY?

The amount of energy you need each day depends on your size, age, gender and level of physical activity. If your weight is below or above the healthy range for your height (see page 34), you're consuming too little or too much energy.

If you consume less energy than you need, your body will use its own stores of carbohydrate, protein and fat for energy, resulting in weight loss. If you consume more energy than you need, it will be mainly stored as extra body fat, resulting in weight gain. A steady weight over a month or more is a good sign that you're balancing your food intake with your body's energy needs.

DAILY ENERGY REQUIREMENTS

Follow the three steps below to estimate your daily energy needs based on your age, gender and height, and how active you are.

STEP 1: Find your approximate basic metabolic rate (the amount of energy your body needs for its basic functions) from the table below, according to your age and gender.

	FEMALES (HEIGHT = 162 CM)		MALES (HEIGHT = 172 CM)	
AGE	KJ	CAL	KJ	CAL
15–22	7900	1900	10900	2600
23–50	7500	1800	9600	2300
51–65	7100	1700	8400	2000

STEP 2: For every 4 cm you are above the average height listed above, add 420 kJ (100 Cal) to the result of step 1.
For every 4 cm you are below the average height listed above, subtract 420 kJ (100 Cal) from the result of step 1.

STEP 3: If you're inactive, subtract 840 kJ (200 Cal) from the result of step 2.
If you're active, add 2100 kJ (500 Cal) to the result of step 2.
If you're exceptionally active, add 4200 kJ (1000 Cal) to the result of step 2.

EXAMPLE: A 40-year-old, 166 cm tall female is an inactive office worker. Approximate daily energy required: (7500 + 420) – 840 = 7080 kJ (1700 Cal).

SOURCE: *The 12345 + Food and Nutrition Plan. A simple guide to healthy eating and weight control*, CSIRO Division of Human Nutrition, Adelaide, Australia and the Anti-cancer Foundation of South Australia, 1992

CARBOHYDRATE

Carbohydrate-rich foods are dietary staples in countries all over the world. Whether they are eaten as rice, flour, potatoes or bread, carbohydrates supply most of our energy.

Carbohydrate is the body's main fuel source, and can supply energy at a fast rate to the brain and muscles. There are three types of carbohydrates found in foods:
- Sugars—in fruit, milk and added to foods
- starches—in grains, legumes and vegetables
- dietary fibre.

SUGARS

Sugars are the smallest or simplest form of carbohydrate, and starches and fibre are larger molecules made up of many sugars joined together in chains. The bonds that hold the sugar units together in sugars and starches can be broken by digestive enzymes.

When you eat foods containing sugars or starches, they are digested in your stomach and mostly broken down into glucose, a single-unit sugar. The glucose is then absorbed into the bloodstream, carried around the body and absorbed by cells that need it. Once it is inside a cell, glucose can be used immediately for energy or it can be stored in muscle or liver cells as glycogen, for later use.

STARCHES

Until recently, it was thought that starches were digested at a much slower rate than sugars, but we now know that this isn't always true. Some processed foods that contain starch but little intact fibre, like regular white or wholemeal bread, are digested at a much faster rate than table sugar because the flour has been ground so finely that digestive enzymes can break it down very fast. These rapidly digested starchy foods produce a faster and higher rise in your blood sugar level than some sugary foods. For these reasons, carbohydrate

Insoluble fibre is found in wholegrain products, such as grain bread, brown rice and wheat bran, and in nuts and some vegetables. Insoluble fibre does not dissolve in water, but it can bind water, which increases the bulk of the food matter in the digestive tract. This extra bulk helps move the food through your system, keeping your digestive system regular, removing waste and preventing constipation. This is one reason why a high fibre intake can help protect you against colon cancer. In addition, the bacteria that are naturally present in the human gut can ferment some of the fibre that reaches the colon, producing certain fatty acids that may help protect you from bowel disease and colon cancer.

HOW MUCH CARBOHYDRATE?

For generally active people (over two years of age), carbohydrate intake should account for at least 55 per cent of the total day's energy intake and should come from a variety of foods.

People who have very active lives, and athletes and people participating in endurance sports, need to eat more carbohydrate in order to ensure that their muscles have a sufficient supply of energy.

GOOD SOURCES OF CARBOHYDRATE

- Starches—bread, foccacia, low-fat muffins, crumpets, pikelets, breakfast cereals, oats, rice, pasta, grains, legumes, corn, pumpkin, potatoes, bananas, plain biscuits and crackers
- Sugars—table sugar, honey, golden syrup, fresh fruit, canned fruit, dried fruit, jam, dairy products
- Fibre—wholegrain bread, muesli, bran, bran cereals, dried fruit, beans, lentils, nuts, seeds, Brussels sprouts, broccoli, passionfruit, strawberries

DAILY CARBOHYDRATE REQUIREMENTS

Use the guide below to estimate your daily carbohydrate needs based on your body weight and activity level.

is no longer classified as being simple or complex, but rather slowly digested (low glycaemic index foods) or rapidly digested (high glycaemic index foods).

DIETARY FIBRE

Dietary fibre is found only in plant foods. Just as there are different vitamins and minerals, there are different types of fibre with different effects in the body. However, there are two main types of fibre: soluble and insoluble.

Soluble fibre either absorbs water or dissolves in water, and can form a gel-like substance in the gut, which slows down the rate of food digestion. Consuming lots of foods that contain soluble fibre, such as oats, oat bran, beans, barley and apples, can help control high blood sugar (glucose) and cholesterol levels, and may also help reduce hunger between meals by slowing down the rate of food digestion.

ACTIVITY LEVEL	CONTINUOUS EXERCISE	GRAMS OF CARBOHYDRATE PER KILOGRAM OF BODY WEIGHT PER DAY
Light	less than 1 hour/day	4.0–4.5
Light–moderate	1 hour/day	4.5–5.5
Moderate	1–2 hours/day	5.5–6.5
Moderate–heavy	2–4 hours/day	6.5–7.5
Heavy	4–5 hours/day	7.5–8.5

EXAMPLE: A 30-year-old, 60 kg female does 1 hour of continuous light exercise each day. Approximate daily carbohydrate required: (4.5 x 60) to (5.5 x 60) = 270–330 g.

SOURCE: *Sports Nutrition Basics*, H. O'Connor & D. Hay, J.B. Fairfax Press, Sydney, Australia, 1998

PROTEIN

While protein is often associated with strength and stamina, too much protein can be unhealthy, especially if it results in a high fat intake.

Protein is part of every body cell and is needed for growth and repair; the maintenance of body structures (muscles, bones, blood vessels, teeth); the production of enzymes and hormones that regulate the body's processes; and the production of antibodies that protect the body from infection and illness. Protein may also be used as an energy source for the body if not enough carbohydrate or fat is available.

All proteins are made up of chains of smaller units called amino acids. Each

different protein has its own unique number and order of amino acids. There are about 20 different amino acids commonly found in proteins. Nine of these amino acids cannot be made in adult human bodies and must be obtained from foods (essential amino acids). The other 11 amino acids can be made in the body or obtained from foods (non-essential amino acids).

If you don't eat enough essential amino acids, your body will obtain them by breaking down other proteins in your

body that contain them, compromising the health of your muscles.

SOURCES OF PROTEIN

Animal foods are the best source of 'complete' proteins, which contain all nine of the essential amino acids.

Plant foods usually contain 'incomplete' proteins, which lack some of the essential amino acids. However, it's possible for vegetarians to get all the essential amino acids they need by eating a variety of plant foods each day, such as grains, nuts,

THE BENEFITS OF HEALTHY EATING • 15

seeds and legumes, especially if they combine them with dairy products and eggs. In fact, many people who live in less-developed countries don't eat much meat and rely on plant foods, such as grains, legumes and vegetables, to meet their protein needs.

Many simple meals containing different protein foods have a complete set of essential amino acids, such as muesli and milk, a peanut butter sandwich, rice and lentil dhal, and baked beans on toast with cheese.

Vegans, who don't eat eggs or dairy products, need to make sure that they consume a good variety of grains, seeds, nuts and legumes each day, in order to obtain sufficient essential amino acids. This is particularly important for vegan women who are pregnant or who are trying to conceive.

HOW MUCH PROTEIN?

Although protein has many vital functions, relatively little protein is needed each day to meet the body's amino acid needs because, unlike carbohydrate, large amounts of protein are not burnt for fuel.

The amount of protein you need depends on your body weight and growth status, but this generally corresponds to 10 to 15 per cent of your daily energy intake. Generally, people in western countries eat more than enough protein.

- Healthy adults who include meat and dairy products or a variety of vegetarian foods in their diet generally need only 0.75 grams of protein per kilogram of body weight each day (53 g of protein for an average 70 kg male).
- Children from 4 years and teenagers up until the age of 18 years need slightly more protein because they are still growing, usually 1 gram of protein per kilogram of body weight each day.

- Pregnant women need more protein for their developing baby— 0.75 grams of protein per kilogram of normal body weight plus an extra 6 grams of protein each day.
- Breast feeding women need even more protein to produce breast milk and to help their body recover from childbirth—0.75 grams of protein per kilogram of normal body weight plus an extra 12 to 16 grams of protein each day.
- Some athletes and very active people undergoing regular, strenuous training, and people suffering from burns or injuries may also need more protein for tissue repair (more than 1 gram of protein per kilogram of body weight per day).

GOOD SOURCES OF PROTEIN

- Animal sources—meat, poultry, fish, seafood, eggs and dairy products
- Plant sources—legumes (beans, lentils, chickpeas), nuts, seeds, grains, grain products, soy milk, tofu, tempeh.

DAILY PROTEIN REQUIREMENTS

Use the guide below to estimate your daily protein needs based on your body weight and growth and repair needs.

CATEGORY	GRAMS OF PROTEIN PER KILOGRAM OF BODY WEIGHT PER DAY	
	MALE	FEMALE
SEDENTARY, INACTIVE PEOPLE		
Children and teenagers (4–18 years)	1.0	1.0
Adults	0.75	0.75
ENDURANCE ATHLETES		
Elite	1.6	1.2
Moderate intensity	1.2	0.9
Recreational	0.85	0.84
WEIGHT TRAINING		
Untrained, beginning of program	1.7	1.3
Trained	1.2	0.9
AVERAGE DAILY CONSUMPTION OF PROTEIN		
Children and teenagers	1–2	1–2
Adults	1–1.5	1–1.5
Athletes	1.5–4	1.5–2.8

EXAMPLES: A 30-year-old, 60 kg female does 1 hour of continuous light exercise each day. Approximate daily protein required: 0.75 x 60 = 45 g.
A 25-year-old, 68 kg male begins a heavy weight training program. Approximate daily protein required: 1.7 x 68 = 116 g.

SOURCE: *Sports Nutrition Basics*, H. O'Connor & D. Hay, J.B. Fairfax Press, Sydney, Australia, 1998

FAT

We all need some fat in our diet, but it is clear that a high intake of dietary fat, particularly saturated fat, increases the risk of serious diseases such as heart disease, stroke and some cancers.

Although many people think that all fat is 'bad', we all need a certain amount of fat to remain in good health. Dietary fat is the most concentrated source of energy in the diet (37 kilojoules per gram) and is a particularly important energy source for babies and young children. Infants start life drinking breast or formula milk, of which fat provides 50 per cent of the calories. This fat helps fuel the rapid growth and development of the brain and body that takes place during the first few years of life. Consequently, low-fat diets are not suitable for children under five years of

age. The need for fat gradually decreases as we age.

Dietary fat is a source of essential fatty acids, which cannot be made in the body in sufficient amounts and are especially important for development in children. Fat is also needed for healthy skin and nerves and is a precursor of prostaglandins, hormone-like substances that regulate many vital bodily processes.

The fat-soluble vitamins A, D, E and K are provided by dietary fat, which also

helps the body absorb these vitamins. Any extra fat that is eaten is stored in the fatty tissues of the body, so that the body has a supply of energy on hand in case its food supply becomes limited. Body fat deposits not only store energy, but also keep us warm and protect our internal organs.

The fat in foods is a mixture of three main types: saturated, monounsaturated and polyunsaturated. These fats vary in their structures and effects on blood cholesterol levels and the risk of heart disease. Foods usually contain a mixture of the three main types of fat, although one is often present in a larger amount (see page 28).

CHOLESTEROL

Cholesterol is a type of fat that is made in the body, but it can also be consumed in the diet from animal products. Most of the cholesterol in the body is found in cell membranes. It is also found in the coating around nerve cells that is needed for them to function properly. The body also needs cholesterol to make vitamin D, bile acids (for proper digestion), and hormones such as testosterone and oestrogen, needed for growth and reproduction.

If your body makes more cholesterol than it needs, the level of cholesterol in your blood rises and fatty deposits can build up in your arteries, leading to heart disease. The amount and type of fat in your diet influences the amount of cholesterol in your blood to a greater extent than the amount of cholesterol you eat.

Although there is one type of cholesterol travelling around the bloodstream, it can be attached to different carrier proteins, called lipoproteins. When determining your risk of heart disease, health professionals are concerned about the level of two types of these cholesterol carriers: low-density lipoprotein (LDL, referred to as 'bad' cholesterol) and high-density lipoprotein (HDL, referred to as 'good' cholesterol). High levels of LDL-cholesterol are a risk factor for heart disease.

HIGH FAT SOURCES

In order to control your fat intake, you need to be aware of hidden and visible fats in foods. Read the nutrient content panel on food labels to help you choose foods that contain less fat.

VISIBLE FATS

- All oils, dripping, vegetable shortening and solid frying fat (100% fat)
- Butter (80% fat); reduced-fat butter (41% fat)
- Margarine (80% fat); reduced-fat margarine (40–50% fat)
- Cream (36% fat); reduced-fat cream (27% fat)
- Cheddar cheese (28–35% fat); reduced-fat Cheddar (24% fat); Brie (29% fat)

HIDDEN FATS

- Peanut butter (52% fat)
- Milk chocolate (27% fat); chocolate-coated biscuits (24% fat); chocolate cake (18% fat)
- Croissant (24% fat)
- Cheesecake (22% fat)
- Doughnut (21% fat)
- Sausages (20% fat)
- Devon (18% fat)
- Toasted muesli (17% fat)
- Meat pie (15% fat)
- Pizza (14% fat)
- Muesli bar (13% fat)

HOW MUCH FAT?

To reduce the risk of heart disease and other health problems, dietary fat should provide no more than 20 to 30 per cent of your daily energy intake, with saturated fat providing no more than 7 per cent of the total fat intake, monounsaturated fat 13 per cent and polyunsaturated fat 10 per cent. This amounts to a total of 50 to 80 grams of fat each day for adult males and 40 to 60 grams for females.

DAILY FAT REQUIREMENTS

Use the guide below to estimate your daily fat needs based on your age, gender and activity level.

CATEGORY	APPROXIMATE GRAMS OF FAT PER DAY (BASED ON AVERAGE BODY WEIGHTS)
Weight loss	25–40
Children and inactive women	30–50
Inactive men	40–60
Active female adults and teenagers	40–70
Active male adults and teenagers	50–80

To calculate what 30% of your daily energy intake amounts to in grams of fat, multiply your daily energy intake in kilojoules by 0.3 and then divide by 37 (1 gram of fat contains 37 kJ).

SOURCE: *Sports Nutrition Basics*, H. O'Connor & D. Hay, J.B. Fairfax Press, Sydney, Australia, 1998

VITAMINS AND MINERALS

No supplement can compare with the vitamins and minerals your body will obtain from
a healthy diet based on plenty of fresh fruits, vegetables and wholegrain products.

VITAMINS

Vitamins are nutrients that are only needed in small amounts, but they have very powerful effects. They are required for the normal functioning of every organ in the body and for many important processes, such as growth, reproduction and tissue repair. Although vitamins are not a source of energy, they are needed to release the energy from dietary carbohydrate, fat, protein and alcohol. Your body can't make most vitamins, so you need to get them from your diet.

There are two classes of vitamins: fat-soluble and water-soluble vitamins. The fat-soluble vitamins (A, D, E and K) can be stored in the body, so consuming too much of them can be toxic and adversely affect your health. Fat-soluble vitamins are fairly stable during cooking and processing, but can be destroyed with exposure to air or light.

The water-soluble vitamins (vitamin C and eight B-group vitamins) dissolve in water, so excessive amounts of most of them are removed from the body in urine. However, very high doses of B vitamins, particularly vitamin B6, can cause toxicity problems. Water-soluble vitamins can be lost by soaking or boiling foods in water and may be destroyed by heat, light or air.

MINERALS

Minerals are nutrients in foods also needed in small amounts for important bodily processes, including the maintenance of the body's fluid balance, the structure of certain compounds, such as hormones, bones and teeth, the regulation of blood pressure, wound healing, and the activity of muscles and nerves. Your body can't make any of the minerals, so you need to get all of them from your diet.

There are two classes of minerals: major minerals and trace elements. The seven major minerals—calcium, sodium, potassium, magnesium, phosphorous, chloride and sulphur— are needed by the body in greater amounts than the trace elements, but both classes are equally important for health.

Nine trace elements have specific deficiency disorders and are therefore considered to be essential dietary factors—iron, copper, zinc, manganese, selenium, iodine, chromium, fluoride and molybdenum.

Minerals are more stable than vitamins, but they can be affected by food processing and preparation methods. The body's absorption of minerals from foods can be reduced or enhanced by other nutrients and components in a meal. For example, dietary fibre can reduce mineral absorption, whereas lactose sugar in milk can enhance calcium absorption. The absorption and functions of many minerals are interrelated, so a deficient or excessive intake of one mineral can affect the absorption and function of others. For example, a high iron intake can reduce zinc absorption. For this reason, high-dose mineral supplements should only be taken under medical supervision.

HOW MUCH OF EACH VITAMIN AND MINERAL?

The amount of vitamins and minerals you need each day depends on your age, gender, body size, physical activity, physiological status, medication use and lifestyle factors (pollution, smoking, stress, alcohol and fat intake). Healthy people should be able to get all the vitamins and minerals they need from a balanced and varied diet.

In many countries, committees of health experts have reviewed all of the scientific

evidence regarding the amounts of vitamins and minerals needed to prevent deficiency and promote good health. Using this data, the experts have been able to calculate recommended dietary intake (RDI) values for some nutrients, which are the amounts needed daily to prevent deficiency in practically all healthy people.

NUTRIENTS IN SUPPLEMENTS

At the moment, the perfect supplement doesn't exist, but it's clear that a balanced diet offers many health benefits.

Whole foods are a complex package of nutrients and other beneficial factors that are not found in supplements. For example, an orange contains vitamin C with carotene, folate, calcium and fibre, but you won't get these other essential elements in a vitamin C pill. Similarly, a glass of milk contains calcium with protein, vitamin D, phosphorous and magnesium—all of the nutrients needed for healthy bones, which aren't always in calcium supplements. Plant foods contain phytochemicals, which have antioxidant properties and may help protect you against cancer, heart disease and diabetes.

Many scientific studies have found that people who regularly eat plenty of fruits and vegetables have a relatively lower risk of some cancers and heart disease, but there is no good evidence to show that supplements can give you the same protection. The benefits of eating a varied, balanced diet are that fresh foods taste great and they contain an effective mixture of nutrients that work in combination to enhance your health and wellbeing.

WHEN YOU MAY NEED A SUPPLEMENT

A lack of energy is a common complaint, which many people feel is due to an inadequate intake of vitamins.

However, this could be due to a lack of sleep or exercise, or too many fatty foods, since vitamin deficiencies are rare. Nonetheless, dietary surveys indicate that many people regularly fail to consume RDI amounts of iron, zinc, calcium or magnesium. While these people may not be strictly deficient in these minerals, low body reserves of these nutrients can increase the risk of developing iron deficiency or osteoporosis over time. On the other hand, some groups of people are at risk of certain vitamin and/or mineral deficiencies simply because they absorb less or eat less than they need.

Some people don't get all the nutrients they need from their diet because they don't eat a balanced diet or they have greater nutrient requirements due to pregnancy, illness or high activity levels. Many people don't eat fruit or vegetables on a daily basis and some people remove a whole food group from their diet, such as meat or dairy products.

Skipping meals, dieting and eating lots of 'junk' foods also contributes to poor nutrition. High intakes of fat and alcohol and certain medications can increase the body's use of certain vitamins and minerals, and some illnesses and medications prevent them from being absorbed. If you need prescription medication for a period of time, ask your doctor whether it is likely to affect your vitamin or mineral needs. Check with your doctor or a dietitian as to whether a supplement could improve your health or prevent a deficiency from developing, but you should also try to improve your diet at the same time.

Even if you don't have a clinical nutrient deficiency, your doctor or dietitian may recommend a supplement if:
• you have been following a vegan diet (eat no animal products) for an extended period of time, as you may be lacking in vitamin B12 and iron

• you are elderly and don't eat much or are housebound
• you are allergic to certain foods, such as dairy products
• you are pregnant or trying to fall pregnant, as you need more folate before conception and also more iron during the first trimester of pregnancy
• you have a high alcohol intake, as this increases the risk of B group vitamin deficiencies
• you are a heavy smoker, as you need more antioxidants
• you take certain medications, such as antacids, anticonvulsants, and cholesterol-lowering drugs, which increase the need for certain micronutrients
• you are an endurance athlete or are very active, as you may need more iron and protein
• you have an eating disorder or low energy intake, as you may have low iron and calcium intakes
• you have a digestive tract disease or have had surgery.

VITAMINS AND MINERALS IN PROCESSED FOODS

Some people think that modern foods are depleted of vitamins and minerals, but supermarkets are full of nutritious foods—fresh, frozen, canned and processed. Vitamins and minerals are even added to some processed foods to replace those that are lost during manufacturing, such as in breakfast cereals and breads, or to increase the food's nutrient content, such as in some milks and drink powders.

However, heat, light and air inactivate some nutrients, and soaking foods in water can wash away some vitamins. The vitamin content of foods also decreases the longer you store them. For this reason, canned and frozen foods, which are usually processed soon after harvesting, contain equal or greater amounts of some nutrients than fresh produce, which may have been stored for a period of time before reaching the supermarket or greengrocer.

During the canning process, food is washed, prepared, sealed into the can and then pressure-cooked to sterilise the food. The absence of light, air and bacteria ensures that the natural flavours, colours and many nutrients are retained. Some minerals can leach out of food into the liquid in the can, such as brine, gravy, sauce, juice or syrup, but often the liquid is consumed with the food so most of these nutrients will be consumed.

Canned fish is a better source of calcium than fresh fish, because the canning process softens the bones so they can be eaten with the fish.

Over the last ten years, the salt content of many canned foods has been gradually reduced to help people consume less sodium, and many salt-free varieties are now available.

TIPS FOR RETAINING VITAMINS DURING COOKING

- Store all food at a cool temperature out of direct sunlight.
- Purchase fresh fruit and vegetables several times a week.
- Store fruit and vegetables in the fridge or a cool place to slow down the rate of nutrient loss.
- Use cooking methods that don't bring food into direct contact with water, such as steaming, pressure cooking, roasting, grilling, stir-frying, baking and microwaving.
- Don't thaw frozen vegetables before cooking and only reheat them until they are tender.

- Cook vegetables for the shortest time possible in the least amount of water. If boiling, bring the water to the boil first, cut up the vegetables and then add to the water. Use the remaining cooking water for soups and sauces.
- Don't use bicarbonate of soda when you are cooking vegetables.
- Don't cook vegetables in brass or copper saucepans, which can react with them.
- Minimise the washing and chopping of foods before cooking. Vegetables should not be cut up or cooked until the last minute.
- Don't soak rice before cooking it.

- Try to eat fruits and vegetables in larger pieces, rather than smaller pieces, including shredded, puréed, mashed or juiced. The smaller the pieces, the more vitamins you lose.
- Serve hot foods immediately—keeping them warm destroys vitamin C.
- Fresh foods don't always contain more nutrients than canned, bottled, frozen or packaged foods. Processed foods can be used with fresh produce to help you make quick, nutritious meals.

THE RECIPE
FOR A HEALTHY DIET

Forget about the complicated figures and calculations—health professionals have devised ten
simple steps to a healthy diet, which are discussed in detail on the following pages.

To stay healthy now and in the future, nutrition authorities recommend that you consume a variety of nutritious foods each day. These should provide you with 55 to 70 per cent of your daily energy as carbohydrate, 10 to 15 per cent as protein, and 30 per cent or less as fat. Unfortunately, most people in western societies are still eating too much fat and are not getting enough physical activity.

	WHAT WE ARE EATING*	WHAT WE SHOULD BE EATING
Energy from carbohydrate	46%	55% or more
Energy from fat	33%	20–30%
Energy from protein	17%	10–15%

*SOURCE: Selected highlights from the 1995 National Nutrition Survey, Australian Bureau of Statistics.

Trying to work out what these numbers mean in terms of the quantities and types of foods we should be eating can be difficult, so health professionals have devised the following general guidelines that highlight the main features of a healthy diet.

It's really not hard to have a healthy balanced diet—it simply means eating more of some foods and less of others. You don't have to give up your favourite indulgences completely, but you might need to treat yourself less frequently, and use healthier versions of your favourite recipes, as seen in this book. No one meal is bad as long as the total mix of foods you consume over a period of days or weeks adds up to an overall healthy diet.

These dietary guidelines have been developed as a result of the findings from scientific studies that have studied the dietary habits of large numbers of people over many years.

Breakfast: Banana bread with maple ricotta (page 69)

Lunch: Low-fat chicken Caesar salad (page 125)

Dinner: Chicken and mushroom risotto (page 196)

The diseases that these people developed over time were then examined. Results from careful laboratory experiments and dietary trials have confirmed these findings.

It's clear that a nutritious diet based on a wide range of plant foods (grain products, fruits, vegetables, legumes, nuts and seeds) offers significant protection against the most common diseases in our society.

STEP 1: EAT A VARIETY OF NUTRITIOUS FOODS EACH DAY

Although scientists continue to make new discoveries about the health benefits of different foods, the basic prescription for healthy eating has been the same for the last 20 years and will hardly change in the future. Many nutrients and other food factors are needed by your body to work together and keep it healthy and functioning normally.

TEN STEPS TO A HEALTHY DIET

1 Eat a variety of nutritious foods each day.
2 Base your diet on grain products, fruits, vegetables and legumes.
3 Eat a diet that is low in fat, particularly saturated fat.
4 Maintain a healthy body weight by balancing food intake with regular exercise.
5 If you drink alcohol, only have moderate amounts.
6 Eat moderate amounts of sugar and foods containing added sugar.
7 Choose low-salt foods and limit your use of table salt.
8 Drink plenty of water throughout the day.
9 Eat calcium-rich foods on a regular basis.
10 Make iron-rich foods a regular part of your diet.

Therefore, the basic principle of a healthy diet is to eat a variety of foods from all of the major food groups each day. This will ensure that you consume the entire range of nutrients that your body needs. Even limiting your intake of one major food group, such as dairy products or meats, can lead to a nutrient deficiency, which may affect your health in the future.

The key to healthy eating is to eat a wide range of foods, in their right proportions, most of the time. Try to eat 30 different foods each day. It's not as difficult as it sounds—muesli, salads, casseroles, stir-fries and sandwiches all contain a variety of foods—yet many people in our society eat less than 15 different foods a day.

STEP 2: BASE YOUR DIET ON GRAIN PRODUCTS, FRUITS, VEGETABLES AND LEGUMES

The healthy diet pyramid is a good guide to help you achieve the main steps for a healthy balanced diet, and is suitable for all healthy people over the age of two, in all ethnic groups. It's also the model for a healthy weight loss diet, as long as you eat sensible portions and use low-fat dairy products and lean protein foods.

The pyramid guide shows you how to eat a balanced diet by selecting a variety of foods from each of the five major food groups each day (fruits, vegetables, cereal products, dairy products, meats and alternatives). Each food group provides

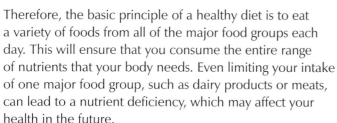

MINIMUM NUMBER OF DAILY SERVES FROM THE FIVE MAJOR FOOD GROUPS NEEDED TO ACHIEVE AT LEAST 70% OF DAILY REQUIREMENTS OF PROTEIN, VITAMINS AND MINERALS

AGE GROUP	BREAD, CEREALS, RICE, PASTA, NOODLES	VEGETABLES, LEGUMES	FRUIT	DAIRY PRODUCTS	MEAT, FISH, POULTRY, EGGS, NUTS, LEGUMES
Children 4–7 years	2	2	1	2	0.5
Children 8–11 years	3	3	1	2	1
Teenagers 12–18 years*	3.5	4	2.5	2.5	1
Adults 19+ years	4	5	2	2	1
Pregnant women	4	5	4	2	1.5
Breast-feeding women*	6	7.5	5	2.5	2

*Average requirement only. Individual needs may differ.

ADAPTED FROM: *The Australian Guide to Healthy Eating—Background information for nutrition educators*, Commonwealth Department of Health and Family Services, Australia, 1998.

some, but not all, of the nutrients you need, so you need different amounts of servings from each food group. You may also be surprised how much healthy food you can eat each day. This is because healthy foods contain fewer calories than fat-laden take-away meals and snack foods.

The bottom layer of the pyramid shows the foods that we should eat in the largest amounts, because they offer so many health benefits. These foods are important sources of energy, vitamins, minerals and fibre, and they also contain other protective compounds, such as antioxidants, phytoestrogens and resistant starch.

The high nutritional quality of these foods is one reason why people who regularly eat plenty of fresh fruit and vegetables are less likely to develop certain cancers.

Eating plenty of wholegrain foods, legumes, fruits and vegetables can also reduce the risk of heart disease, diabetes and weight gain. These foods contain relatively few calories, so by basing your meals and snacks on these foods, it's possible to lose weight without going hungry (as long as you don't add lots of mayonnaise and sour cream).

Rather than eating the same types of fruits and vegetables each week, try to eat a variety of different-coloured fruits and vegetables. This may help protect you from more diseases.

The recipes in this book will help you explore the wide variety of fruits and vegetables, legumes and grain products that are readily available in supermarkets. Healthy eating isn't about depriving yourself of great-tasting foods. Even if you are sensitive to wheat or certain fruits and vegetables, there are

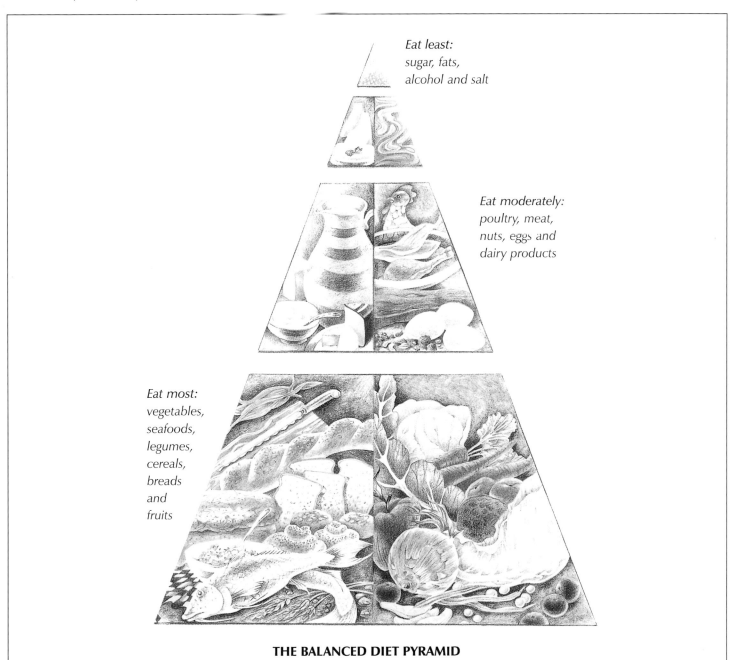

Eat least:
sugar, fats,
alcohol and salt

Eat moderately:
poultry, meat,
nuts, eggs and
dairy products

Eat most:
vegetables,
seafoods,
legumes,
cereals,
breads
and
fruits

THE BALANCED DIET PYRAMID

TOP OF PYRAMID: EAT LEAST

INDULGENCES OR EXTRAS:
NO MORE THAN 1–2 SERVES PER DAY

1 serve = 1 small doughnut
- 4 plain sweet biscuits
- 1 small slice of cake
- ½ small bar (25 g) chocolate
- 1½ scoops ice cream
- 1 can (375 ml) soft drink
- ⅓ meat pie or pasty (60 g)
- 12 (60 g) hot chips
- 1 small packet (30 g) chips
- 2 tablespoons cream or mayonnaise
- 1 tablespoon butter, margarine or oil
- 200 ml wine, 400 ml beer or 600 ml light beer (1.5 standard drinks)

MIDDLE OF PYRAMID: EAT MODERATELY

LEAN MEATS AND ALTERNATIVES:
1–2 SERVES PER DAY

1 serve = 65–100 g cooked meat
(2 small chops, 2 slices roast meat,
½ cup mince)
- 80–120 g cooked fish
- 2 small eggs
- ⅓ cup nuts
- ¼ cup seeds

LOW-FAT MILK AND DAIRY PRODUCTS:
2 SERVES PER DAY (ADULTS) 4 OR MORE
SERVES PER DAY (CHILDREN
AND TEENAGERS)

1 serve = 1 cup (250 ml) milk
- ½ cup (125 ml) evaporated milk
- 2 slices (40 g) cheese
- 1 tub (200 g) yoghurt

BOTTOM OF PYRAMID: EAT MOST

FRUIT: 3 OR MORE SERVES
PER DAY

1 serve = 1 medium piece fruit
(apple, banana, orange, pear)

- 2 small pieces fruit (apricots, kiwi fruit, plums)
- ½ cup grapes
- 1 cup diced or canned fruit
- 1½ tablespoons sultanas
- 4 dried apricots
- ½ cup (125 ml) fruit juice

VEGETABLES, INCLUDING LEGUMES:
4 OR MORE SERVES PER DAY

1 serve = 1 cup salad vegetables
- ½ cup cooked or raw vegetables
- ¾ cup (185 ml) vegetable juice
- 1½ cup cooked legumes
- 1 small potato

GRAIN PRODUCTS:
5 OR MORE SERVES PER DAY

1 serve = 2 slices bread (60 g)
- 1 medium bread roll
- 1 cup cooked rice, pasta or noodles
- 1 cup cooked porridge
- 1⅓ cups ready-to-eat breakfast cereal
- ½ cup natural muesli

still plenty of foods at the bottom of the pyramid that you can eat. The middle layer of the diet pyramid contains protein-rich foods, which should be low in fat and eaten in moderation. All of these foods, except dairy products, contain iron and zinc—minerals that many people don't eat enough of. These foods help to keep your blood, bones, skin and muscles strong and healthy, but large portions are usually not needed

(a palm-sized serving of lean meat is generally sufficient).

The foods and drinks at the top of the pyramid should be eaten in the smallest quantities, because they contain many calories but relatively few vitamins and minerals.

Eating the pyramid way isn't difficult because supermarkets are full of healthy food all year round. If you eat well and

exercise regularly most of the time, you have room for a small indulgence each day, such as a glass of wine or a small serve of ice cream. Some healthy treats, such as a cup of low-fat frozen yoghurt, can even count as one serve of dairy food. There's room to have your cake and eat it too, particularly if it's a low-fat treat, but by filling up with a regular supply of healthy foods, you probably won't crave the less healthy foods at the top of the pyramid.

A HEALTHY MENU FOR A DAY

BREAKFAST

Start with an orange, grapefruit, melon or paw paw
- A bowl of wholegrain cereal or untoasted muesli and
- 2 slices of wholegrain toast
    or
- Baked beans and fresh tomato on toast
    or
- 1 bowl of porridge (use fruit instead of sugar to sweeten)
    or
- A banana smoothie made with low-fat milk and honey

BETWEEN-MEAL SNACKS

Keep your energy levels high with low-fat yoghurt, fresh or dried fruit

LUNCH

Accompany your lunch with a couple of glasses of water
- A lentil burger on wholegrain bread with salad
    or
- California rolls with miso soup
    or
- A bowl of chunky vegetable soup with a bagel
    or
- Niçoise salad with oil-free dressing
    or
- Baked potato with salmon, capers and low-fat yoghurt
    or
- Roll-up with hummus, tabbouleh and skin-free chicken
- Finish with a piece of fruit

DINNER

Don't make this the big meal—spread out your eating evenly
- Barbecued fillet steak with spicy chutney and chargrilled vegetables
    or
- Chilli con carne with rice
    or
- Mushroom risotto
    or
- Chargrilled tuna or salmon with salsa, steamed potatoes and vegetables
    or
- Spicy vegetables with steamed couscous
- Finish with poached fruit, a baked apple or a grilled banana with low-fat yoghurt

DID YOU KNOW?

Legumes or pulses were important foods for our ancestors long before wheat became a dietary staple. Legumes have fewer calories than many foods and are a great source of protein, vitamins and minerals. They also contain soluble fibre and slowly digested carbohydrate, which provides a slow, sustained stream of energy. If eaten regularly, they can help reduce high blood cholesterol levels and will be less likely to cause flatulence.

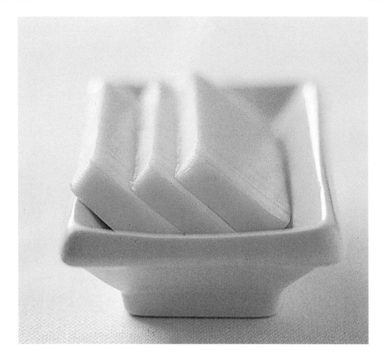

STEP 3: EAT A DIET THAT IS LOW IN FAT, PARTICULARLY SATURATED FAT

Dietary guidelines advise people to limit their fat intake, because high-fat diets:
- increase the risk of weight gain (because fat contains more calories per gram than either carbohydrate or protein, and is also less filling)
- increase the risk of developing certain cancers and adult-onset diabetes
- increase blood cholesterol levels and the risk of heart disease and stroke—two major causes of death in our society.

Many people in our society are overweight and consume too much fat. Heart disease is a major cause of premature death in men and women. A high level of cholesterol in your bloodstream can result in fatty deposits building up inside your arteries (atherosclerosis). If these fatty deposits keep growing over time, they can eventually restrict the blood flowing through your arteries.

ARE SOME FATS HEALTHIER THAN OTHERS?
The fat in foods is a mixture of three types of fat: saturated, monounsaturated and polyunsaturated. These fats vary in the effects they have on blood cholesterol and their relationship to heart disease.
- Saturated fats tend to increase the amount of cholesterol in your blood to a greater extent than dietary cholesterol and their intake should be limited. Saturated fats are found mainly in animal produce, such as dairy products, meat, poultry and lard, and in many processed foods, such as biscuits, pies, cakes, pastries and chocolate. Coconut and palm oil are also high in saturated fat.
- Monounsaturated fats can help lower the level of cholesterol in the blood, if your total and saturated fat intake is low. Monounsaturated fats are found in avocados, olive oil, canola oil, sunola oil, monounsaturated margarines and nuts.
- Polyunsaturated fats can help reduce the level of blood cholesterol if they are used in place of saturated fat as part of a low-fat diet. Polyunsaturated fats are found in sunflower oil, safflower oil, soya bean oil, evening primrose oil, linseed oil, fish oils, polyunsaturated margarines, mackerel, tuna and salmon.

Health professionals recommend that fats provide no more than 30 per cent of your total daily energy intake, with saturated fat providing 7 per cent of the total fat intake, monounsaturated fat 13 per cent and polyunsaturated fat 10 per cent. It's not so important to achieve these exact percentages, but monounsaturated and polyunsaturated fats should be consumed in greater proportions than saturated fat.

An easy way to increase your intake of healthy fats without blowing your daily fat budget is to eat fish that is rich in omega-3 polyunsaturated fatty acids, such as sardines, herrings, mackerel, tuna and salmon, two to three times a week. These fish are readily available fresh, canned or bottled in brine, so it's easy to eat them regularly. Make sure you use low-fat cooking methods to prepare them. Regular consumption of fish can also help reduce high blood pressure and triglyceride levels and reduce the risk of blood clots and strokes. It may also help alleviate depression and arthritis.

TIPS FOR REDUCING YOUR FAT INTAKE
- Cut down your fat intake gradually by making a series of small changes. Stick with each change for a few weeks, and you'll soon like the taste of low-fat foods.

- Learn to read food labels so you can identify high-fat foods. As a general rule, low-fat snacks contain no more than 5 grams of fat per serve, and low-fat meals contain no more than 10 grams per serve. Food labels will also show you which reduced-fat foods are still relatively high in fat and calories.
- Switch from full-fat dairy products to low-fat and reduced-fat varieties. Healthy children over the age of five years can switch from full-fat to reduced-fat milk.
- Substitute added fats (butter, margarine, mayonnaise, salad dressing, sour cream) with low-fat alternatives (vinegar, oil-free dressings, mustard, salsa, lemon juice). Flavour your foods with herbs, spices, low-fat relishes and sauces.
- Choose fresh fish or fish canned in brine or spring water, not oil.
- Choose lean cuts of meat and poultry, and remove any skin and visible fat before cooking.
- Fill up on vegetables and grain products at lunch and dinner, and eat small portions of meat, chicken or fish.
- Avoid fried foods and fatty snacks.
- Some healthy-looking foods, such as toasted muesli and muffins, are high in fat. Make your own versions of your favourite foods (low-fat grilled pitta pizzas, hamburgers, burrito wraps) using your imagination or the recipes in this book.
- Pack low-fat foods to take with you to work or school or when travelling so you have something healthy on hand.

- Fill sandwiches with plenty of juicy salad vegetables so that you don't need margarine, and add a small serving of lean meat, skinless chicken, fish or reduced-fat cheese.
- When you have to eat on the run, choose lower-fat foods:
  — healthy sandwiches or salads (skip the margarine and fatty dressings; choose filling wholegrain breads)
  — Asian food (steamed rice, mixed vegetable dishes, lean meat or seafood stir-fries)
  — pasta with tomato-based sauces
  — pizza with low-fat toppings
  — pitta bread with meat, tabbouleh and fresh salad.
- At dinner parties and social events, limit your intake of fatty hors d'oeuvres (cream dips, crackers, peanuts, chips, vol au vents). Fill up on fresh vegetables, low-fat dips, and non-alcoholic drinks.
- When dining out:
  — choose low-fat dishes rather than dishes that are crumbed and fried, and dishes with low-fat sauces rather than creamy ones
  — trim any fat from meat and poultry
  — don't go overboard at a smorgasbord—fill up on salads and clear soup
  — skip creamy desserts or share them with someone else
  — swap garlic bread for fresh crusty bread with a thin scrape of butter.

LOW-FAT COOKING

Choosing low-fat foods is just one aspect of following a healthy diet—you also have to prepare them in a healthy way. You may think you're doing the right thing when you choose brown rice over white, but if you're making a dish like fried rice with lots of oil and ham, you may still be eating a high-fat meal.

Healthy, carbohydrate-rich foods, like potatoes, bread and pasta, have been falsely accused of being fattening foods, but it's really the accompaniments that are fattening (butter on bread, sour cream on potatoes, creamy pasta sauces).

You have to eat a considerable amount of carbohydrate before it's turned into fat, whereas dietary fat is readily stored as body fat. The secret to tasty low-fat cooking is to use cooking techniques that maintain the flavour of the food without adding any extra, unnecessary fat.

LOW-FAT INGREDIENTS

It's possible to lower the fat content of many dishes without reducing the flavour by using simple substitutions. The table opposite contains alternatives for high-fat ingredients. By using a mix of low-fat substitutes and spices and flavourings, the low-fat recipe can taste even better.

The two main ways to reduce a recipe's fat content are to switch to low-fat cooking techniques and to replace some or all of the high-fat ingredients with low-fat alternatives.

LOW-FAT COOKING TECHNIQUES

MEAT, POULTRY, FISH AND SEAFOOD

- Use non-stick pans and low-fat cooking methods requiring little or no fat or oil (dry-fry, stir-fry, grill, roast on a rack, steam, poach, microwave, simmer in low-fat sauce).
- As little as one tablespoon of oil is enough to brown or stir-fry enough meat for four people. Brush the base of the pan with oil, instead of pouring oil into the pan. Stock can also be used in place of oil for meat dishes.
- Grilling and barbecuing trim meat with low-fat marinades produces flavoursome meals. Marinate chicken breast fillets or lean meat in fruit or wine and herbs before grilling on the barbecue.
- Bake fish fillets or kebabs in foil with seasoning and lemon juice.
- Use a rack when grilling or roasting meat so the fat drips away.
- Cook legs of lamb in a roasting pan with a little water, wine or stock.

SOUPS, MIXED DISHES, SAUCES

- Let home-made soups, casseroles, mince dishes and stews cool until the fat solidifies on top. Then remove the fat before adding vegetables and reheating.
- Substitute low-fat ingredients for high-fat ones in recipes.
- Use low-fat, tomato-based sauces instead of creamy or cheesy ones.
- Use low-fat ricotta cheese with a sprinkle of Parmesan in cheese dishes.
- Use evaporated skim milk for creamy soups.
- Use puréed vegetables to thicken sauces.
- Use barley, lentils or potatoes to thicken casseroles or stews.

VEGETABLES

- Pre-cook potatoes in the microwave or oven, then crisp on the barbecue.
- Brown microwaved vegetables under the griller for crispness without the fat (if necessary, brush with a little oil first).
- Stir-fry vegetables in a little water and salt-reduced soy sauce.

HIGH-FAT INGREDIENT	REDUCED- OR LOW-FAT ALTERNATIVE
Milk, yoghurt	Use low-fat varieties.
Whipped cream	Use evaporated skim milk and chill before whipping. Whip low-fat ricotta cheese with icing sugar and low-fat milk or fruit juice.
Sour cream	Use low-fat yoghurt or buttermilk. Blend cottage cheese with skim milk and lemon juice or vinegar. Mix low-fat evaporated milk with lemon juice.
Whole eggs	Use 2 egg whites or ¼ cup of egg substitute for 1 egg. If the recipe needs a few eggs, keep at least one or two whole eggs to maintain texture. Replace 3 whole eggs with 1 whole egg and 4 egg whites. Before you add the fresh egg whites, whisk them slightly.
Cream cheese	Use low-fat cream cheese or low-fat fromage frais. Use blended low-fat cottage cheese.
Cheese	Use smaller amounts of lower-fat varieties. Choose low-fat ricotta or cottage cheese. Instead of a Cheddar cheese topping, mix a little grated Parmesan with oats, bran or wheat germ.
Butter or margarine	Use small amounts of reduced-fat varieties (but not for baking). Use lower-fat alternatives (chutney, cottage cheese, a little avocado) for sandwiches or only butter one slice of bread.
Oil	Use less oil or use olive oil spray, stocks and juices for stir-frying or sautéing. In cakes, replace oil with an equal amount of fruit purée and one-third of the oil—use puréed prunes, dried apricots or apple.
Mayonnaise /salad dressings	Use non-fat varieties. Make your own low-fat dressings (vinegar, herbs, lemon juice, ricotta, tomato paste) or sauces (low-fat yoghurt, buttermilk, mustard).
Coconut cream or milk	Use reduced-fat versions. Use low-fat yoghurt and a little desiccated coconut.
Pastry	Use filo pastry, brushing every 3–4 layers with oil, juice, low-fat yoghurt or concentrated stock. Mix cooked rice with egg white and pat onto a lightly oiled pie dish. Bake before using as a pastry base.
Sweet pie crust or slice base	Combine plain reduced-fat sweet biscuits or wafer biscuits with dried fruit (apricots, prunes or figs) in a food processor until the mixture forms a ball. For 150 g biscuits, you need 75 g fruit. You may need to vary the amounts depending on the fruit's moisture.
Cakes and biscuits	Minimum fat needed for biscuits is 2 tablespoons per cup of flour. Replace oil with an equal amount of fruit purée plus one-third of the oil. Use non-stick pans.
Meat and poultry	Buy lean cuts and remove any visible fat before cooking. Remove the skin and fat under the skin from poultry beforecooking. Keep portions small and fill up with vegetables and legumes.

SOURCE: *Winning Tastes*, National Heart Foundation of Australia, 1993

STEP 4: MAINTAIN A HEALTHY BODY
WEIGHT BY BALANCING FOOD INTAKE WITH REGULAR EXERCISE

People come in all shapes and sizes, and there is a range of healthy weights for each height. When deciding whether or not your weight is healthy, you need to consider how much body fat you have and where it's located. Body weight alone isn't always a good indication of body fatness—some thin-looking people can have a lot of fat but little muscle.

Firstly, use the chart opposite to see if your current weight is within the healthy range for your height. Since muscle and bone weigh more than fat, the higher weights in the healthy range typically apply to people with larger, muscular frames, whereas the lower end of the range applies to people with less muscle and smaller frames.

Secondly, for adults aged 20 to 69 years, you can estimate your body fat level by calculating your body mass index (BMI), which is your weight in kilograms divided by your height in metres squared. In general, the greater your BMI, the greater your risk of serious health problems (see example page 36).

Thirdly, using a tape measure, measure the circumference of your waist and hips. People who carry more fat around their mid-section (apple shaped) rather than on their lower body (pear shaped) have a greater risk of heart disease and diabetes.

Although it's often hard for women to lose the fat from their hips and thighs, this lower body fat isn't as detrimental to health as the classic 'beer gut', upper body/abdominal fat. See your doctor or a dietitian if you want a more accurate assessment of your body fat level, particularly if you're very active. Body weight is often a poor indication of body fatness in athletes because changes in their weight, even up to 2 kilograms at a time, can be due to fluid and carbohydrate lost from the body and increased muscle mass.

Weight gain with age is a common problem in our society. Currently, in Australia, it's estimated that two thirds of the adult population is overweight or obese, and in the UK three out of four adults are regarded as being overweight.

Besides being bad for self-esteem and your general feeling of wellbeing, being overweight and inactive increases your risk of many illnesses, including heart disease, diabetes, gallstones, degenerative joint disease and some cancers. You can greatly reduce your risk of these problems by staying active and maintaining your weight within the healthy weight range for your height. The good news is that you don't need to be skinny or at the lowest end of the weight range in order to be

SOME HEALTH PROBLEMS THAT CAN OCCUR AT EITHER EXTREME OF THE WEIGHT RANGE

OVERWEIGHT OR OBESE

High blood pressure
High blood cholesterol
Sleep disorders
Breathing problems
Arthritis
Diabetes
Heart disease and stroke
Cancer (breast, uterus, prostate, colon)
Gall bladder disease, gallstones

UNDERWEIGHT

Delayed development (children and teenagers)
Decreased immunity
Menstrual irregularities
Increased risk of anaemia and osteoporosis
Malnutrition
Less energy and vitality
Depression
Risk of early death (if very underweight)

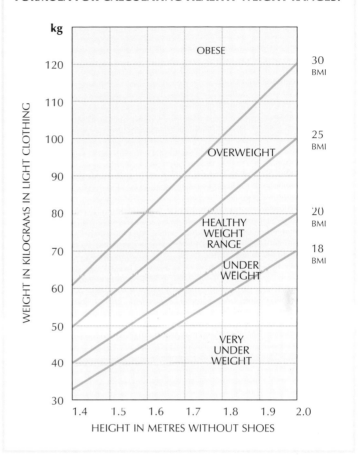

HEALTHY WEIGHT RANGE GRAPH FOR MEN AND WOMEN FROM 18 YEARS ONWARDS BASED ON THE BODY MASS INDEX, OR BMI (WEIGHT/HEIGHT²), WHICH IS A FORMULA FOR CALCULATING HEALTHY WEIGHT RANGES.

healthy—being underweight may also adversely affect your health.

HOW MUCH WEIGHT SHOULD I LOSE?

If you are overweight, you should aim to get your weight into the healthy weight range. Even maintaining your weight at the top end of the healthy range for your height can significantly improve your health, and should be achievable by most overweight adults.

An overweight person who reduces their weight by 2 BMI units and increases their general activity will significantly improve their health relative to when they were overweight.

Losing weight slowly by making gradual changes in your dietary and exercise habits is the best way to achieve a healthy weight and lifestyle you can maintain. Gradual weight loss will help you lose body fat rather than muscle. You should aim to lose only 1 to 2 kilograms (2–4 lbs) per week if you are very overweight or 0.5 to 1 kilogram (1–2 lbs) per week if you are only slightly overweight.

It may have taken you years to gain 5 kilograms, so you can't expect to lose it all in a month. This could require drastic

measures, such as very restricted diets or liquid-only diets, which could adversely affect your health.

It's also important to remember that the closer you are to your ideal weight, the more difficult it can be to lose weight, simply because you've got less to lose. Also, our body shapes are genetically determined—some people naturally need more body fat to remain healthy than others.

If your weight is normal for your height, and you have to diet and exercise excessively to lose even 2 kilograms, it's likely that you're trying to maintain a body weight that's unnaturally low for you. A dietitian can establish an ideal body fat level that you can achieve with a healthy diet and exercise program so that you won't have trouble maintaining these habits over time.

If you decrease your fat intake and begin weight training, you may not lose any body weight (as shown on the scales), but you can lose body fat, which is more important for your health. So instead of spending money on diet pills and powders, take up some active leisure pursuits and purchase fresh, healthy foods.

WHAT'S THE BEST WAY TO LOSE WEIGHT?

To achieve a healthy body weight you have to balance your energy intake with the amount of energy your body needs. So in order to lose weight, you can eat less energy and/or increase your physical activity. However, it's much harder to lose weight simply by eating less, and may even be counterproductive in the long term.

People who have managed to lose a lot of weight and keep it off for many years will tell you that increasing your physical activity is essential for lasting weight loss. Rather than taking up jogging or other difficult forms of exercise, which are hard to stick to and leave you too tired to keep moving the rest of the day, you can burn more calories simply by going for regular long walks (at least 30 minutes a day) and by being generally more active (take the stairs, park your car further from work, go bowling instead of to the movies).

Trying to lose weight by eating less food is difficult and usually doesn't last long, because the body is designed to protect itself against food shortages with increased hunger and a lower metabolic rate, meaning that you feel hungrier but you're burning less energy. The persistent hunger will make even the most resolved dieter constantly think about food, and often within a month people end up breaking their diet by bingeing on their favourite high-calorie foods.

There's no need to feel like a failure if this happens to you, because your body has driven you to eat to increase its chances of survival. The body doesn't know if there's a famine coming so it has developed stronger mechanisms to stop people eating less energy than they need. There's always room to store more fat, so our bodies don't have the same defences against overeating.

These natural mechanisms are a problem for modern people because we have so many opportunities to overeat and under-exercise. Up until the last 50 years, people were generally more active, and fewer people were overweight.

Although there's no single method of losing weight that will suit everyone, there are three habits that will increase your chance of success:
• eating balanced, healthy meals
• limiting fat and alcohol intake
• being physically active.

IS IT POSSIBLE TO EAT MORE AND STILL LOSE WEIGHT?

Many of us think that losing weight is a matter of starving yourself, but this isn't true. One of the best things you can do to help control your weight is to give yourself permission to eat three healthy meals a day, which will help stop you craving less nutritious foods. By eating regular low-fat meals and keeping active, you will keep your internal engine running and burning calories.

Rather than trying to restrict your food intake, focus on making better food choices, using the healthy diet pyramid (page 25) as a guideline, and eat to a comfortable level of fullness. Basing your diet on the low-fat foods at the bottom of the pyramid means you can control your calorie intake without going hungry. These foods contain fewer calories per gram than fatty foods, so it's possible to eat filling meals and reduce your calorie intake at the same time. You just have to make a conscious effort to choose the right foods and prepare them using low-fat methods.

LIMIT YOUR FAT AND ALCOHOL INTAKE

Fat and alcohol contain more energy per gram than carbohydrate or protein, with fat containing over twice as much energy per gram. Even small amounts of fatty foods and alcoholic drinks contain a lot of calories, making it much easier to consume more calories than you need.

Worse still, many research studies have shown that fat and alcohol don't make you feel as full as the same amount of calories from carbohydrate and protein, and they are also more effective at increasing body fat stores. It's hardly surprising that many research studies have found that people who eat high-fat diets are more likely to be overweight than people with low fat intakes. So an effective way of reducing your calorie intake without going hungry is to limit your intake of fat and alcohol.

WEIGHING UP YOUR HEALTH RISKS

BODY MASS INDEX	CLASSIFICATION	HEALTH RISK	
less than 18.5	Underweight	Risk of health problems	
18.5–24.9	Healthy		
25–29.9	Overweight	Risk of health problems	(Health risk is further increased if waist
30–39.9	Obese	Significant health risk	circumference is more than 101 cm
40 or more	Extremely obese	Serious health risk	for men or 96 cm for women.)

EXAMPLE: A man who weighs 80 kg is 175 cm. BMI = $80 \div 1.75^2 = 80 \div 3.0625 = 26.1$ kg/m^2
By losing 5 kg, he will bring his BMI down to 24.5 ($75 \div 1.75^2$) and reduce his risk of health problems.

ISN'T CARBOHYDRATE FATTENING?

Carbohydrate-rich foods, like bread and potatoes, are often claimed to be fattening, but, as we've said, it's the fat that's added to them that is fattening, not the carbohydrate itself. This extra fat provides lots of calories, but doesn't increase fullness and is readily stored as body fat. Although it's possible to gain weight if you eat more carbohydrate than you need, it's much easier to overeat high-fat foods.

Some foods that are sweet but rich in fat have wrongly been classified as carbohydrate-rich foods, like cakes, pastries, ice cream and chocolate. Although they contain sugar, fat provides most of the calories in these foods. Refined sugar shouldn't be a major part of your diet, but because sugar contains less energy than fat, you can add small amounts of sugar to your low-fat meals to make them more palatable.

However, if you want to lose weight, it's a good idea to cut back on extra sugar where you can. If you have a craving for something sweet, satisfy it with a sweet low-fat food like fruit or low-fat yoghurt.

A GUIDE FOR ESTIMATING YOUR DAILY FAT AND KILOJOULE INTAKES

If you want to lose weight, aim to make fat less than 30% of your daily energy intake (not suitable for children).

FOR WOMEN WHO WANT TO LOSE	DAILY ENERGY INTAKE (kJ)	DAILY FAT INTAKE
Less than 5 kg	5000	30–35 g
Between 5 and 15 kg	6000	35–40 g
More than 15 kg	7000	40–50 g

Men add 500 kJ and 5 g fat.

SOURCE: *Australian Slimming Magazine*, September 2000

INCREASING THE FILLING POWER OF YOUR LOW-FAT DIET: MORE FULLNESS FOR FEWER CALORIES

If you eat a low-fat diet but can't lose weight, you're probably still eating more calories than you need. By choosing the most filling low-fat foods, you can reduce your calorie intake without going hungry.

Low-fat foods that are high in fibre or are less refined are more difficult to chew and swallow. Therefore, they take longer to eat, giving your brain time to register the growing level of fullness in your stomach. Not only do these filling foods help you eat less, they tend to keep you full for longer because they are slowly digested.

Many of the foods in modern super-markets are soft and tasty, and can be eaten and digested very quickly. Perhaps this is one reason why it's now so easy to gain weight. Because you may be used to these soft foods, you may initially find whole foods a little unpalatable. But if you make small changes and stick with them for a few weeks, you'll soon learn to like their taste. Also, remember to drink plenty of water throughout the day to help fill your stomach.

'LITE' CALORIES STILL COUNT

The food industry is helping people lower their fat intake by making reduced-fat versions of high-fat products. However, reduced-fat foods are not always lower in calories, because some ingredients that replace fats in foods are also high in calories. Many people believe they can eat larger portions of 'lite' foods and still consume fewer calories than if they had eaten a normal portion of the high-fat version.

Unfortunately, this isn't true and probably explains why some people don't lose weight on a low-fat diet. It's important to learn to interpret the information on food labels because some terms are confusing. A reduced-fat food contains less fat than the regular version, but it may still be high in fat and/or calories. The word 'lite' on a food label can mean that the product

LOW FAT, FEWER CALORIES	HIGH FAT, MORE CALORIES
1 slice of wholegrain bread 255 kJ (60 Cal), 1 g fat	1 slice of wholegrain bread thickly spread with butter 560 kJ (135 Cal), 9 g fat
1 medium potato, boiled 335 kJ (80 Cal), 0 g fat	1 medium potato, boiled, with 1 tablespoon sour cream 640 kJ (155 Cal), 8 g fat 1 small serve of French fries 1155 kJ (275 Cal), 16 g fat
1 cup pasta with 125 g tomato sauce 910 kJ (215 Cal), 1 g fat	1 cup pasta with 125 g creamy sauce 1440 kJ (345 Cal), 14 g fat
1 cup steamed white rice 990 kJ (235 Cal), 0 g fat	1 cup fried rice 1735 kJ (415 Cal), 16 g fat
1 big handful of sultanas 385 kJ (90 Cal), 0 g fat	1 big handful of chocolate-covered sultanas 550 kJ (130 Cal), 5 g fat
1 medium lean pork chop, grilled 715 kJ (170 Cal), 7 g fat	1 medium pork chop, not trimmed of any fat, grilled 975 kJ (235 Cal), 15 g fat

LESS FILLING	MORE FILLING
FOODS	
Fruit juice, fruit purée, soft canned fruit,	Fresh, crunchy fruit, unpeeled dried fruit
Soft white or wholemeal bread crackers,	Crunchy or grainy bread, rice cakes
White pasta or white rice	Brown pasta or brown rice
Mashed potatoes, potato chips	Whole boiled or steamed potatoes, unpeeled
Minced or processed meat, thin strips	Large strips, slices or chunks of meat, steaks
Natural muesli	Porridge
Light breakfast cereals and cereal bars	Bran-based breakfast cereals
Fish spread	Fresh or canned fish
Finely strained or puréed soups	Soups with large chunks of meat and vegetables
Canned legumes (baked beans, etc)	Boiled dry legumes
Soft cakes and slices	Crunchy or thicker cakes and slices
MEALS	
Cornflakes, skim milk and sugar	Porridge, skim milk and fresh fruit slices
White bread, chicken and lettuce sandwich	Grainy bread, lean beef and crunchy salad sandwich
Mashed potatoes, pork chops, peas	Whole potatoes, grilled pork steak, steamed vegetables

either has a light colour or contains less fat than the regular version. A food that is 90 per cent fat-free still contains 10 per cent of its weight or energy content as fat.

CRASH DIETS—NOT A HEALTHY WAY TO LOSE WEIGHT

In recent times, one fad diet after another has claimed to be the most effective weight loss method, and new diet books are still becoming best sellers. Why are there so many fad diets? The simple answer is that they don't achieve lasting weight loss. Typically, fad diets require very specific meals and may be deficient in nutrients, especially if they restrict entire food groups, such as grain or dairy products. Although their methods vary, fad diets all produce weight loss by significantly reducing your normal energy intake.

None of these diets magically melt fat away. You can lose weight eating any combination of foods, if you keep eating fewer calories than normal. However, fad diets are usually only something you can stick to for a short time, so they don't help you make lasting changes

that will improve your health and weight. Many women go on a rapid weight loss diet before an important event, but they may put on even more weight when they start eating normally again. Rapid weight loss diets are not a healthy way of losing weight.

Before trying a high-protein diet, liquid meal replacements or any other diet fad, find out if it has any side effects. If

you stick to a low-calorie diet for more than a month, you'll lose some weight, but it will be mostly water, not body fat. As time progresses, weight loss will occur more slowly and side effects may appear, such as increased hunger, cravings, irritability, tiredness and light-headedness. High-protein diets can also be harmful to the kidneys, as they have to work harder to remove the extra waste products from the body.

NOT ALL LITE FOODS ARE LOW IN CALORIES

LIGHT OR LITE	This can refer to the colour or texture of a product or its calorie or nutrient content. Read the food label to check which feature this refers to. If 'lite' refers to the calorie or fat content, then the product must also be reduced or low in energy and fat.
REDUCED-FAT	The product must contain 25% less fat than the regular version. Some reduced-fat versions of high-fat foods like margarine are still high in fat and calories.
LOW-FAT	Solid foods must contain no more than 3 grams of fat per 100 grams. Liquids must contain no more than 1.5 grams of fat per 100 grams. Some low-fat foods are not lower in calories because the fat has been replaced with sugar and other high-calorie ingredients. Use the nutrient information on food labels to help you select low-fat, lower-calorie foods.

BE PREPARED TO EAT WELL

We all lead busy, stressful lives and many people come home to find the fridge empty or they are simply too tired to cook. You can make it easier to follow a low-fat diet by stocking your pantry, fridge and freezer with low-fat foods and ingredients that can be quickly prepared to make nutritious meals.

FOR THE PANTRY

Breads, low-fat crispbreads and crackers, rice cakes, natural muesli, breakfast cereals, porridge oats, low-fat breakfast cereal bars, reduced-fat muesli bars, rice, pasta, noodles, canned spaghetti, couscous, polenta, quick-cooking grain mixes, risotto rice, low-fat muffin and pancake mixes, dried fruit, nuts and seeds, wheat germ, oat bran, potatoes, low-fat microwave popcorn, low-fat pretzels, canned legumes (lentils, beans, baked beans, chickpeas), vacuum-packed legumes, canned vegetables, canned fish in brine, bottled pasta sauces, low-fat casserole sauces, long-life reduced-fat or low-fat milks, light evaporated milk, soy sauce, oyster sauce, vinegar, dried herbs and spices, stock cubes or long-life stocks, low-fat soups (canned, sachets, packets), baking ingredients (flour, sugar), spray oils, olive oil, yeast extract spreads, jam, honey, low-fat drinking chocolate mixes, diet jelly

FOR THE FRIDGE

Fresh fruit and vegetables, juices, mineral water, reduced-fat or low-fat dairy products or soy-alternatives (milk, cheese, yoghurt, custard), tofu, tempeh, smoked salmon, reduced-fat margarine, eggs, reduced-fat processed meat slices, fresh pasta (ravioli, tortellini, lasagne sheets), fresh noodles, sauces, minced herbs, tomato paste, curry paste, mustard, fat-free dressings and mayonnaise

FOR THE FREEZER

Any type of bread, pitta bread or pizza bases, English muffins, bagels, fruit loaf, filo pastry, skinless chicken fillets, fish fillets, marinara mix, lean meats (mince, steaks, etc), frozen vegetables, frozen vegetable stir-fry mixes, thick-cut 97% fat-free oven fries, grated reduced-fat cheese, frozen berries, sorbet, gelato, low-fat frozen fruit desserts

PROBLEMS WITH SOME COMMON WEIGHT-CONTROL PRODUCTS

In addition to low-calorie diet books, many other products are marketed for weight loss. Unfortunately, most of them don't promote fat loss and some may jeopardise your health. Below are some common products that should not be used in place of a healthy balanced diet if you're trying to lose weight.

LAXATIVES AND DIURETICS

- These don't prevent you from absorbing food.
- They cause water loss rather than fat loss, so your normal weight will return once you drink enough fluid.
- Long-term use of such products can lead to dangerous losses of water, sodium and potassium, which can cause death.

SUPPLEMENTS CLAIMED TO SUPPRESS APPETITE, INCREASE FAT METABOLISM OR BLOCK FAT ABSORPTION

- As yet, there is no scientific evidence that use of these supplements alone results in weight loss.
- They often contain only minute amounts of the ingredients claimed to produce the beneficial effects.

FIBRE SUPPLEMENTS

- These are claimed to help reduce appetite by filling the stomach, but must be taken with lots of water.
- They can cause constipation, bloating, and flatulence.
- Excessive use can cause gut problems and reduced absorption of iron, zinc and calcium.
- Natural high-fibre foods may be more beneficial for weight control by decreasing the amount of food that is consumed at meals and increasing fullness between meals.

MEAL REPLACEMENT DRINKS AND BARS

- These are often low in calories and/or carbohydrate, and don't contain all important vitamins and minerals.
- They are not as filling as a wholesome low-fat meal and don't contain all the important vitamins and minerals.
- They can lead to hunger between meals and increased risk of snacking.
- There is no scientific evidence that they are useful for long-term weight loss.

MODIFIED FASTING (VERY LOW-CALORIE DIETS) AND LOW-CARBOHYDRATE DIETS

- Due to low calorie intake, these diets can lead to rapid weight loss, but this is mostly water.
- Side effects include dizziness, fatigue, depression, hair loss, nervousness and skin problems.
- With time, loss of muscle mass will cause the body to run on less energy and slow the rate of weight loss.
- They are difficult to maintain due to boredom, hunger and side effects.

TIPS FOR A HEALTHY APPROACH TO WEIGHT LOSS

- Make realistic changes to your eating and activity habits in a series of small steps. Set gradual goals you can achieve and measure. For example, first switch from full-fat to reduced-fat dairy products. Once you've mastered this, change to low-fat dairy products. Focus on changes you know you can stick to.

- Be prepared to eat healthily. Stock your pantry and fridge with healthy foods on hand for fast meals and snacks. Cook extra portions of healthy meals to store in the freezer, so you can reheat them when you don't have time to cook. Plan a menu for the week and take healthy foods with you to eat at work or school.

- Try to eat regular, balanced meals containing a variety of healthy foods. Focus on what you can eat, rather than what you shouldn't eat. Eat at a slow pace to a comfortable level of fullness. This will give you time to register how much you've eaten. Wait a while before deciding whether or not to eat a second helping.

- Make your meals as filling as possible by choosing less refined foods. Include a little protein with your high-carbohydrate meals (for example, low-fat milk with breakfast cereal, lean beef and salad on your sandwich).

- Restrict your alcohol intake. This will help keep your calorie intake and blood pressure down.

- Become aware of times when you are likely to overeat, such as when you're stressed or bored, or when there is free food around, and check if you're really hungry before you eat anything. Finding tasks to keep you busy can help you feel happier and productive, and you'll have less time to snack.

- Don't give up if you have problems, just get back on track as soon as you can. Learn to think positively and find ways of dealing with your emotions other than eating. Regular exercise and yoga can be great stress-relievers. Don't weigh yourself every day.

- Aim for at least 30 minutes of moderate activity on most days. Find activities that you enjoy so you'll look forward to doing them. If you haven't been physically active, build up to 30 minutes gradually and look at ways to increase your general daily activity. It's harder to eat if you're out of the house exercising.

- Develop a strategy for eating healthily at social occasions. Bring some suitable foods with you, if appropriate, or have a healthy snack beforehand so you're not hungry at the party.

- Drink plenty of water throughout the day. This can help keep your appetite down, as sometimes it's easy to confuse thirst for hunger.

STEP 5: IF YOU DRINK ALCOHOL, ONLY HAVE MODERATE AMOUNTS

Unlike the other nutrients, we can do without alcohol altogether. Alcoholic drinks provide 'empty calories'— lots of energy, but few vitamins or minerals. However, a low to moderate intake with some alcohol-free days each week appears to be fine for most healthy people.

Another good reason to limit your alcohol intake is that alcohol can cause weight gain, because it provides energy (29 kJ per gram) and suppresses the body's use of carbohydrate and fat as fuel. The body can't store alcohol, because it's a toxin and causes cell damage, so your body has to burn off any alcohol that's in your system. While this is happening, any fat in your system won't be needed for energy and will be stored as body fat.

Unlike the other nutrients, alcohol is also a drug that has short-term effects immediately after ingestion—and being a drug, there are many myths and claims associated with its effects. For example, some people believe that alcoholic drinks will make you feel warm in cold weather. Although some alcoholic drinks can have an initial warming effect, alcohol metabolism increases heat loss from the body, so you may end up feeling colder. Another myth is that alcohol helps fight a cold, but it can actually suppress the body's immune system and interfere with the effects of any medication.

In recent times, wine has been promoted as being helpful for heart health. However, this is a controversial issue. The regular

consumption of moderate to high amounts of alcohol may, in fact, cause cardiovascular problems. Even a low to moderate intake of alcohol has some harmful effects, including headaches, disrupted sleep and reduced alertness, coordination and mental activity.

Alcohol consumption at any level tends to raise your blood pressure and can also raise your blood triglyceride level—both of these factors over time may increase the risk of heart disease. In addition, alcohol can interact with many prescription and over-the-counter

medications and can be dangerous if consumed with tranquilisers, sleeping pills, antihistamines and aspirin.

Over time, moderate to heavy alcohol use increases the risk of death from heart attack or stroke, and cancers of the digestive system.

If you choose to drink alcohol, do so only in moderation. You should be particularly careful if you have diabetes, high blood pressure or high cholesterol levels. People taking medication to lower their blood pressure should avoid

alcohol or restrict their intake to one or two drinks per day at most. Alcohol should be entirely avoided by children, pregnant or breast-feeding women, and women trying to conceive.

A moderate alcohol intake is defined as two to four standard drinks a day for men and one to two standard drinks a day for women, with some alcohol-free days each week. People over the age of 65 years are advised to consume only one standard drink a day. A standard alcoholic drink contains eight to 10 grams of alcohol.

STEP 6: EAT MODERATE AMOUNTS
OF SUGAR AND FOODS CONTAINING ADDED SUGAR

Sugars, like starches, are carbohydrates, which serve as the body's main energy source. Like salt, sugars are found naturally in foods (intrinsic or natural sugars) or can be added to foods (extrinsic or refined sugars).

Taste is only one of the important roles that sugars play in food. They are also used to preserve jams, cereals, cakes, biscuits and drinks, and add texture and colour to baked goods and dairy products. Sugar is also a source of energy for the yeast that causes bread to rise, and helps balance acidity in tomato sauces and salad dressings.

Most of the sugar in our diet comes from processed foods and drinks (biscuits, cakes, breakfast cereals, jams, sauces, cordial, soft drinks), rather than from table sugar that is added to drinks and foods.

There are a number of different sugars that occur naturally in foods:
* glucose
* fructose
* sucrose
* maltose
* lactose.

Once consumed and in the body, there is little difference between most of these sugars in their effects on the body in healthy people. During digestion, all sugars and starches are broken down into glucose and fructose (except lactose, which is broken down into galactose and glucose). Glucose and fructose are small enough to be absorbed through the small intestine into the bloodstream and then delivered to the body's cells for immediate use as energy or storage as glycogen (in muscles or the liver) to be broken down for later fuel needs.

However, in terms of healthy eating, you should be eating most of the sugar in your diet from foods like fruit and dairy products that contain other valuable nutrients, rather than from refined sugar (table or added to processed foods) that doesn't contain any vitamins or minerals.

SUGAR: FRIEND OR FOE?
In the past, refined sugar was thought to be the cause of common western diseases, such as obesity, heart disease and diabetes, and was also thought to be responsible for hyperactivity in children.

Refined sugar was assumed to be responsible for these disorders simply because western societies ate so much of it. Subsequently, a lot of research has been conducted to find out whether these claims are true.

Sugar is one of the most extensively studied nutrients, and we now know that it doesn't cause obesity, heart diease, diabetes, or hyperactivity. Studies in which sugar has been given to children with attention deficit disorder or hyperactivity have consistently shown that sugar does not worsen behaviour or decrease attention span in these children.

However, sugar can contribute to tooth decay when it is consumed in soft drinks, fruit juice, sticky lollies and dried fruit, but not when in the form of fresh fruit like apples.

You may also need to watch your intake of refined sugar if you're trying to lose weight or if you regularly eat a lot of sugary foods that might prevent you consuming all the vitamins and minerals you need.

HOW MUCH SUGAR?
For most people, a moderate amount of refined sugar as part of a varied diet won't cause health problems or weight gain. In fact, adding a little sugar to some bland foods, like porridge, may make it easier for you to stick to a healthy low-fat diet. However, table sugar, soft drinks and other sweet 'junk' foods remain at the top of the dietary pyramid

HEALTHIER SOURCES OF SUGAR	LESS DESIRABLE SOURCES OF SUGAR
	(SUGAR WITH FAT OR SUGAR WITHOUT OTHER NUTRIENTS)
EAT IN MODERATION	EAT LESS
Fruit (dried, canned, jellied)	Soft drinks, cordials
Fruit juices	Sweet alcoholic beverages, beer
Yoghurt, custard, flavoured milk	Chocolate, lollies, syrups, topping
Breakfast cereals	Jelly, ice cream, jam, glacé fruit
Fruit and yoghurt snack bars	Biscuits, cakes, pastries, puddings

and should only be eaten occasionally. Rather than reaching for the table sugar, try to get sweetness from foods containing natural sugars, like fruit or yoghurt, because they also give you other valuable nutrients.

If you want to lose weight, first concentrate on reducing your fat intake and becoming more physically active. Then reduce any unnecessary sugar in your diet (for example, soft drinks, cordials, sugar added to tea or coffee) by using sugar-free products or leaving it out altogether.

Fat contains more than twice the amount of energy per gram (37 kJ or 9 Cal per gram) than sugar does (16 kJ or 4 Cal per gram). So you can cut more calories from your diet by reducing your fat intake than you can by reducing your sugar intake. Limit your intake of foods that are high in both fat and refined sugar, like biscuits, cakes and chocolate. When you feel like a sweet treat, choose a healthy food such as low-

fat yoghurt, fruit, fruit loaf or mineral water flavoured with fruit juice.

Honey contains a few more vitamins and minerals than table sugar, but it should be treated in the same way—eaten only in moderation.

SUGAR AND FOOD LABELS

The nutrition panel on a label lists the total amount of sugar that is either naturally present or has been added to the food during processing (per average serve and per 100 grams). The ingredient list on the food label will show any sources of sugar that have been added to the food, such as cane sugar, honey, fructose, fruit juice concentrate, treacle, malt/maltose and dextrose. Sugar is not allowed to be added to foods labelled as containing 'no added sugar' or 'without added sugar'. A low-sugar food must contain less than 5 grams of sugar per average serve.

SUGAR SUBSTITUTES

Many sweet-tasting substances are now used instead of sugar to produce reduced-sugar products for people trying to control their weight or blood sugar levels. These substances are either reduced-calorie sweeteners (isomalt and sugar alcohols) or artificial, non-nutritive sweeteners (for example: aspartame, cyclamate, saccharin, acesulphame-K, sucralose).

Unlike 'nutritive' or sugar-containing sweeteners, such as table sugar, honey and golden syrup, and reduced-energy sweeteners, artificial sweeteners are intensely sweet and don't provide any calories because they are used in very small amounts.

Sugar alcohols (sorbitol, mannitol, xylitol, maltitol, lactitol) and isomalt are mainly used to sweeten 'diet' products because they are not completely absorbed in the intestine and therefore provide fewer calories than normal sugars.

Sugar alcohols occur naturally in plums, apples and other foods, or they can be produced commercially from carbohydrates such as sucrose, glucose and starch. Apart from adding a sweet taste, sugar alcohols also add bulk and texture to foods, provide a cooling effect or aftertaste, and help retain moisture in foods. When consumed in large amounts, sugar alcohols can have a laxative effect, and are only used in small amounts in products, such as sugar-free chewing gum and lollies.

Sucralose is a reduced-calorie sweetener made from a sugar that can't be digested and so passes through the body without being absorbed. It is about 600 times sweeter than sugar, so it's used in tiny amounts, replacing the calories that would normally be provided by sugar, in foods like jams, confectionery and cakes. Sucralose can be used in home cooking to replace sugar in cakes and desserts because it's stable at high temperatures. Foods containing sucralose are safe for consumption in normal-sized portions by healthy adults and children, and people with diabetes.

Sugar substitutes can be purchased from the supermarket in tablet or granule form to be used at home in place of sugar to sweeten drinks and foods. These artificial sweeteners can replace sugar in most foods, resulting in a reduction of the food's calorie content of approximately 67 kilojoules (16 Calories) per teaspoon.

However, sweeteners used as a substitute for table sugar are less popular than the artificial sweeteners that are used in confectionery and soft drinks. Recent surveys indicate that nearly one in three Australian people regularly drink 'diet' soft drinks.

One of the most common sweeteners is aspartame, which is used as an ingredient in breakfast cereals, soft drinks and desserts. Aspartame is about 200 times sweeter than sugar. Tiny amounts of aspartame produce a satisfactory level of sweetness, so calories can be substantially reduced or almost eliminated by using aspartame in place of sugar.

Aspartame also enhances fruit flavours and doesn't increase blood sugar levels or contribute to tooth decay. However, it contains the natural amino acid phenylalanine and, therefore,

FAT REDUCTION VERSUS SUGAR REDUCTION

Reducing your fat intake can cut more calories from your diet than reducing your sugar intake because fat contains more calories per gram and is often consumed in larger amounts than sugar. However, if you have a high intake of fat and sugar, particularly sugar-rich drinks, you may need to cut down on both.

HIGH-FAT	LOW-FAT	HIGH-SUGAR	LOW-SUGAR
Regular margarine 2 teaspoons = 250 kJ	Low-fat cottage cheese 35 kJ	Table sugar 2 teaspoons = 134 kJ	Artificial sweetener 17 kJ
Full-cream milk 1 cup = 700 kJ	Skim milk 377 kJ	Regular soft drink 375 ml = 657 kJ	Sugar-free soft drink 8 kJ
Lamb chop, untrimmed, fried 2 small chops = 1340 kJ	Grilled, trimmed of fat 688 kJ	Regular cordial 1 cup = 463 kJ	Sugar-free cordial 15 kJ
Sour cream 2 tablespoons = 605 kJ	Low-fat yoghurt 92 kJ	Regular jam 1 tablespoon = 289 kJ	Sugar-free jam 21 kJ

aspartame-containing products are not suitable for consumption by people with phenylketonuria, who can't metabolise phenylalanine.

DO SUGAR SUBSTITUTES HAVE ANY BENEFITS FOR WEIGHT CONTROL OR HEALTH?

- Weight control—most people use artificial sweeteners for weight control purposes, but they don't produce weight loss or prevent weight gain in most people who use them. There are three main reasons for this: most people simply add artificially sweetened products to their diet rather than using them instead of sugar-rich versions; some sugar-free products still contain high amounts of fat and calories; and many people wrongly think that by using sugar-free products they have spared enough calories to allow them to eat larger than normal portions of other foods. Sugar substitutes may be helpful for weight control if you use normal portions of them in place of foods you eat regularly in your low-fat diet, such as yoghurts, soft drinks and sugar sprinkled on cereal.

- Tooth decay—instead of preventing tooth decay by replacing sugar, some artificial sweeteners can erode tooth enamel because they are acidic.

- Diabetes—people with diabetes don't have to totally avoid sugar because small amounts of sugar won't disturb their blood sugar level. However, if you have diabetes, you still need to eat less sugar than most people consume. If you choose artificially sweetened foods, use a variety of sweeteners and make sure you eat normal-sized portions.

- Other diseases—there is no strong scientific evidence to suggest that the regular use of artificial sweeteners in normal amounts causes cancer, multiple sclerosis or any other diseases.

STEP 7: CHOOSE LOW-SALT FOODS AND LIMIT YOUR USE OF TABLE SALT

Table salt contains 40 per cent sodium and 60 per cent chloride and its chemical name is sodium chloride. A teaspoon of salt weighs 5 grams (1/8 oz) and contains 2 grams (1/16 oz) of sodium.

Sodium and chloride are both minerals with important roles in the body. Sodium is needed to regulate the body's fluid balance and blood pressure and for the proper functioning of nerves and muscles. Chloride is also needed to maintain normal fluid balance and blood pressure, and is a component of the stomach's digestive juices.

A certain amount of sodium chloride is needed for the normal functioning of the body, but most people consume far more than they need, mainly because salt is added to so many processed foods. The recommended intake of sodium for adults is between 0.9 and 2.3 milligrams per day or a maximum of one teaspoon of salt per day. However, in western countries many people consume more than 2.5 teaspoons of salt a day.

Health authorities advise against consuming too much salt because a high salt intake increases the risk of developing high blood pressure (hypertension), which in turn increases the risk of early death from heart disease or stroke. Almost half of the population of western countries develop high blood pressure with age. Scientists estimate that if most people simply cut their salt intake by 30 per cent, there would be a 16 per cent fall in deaths due to heart disease and a 50 per cent reduction in the number of people requiring treatment for hypertension.

In addition to protecting you from hypertension as you get older, there are other good reasons to control your salt intake, even if your blood pressure is normal. An excessive intake of salt will increase your fluid needs and may contribute to osteoporosis and kidney stones. In addition, the drugs that are prescribed to lower blood pressure have adverse side effects,

SHOPPING

- Use the nutrient information on food labels to help you compare the sodium or salt content of different foods. Choose 'reduced-salt', 'salt-free' or 'no added salt' products.
- Choose frozen or fresh vegetables rather than canned.
- Choose fish or vegetables canned in water rather than brine.
- Buy unsalted nuts and low-salt snack foods (fresh fruit, yoghurt, rice cakes).

COOKING

- Don't add salt to meals before or after cooking.
- Don't add salt to the water when boiling vegetables, rice or pasta.
- Flavour foods with low-salt seasonings, such as lemon juice and rind, herbs, spices, garlic, chilli, pepper, wine and onions.
- Use unsalted butter or margarine for baking cakes and biscuits.

EATING

- Don't add table salt to your meals.
- Limit your intake of salty take-away foods and snacks. Replace them with healthy salt-free choices.
- Replace processed or smoked meat and fish with freshly roasted meat or poultry slices and fresh fish.
- Limit your intake of gherkins, olives and other pickled vegetables. Replace them with fresh vegetables.
- Squeeze fresh lemon juice on vegetables, fish, rice or pasta for a refreshing taste.
- Limit the amounts of salty sauces, spreads and cheeses you add to foods.
- Add some salt-free garlic-and-herb seasoning to soup to liven up the flavour.
- When eating out, choose freshly made dishes, such as steaks or fish, that aren't swimming in sauce, and ask the chef not to add any salt.

such as nausea, cramps and reduced blood sugar control, so prevention is better than the cure.

The best way to prevent hypertension is to have a healthy diet with a low to moderate salt intake, as well as remaining physically active and maintaining a healthy body weight.

WHAT IS HIGH BLOOD PRESSURE?
Blood pressure refers to the amount of force exerted by the blood against artery walls while it is circulating around the body. A blood pressure measurement consists of two numbers. The first number represents systolic blood pressure, which is the pressure in your blood vessels created by the contraction of your heart. The second number represents diastolic blood pressure, which is the pressure in your blood vessels when your heart is relaxing in between heart beats (contractions). Optimal blood pressure is less than 110/70.

You should have your blood pressure measured when you're feeling calm and relaxed because stress, anxiety or exercise can elevate both systolic and diastolic blood pressure by up to 20 units (mmHg) on both readings. For this reason, a high blood pressure measurement on one occasion should be re-checked on another day, especially before any medication is prescribed.

RISK FACTORS FOR HIGH BLOOD PRESSURE
- Genetics—if high blood pressure runs in your family, you may have a greater risk
- A high salt intake
- A high alcohol intake (either regularly or infrequent binges)
- Excess body weight
- Older age
- Smoking
- Being inactive
- Regularly feeling stressed.

REDUCING SALT INTAKE
To significantly lower your salt intake you need to choose low-salt foods and stop using the salt shaker at meals and while cooking. You can cut your salt intake significantly if you use reduced-salt versions of foods that you eat regularly, such as bread, spreads, cheese and breakfast cereals.

Gradually switch to using salt-reduced products to give your taste buds time to adjust. After a few weeks you won't miss the salt. Humans are not born with a preference for salt, but we learn to like it by eating salty foods. You can retrain your taste buds to like the natural flavours of healthy foods without the salt.

Use the nutrient information on food labels to help you choose lower-salt varieties. If a product's salt content has been reduced, one of the following terms will appear on the label:

- reduced-salt contains less than 75 per cent of the salt in the regular version
- low-salt contains less than 120 milligrams of sodium per 100 grams of food
- no added salt or unsalted means no salt has been added during processing, but this doesn't mean that the product is sodium-free
- reduced-sodium contains at least 25 per cent less sodium than the regular version, but it may still be high in sodium, so use sparingly
- low-sodium contains 120 milligrams or less of sodium per 100 grams of food
- sodium-free contains 5 milligrams or less of sodium per serve.

STEP 8: DRINK PLENTY OF WATER THROUGHOUT THE DAY

Water is the second most essential compound for our survival, with oxygen being the first. An average healthy adult can survive for about eight weeks without food, but can only live for a few days without water.

Water accounts for 50 to 70 per cent of our body weight, with the percentage being greater in infants than adults. A loss of as little as 10 per cent of body water due to excessive vomiting or diarrhoea is a serious health risk in adults, and could be fatal in a young child.

There's so much water in your body because it plays a vital role in all bodily processes—it's involved in metabolic reactions and also provides the medium in which these reactions occur.

Water is needed for the digestion and absorption of food, maintaining a normal temperature in the body, and for the lubrication and protection of body joints. As a major component of blood, water helps deliver nutrients to body cells and transports waste to the kidneys for excretion. Water also helps prevent urinary tract infections by flushing toxins out of the body.

Water also contains small amounts of essential minerals, such as sodium, potassium, calcium, copper and magnesium, depending on the mineral content of the rock or soil from where it has come. Hard water contains higher levels of these minerals than soft water.

SHOULD I INCREASE MY SALT INTAKE WHEN I SWEAT?
Unless recommended by a doctor, there is no need to increase your salt intake in hot weather or when exercising. The body itself carefully adjusts the salt content of sweat according to its own salt balance. Increasing your salt intake under these conditions can, in fact, cause dehydration and cramps. Most people eat far more salt than they need, so it's better to concentrate on drinking more water when you're hot and sweaty.

Only a small number of endurance athletes and people with certain medical conditions that cause excessive sweating or diarrhoea may need to increase their salt intake.

SALT AND FOOD LABELS
Eating less salt is easier than you think. Supermarket shelves contain reduced-salt varieties of many popular foods. You can't always tell if a food is high in salt by its flavour because some sweet-tasting foods contain lots of salt.

HOW MUCH WATER?
The body can't store water so a regular intake of liquid throughout the day is essential to replace the fluid that's constantly being lost from your body.

In normal conditions, adults need about 2 to 3 litres of water a day (8 to 12 glasses of water), but much more fluid is needed when the body's losses are greater, such as in hot, dry weather, at high altitudes, and during strenuous physical activity.

Sweating is the body's way of getting rid of extra heat, and sweating rates increase as the environment gets drier or when the body's temperature rises (due to exercise or illness). If you don't drink enough fluid to replace your sweat losses, you will become dehydrated.

A loss of only 2 per cent of body weight as water (mild dehydration—1.4 kg (3 lb 2 oz) for a 70 kg (15½ lb) person) will lower your blood volume and reduce your capacity to perform physical and mental tasks, even before you feel badly affected. It's quite easy to lose a litre or more of fluid during an hour or two of hard physical activity.

Unfortunately, thirst isn't a good indication of your body's fluid needs, because you're already slightly dehydrated by the time you feel thirsty. Drinking plenty of water throughout the day is the best way to meet your daily fluid needs and avoid dehydration. You'll also obtain some fluid from the foods and other drinks you consume, such as milk, fruits, vegetables, meats, porridge and bread.

Infants and children need more fluid than adults and therefore have a greater risk of dehydration. Children should take a drink bottle or two to school or sport, and should be encouraged to drink water throughout the day. If they don't like plain water, flavour it with a little juice to encourage drinking.

FACTORS THAT INCREASE FLUID LOSS OR FLUID NEEDS
- Hot, dry temperatures
- Fever, diarrhoea and vomiting
- Exercise and physical labour
- Low-calorie and high-protein diets
- High salt or fibre intake
- Alcohol consumption
- Caffeine consumption
- Pregnancy and breast feeding

IS BOTTLED WATER BETTER THAN TAP WATER?
Bottled water comes in different forms, including mineral, spring and distilled tap water. Although bottled waters are often marketed as being fresh and pure, they may not necessarily be any safer or healthier than tap water.

In several instances, bottled water has been found to contain higher than recommended levels of bromate. Too much bromate can cause a number of health problems, including nausea, diarrhoea, kidney and nerve problems.

If you are concerned about the purity of your tap water, you can use a simple activated charcoal water filter that will remove chlorine and other bad-tasting substances from the water. These simple filters also keep more minerals in the water than complicated filter units, distillation units or water softeners (ion exchange units), which remove contaminants as well as calcium and magnesium and replace them with sodium.

STEP 9: EAT CALCIUM-RICH FOODS ON A REGULAR BASIS

Calcium is needed to maintain the strength of your bones and teeth, is required for normal blood pressure and blood clotting, and for the proper functioning of nerves and muscles. Most of the calcium in your body is found in your skeleton, where it maintains bone strength and acts as a reservoir from which calcium can be drawn when it is needed by other parts of the body.

Bone is a living tissue that is constantly changing. It has a web-like structure, which makes it a strong but light shock-absorbing material. Most of your bone mass is formed during childhood, when the skeleton rapidly increases in thickness and strength.

Our bones generally stop growing in length when we are between 16 and 18 years of age, but continue to grow in strength up until our early thirties. Between the ages of 16 and 30, depending on your genes and dietary habits, your bones will have reached their maximum strength and thickness (peak bone mass). Between the ages of 35 and 45, bone breakdown begins to exceed bone formation as part of the natural ageing process, but an adequate calcium intake can reduce this rate of bone loss.

If enough bone is lost over time, the skeleton becomes weaker and fractures more easily, resulting in osteoporosis. Even though they may have been losing bone mass for years, many people don't realise they have osteoporosis until they have experienced the first of possibly many fractures.

Many children and adults regularly don't eat the recommended amount of calcium each day and are at risk of developing osteoporosis. Women have a greater risk than men because they generally have a smaller bone mass and have an accelerated rate of bone loss for about five years after menopause. Osteoporosis can also occur in younger people, particularly in young women who have lost a lot of weight and not had their menstrual periods for a while. As with postmenopausal women, the lower level of oestrogen in their body prevents calcium from being retained in their bones.

REDUCING THE RISK OF OSTEOPOROSIS
- Regularly eat calcium-rich foods.
- Get adequate exposure to sunlight (several hours a week). Your body needs vitamin D to absorb calcium.
- Do at least 30 minutes of physical activity each day. Weight-bearing exercise (such as walking, weight training, tennis, low-impact aerobics) helps keep your bones strong.
- Limit your intake of alcohol to one to two standard drinks a day, with alcohol-free days each week.
- Don't smoke.
- Limit your intake of salt and caffeine.
- Don't consume excess protein.

- Women shouldn't lose so much weight that their menstrual periods stop.

SOURCES OF CALCIUM
Dairy products, such as milk, cheese and yoghurt, are the richest sources of dietary calcium, and they also provide the other essential nutrients for healthy bones (protein, magnesium and phosphorous). Just three serves of dairy products a day supplies all the calcium most healthy people need (one serve equals 250 ml (1 cup) of milk; 200 g (6½ oz) of yoghurt; or 35 g (1 oz) of hard cheese). There are dairy products to suit everyone's tastes, and low-fat varieties for those trying to reduce their fat and cholesterol intake.

Other sources of calcium include calcium-enriched soy milk and tofu, canned salmon or sardines eaten with their bones, canned crab meat, some green vegetables (broccoli and Chinese cabbage), calcium-enriched drinking powders, dried figs, spinach, sweet potatoes and grains. However, more of the calcium in dairy foods is absorbed by the body than the calcium in cereals and vegetables because absorption is impaired by certain compounds in plant foods (tannins, fibre and oxalates).

CALCIUM AND LACTOSE INTOLERANCE
If you have lactose intolerance and can't drink large amounts of cow's milk, try to consume smaller amounts of dairy products throughout the day. Full-cream milk will be easier for you to digest than skim milk. Lactose-reduced milks are also available. Most cheeses don't contain much lactose and you can reduce the amount of lactose in yoghurt by storing it in the fridge for a while.

If you choose to avoid dairy products, you will need to consume larger amounts of the other calcium-containing foods listed above. Include calcium in your main meals and snacks by adding some dried figs or raw almonds to breakfast cereals, desserts and yoghurt, or some cheese, salmon or crab meat to salads.

CALCIUM SUPPLEMENTS
If you can't consume enough calcium on a regular basis, your doctor may recommend a calcium supplement, particularly if you have a higher risk of bone loss. You should look for a calcium-only supplement rather than a multivitamin and mineral tablet, which typically contain small amounts of calcium. Avoid calcium supplements that also contain iron and magnesium—these minerals actually reduce the amount of calcium that your body will absorb. While taking supplements, make sure that you don't take high-dose calcium supplements (more than 800 mg a day) or calcium supplements containing vitamin D on a regular basis (to avoid vitamin D toxicity and imbalances in other minerals).

INCREASING CALCIUM INTAKE

- Read the ingredient list and nutrition information on food labels to compare the calcium content of different products, and choose calcium-enriched breakfast cereals, drinking powders and dairy products.
- Eat yoghurt instead of ice cream for snacks or dessert—

you'll get more calcium as well as less fat and calories.

- For breakfast, add calcium-enriched low-fat milk and drinking powder to your cereal instead of full-cream milk and sugar.
- Use low-fat cheese on bread instead of butter and drink a calcium-enriched low-fat milk instead of full-fat milk.

STEP 10: MAKE IRON-RICH FOODS A REGULAR PART OF YOUR DIET

Iron is needed for a healthy immune system, for producing energy from the nutrients you eat, for metabolising drugs and protecting your cells from damage caused by free radicals. Iron is also essential for transporting oxygen around the body, because it is a component of the body's two main oxygen-carrying proteins: haemoglobin and myoglobin.

Haemoglobin is the protein in red blood cells that takes oxygen from the lungs to the body's cells, and then takes carbon dioxide back to the lungs to be exhaled from the body.

Myoglobin is a protein found in muscles. It stores oxygen until needed by the muscles to contract and move.

IRON DEFICIENCY
In western countries, people's diets are more likely to be deficient in iron, zinc, calcium or dietary fibre than any other nutrients. Dietary surveys indicate that many people don't eat iron-rich foods on a regular basis, and sales of red meat have fallen over the last three decades. In fact, iron deficiency is the most common nutrient deficiency in the world.

Symptoms of iron deficiency include feeling constantly tired and lethargic, depression, a lack of concentration, and greater difficulty in performing and recovering from exercise. However, these symptoms could be due to other factors, such as a virus, lack of sleep or lack of carbohydrate. A doctor needs to take a blood test to confirm iron deficiency. Don't self-diagnose iron deficiency because problems can arise from the use of iron supplements when you're not actually deficient.

Although iron deficiency can lead to the serious condition of anaemia, not everybody with iron deficiency is actually anaemic. Anaemia only occurs when the body's iron stores are depleted, which may take several years, because the body tries to compensate for falling iron stores by absorbing more of the iron you eat. As the body's iron stores continue to fall, less haemoglobin is made by the body and the red blood cells that are formed are pale and small and not able to carry as much oxygen.

At this stage, symptoms include fatigue, weakness, headaches, decreased ability to perform physical or mental work, an increased risk of illness and infection, and impaired mental development in infants and young children.

WHO'S AT RISK OF IRON DEFICIENCY?
• Teenage girls and women of reproductive age lose more iron from their bodies than men due to menstruation, and also tend to eat less iron. About one-third of these women consume less than 70 per cent of the recommended daily intake of iron.

- Pregnant women need much more iron for the growth and development of their baby as well as to increase their own blood supply.
- Infants and children up to six years old have higher iron needs due to their rapid growth rates. Iron stores at birth are sufficient to meet their needs for the first four to six months, but after this time infants need iron-fortified formula or cereals. Toddlers who are fussy eaters may not consume enough iron.
- Vegetarians consume iron in plant foods, but the body does not absorb this as efficiently as the iron found in meat.
- Teenage boys are growing rapidly and may not eat enough iron.
- Athletes have high iron needs for growing muscle and energy production, and may also be losing iron through sweat. They may have low iron intake due to poor dietary habits, little time to eat or drastic weight loss practices.

SOURCES OF IRON

Iron is found in both plant and animal foods, but occurs in two different chemical forms—haem iron and non-haem iron. Most of the iron in animal products is haem iron, which is the same kind of iron found in haemoglobin and myoglobin, and our bodies absorb this more efficiently than non-haem iron.

Good sources of haem iron include meat, poultry, fish and seafood. Red meat, oysters and mussels have particularly high levels of this type of iron.

Non-haem iron is found in eggs, legumes, fortified breakfast cereals and drinking powders, wholegrain bread, leafy green vegetables, nuts and seeds.

It's possible to increase the absorption of non-haem iron by combining it with certain foods. For example, the muscle proteins in meat, poultry and fish increase the absorption of non-haem iron by up to three times. So you can absorb more of the non-haem iron in a plant food, such as rice or bread, by eating it with some meat, chicken or fish. Vitamin C also increases the absorption of non-haem iron up to three times if eaten in the same meal. So add some strawberries or kiwi fruit to your iron-enriched breakfast cereal, have a glass of orange juice with your sandwich or add lots of capsicum and spinach to your stir-fries.

On the other hand, some substances can reduce the absorption of non-haem iron, such as tannin in tea, phytates in grains and oxalates in spinach, and compounds in soy foods. For example, the tannin in one large cup of black tea reduces non-haem iron absorption by around 50 per cent. The presence of these compounds means that only a small amount of iron in the diet is actually absorbed. This means that you need to be extra careful about eating plenty of iron if you are vegetarian or have higher iron needs. Drink less strong tea or coffee in between meals and look for iron-enriched products in your supermarket, including breakfast cereals, pasta, breads and drinking powders.

Some soy milks may be fortified with iron, but this iron is not well absorbed. However, the iron in processed soy foods, such as miso, tempeh and tofu, tends to be better absorbed.

RED MEAT AND IRON

During the last three decades, the consumption of red meat in western countries has fallen because people have less time to cook and some people think meat is unhealthy or fattening. However, this isn't the case. There are now many lean cuts of meats available, which can be cooked quickly, and meat is a filling and nutritious food—a factor that is particularly beneficial if you're trying to control your weight. Some people think that meat is heavy or fattening because they eat very large portions, but all you really need is 100 to 150 grams (3–5 oz) of meat, three to four times a week (two to three slices of roast meat, ½ cup of cooked meat strips or mince, or 2 lean lamb chops).

Many people these days are also not used to eating filling foods. They have grown up eating white bread, fruit juice, and other foods that don't need much chewing. You can make meat less difficult to eat by using mince or

THE IRON CONTENT OF COMMON PROTEIN-RICH FOODS

FOOD (SERVE SIZE)	FAT (grams)	IRON (milligrams)	ENERGY (kJ)
Lean beef (100 g/3 oz)	1.8	2.4	450
Lean lamb (100 g/3 oz)	4.2	2.3	501
Eggs (2 large = 100 g/3 oz)	10.9	1.8 *	632
Baked beans (100 g/3 oz)	0.5	1.6 *	285
Canned red salmon (100 g/3 oz)	12.0	1.2	815
Lean pork (100 g/3 oz)	1.7	1.0	438
Skinless chicken (100 g/3 oz)	3.3	1.0	466
Tofu (100 g/3 oz)	0.4	0.4 *	107
Cheddar cheese (100 g/3 oz)	33.8	0.0	1690

* Contain non-haem iron, so not all of this iron will be absorbed.

ADAPTED FROM: *The Role of Red Meat in Healthy Australian Diets*, Meat and Livestock, Australia, 2001

COMBINING IRON WITH VITAMIN C

HAEM-IRON	NON-HAEM IRON	VITAMIN C
Lean beef	Nuts, sesame seeds	Orange juice
Lean lamb	Legumes	Guava juice
Lean pork	Muesli	Drinks with added vitamin C
Skinless chicken or turkey	Wholemeal or grain bread	Fresh citrus fruit
(darker meat)	Iron-enriched breakfast cereals	Pawpaw, mangoes
Liver, liverwurst	Iron-enriched pasta	Kiwi fruit
Heart	Dried fruit	Fresh berries
Fish	Spinach	Pineapple
Oysters	Eggs	Capsicum, spinach
Mussels	Cocoa powder	Parsley, tomatoes
Scallops	Iron-enriched drinking powders	Broccoli, cauliflower
Canned crab	Curry powder	Cabbage, Asian greens
		Sprouts

thin strips of meat. Another common misconception is that meat stays in your stomach a long time and can't be broken down, but this is also not true. Your stomach is full of digestive acids, which efficiently break down all food matter, except some fibres.

Including lean meat in your diet is one of the easiest ways to consume all of the iron, zinc, vitamin B12, essential fatty acids and protein you need.

A WORD OF CAUTION

Not everyone needs extra iron. Some people have a genetic disorder called haemochromatosis, which means they have an excessively high iron level in their body. It is the most common genetic disorder in Caucasians living in North America, Europe and Australasia,

TIPS TO HELP BOOST YOUR IRON INTAKE

- Eat meals containing lean red meat or liver three to four times a week. A small serve (100 to 150 grams/3–5 oz) is enough.
- Read the ingredient list and nutrient panel on food labels to help you identify foods with added iron (such as pasta, breakfast cereals, breads and drinking powders). Consume these in place of non-enriched versions.
- Add some vitamin C or haem iron such as meat, poultry, fish or seafood to foods containing non-haem iron, such as legumes, eggs, breakfast cereals, rice, pasta, bread or spinach. For example, add tomatoes and capsicum to a spinach omelette, and sprinkle some dried apricots and fresh fruit on your iron-enriched breakfast cereal and serve with a glass of guava or orange juice. See the lists above to help you mix and match foods containing iron with those containing vitamin C.
- If you are a vegetarian, make sure you eat some good sources of non-haem iron at main meals, such as eggs, legumes, spinach, iron-fortified pasta or breakfast cereals.
- Avoid strongly brewed tea, especially with your meals. Drink weak tea in between meals.
- Don't add unprocessed wheat bran to your meals. Look for bran-rich breakfast cereals with added iron.

affecting approximately one in 300 people. The symptoms experienced by these people are related to the amount of iron in their body. Initially they may experience lethargy and fatigue, but rising iron levels can lead to heart and liver damage, diabetes and some types of cancer. Early diagnosis and regular treatment can reduce this risk.

Treatment of haemochromatosis involves regularly donating blood and avoiding a high-iron diet and combinations of foods that enhance iron absorption. If you have a family history of this disorder, see your doctor, who can test whether you or your children are also at risk.

BREAKFAST

BREAKFAST

A healthy, nourishing breakfast is the best start to the day that you can give your body. It will boost your energy levels and help you cope with the challenges of the day ahead.

Breakfast is, literally, the meal that breaks the fast of the previous night. We all know that breakfast is an important meal because it replenishes our fuel stores and recharges the brain and body. And yet it still seems to be the most neglected time, the meal least thought is given to. Many people are on 'autopilot' as they reach for a cup of coffee and grab a cereal bar or piece of toast on the way out the door. However, a healthy breakfast can be tasty, something to look forward to and enjoy before dealing with the demands of a busy day.

Compared to people who regularly skip breakfast, breakfast-eaters tend to consume more vitamins and minerals and less fat, and have lower blood cholesterol and a lower body weight. This is because breakfast-skippers tend to overeat later in the day, and often choose fatty snacks because they are the easiest option.

For everyday breakfasts, try to keep the fat content down, and include carbohydrates in the form of fruit, cereal or bread. The small amount of time it takes to make up your own Puffed corn cereal (page 62) gives you satisfaction in knowing exactly what you are eating,

and knowing that it contains no added sugar or preservatives. If you soak your Bircher muesli (page 63) overnight, no preparation is needed the next morning.

Weekends may be a more leisurely affair when breakfast becomes brunch, a time to relax and savour food. When stone fruits are in season, enjoy Grilled fruit with cinnamon toast (page 67). When you are making Banana bread (page 69), make a double quantity, and freeze one loaf. Then, for your weekend brunch, simply defrost the bread, warm it in the oven and serve it dolloped with delicious maple ricotta and fresh seasonal fruit.

Enjoy boiled or poached eggs, not more than twice a week, and serve with lean bacon only as a rare treat. Eggs are an excellent source of nutrients and protein. However, they may need to be eaten in moderation if you are watching your weight or blood cholesterol level.

A great way of incorporating fibre into the diet is to leave the skin on fruit, choose wholegrain breads and cereals, and drink lots of water to enhance the beneficial effects of fibre. Both soluble fibre (found in fruit, vegetables, oats, barley and legumes) and insoluble fibre (found in the skins of fruit and vegetables, wholegrains and nuts) help to lower high blood cholesterol and help prevent bowel disorders and diseases.

When buying cereal from a supermarket, read the nutrition panel on the packet and choose one that is wholegrain, low in fat and added salt and sugar. Often these are the plainer cereals, such as:
• rolled oats
• wheat germ
• natural rather than toasted muesli
• wholewheat breakfast biscuits
• bran flakes
• processed cereals based on whole wheat, oats and barley.

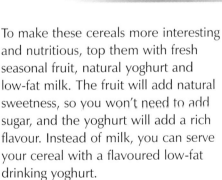

To make these cereals more interesting and nutritious, top them with fresh seasonal fruit, natural yoghurt and low-fat milk. The fruit will add natural sweetness, so you won't need to add sugar, and the yoghurt will add a rich flavour. Instead of milk, you can serve your cereal with a flavoured low-fat drinking yoghurt.

If your preference is toast or muffins, then choose wholegrain varieties, and spread them with only a little butter or margarine, if any. Below are some nutritious toppings for your toast:
- cottage cheese with fresh tomatoes
- ripe avocado with a squeeze of lemon
- low-fat cream cheese and banana
- baked beans
- ricotta and chopped fresh dates.

BREAKFAST DRINKS

Smoothies provide a fast, healthy fix for those who don't have time to sit down to breakfast. Simply blend your favourite combination, including ingredients such as:
- fresh seasonal fruit (berries, bananas, mango, rockmelon)
- natural or low-fat fruit yoghurt
- wheat germ
- an egg
- honey
- oat bran
- a breakfast wheat biscuit.

Fresh fruit juices are another delicious way to include fruit in the diet. Enjoy a freshly squeezed orange juice to start the day, or try a fruit, vegetable and herb combination:
- orange, pineapple and mint
- apple and ginger
- strawberry and pear
- watermelon and passionfruit pulp
- rockmelon and mint
- beetroot, apple and parsley.

Tea and coffee are common breakfast beverage choices. Both contain caffeine (tea about half the amount of coffee). Caffeine stimulates the central nervous system and may increase the heart rate, which can give a 'wake up' jolt in the mornings. However, caffeine is also a diuretic that promotes fluid loss from the body. It is recommended that coffee and tea be enjoyed in moderation—no more than three or four cups a day. There is a large range of caffeine-free and herbal teas available, as well as decaffeinated coffee and coffee substitutes.

Serves 4

Preparation time:
10 minutes + standing + chilling

Cooking time: 5 minutes

Easy

185 g (1 cup) instant couscous
500 ml (2 cups) apple and
   blackcurrant juice
1 cinnamon stick
250 g (8 oz) raspberries
250 g (8 oz) blueberries
250 g (8 oz) strawberries, halved
2 teaspoons grated lime rind
1 tablespoon finely shredded fresh mint
200 g (6½ oz) low-fat plain yoghurt
2 tablespoons maple syrup

NUTRITION PER SERVE

- Protein 8.5 g;
- Fat 3 g;
- Carbohydrate 70 g;
- Dietary Fibre 7 g;
- Cholesterol 8 mg;
- 1448 kJ (346 Cal)

VARIATION: Try using orange juice and dried fruits or fresh mango, peach, pear and apple.

MIXED BERRY COUSCOUS

This sweet couscous makes a delicious breakfast or dessert, providing a refreshing mix of carbohydrate, fibre, vitamin C, calcium and antioxidants.

1   Place the couscous in a bowl. Pour the apple and blackcurrant juice into a small saucepan and add the cinnamon stick. Bring to the boil, then remove from the heat and pour over the couscous. Cover with plastic wrap and leave for 5 minutes, or until the liquid has been absorbed. Remove the cinnamon stick. Chill.

2   Separate the couscous grains with a fork, add the berries, lime rind and mint, and gently fold through. Spoon the mixture into four bowls. Top with a large dollop of yoghurt and drizzle with the maple syrup. Serve the couscous chilled.

Serves 4

Preparation time: 5 minutes

Cooking time: 20 minutes

Easy

600 g (6 cups) rolled oats
55 g (½ cup) rolled rice flakes
60 g (½ cup) rolled barley
60 g (½ cup) rolled rye
30 g (½ cup) millet flakes

STEWED RHUBARB
350 g (12 oz) rhubarb
95 g (½ cup) soft brown sugar
¼ teaspoon ground mixed spice

NUTRITION PER SERVE

- Protein 5.5 g
- Fat 3.5 g;
- Carbohydrate 37 g;
- Dietary Fibre 4.5 g;
- Cholesterol 0 mg;
- 858 kJ (205 Cal)

PORRIDGE with stewed rhubarb

This recipe provides a more nutritious version of traditional porridge. It's rich in slowly digested carbohydrate and soluble fibre—great for keeping hunger at bay.

1   Place all the porridge ingredients in a large bowl and mix together well. Store in a large airtight jar until ready to use.

2   To make enough porridge for four, place 200 g (2 cups) of the porridge mixture in a saucepan with 1.25 litres water. Bring to the boil, then reduce the heat and simmer over medium heat, stirring frequently, for 15 minutes, or until the porridge is thick. (If it is too thick, add a little skim milk.)

3   To make the stewed rhubarb, cut the rhubarb into 2 cm (¾ in) lengths. Place in a saucepan with the sugar, mixed spice and 250 ml (1 cup) water. Slowly bring to the boil, stirring to dissolve the sugar, then reduce the heat and simmer for 10 minutes, stirring often. Serve hot or cold with the porridge.

NOTES: The dry porridge mixture makes about 8 cups (enough for 16 serves). It can be stored in a large airtight jar or container for up to 2 months.
    The cooking time of the porridge will decrease considerably if you use quick-cooking oats (one-minute oats), so make sure you check the packet carefully when you buy the rolled oats.

Serves 20 (Makes about 1.5 kg/
3 lb 5 oz)

Preparation time: 10 minutes

Cooking time: 15 minutes

Easy

85 g (3 oz) puffed corn
85 g (3 oz) puffed millet
400 g (13 oz) dried fruit and nut mix
180 g (6 oz) unprocessed natural bran
60 g (2 oz) flaked coconut
60 g (1/3 cup) pepitas
185 ml (3/4 cup) maple syrup
70 g (1 cup) processed bran cereal
400 g (13 oz) dried fruit salad mix,
   chopped

NUTRITION PER SERVE

• Protein 5 g;
• Fat 4 g;
• Carbohydrate 47 g;
• Dietary Fibre 9 g;
• Cholesterol 0 mg;
• 965 kJ (231 Cal)

PUFFED CORN CEREAL

The ingredients of this breakfast cereal come from four food groups and provide carbohydrate, fibre, B vitamins, vitamin A, and magnesium.

1 Preheat the oven to moderate 180°C (350°F/Gas 4). Spread out the corn, millet, fruit and nut mix, bran, coconut and pepitas in a large roasting tin.

2 Pour the maple syrup over the puffed corn mixture and stir until the dry ingredients are well coated.

3 Stir in the bran cereal and fruit salad mix and bake for 15 minutes, or until golden, turning the cereal several times during cooking. Cool completely.

Serves 6

Preparation time: 5 minutes + chilling

Easy

300 g (3 cups) rolled oats
250 ml (1 cup) skim milk
100 g (3½ oz) low-fat plain yoghurt
100 ml (½ cup) orange juice
60 g (¼ cup) sugar

125 g (½ cup) low-fat plain yoghurt
2 grated apples
2 cups chopped mixed fresh fruit, such as
    banana, peach, apricot, melon, apple
    or strawberries

POWER THROUGH YOUR MORNING
Unlike many commercially-produced breakfast cereals, home-made muesli has a low glycaemic index (GI), so the carbohydrates it contains are converted into energy slowly. High-fibre, low-GI breakfasts provide a sustained source of energy throughout the morning, so they keep you feeling full longer, and reduce the tendency to snack on sugary foods during the morning. You may also find that you perform better at work or school—research indicates that children who consume a low-GI breakfast score better on attention and memory tasks over the following few hours than kids who eat a high-GI breakfast. Hallmarks of a low-GI breakfast cereal include good levels of fibre; nuts and seeds to provide protein and healthy fats; and only minimal amounts of processed grains or added sugars.

BIRCHER MUESLI

NUTRITION PER SERVE

- Protein 9 g;
- Fat 5 g;
- Carbohydrate 60 g;
- Dietary Fibre 6 g;
- Cholesterol 4.5 mg;
- 1319 kJ (315 Cal)

1 Place rolled oats, milk, yoghurt, orange juice and sugar in a bowl, and mix together well. Cover and refrigerate for 4 hours, or overnight. Serve with plain yoghurt, grated apples and 2 cups chopped mixed fresh fruit. Drizzle with a little honey, if desired.

Serves 4

Preparation time: 20 minutes + chilling

Cooking time: 15 minutes

Easy

500 g (1 lb) watermelon, cut into large
    cubes
260 g (8 oz) honeydew melon, cut into
    large cubes
½ small pineapple, cut into large pieces
1 mango, cut into 2 cm (¾ in) cubes
250 g (8 oz) strawberries, halved
5 g (¼ cup) small fresh mint sprigs

LEMON GRASS SYRUP
125 ml (½ cup) lime juice
45 g (¼ cup) soft brown sugar
1 stem lemon grass, white part only,
    thinly sliced
2 tablespoons grated fresh ginger
1 vanilla bean, split

NUTRITION PER SERVE

- Protein 3.5 g;
- Fat 0.5 g;
- Carbohydrate 40 g;
- Dietary Fibre 6 g;
- Cholesterol 0 mg;
- 797 kJ (190 Cal)

NOTE: If you prefer your syrup
without the lemon grass pieces but
like the flavour, bruise the white part
of the lemon grass with a rolling pin.
Remove the lemon grass along with
the vanilla bean.

FRUIT SALAD in lemon grass syrup

This is a refreshing blend of fresh fruit, providing vitamin C, antioxidants,
fibre and potassium. Serve with low-fat yoghurt for a calcium boost.

1   Place the fruit and mint in a bowl and mix gently.

2   To make the syrup, place the lime juice, sugar and 125 ml (½ cup) water in a
    small saucepan and stir over low heat until the sugar dissolves. Add the lemon
    grass, ginger and vanilla bean. Bring to the boil, then reduce the heat and
    simmer for 10 minutes, or until reduced. Remove the vanilla bean, pour the
    syrup over the fruit and refrigerate until cold.

Serves 6

Preparation time: 15 minutes

Cooking time: 20 minutes

Easy

150 g (5 oz) English spinach leaves
1 garlic clove, crushed
2 eggs
2 egg whites
60 ml (¼ cup) skim milk
2 tablespoons grated Parmesan
70 g (2 oz) low-fat feta, cut into 1 cm
   (½ in) cubes (you should have
   18 cubes)

NUTRITION PER SERVE

- Protein 8 g;
- Fat 5 g;
- Carbohydrate 0 g;
- Dietary Fibre 0.5 g;
- Cholesterol 100 mg;
- 336 kJ (80 Cal)

SPINACH AND FETA FRITTATAS

These are lower-fat cheese frittatas, full of protein, calcium, vitamin A and riboflavin. The spinach provides extra taste and minerals.

1 Preheat the oven to moderately hot 200°C (400°F/Gas 6). Place the washed spinach leaves and garlic in a saucepan, cover and steam for 3–5 minutes, or until the spinach is wilted.

2 Cool the spinach slightly and squeeze any excess liquid out of the leaves, then roughly chop. Place the eggs, egg whites, skim milk and Parmesan in a bowl, and whisk to combine. Stir in the spinach. Season with salt and ground black pepper.

3 Spoon the spinach mixture into six 125 ml (½ cup) non-stick muffin holes, filling each three-quarters full.

Place three cubes of low-fat feta on top and press lightly into the mixture. Bake for 15 minutes, or until the frittatas are golden and set. Serve immediately.

NOTE: The mixture has a soufflé effect and will deflate quite quickly.

Serves 4

Preparation time: 15 minutes

Cooking time: 30 minutes

Easy

150 g (¾ cup) basmati rice
500 ml (2 cups) milk
4 cardamom pods, bruised
½ cinnamon stick
1 clove
3 tablespoons honey
1 teaspoon vanilla essence

CITRUS COMPOTE
2 ruby grapefruit, peeled and segmented
2 oranges, peeled and segmented
3 tablespoons orange juice
1 teaspoon grated lime rind
3 tablespoons honey
8 fresh mint leaves, finely chopped

NUTRITION PER SERVE

- Protein 9 g;
- Fat 2.5 g;
- Carbohydrate 81 g;
- Dietary Fibre 3 g;
- Cholesterol 9 mg;
- 1575 kJ (375 Cal)

CREAMED RICE
with citrus compote

This is a low-fat version of traditional creamed rice. It's based on slowly digested carbohydrate (rice), topped with vitamin C, fibre, potassium, antioxidants and soothing mint.

1 Cook the rice in a large saucepan of boiling water for 12 minutes, stirring occasionally. Drain and cool.

2 Place the rice, milk, cardamom pods, cinnamon stick and clove in a saucepan and bring to the boil. Reduce the heat to low and simmer for 15 minutes, stirring occasionally, until the milk is absorbed and the rice is creamy. Remove the spices, then stir in the honey and vanilla.

3 To make the compote, combine the ruby grapefruit, orange, orange juice, lime rind, honey and mint, and stir until the honey has dissolved. Serve with the rice.

Serves 4

Preparation time: 10 minutes

Cooking time: 10 minutes

Easy

2 tablespoons low-fat margarine
1½ teaspoons ground cinnamon
4 thick slices brioche
4 ripe plums, halved and stones removed
4 ripe nectarines, halved and stones removed
2 tablespoons warmed blossom honey

NUTRITION PER SERVE

- Protein 9 g;
- Fat 13 g;
- Carbohydrate 66 g;
- Dietary Fibre 7 g;
- Cholesterol 41 mg;
- 1730 kJ (415 Cal)

GRILLED FRUIT with cinnamon toast

More filling and nutritious than toast and jam, and with less fat than French toast, this recipe is a great source of vitamin C, potassium, beta-carotene and fibre.

1 Place the margarine and 1 teaspoon of the ground cinnamon in a bowl and mix until well combined. Grill the brioche on one side until golden. Spread the other side with half the cinnamon spread, then grill until golden. Keep warm in the oven.

2 Brush the plums and nectarines with the remaining spread and cook under a grill until the spread is bubbling and the fruit is tinged at the edges.

3 To serve, place 2 plum halves and 2 nectarine halves on each toasted slice of brioche. Dust with the remaining cinnamon and drizzle with the warmed honey. Dollop with a little fromage frais, if desired.

NOTE: Canned plums or apricots may be used in place of fresh stone fruits.

Serves 4

Preparation time: 15 minutes

Easy

4 plum (Roma) tomatoes, halved
2 large field mushrooms, halved
oil spray
8 slices low-fat bacon
    (we used 97% fat-free)
160 g (5¾ oz) low-fat cottage
    cheese
2 tbs chopped flat-leaf (Italian)
    parsley
1 tbs snipped chives
8 slices ciabatta bread, cut thickly at
    an angle and toasted
balsamic vinegar, to drizzle

NUTRITION PER SERVE

- Fat 3.5 g;
- Carbohydrates 36.6 g;
- Protein 20.3 g
- 1090 kJ (259 Cal);

CIABATTA BREAKFAST TOASTS

These crunchy toasts are great for breakfast or as a snack. The mix of plant foods and bacon provides a range of vitamins and minerals plus antioxidants and protein. Ciabatta is an oval-shaped, dense, crusty Italian bread. It is available from delicatessens. If you can't find it, you can use sourdough or another type of bread.

1 Preheat the broiler (grill). Place the tomatoes, cut-side-up, and the mushrooms on a large baking tray. Lightly spray with the oil. Season well with black pepper.

2 Pat the bacon dry with paper towels and place on the tray. Broil the tomatoes, mushrooms and bacon for 5–8 minutes, or until cooked. Turn the bacon slices once and remove them as they cook and become crisp.

3 Combine the cottage cheese, parsley and chives. Spread thickly over the toasted bread. Arrange the tomatoes, mushrooms and bacon over the top. Drizzle (or spray) with a little balsamic vinegar.

Makes 10–12 slices

Preparation time: 10 minutes

Cooking time: 55 minutes

Easy

80 ml (⅓ cup) strong coffee
125 g (⅔ cup) soft brown sugar
1 egg
1 egg white
60 ml (¼ cup) vegetable oil
1 teaspoon vanilla essence
3 ripe bananas, mashed
125 g (1 cup) plain flour
250 g (2 cups) self-raising flour
½ teaspoon baking powder
1 teaspoon ground ginger
½ teaspoon ground nutmeg
1 teaspoon ground cinnamon
1 teaspoon bicarbonate of soda
200 g (6½ oz) low-fat ricotta
2 tablespoons maple syrup
fresh fruit, to serve

BANANA BREAD
with maple ricotta

This reduced-fat banana bread provides carbohydrate, protein and minerals, and is topped with calcium, fibre and antioxidants.

1 Preheat the oven to warm 170°C (325°F/Gas 3). Lightly grease a 22 x 12 cm/8½ x 4¾ in) loaf tin and line the base with baking paper. Heat the coffee in a small saucepan over low heat, add the brown sugar and stir until the sugar has dissolved.

2 Place the egg, egg white, oil and vanilla in a bowl and beat until just combined. Add the coffee mixture and banana.

3 Sift the flours, baking powder, ginger, nutmeg, cinnamon and bicarbonate of soda onto the mixture and stir gently to combine—do not overbeat. Spoon the mixture into the prepared loaf tin. Bake for 50 minutes, or until a skewer comes out clean when inserted into the centre. Leave in the tin for 10 minutes before turning out onto a wire rack to cool completely.

NUTRITION PER SLICE (12)

- Protein 8 g;
- Fat 7 g;
- Carbohydrate 45 g;
- Dietary Fibre 3.5 g;
- Cholesterol 22.6 mg;
- 1135 kJ (270 Cal)

4 Combine the ricotta and maple syrup in a small bowl. Cut the banana bread into thick slices and serve with the maple ricotta and fresh fruit.

Serves 4

Preparation time: 10 minutes

Cooking time: 40 minutes

Easy

BERRY SAUCE
60 g (¼ cup) sugar
2 teaspoons lemon juice
250 g (8½ oz) raspberries

40 g (⅓ cup) buckwheat flour
100 g (⅔ cup) wholemeal plain flour
1½ teaspoons baking powder
25 g (¼ cup) rolled oats
1 egg yolk
375 ml (1½ cups) buttermilk
3 egg whites
raspberries, to serve

NUTRITION PER SERVE

- Protein 13 g;
- Fat 5 g
- Carbohydrate 51 g
- Dietary Fibre 7.5 g
- Cholesterol 53.5 mg
- 1255 kJ (300 Cal)

OATY BUCKWHEAT PANCAKES

These nourishing pancakes contain slowly digested carbohydrate, fibre and protein.

1 To make the sauce, place the sugar, lemon juice and ¼ cup (60 ml) water in a saucepan over medium heat and bring to the boil. Add the raspberries and cook over low heat for 3 minutes. Cool, then purée in a food processor for 10 seconds.

2 Sift the flours into a bowl and return the husks to the bowl. Add the baking powder and rolled oats and combine. Make a well in the centre. Combine the egg yolk and buttermilk and add to the dry ingredients all at once. Stir to form a smooth batter. Whisk the egg whites until firm peaks form, then fold into the batter.

3 Heat a non-stick frying pan over medium–high heat and brush lightly with butter. Pour ¼ cup (60 ml) batter into the pan and swirl to form a 10 cm (4 in) circle. Cook for 1–2 minutes, or until bubbles appear on the surface. Turn and cook for 1–2 minutes, or until light brown. Transfer to a plate and keep warm. Repeat to make 8 pancakes. Serve with the berry sauce and raspberries.

Serves 4

Preparation time: 5 minutes

Easy

12 strawberries, cut into thin slices
4 kiwi fruit, peeled and cut into thin slices
160 g (5 oz) low-fat muesli
400 g (13 oz) 99.8% fat-free natural
    yoghurt
1⅓ cup (360 ml) milk
2½ tablepoons honey

OATS FOR HEART HEALTH

Oats are well known for their cholesterol-lowering actions, which are largely due to the soluble fibre that oat bran provides—and particularly to a compound called beta-glucan, which helps lower cholesterol by binding with bile acids and aiding their removal from the body. Eating a bowl of oat bran or oatmeal cereal each day provides around 3 grams of soluble fibre, and could lower your cholesterol levels by between 8 and 23%. Oats also contain other constituents that play a role in reducing cholesterol levels, including polyunsaturated fatty acids to help offset saturated fat intake, and antioxidant compounds called avenanthramides that protect cholesterol from oxidation and help prevent the build-up of fatty plaque in the arteries.

BREAKFAST DELUXE

NUTRITION PER SERVE

• Protein 16 g;
• Fat 6 g;
• Carbohydrate 54 g;
• Dietary Fibre 7 g;
• Cholesterol 11 mg;
• 1370 kJ (325 Cal)

1   Divide the strawberry slices, kiwi fruit slices, muesli and yoghurt among four glasses. Repeat these layers, finishing with some fruit. Pour ⅓ cup (80 ml) milk into each glass, then drizzle each with 2 teaspoons honey. Serve with a spoon.

Serves 4

Preparation time: 10 minutes

Cooking time: 25 minutes

Easy

200 g (6½ oz) low-fat ricotta
1 egg
1 egg white
125 ml (½ cup) skim milk
75 g (½ cup) wholemeal self-raising flour
420 g (14 oz) can corn kernels, drained
3 spring onions, chopped
2 tablespoons snipped fresh chives
cooking oil spray
100 g (3 oz) low-fat ricotta, extra
100 g (⅓ cup) spicy tomato chutney

NUTRITION PER SERVE

- Protein 16 g
- Fat 9 g
- Carbohydrate 40 g
- Dietary Fibre 6.5 g
- Cholesterol 77 mg
- 1305 kJ (311 Cal)

RICOTTA CORN FRITTERS

This delicious, reduced-fat fritter recipe is a great source of protein, calcium, vitamin A and B vitamins.

1 Place the ricotta, egg, egg white and milk in a bowl, and beat together until smooth. Stir in the flour, corn kernels, spring onion and chives. Season well with salt and ground black pepper.

2 Spray a non-stick frying pan liberally with cooking oil. Add heaped tablespoons of the mixture to the pan, four at a time, and flatten to about 1.5 cm (½ in) thick. Cook for 3–4 minutes each side. Drain on paper towels. Serve the fritters in a stack of three and top with a tablespoon of ricotta and a tablespoon of spicy tomato chutney.

Serves 4

Preparation time: 10 minutes

Cooking time: 10 minutes

Easy

400 g (13 oz) can baked beans
200 g (4 cups) baby English spinach leaves
4 bagels, halved
250 g (1 cup) low-fat cottage cheese

BAGELS with baked beans

These bagels are a low-fat savoury breakfast, providing slowly released carbohydrate energy, fibre, protein, phytochemicals and calcium—an excellent meal at any time of day.

1 Place the baked beans in a small saucepan and cook over medium heat for 3 minutes, or until warmed.

2 Place the washed spinach in a medium saucepan, cover and cook over medium heat for 2 minutes, or until wilted.

3 Toast the bagel halves and top with the cottage cheese and spinach. Spoon the baked beans over the top, and season with ground black pepper.

NUTRITION PER SERVE

- Protein 17 g;
- Fat 2 g;
- Carbohydrate 58 g;
- Dietary Fibre 6 g;
- Cholesterol 18 mg;
- 1780 kJ (424 Cal)

Serves 4

Preparation time: 10 minutes

Cooking time: 20 minutes

Easy

4 mushrooms
10 g (3½ oz) butter
4 Roma tomatoes, halved
3 tablespoons balsamic vinegar
4 eggs, lightly beaten
4 egg whites, lightly beaten
60 ml (¼ cup) skim milk
2 tablespoons snipped fresh chives
8 slices wholegrain bread

GRILLED MUSHROOMS with scrambled eggs

This is a more nutritious version of traditional scrambled eggs—a good source of high-quality protein, vitamin A, folate and antioxidants.

1 Trim the mushroom stalks to 2 cm (¾ in) above the cap. Brush the mushrooms with paper towels to remove any dirt and grit.

2 Melt the butter in a small saucepan over low heat until it begins to foam.

3 Brush both sides of the mushrooms with the melted butter and place on a non-stick baking tray with the tomato halves. Drizzle the mushrooms and tomato with the balsamic vinegar, sprinkle with salt and ground black pepper, then place under a medium grill for 10–15 minutes, or until tender.

4 Meanwhile, place the eggs, egg whites, milk and chives in a bowl, and whisk to combine. Pour the mixture into a non-stick frying pan and cook over low heat for 5 minutes, or until the egg begins to set, then gently stir with a wooden spoon to scramble.

5 Toast the wholegrain bread until golden brown, then cut on the diagonal. Serve with the mushrooms, tomato and scrambled eggs.

NUTRITION PER SERVE

- Protein 17 g;
- Fat 8.5 g;
- Carbohydrate 26 g;
- Dietary Fibre 4 g;
- Cholesterol 187 mg;
- 1056 kJ (252 Cal)

Serves 4

Preparation time: 10 minutes

Cooking: 20 minutes

Easy

200 g (6½ oz) pitted prunes
200 g (6½ oz) fresh dates, pitted
  and halved
400 g (13 oz) dried fruit salad mix
500 ml (2 cups) apple juice
1 tablespoon ground cinnamon
3 tablespoons sugar
4 crumpets
20 g (½ oz) butter
200 g (6½ oz) low-fat vanilla fromage
  frais or whipped yoghurt

FRUIT COMPOTE with crumpet fingers

High in carbohydrates, this recipe is full of energy and fibre, as well as a wide variety of vitamins and minerals.

1   Place the prunes, dates and dried fruit salad mix in a saucepan with the apple juice. Bring to the boil, then reduce the heat and simmer for 15 minutes, or until the fruit is plump and tender.

2   Place the ground cinnamon and sugar in a small bowl, and mix together well.

3   Toast the crumpets for 3 minutes each side, or until golden brown, then spread lightly with the butter. Sprinkle with the combined sugar and cinnamon, then cut into fingers.

4   Spoon the compote into four serving bowls and top with a spoonful of fromage frais. Stack the crumpet fingers on a side plate and serve.

NOTE: Any combination of dried fruits can be used in the compote.

NUTRITION PER SERVE

- Protein 7 g;
- Fat 7 g;
- Carbohydrate 169 g;
- Dietary Fibre 16 g;
- Cholesterol 13 mg;
- 3255 kJ (775 Cal)

Serves 4

Preparation time: 10 minutes

Easy

90 g (3¼ oz) peeled and cored fresh
  pineapple
1 banana
3 kiwi fruit, peeled and sliced
250 ml (1 cup) unsweetened tropical
  fruit juice
2 ice cubes

NUTRITION PER SERVE

- Protein 1.5 g;
- Fat 0.3 g;
- Saturated fat 0 g;
- Carbohydrate 17.9 g;
- Fibre 2 g;
- Cholesterol 0 mg
- 365 kJ (87 Cal);

FRESH FRUIT SLUSHY

This drink is high in fibre with around three times the fibre you'd get in many commercial fruit juices. It also provides over 100 per cent of daily needs for vitamin C.

1 Cut the pineapple and banana into chunks. Put in a blender with the kiwi fruit, fruit juice and ice cubes and blend until smooth. Pour into four glasses and serve.

NOTE: If fresh pineapple is not available, replace with tinned sliced pineapple in natural juice.

Try adding a frozen banana for an extra thick slushy.

FRUIT MUFFINS

Lower in fat and calories than most commercial varieties, these tangy muffins are a great source of fibre, potassium and phosphorus. Serve them with some fruit yoghurt to boost the calcium content.

NUTRITION PER MUFFIN

- Protein 6 g;
- Fat 3.5 g;
- Carbohydrate 28 g;
- Dietary Fibre 5 g;
- Cholesterol 16.5 mg;
- 700 kJ (170 Cal)

1 Preheat the oven to moderate 180°C (350°F/Gas 4). Grease twelve 125 ml (½ cup) muffin holes. Soak the dried fruit with 60 ml (¼ cup) boiling water for 5 minutes.

2 Sift the flour and baking powder into a large bowl, returning the husks to the bowl. Stir in the oat bran and sugar and make a well in the centre.

3 Combine the milk, egg and oil in a jug. Add the soaked fruit and milk mixture all at once to the dry ingredients. Fold in gently using a metal spoon, until just combined—do not overmix.

4 Divide the mixture evenly among the muffin holes. Bake for 20 minutes, or until the muffins are risen and golden, and a skewer inserted into the centre comes out clean. Cool for a few minutes in the tin, then turn out onto a wire rack. Serve warm or at room temperature.

Makes 12

Preparation time:
15 minutes + 5 minutes soaking

Cooking time: 20 minutes

Easy

160 g (1 cup) chopped mixed dried fruit (apricots, dates, peaches or fruit medley with peel)
225 g (1½ cups) wholemeal self-raising flour
1 teaspoon baking powder
150 g (1 cup) unprocessed oat bran
60 g (⅓ cup) soft brown sugar
300 ml (1¼ cups) skim milk
1 egg
1 tablespoon oil

Serves 6

Preparation time:
15 minutes + 1 hour standing

Cooking time: 20 minutes

Easy

200 g (6½ oz) plain flour
1½ tablespoons caster (superfine) sugar
1 tablespoon baking powder
½ teaspoon salt
50 g (½ cup) rolled oats
1 egg yolk
350 ml (1½ cups) reduced-fat milk
2 teaspoons reduced-fat dairy
    spread, melted
3 egg whites
100 g (3½ oz) low-fat ricotta
2 tablespoons low-fat vanilla yoghurt
60 ml (¼ cup) maple syrup, plus extra
    to serve

WAFFLES with maple syrup and ricotta

These waffles are a sweet, nutritious breakfast alternative, providing niacin and minerals.
Top them with berries or other fruit for a burst of vitamin C and antioxidants.

NUTRITION PER SERVE

- Protein 11 g;
- Fat 5 g;
- Carbohydrate 47 g;
- Dietary Fibre 2 g;
- Cholesterol 43 mg;
- 1165 kJ (280 Cal)

1 Sift the flour, sugar, baking powder and salt into a bowl, then stir in the oats. Add the combined egg yolk and milk with the dairy spread and stir until combined.

2 Whisk the egg whites in a clean, dry bowl until soft peaks form, then gently fold into the batter with a metal spoon. Cover and leave for 1 hour. Beat together the ricotta, yoghurt and maple syrup until smooth.

3 Preheat a waffle maker. Pour one-sixth of the mixture, or enough to fill, into the waffle maker and cook for 2–3 minutes. Repeat with the remaining mixture to make six waffles. To serve, place each waffle on a serving plate, top with some ricotta mixture and drizzle with the extra maple syrup.

NOTE: The number of waffles you make may vary, depending on the size of your waffle maker.

Serves 4

Preparation time:
30 minutes + 30 minutes standing

Cooking time: 20 minutes

Easy

60 g (1/2 cup) plain flour
2 eggs
250 ml (1 cup) skim milk
canola oil spray
2 teaspoons caster sugar

COMPOTE
100 g (3 1/2 cup) whole dried apricots
60 ml (1/4 cup) port or Muscat
2 firm pears, peeled, cored and quartered
1 vanilla bean, split
2 cinnamon sticks
425 g (14 oz) can pitted prunes in syrup,
    drained, syrup reserved

CREPES with warm fruit compote

A wonderful breakfast or winter dessert, these crepes provide energy with fibre,
vitamin A, potassium, calcium, phosphorus and a little iron.

1   Place the flour in a bowl and
    gradually add the combined
    eggs and milk, whisking to remove
    any lumps. Cover and leave for
    30 minutes.

2   Meanwhile, cook the apricots and
    port in a covered saucepan over
    low heat for 2–3 minutes, or until
    softened. Scrape the seeds from the
    vanilla bean and add to the pan
    with the pod, cinnamon, pear
    and prune syrup. Simmer, stirring
    occasionally, for 4 minutes, or until

the pear is soft. Add the prunes and
simmer for 1 minute.

3   Heat a 20 cm (8 in) non-stick crepe
    pan or frying pan over medium heat.
    Lightly spray with oil. Pour 60 ml
    (1/4 cup) batter into the pan and swirl
    over the base. Cook for 1 minute, or
    until the underside is golden. Turn
    and cook for 30 seconds. Transfer to
    a plate and keep warm. Repeat to
    make 8 crepes. Fold the crepes into
    triangles and scatter with the sugar.
    Serve with the compote.

NUTRITION PER SERVE

- Protein 9 g;
- Fat 4 g;
- Carbohydrate 59 g;
- Dietary Fibre 6 g;
- Cholesterol 92 mg;
- 1340 kJ (320 Cal)

Serves 2

Preparation time: 10 minutes

Cooking time: 10 minutes

Easy

6 egg whites
6 eggs
2 tablespoons low-fat ricotta
2 tablespoons chopped fresh dill
420 g (14 oz) fresh asparagus, cut into
　5 cm (2 in) lengths
100 g (3½ oz) smoked salmon,
　thinly sliced
lemon wedges, to garnish
fresh dill sprigs

NUTRITION PER SERVE

- Protein 25 g;
- Fat 9 g;
- Carbohydrate 2 g;
- Dietary Fibre 1.5 g;
- Cholesterol 298 mg;
- 810 kJ (195 Cal)

CHOOSE A LOW GI BREAKFAST
Avoid sugary, processed cereals, muffins
and pastries at breakfast time as they
tend to have a high glycaemic index (GI).
Instead go for a wholesome meal that
offers a combination of low-fat protein
and complex carbohydrates—you'll find
you've got more energy to get you
through your day, and over time your
skin will start to show the benefits too.

OMELETTE with asparagus, smoked salmon and dill

This recipe is packed full of essential nutrients—high-quality protein,
fat-soluble vitamins, calcium, choline, folate and antioxidants.

1　Whisk the egg whites until foaming. In a separate bowl, whisk the whole eggs
　and ricotta. Add the whites. Season with salt and pepper, and stir in the dill.

2　Bring a saucepan of lightly salted water to the boil. Add the asparagus and cook
　for 1–2 minutes, or until just tender. Drain and refresh in iced water.

3　Heat a non-stick 24 cm (9½ in) frying pan over low heat and spray lightly with
　oil spray. Pour in half the egg mixture and arrange half the asparagus on top.
　Cook over medium heat until the egg is just setting. Flip one side onto the other
　and transfer to a serving plate. Repeat with the remaining mixture and asparagus.

4　To serve, top the omelettes with smoked salmon, and garnish with lemon
　wedges and a sprig of dill.

Serves 4

Preparation time: 15 minutes

Cooking time: 20 minutes

Easy

250 g (9 oz) yellow or red cherry
   tomatoes, halved
4 eggs, lightly beaten
4 tablespoons chopped mixed herbs
   (parsley, chives, oregano)
2 egg whites
oil spray
30 g (¼ cup) grated
   low-fat Cheddar
1 handful baby rocket (handful
   arugula) leaves
4 whole wheat (wholemeal) or
   wholegrain English muffins, halved
   and toasted

HERB OMELETTE

This full-flavored dish is easy to prepare and is a good source of protein,
vitamin A, antioxidants, folate and other B-group vitamins, and many minerals.

NUTRITION PER SERVE

- Protein 1.5 g;
- Fat 0.5 g;
- Carbohydrate 27 g;
- Dietary Fibre 4 g;
- Cholesterol 0 g;
- 500 kJ (120 Cal)

1 Preheat the oven to 350°F
   (180°C/Gas 4). Line a baking tray
   with baking paper. Place the
   tomatoes, cut-side-up, on the
   prepared tray. Season well with sea
   salt and ground black pepper.
   Bake for 15 minutes, or until
   softened. Reserve about one-third of
   the tomatoes for garnish.

2 Whisk together the eggs and mixed
   herbs in a bowl. Beat the egg
   whites in a small bowl with electric
   beaters until soft peaks form.
   Gently whisk the egg whites into the
   egg and herb mixture.

3 Preheat a broiler (grill). Heat an
   omelette pan or small frying pan
   with an 22 cm (8½ in) diameter
   (across the base) and lightly spray
   with the oil. Pour in half of the egg
   mixture and leave for 1–2 minutes,
   or until lightly browned underneath.

4 Scatter over half the cheese and
   place the pan under the broiler for
   1 minute, or until the egg is set and
   the cheese is melted. Top with half
   of the remaining tomatoes and half
   of the arugula. Fold the omelette in
   half and carefully slide from the pan
   onto a plate. Scatter over half of the
   reserved tomatoes.

5 Gently re-whisk the remaining egg
   mixture, then cook a second
   omelette in the same way as the
   first. Serve with the muffins.

NOTE: Use baby spinach instead of
rocket, if preferred. Use eggs
enriched with omega-3 essential fatty
acids to get more good fats in your
diet. These are available in
most supermarkets.

Serves 4

Preparation time: 10 minutes

Cooking time: 14 minutes

Medium

20 g (1/2 oz) soy margarine
200 g (6 1/2 oz)button mushrooms, sliced
1 clove garlic, crushed
2 spring onions, chopped
400 g (13 oz) firm tofu, drained
    and crumbled
1 teaspoon tamari
1 tablespoon finely chopped fresh parsley
8 thick slices soy and linseed bread

NUTRITION PER SERVE

- Protein 22 g;
- Fat 13.5 g;
- Carbohydrate 39 g;
- Dietary Fibre 7.5 g;
- Cholesterol 0 mg;
- 1535 kJ (365 Cal)

NOTE: Some types of tofu are processed using calcium sulphate and others with nigari, a traditional Japanese preparation that predominantly consists of magnesium chloride. So, check the label on your tofu before you buy it—the calcium sulphate variety provides around four times more calcium!

SCRAMBLED TOFU
with mushrooms

This is a nourishing vegetarian meal. The tofu and bread are a great source of protective phytochemicals, and the mushrooms provide vitamin B12.

1   Melt half the soy margarine in a large frying pan. Add the mushrooms and cook over high heat for 5 minutes, or until they start to lose their moisture. Add the garlic and cook for 5 minutes, or until the liquid has evaporated. Remove from the pan.

2   Melt the remaining soy margarine in the pan. Add the spring onion and cook for 30 seconds, or until just wilted. Add the tofu, tamari and mushrooms and cook, stirring gently, for 2 minutes, or until the tofu is heated through. Stir in the parsley and season with black pepper.

3   Lightly toast the bread and serve with the scrambled tofu.

Serves 4–6

Preparation time:
10 minutes + 15 minutes standing

Cooking time: 20 minutes

Easy

125 g (1 cup) plain flour
50 g (½ cup) soy flour
1 tablespoon baking powder
½ teaspoon salt
2 tablespoons sugar
65 g (¼ cup) silken tofu
435 ml (1¾ cups) vanilla soy milk
50 g (2 oz) soy spread or margarine,
  melted and cooled
500 g (1 lb) raspberries
½ cup (125 ml) maple syrup
icing (confectioners') sugar, for dusting

SOY PANCAKES
with maple raspberries

This is a great recipe for vegetarians. The pancakes are full of protective soy phytochemicals, carbohydrate energy and fibre. Topped with berries, they provide vitamin C and antioxidants.

NUTRITION PER SERVE (6)

- Protein 9 g;
- Fat 12 g;
- Carbohydrate 50 g;
- Dietary Fibre 6 g;
- Cholesterol 0 mg;
- 1372 kJ (328 Cal)

1 Sift the flours, baking powder and salt into a large bowl, then stir in the sugar. Place the tofu, soy milk and 1 tablespoon of the melted soy spread in a food processor and combine until smooth. Add to the dry ingredients and mix well. Cover and leave for 15 minutes.

2 Heat some of the soy spread in a frying pan over medium heat.

Making two pancakes at a time, drop 2 tablespoons of batter in the pan per pancake and cook for 1–2 minutes, or until bubbles form on the surface. Turn and cook for 1 minute, or until golden. Keep warm and repeat with the remaining batter.

3 Place the raspberries and maple syrup in a saucepan and stir to coat.

Gently cook for 1–2 minutes, or until the berries are warm and well coated in the syrup.

4 Place 2 or 3 pancakes on each plate, top with the raspberries and dust with sugar.

Serves 4

Preparation time: 20 minutes

Cooking time: 1 hour 15 minutes

Medium

4 Roma tomatoes, halved lengthways
1 tablespoon olive oil
1 tablespoon balsamic vinegar
1 teaspoon sugar
1 tablespoon chopped fresh oregano
4 tablespoons chopped fresh herbs
   (oregano, sage, rosemary, parsley)
310 g (1¼ cups) low-fat ricotta
185 g (1½ cups) self-raising flour
25 g (¼ cup) grated Parmesan
30 g (¼ cup) grated low-fat Cheddar
3 large spring onions, finely chopped
1 egg
250 ml (1 cup) low-fat milk
2 egg whites
fresh oregano sprigs

CHEESE WAFFLES with herbed ricotta and roast tomato

NUTRITION PER SERVE

- Protein 28 g;
- Fat 14 g;
- Carbohydrate 42 g;
- Dietary Fibre 3.5 g;
- Cholesterol 93 mg;
- 1800 kJ (430 Cal)

This is a savoury waffle recipe containing high-quality protein, calcium, phosphorus (great for bones and teeth), vitamin A, niacin and folate.

1 Preheat the oven to warm 160°C (315°F/Gas 2–3). Place the tomato halves on a lightly greased baking tray and drizzle with olive oil and balsamic vinegar. Sprinkle with the sugar, oregano and some salt. Bake for 1 hour, or until very soft.

2 Fold the chopped herbs into the ricotta. Season with salt and black pepper. Using two tablespoons, shape the ricotta into quenelle shapes. Refrigerate until needed.

3 Place the flour, Parmesan, Cheddar, spring onion, egg and milk in a bowl. Season, then mix well. Whisk the egg whites until soft peaks form, then gently fold into the cheese and egg mixture.

4 Preheat a waffle maker and brush lightly with oil. Pour in 80 ml (⅓ cup) batter and cook until golden on both sides. Keep warm while you cook the remaining waffles. Arrange two waffle halves on each plate with two tomato halves and two ricotta quenelles. Garnish with oregano.

TOMATO SAUCE
1 tablespoon olive oil
1 clove garlic, crushed
3 vine-ripened tomatoes (about
    300 g/10 oz), peeled, seeded
    and chopped

1/2 teaspoon olive oil
4 eggs
Tabasco sauce, to taste
2 tablespoons snipped fresh chives
4 slices thick multigrain bread
20 g (1/2 oz) margarine

EGGS EN COCOTTE

NUTRITION PER SERVE

- Protein 11 g;
- Fat 15 g;
- Carbohydrate 20 g;
- Dietary Fibre 3 g;
- Cholesterol 187.5 mg;
- 1075 kJ (255 Cal)

This delicious and satisfying meal is densely packed with nutrients from the eggs, vitamin C and antioxidants from the sauce, and B vitamins and carbohydrate from the bread.

1 Preheat the oven to moderate 180°C (350°F/Gas 4). To make the tomato sauce, heat the oil in a heavy-based frying pan. Add the garlic and cook for 1 minute, or until it begins to turn golden. Add the tomato and season with salt and ground black pepper. Cook over medium heat for 15 minutes, or until thickened.

2 Grease four 125 ml (1/2 cup) ramekins with the oil, then break 1 egg into each, trying not to break the yolk. Pour the sauce around the outside of each egg so the yolk is still visible. Add a little Tabasco, sprinkle with the chives and season.

3 Place the ramekins in a deep baking dish and pour in enough hot water to come halfway up the side of the ramekins. Bake for 10–12 minutes, or until the egg white is set. Toast the bread and lightly spread with the margarine, then cut into thick fingers. Serve immediately with the egg.

SNACKS & DRINKS

SNACKS & DRINKS

Following a healthy diet doesn't mean giving up snacks and tasty drinks, it just means making better choices when hunger strikes or you crave a sweet treat.

Sometimes you may feel too hungry to wait for your next main meal before you eat again, or you may start to feel a little sluggish and in need of an energy boost. Because this often happens when you don't have a lot of time to prepare food, an easy alternative is to reach for a packaged snack food like potato chips or a chocolate bar to satisfy your hunger or craving. However, these processed snack foods are generally high in fat, sugar and salt. They may provide a quick-fix for your hunger, but they don't supply you with many nutrients or a lasting energy supply.

There are many healthier alternatives to processed snack foods, which will satisfy your hunger and taste cravings, and provide you with energy until your next main meal.

One of the best and easiest to prepare snack foods is fresh fruit. Most fruit is easy to transport, and the only preparation needed is washing or chopping. Leave the skin on fruit such as apples or pears to increase dietary fibre, and choose fruit at the peak of its season, when its flavour is fully developed and the taste and texture are at their best. If you've got a little more time to prepare your snack, try a fresh

fruit salad topped with low-fat yoghurt and a handful of sunflower seeds.

Among the less healthy processed foods, there are plenty of low-fat snack foods in supermarkets and health food stores that you can choose for a quick, healthy snack. Use the nutritional information on food labels to help you choose products that contain relatively low amounts of fat. Not only is it important to be aware of what you are eating, you might be surprised by the amount of fat, sugar and salt some supposedly healthy foods contain.

Some examples of healthy snacks on the run are:
- reduced-fat muesli bars
- dried fruit
- rice crackers
- puffed rice/corn cakes
- breakfast cereal bars
- low-fat yoghurt
- low-fat frozen yoghurt
- low-fat fruit muffins
- pretzels
- microwave popcorn.

For a snack to accompany fresh vegetable sticks, take one of your favourite dip recipes and make it with less fat:
- make hummus by blending the chickpeas with water or vegetable stock rather than oil
- use low-fat plain yoghurt rather than full-fat yoghurt to make tzatziki
- use light sour cream and reduced-salt French onion soup mix to make French onion dip
- use Indian or Moroccan spice blends to add flavour to vegetable and bean purées and serve them as a dip, such as sweet potato with ras el hanout, or red lentil dahl with garam masala
- make use of fresh herbs to enhance the flavour of your dips or tomato salsas

- serve the dips with rice crackers, crisp wedges of pitta bread, or thinly sliced toasted Italian bread.

HEALTHY SNACK IDEAS

There are many ways of making your favourite snack foods a little more healthy, simply by using different cooking methods, and reducing the fat while adding different seasonings to make up for any changes in texture and flavour.

- Wash and dry potatoes, cut them into wedges, leaving the skin on (which contains nutrients and dietary fibre), lightly spray them with olive oil and sprinkle with Cajun spice powder or lemon pepper, then bake in a hot oven until cooked through and crisp.
- Cook popcorn without any oil in a paper bag in the microwave, or in a saucepan on the stove using a minimum of oil. Instead of seasoning the popcorn with salt, try chilli powder, garlic and dried herbs, or a light sprinkling of grated Parmesan cheese.

- Mix diced fresh tomato with balsamic vinegar, chopped fresh basil and cracked black pepper, then pile it onto toasted Italian bread.
- Spread toasted crumpets with low-fat ricotta, top with sliced banana and drizzle with honey.
- Spoon some hot baked beans onto toasted English muffins.
- Make your own pizzas using pitta bread topped with tomato paste, fresh basil and slices of roasted vegetables such as eggplant, sweet potato and zucchini. Sprinkle the pizzas with a little grated light mozzarella cheese and bake or grill until the pizzas are golden and crisp.
- Marinate chicken wings with soy sauce, grated fresh ginger and crushed garlic, then bake on a rack in a baking dish until cooked through. Serve hot or cold.
- Fill triangles of wholemeal filo pastry with leftover curry, seal and lightly spray with olive oil, then bake until golden and heated through. Serve with low-fat natural yoghurt flavoured with ground coriander.

DRINK UP

Drinking plenty of fluid regularly throughout the day is a great way of keeping your brain and tissues well hydrated and functioning at their best, and can help keep hunger at bay.

This is especially important if you are exercising. While exercising, you should regularly replace any fluid lost as sweat, to avoid cramps, fatigue and headaches. As a general guideline, drink lots of water, limit your consumption of drinks containing caffeine, avoid soft drinks that contain large quantities of sugar, and limit your consumption of alcohol.

If you're looking for some taste as well as refreshment, try:
- fresh fruit juices
- low-fat fruit smoothies
- soda water flavoured with fresh fruit purée
- sports drinks (for a long exercise session)
- herbal tea—hot or iced
- mineral water flavoured with fresh lemon or lime juice.

Serves 20

Preparation time: 10 minutes

Cooking time: 20 minutes

Easy

170 g (5½ oz) puffed corn
400 g (13 oz) packet dried fruit and
   nut mix
95 g (1¼ cups) unprocessed natural bran
55 g (1 cup) flaked coconut, toasted
60 g (⅓ cup) pepitas
260 g (¾ cup) honey

NUTRITION PER SERVE

• Protein 4 g;
• Fat 7.5 g;
• Carbohydrate 28.5 g;
• Dietary Fibre 4.5 g;
• Cholesterol 0 mg;
• 820 kJ (195 Cal)

PUFFED CORN SNACK MIX

More nutritious than regular popcorn, this snack provides good amounts of fibre, vitamin E and beta-carotene.

1 Preheat the oven to moderate 180°C (350°F/Gas 4). Line four baking trays with baking paper. Place the puffed corn, dried fruit and nut mix, bran, coconut and pepitas in a large bowl, and mix together well.

2 Heat the honey in a small saucepan over low heat for 3 minutes, or until it thins to a pouring consistency. Pour over the puffed corn mixture and stir until all the dry ingredients are well coated with the honey.

3 Spread the mixture onto the lined baking trays in a single layer and bake for 15 minutes, or until golden, turning the cereal several times during cooking. Cool completely before storing in an airtight container in a cool, dark place.

Serves 3–4

Preparation time: 15 minutes

Cooking time: 30 minutes

Easy

500 g (1 lb) pumpkin, cut into
    2 cm (¾ in) cubes
300 g (10 oz) orange sweet potato, cut
    into 2 cm (¾ in) cubes
2 teaspoons honey
1 teaspoon ground cumin
1 teaspoon ground coriander
½ teaspoon ground cinnamon
1 clove garlic
2 tablespoons chopped fresh
    flat-leaf parsley
2 tablespoons chopped fresh
    coriander leaves
½ teaspoon grated orange rind
2 teaspoons white vinegar

NUTRITION PER SERVE (4)

- Protein 4.5 g;
- Fat 1 g;
- Carbohydrate 22 g;
- Dietary Fibre 3.5 g;
- Cholesterol 0 mg;
- 470 kJ (110 Cal)

PUMPKIN AND SWEET POTATO DIP

This low-fat dip tastes great alone or with fresh carrot and celery sticks, and is an excellent source of potassium, folate and antioxidants.

1   Preheat the oven to moderate 180°C (350°F/Gas 4). Line a large baking tray with baking paper, place the pumpkin and sweet potato on the tray, drizzle with the honey and sprinkle the cumin, coriander and cinnamon over the top. Cook in the oven for 5 minutes, then turn the vegetables, making sure they are well coated, and cook for another 25 minutes, or until soft and golden brown. Cool.

2   Place the roasted vegetables, garlic, parsley, coriander leaves, orange rind and vinegar in a food processor, and process until smooth. With the motor still running, slowly add 60 ml (¼ cup) hot water to the processor in a thin stream until the mixture is smooth and 'dippable'. Serve at room temperature with crudités and pitta crisps.

Serves 2

Preparation time: 10 minutes

Cooking time: Nil

Easy

1/2 rockmelon
4 peaches
600 ml (2 1/2 cups) orange juice
12 ice cubes
1 tablespoon lime juice

NUTRITION PER SERVE

• Protein 3 g;
• Fat 0.5 g;
• Carbohydrate 23 g;
• Dietary Fibre 5 g;
• Cholesterol 0 mg;
• 465 kJ (110 Cal)

PEACH AND ROCKMELON JUICE

A refreshing thirst quencher, this drink provides sweet natural sugar for energy and a boost of vitamin C, beta-carotene, folate, potassium and fibre.

1 Peel the rockmelon, remove the seeds and roughly chop the flesh into bite-sized pieces. Cut a cross in the base of the peaches. Place them in a heatproof bowl and cover with boiling water. Leave for 1–2 minutes, then remove with a slotted spoon, cool slightly and peel. Halve, remove the stone, and chop the flesh into bite-sized pieces.

2 Place the fruit in a blender with the orange juice and ice cubes, and blend until smooth. If the juice is too thick, add a little iced water. Stir in the lime juice and serve immediately.

Serves 2–3

Preparation time: 5 minutes

Cooking time: Nil

Easy

2 ripe bananas, roughly chopped
200 g (6½ cups) fresh or frozen
    mixed berries
1 tablespoon oat bran
3 tablespoons low-fat vanilla fromage
    frais or whipped yoghurt
500 ml (2 cups) skim milk

BANANA AND BERRY SMOOTHIE

A nutritious snack or breakfast, this drink provides carbohydrate energy, soluble fibre, vitamin C, calcium and flavonoids.

NUTRITION PER SERVE (3)

- Protein 8 g;
- Fat 1 g;
- Carbohydrate 30 g;
- Dietary Fibre 3.5 g;
- Cholesterol 5 mg;
- 660 kJ (155 Cal)

1 Place the chopped banana, berries, oat bran, vanilla fromage frais and skim milk in a blender, and blend for 2 minutes, or until thick and creamy.

NOTE: The smoothie will be thicker if you use frozen berries. You may need to add an extra 125 ml (½ cup) skim milk to thin it down.

SOY AND CALCIUM

Although soy milk can replace cow's milk in many ways—and is superior from the perspective of heart health—it doesn't naturally contain a great deal of calcium. To ensure that you don't miss out on this vital nutrient, make sure to choose a soy drink that has been fortified with extra calcium. Without it, a cup of soy milk contains about 95mg of calcium—but the calcium-fortified variety provides around 375 mg per cup, making it much easier to reach your daily calcium target of at least 1000mg.

Serves 4

Preparation time:
5 minutes + 10 minutes soaking

Cooking time: Nil

Easy

10 dried apricot halves
200 g (13 oz) fresh or frozen raspberries
1 banana, roughly chopped
1 mango, chopped
500 ml (2 cups) orange juice
1 tablespoon fresh mint leaves
6 ice cubes

NUTRITION PER SERVE

- Protein 2 g;
- Fat 1 g;
- Carbohydrate 33 g;
- Dietary Fibre 5 g;
- Cholesterol 0 mg;
- 615 kJ (145 Cal)

FRUIT FRAPPE

This drink is a refreshing antioxidant cocktail, which makes a substantial snack or light meal, rich in vitamin C, vitamin A, vitamin B6, fibre and flavonoid antioxidants.

1 Place the dried apricots in a heatproof bowl. Cover with 60 ml (¼ cup) boiling water for 10 minutes, or until plump. Drain, then roughly chop.

2 Place the chopped apricots, raspberries, banana, mango, orange juice, mint leaves and ice cubes in a blender, and blend until thick and smooth.

Serves 4

Preparation time:
20 minutes + 45 minutes refrigeration

Cooking time: 10 minutes

Medium

8 spring onions, chopped
30 g (1 cup) roughly chopped fresh
    flat-leaf parsley
15 g (½ cup) fresh coriander leaves
2 teaspoons ground coriander
2 teaspoons ground cumin
¼ teaspoon chilli powder
2 cloves garlic, crushed
300 g (10½ oz) can chickpeas, rinsed
    and drained
plain flour, for coating
oil, for deep-frying
4 tablespoons ready-made hummus
4 rounds Lebanese bread
200 g (7 oz) ready-made tabbouleh

FALAFEL ROLLS

If plain sandwiches don't tempt you, then satisfy your hunger with this nutritious dish.
These rolls provide plenty of fibre, and good amounts of folate, vitamin C and iron.

1 Place the spring onion, parsley and fresh coriander in a food processor, and process until finely chopped.

2 Add the spices, garlic and chickpeas, and process to a smooth paste. Shape into 12 patties. Coat lightly in flour and refrigerate for 45 minutes.

3 Fill a deep heavy-based saucepan one-third full of oil and heat to 180°C (350°F), or until a bread cube browns in 15 seconds when dropped into the oil. Cook the falafel in batches for 2–3 minutes, or until dark gold and cooked through. Drain.

4 To serve, spread the hummus over the four rounds of Lebanese bread, top with the tabbouleh and three falafel each. Roll up securely and serve wrapped in paper.

NOTE: You can reduce the fat content of this dish by using reduced-fat hummus, and salad rather than tabbouleh.

NUTRITION PER SERVE

- Protein 15 g;
- Fat 21.5 g;
- Carbohydrate 63 g;
- Dietary Fibre 10.5 g;
- Cholesterol 0 mg;
- 2095 kJ (500 Cal)

Makes 1 litre (4 cups)

Preparation time: 8 minutes

Easy

80 g (2¾ oz) chopped
  fresh pineapple
110 g (3¾ oz) chopped papaya
2 chopped bananas
125 ml (½ cup) coconut milk
250 ml (1 cup) orange juice
100 g (3½ oz) ice cubes

NUTRITION PER 100 mL

- Protein 9 g;
- Fat 27 g;
- Carbohydrate 100 g;
- Dietary Fibre 13 g;
- Cholesterol 0 mg;
- 2840 kJ (680 cal)

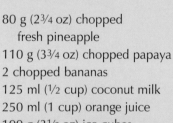

TROPICAL THICKSHAKE

1 Put pineapple, papaya, bananas, coconut milk and orange juice in a food
   processor or blender. Blend for 1–2 minutes, or until the fruit is puréed. ice
   cubes and process in bursts for 5 minutes, or until the ice is crushed. Garnish
   with banana slices.

Serves 4

Preparation time: 5 minutes

Cooking time: Nil

Easy

500 ml (2 cups) apricot nectar, chilled
500 ml (2 cups) soda water, chilled
250 ml (1 cup) apple juice, chilled
250 ml (1 cup) orange juice, chilled
8 ice cubes

FRUIT SPRITZER

More nutritious than soft drink, this sparkling drink provides vitamin C, potassium and beta-carotene.

1   Place the apricot nectar, soda water, apple juice, orange juice and ice cubes in a large jug and stir until combined.

2   Pour into glasses and serve.

NUTRITION PER SERVE

• Protein 0.5 g;
• Fat 0.2 g;
• Carbohydrate 30 g;
• Dietary Fibre 0 g;
• Cholesterol 0 g;
• 505 kJ (120 Cal)

Serves 4

Preparation time:
40 minutes + 5 minutes soaking

Cooking time: 2 minutes

Medium

50 g (2 oz) dried rice vermicelli
200 g (13 oz) frozen soya beans
16 square (15 cm/6 in) rice
    paper wrappers
1 courgette (zucchini), julienned
1 small cucumber, julienned
1 carrot, grated
20 g (1 cup) fresh mint, julienned
100 g (3½ oz) tofu, cut into 1 cm wide
    batons

DIPPING SAUCE
80 ml (⅓ cup) fish sauce
2 tablespoons chopped fresh coriander
    leaves
2 small red chillies, finely chopped
2 teaspoons soft brown sugar
2 teaspoons lime juice

NUTRITION PER SERVE

- Protein 13 g;
- Fat 5.5 g;
- Carbohydrate 46.5 g;
- Dietary Fibre 5.5 g;
- Cholesterol 0 mg;
- 1200 kJ (285 Cal)

RICE PAPER ROLLS
with dipping sauce

This vegetarian snack is full of vitamin C, folate and beta-carotene,
with some iron and calcium.

1 Soak the vermicelli in hot water for
   5 minutes, or until soft. Drain and
   cut into 5 cm lengths. Bring a
   saucepan of water to the boil,
   add the soya beans and cook
   for 2 minutes. Drain well.

2 Working with no more than two
   wrappers at a time, dip each rice
   paper wrapper in warm water for

10 seconds. Drain, then lay out
on a flat work surface.

3 Place a small amount of vermicelli
   on the bottom third of each
   wrapper, leaving a 2 cm (¾ in)
   border either side. Top with a little
   zucchini, cucumber, carrot, soya
   beans, mint and 2 batons of tofu.
   Keeping the filling compact and

neat, fold in the sides and roll
up tightly. Seal with a little water.
Cover with a damp cloth.

4 To make the dipping sauce,
   combine the fish sauce,
   coriander, chilli, sugar, lime
   juice and 2 tablespoons water
   in a small bowl. Serve with the
   rice paper rolls.

Serves 3–4

Preparation time: 10 minutes

Cooking time: Nil

Easy

400 g (13 oz) can cannellini beans, rinsed and drained
400 g (13 oz) can chickpeas, rinsed and drained
1½ teaspoons ground cumin
3 cloves garlic, crushed
2 tablespoons chopped fresh flat-leaf parsley
60 ml (¼ cup) lemon juice
1 teaspoon grated lemon rind
1 tablespoon tahini

NUTRITION PER SERVE (4)

- Protein 11 g;
- Fat 5 g;
- Carbohydrate 19 g;
- Dietary Fibre 9 g;
- Cholesterol 0 mg;
- 675 kJ (160 Cal)

CANNELLINI BEAN AND CHICKPEA DIP

This filling dip is an excellent source of fibre and slowly digested starch. Eat it with fresh vegetables for an antioxidant boost.

1 Place all the ingredients in a food processor and process for 30 seconds. With the motor still running, slowly add ¼ cup (60 ml) hot water to the processor in a thin stream until the mixture is smooth and 'dippable'. Serve at room temperature with crudités and pitta crisps.

Serves 4–6

Preparation time: 10 minutes +
freezing time

Easy

1 large watermelon
250 g (8 oz) hulled strawberries
2 teaspoons caster sugar

NUTRITION PER SERVE (6)

- Protein 1.5 g;
- Fat 0.5 g;
- Carbohydrate 19 g;
- Dietary Fibre 3 g;
- Cholesterol 0 mg;
- 375 kJ (90 Cal)

STRAWBERRY AND WATERMELON SLUSHY

1 Peel and seed a large watermelon to give 2 kg (4 lb) flesh and place it in a bowl.
Add strawberries and caster sugar. Blend in batches in a blender or food
processor until smooth, then pour into a shallow metal tray. Cover with plastic
wrap and freeze for 2–3 hours, or until the mixture begins to freeze. Remove
from the freezer and return to the blender. Whiz quickly to break up the ice,
pour into a jug and serve immediately.

Serves 2

Preparation time: 15 minutes

Cooking time: Nil

Easy

185 g (3/4 cup) low-fat peach and
   mango yoghurt
185 ml (3/4 cup) apricot nectar, chilled
60 g (1/2 cup) fresh or frozen raspberries
300 g (1 1/2 cups) diced fresh peaches
8 large ice cubes
fresh peach wedges, to serve

NUTRITION PER SERVE

- Protein 6.5 g;
- Fat 0.5 g;
- Carbohydrate 36 g;
- Dietary Fibre 4.5 g;
- Cholesterol 3 g;
- 750 kJ (180 Cal)

PEACHY KEEN

This drink is a great dessert or snack. It's low in fat but high in flavour,
vitamin C, beta-carotene and healthy flavonoids.

1 Place the yoghurt, apricot nectar, raspberries, peaches and ice in a blender
   and blend until smooth.

2 Serve with the peach wedges.

Serves 4

Preparation time: 10 minutes

Cooking time: Nil

Easy

125 g (½ cup) passionfruit pulp
185 ml (¾ cup) lime juice cordial
750 ml (3 cups) ginger ale
crushed ice

NUTRITION PER SERVE

- Protein 0.5 g;
- Fat 0 g;
- Carbohydrate 40 g;
- Dietary Fibre 1.7 g;
- Cholesterol 0 g;
- 700 kJ (170 Cal)

PASSIONFRUIT LIME CRUSH

More nutritious than a regular cordial drink, this tangy mix provides a burst of sweet energy with fibre, beta-carotene and small amounts of minerals.

1 Combine the passionfruit pulp, lime juice cordial and ginger ale in a large jug. Mix well.

2 Pour into glasses filled with crushed ice. Serve immediately.

Serves 4

Preparation time: 10 minutes

Cooking time: Nil

Easy

440 ml (1¾ cups) coffee-flavoured
   soy milk, chilled
2 bananas, sliced
8 large ice cubes
1 teaspoon drinking chocolate
¼ teaspoon ground cinnamon

NUTRITION PER SERVE

- Protein 4 g;
- Fat 3.5 g;
- Carbohydrate 19 g;
- Dietary Fibre 1.5 g;
- Cholesterol 0 g;
- 520 kJ (125 Cal)

BANANA SOY LATTE

This drink has less fat than a chocolate smoothie and more nutrients than iced coffee, plus good amounts of calcium, phosphorus and potassium.

1 Place the soy milk and sliced bananas in a blender and process until smooth.

2 With the blender running, add the ice cubes one at a time until well incorporated and the desired consistency is reached.

3 Pour into tall chilled glasses and sprinkle generously with the drinking chocolate and ground cinnamon.

Serves 6

Preparation time: 10 minutes

Cooking time: 40 minutes

Easy

6 potatoes
1 tablespoon oil
½ teaspoon chicken or vegetable
  stock powder
25 g (¼ cup) dry breadcrumbs
2 teaspoons chopped fresh chives
 1 teaspoon celery salt
¼ teaspoon garlic powder
½ teaspoon chopped fresh rosemary

NUTRITION PER SERVE

- Protein 4 g;
- Fat 2.5 g;
- Carbohydrate 22.5 g;
- Dietary Fibre 3 g;
- Cholesterol 0 mg;
- 555 kJ (135 Cal)

CRUNCHY WEDGES

1 Preheat the oven to moderately hot 200°C (400°F/Gas 6). Cut potatoes into eight wedges each. Dry, then toss with oil. Combine stock powder, breadcrumbs, chives, celery salt, garlic powder and rosemary. Add the wedges and toss. Spread on greased baking trays and bake for 40 minutes, or until golden.

Makes 20–25

Preparation time: 1 hour + cooling

Cooking time: 1 hour 5 minutes

Difficult

125 ml (½ cup) olive oil
6 spring onions, chopped
150 g (¾ cup) long-grain rice
15 g (¼ cup) chopped fresh mint
2 tablespoons chopped fresh dill
170 ml (⅔ cup) lemon juice
35 g (¼ cup) currants
40 g (¼ cup) pine nuts
240 g (8 oz/about 50) packaged
    vine leaves
2 tablespoons olive oil, extra

DOLMADES

This snack provides monounsaturated fat, some beta-carotene, niacin and minerals.

1 Heat the oil in a pan over medium heat. Cook the spring onion for 1 minute. Stir in the rice, mint, dill and half the lemon juice, then season. Add 250 ml (1 cup) water and bring to the boil. Reduce the heat, cover and simmer for 20 minutes. Remove the lid, fork through the currants and pine nuts, cover with a paper towel, then the lid, and leave to cool.

2 Rinse and separate the vine leaves. Drain, then dry on paper towels. Trim any thick stems. Line the base of a 20 cm (8 in) pan (with a lid) with any torn or misshapen leaves.

3 Place each leaf shiny side down. Spoon a tablespoon of filling into the centre, bring in the sides and roll up tightly from the stem end. Place seam side down with the stem end closest to you in pan, tightly, in a single layer.

4 Pour in the remaining lemon juice, extra oil and 185 ml (¾ cup) water to just cover the dolmades. Cover with an inverted plate. Place a can on the plate to compress the dolmades. Cover with the lid.

5 Bring to the boil, then reduce the heat and simmer for 45 minutes. Allow to cool in the pan. Serve at room temperature.

NUTRITION PER SERVE (25)

- Protein 1.5 g;
- Fat 7.5 g;
- Carbohydrate 6 g;
- Dietary Fibre 1 g;
- Cholesterol 0 mg;
- 380 kJ (90 Cal)

Makes 16–20

Preparation time: 10 minutes + cooling

Cooking time: 25 minutes

Easy

60 g (2 cups) puffed rice cereal
150 g (1½ cups) rolled oats
30 g (¼ cup) sunflower seeds
40 g (¼ cup) sesame seeds
200 g (7 oz) packet dried fruit medley
60 g (⅓ cup) rice flour
125 ml (½ cup) liquid glucose
90 g (¼ cup) honey

NUTRITION PER BAR (20)

- Protein 2.5 g;
- Fat 3 g;
- Carbohydrate 25 g;
- Dietary Fibre 1.5 g;
- Cholesterol 0 mg;
- 560 kJ (135 Cal)

FRUIT BARS

A great snack when you're on the run, these fruit bars provide carbohydrate, unsaturated fat, beta-carotene, vitamin E and minerals.

1 Preheat the oven to moderate 180°C (350°F/Gas 4). Line the base and two long sides of a 29 x 19 cm (11½ x 7½ in) tin with baking paper. Place the puffed rice cereal, rolled oats, sunflower seeds, sesame seeds, dried fruit and rice flour in a bowl, and mix together well.

2 Place the liquid glucose and honey in a small saucepan and heat gently over medium heat for 2 minutes, or until runny. Stir the syrup into the dry ingredients and mix well to coat.

3 Press the mixture firmly into the tin. Place a sheet of baking paper over the mixture and use the back of a spoon or a measuring cup to spread it evenly. Remove the top sheet of baking paper. Bake for 20 minutes, or until golden brown. Leave to cool and crisp in the tin, before lifting out and cutting into fingers. Store in an airtight container in the refrigerator.

NOTE: Liquid glucose is available from health food stores.

VARIATION: Any low-fat sports breakfast cereal can be used in this recipe.

Serves 6

Preparation time: 15 minutes

Cooking time: 25 minutes

Easy

200 g (6½ oz) courgette (zucchini), cubed
250 g (8 oz) pumpkin, cubed
300 g (10 oz) potato, cubed
100 g (3½ oz) broccoli florets
3 teaspoons oil
1 small onion, chopped
1 small red pepper (capsicum), chopped
2 tablespoons finely chopped
  fresh parsley
3 eggs
2 egg whites

VEGETABLE FRITTATA

A nourishing snack or meal with a greater range of nutrients than scrambled eggs, this dish is a good source of vitamin A, folate, vitamin B12 and high-quality protein.

NUTRITION PER SERVE

- Protein 8 g;
- Fat 5 g;
- Carbohydrate 10.5 g;
- Dietary Fibre 3 g;
- Cholesterol 93.5 mg;
- 510 kJ (120 Cal)

1   Steam the courgette (zucchini), pumpkin, potato and broccoli until tender, then transfer to a bowl.

2   Heat 2 teaspoons of the oil in a non-stick frying pan, about 22 cm (8½ in) diameter. Add the onion and pepper (capsicum), and cook for 3 minutes, or until tender. Transfer to the bowl of steamed vegetables, along with the chopped parsley.

3   Brush the pan with the remaining oil. Return all the vegetables to the pan and spread out with a spatula to an even thickness. Beat the eggs and whites together and pour into the pan, tilting to distribute evenly.

4   Cook over medium heat until the egg is almost set, but still runny on top. Wrap the handle of the pan in a damp tea towel to protect it and place the pan under the grill to cook the frittata top (pierce gently with a fork to make sure it is cooked through). Cut into wedges and serve.

Serves 4

Preparation time: 5 minutes

Easy

3 sliced kiwi fruit
90 g (3¼ oz) peeled and cored
   pineapple chunks
1 banana
250 ml (1 cup) tropical fruit juice
2 ice cubesd

SELECTION AND STORAGE OF KIWI FRUIT

Buy kiwi fruit quite firm and you'll be able to keep them in the refrigerator for 4–5 weeks—bring them out to ripen at room temperature when you want sweet, soft, lush fruit.

To speed ripening, put kiwi fruit in a paper bag at room temperature with a banana or an apple, as these fruits produce ethylene gas which accelerates fruit ripening.

When ripe, kiwi fruit should give slightly when pressed and can be eaten simply cut in half and the flesh scooped out with a teaspoon. Steer clear of overly soft fruit or any whose skins are wrinkled, as this indicates they are well and truly past their prime.

KIWI DELIGHT

This is a superb and simple way to boost your day.

NUTRITION PER SERVE

• Protein 2 g;
• Fat 0.5 g;
• Carbohydrate 18 g;
• Dietary Fibre 3 g;
• Cholesterol 0 mg;
• 340 kJ (80 Cal)

1 Blend kiwi fruit, peeled and cored pineapple chunks, banana, tropical fruit juice and ice cubes in a blender until smooth. Pour into glasses and serve.

Serves 4

Preparation time: 5 minutes

Cooking time: Nil

Easy

60 g (2¼ oz/½ mango) mango flesh
  cut into chunks,
2 tablespoons oat bran
500 ml (2 cups) no-fat soy milk
2 tablespoons honey
60 g (¼ cup) fat-free natural yoghurt

GET UP AND GO SMOOTHIE

The oat bran in this recipe makes it more of a snack than a drink.

NUTRITION PER SERVE

- Protein 7 g;
- Fat 1 g;
- Carbohydrate 25 g;
- Dietary Fibre 2 g;
- Cholesterol 1 mg;
- 560 kJ (135 Cal)

1 Blend mango flesh, oat bran, no-fat soy milk, honey and fat-free natural yoghurt in a blender until smooth. Pour the smoothie into glasses and serve with a spoon.

SELECTION AND STORAGE OF MANGOES

The size of a mango depends upon type, not quality or ripeness. When ripe, mangoes should yield slightly to pressure and their stem end should emit sweet, fragrant, tropical smells. According to type, the skin colour will deepen and may develop pink or red patches. Black speckles on the skin can indicate damaged flesh underneath or over-ripeness; avoid fruits with loose or wrinkled skin as these are past their best.

Under-ripe fruit will continue to ripen at room temperature, and once ripe, should be stored in the refrigerator and used within 1–2 days.

Serves 4-6

Preparation time: 30 minutes

Easy

200 g (1 cup) sushi rice
2 tablespoons white rice vinegar
1 tablespoon sugar
4 nori sheets
2–3 fillings from a selection of thinly
  sliced sashimi tuna, cooked and
  peeled prawns (shrimp), fresh or
  smoked salmon, sliced cucumber,
  pickled daikon, sliced avocado and
  blanched English spinach
wasabi
Japanese soy sauce for dipping

SUSHI HAND ROLLS

Nori is dried or toasted seaweed and is usually sold in sheets. It comes in a wide range of colours and textures depending on the type of seaweed used.

1 Rinse the sushi rice until it runs clear. Put in a pan with 310 ml (1¼ cups) water and bring to the boil. Simmer, covered, over very low heat for 12 minutes, or until the water is absorbed. Remove from the heat. Leave for 15 minutes.

2 Mix together the white rice vinegar, sugar and a pinch of salt until dissolved, then stir through the rice.

Put in a bowl and cool. Cover with a damp cloth.

3 Cut nori sheets into quarters. Put a square of nori in the palm of your hand and place 1½ tablespoons of rice in the centre. Lightly spread wasabi over the rice and top with 2–3 fillings of your choice. Roll into a cone shape and serve with Japanese soy sauce for dipping.

NUTRITION PER SERVE

- Protein 7 g;
- Fat 2 g;
- Carbohydrate 22 g;
- Dietary Fibre 2.5 g;
- Cholesterol 37.5 mg;
- 575 kJ (135 Cal)

Serves 4

Preparation time:
20 minutes + 30 minutes rising

Cooking time: 15 minutes

Easy

125 g (1 cup) plain flour
150 g (1 cup) wholemeal plain flour
2 teaspoons dried yeast
½ teaspoon sugar
2 tablespoons natural yoghurt
2 tablespoons tomato paste
1 clove garlic, crushed
1 teaspoon dried oregano
80 g (3 oz) lean shaved ham
2 tablespoons grated light mozzarella
rocket leaves, chopped, to serve
extra virgin olive oil, to drizzle

NUTRITION PER PIZZETTE

• Protein 17 g;
• Fat 5 g;
• Carbohydrate 45 g;
• Dietary Fibre 6 g;
• Cholesterol 23 mg;
• 1235 kJ (295 Cal)

PIZZETTE

With much less fat per mouthful than commercial pizzas, this is a good
source of protein.

1 Sift the plain flour into a bowl,
then add the wholemeal plain flour,
yeast, sugar and ½ teaspoon salt.
Make a well in the centre, add
½ cup (125 ml) water and the
yoghurt, and mix to a dough.
Knead on a lightly floured surface
for 5 minutes, or until smooth and
elastic. Cover with a tea towel and
rest in a warm place for 20–30
minutes, or until doubled in size.

2 Preheat the oven to moderately hot
200°C (400°F/Gas 6). Punch down
the dough and knead for 30 seconds,
then divide into four portions. Roll
each portion into a 15 cm (6 in)
round and place on a baking tray.

Combine the tomato paste, garlic,
oregano and 1 tablespoon water.
Spread over each base, then top
with the ham and mozzarella. Bake
for 12–15 minutes, or until crisp
and golden on the edges.

3 Just before serving, top with rocket
and drizzle with the oil.

Serves 8 (Makes 2 cups)

Preparation time: 15 minutes

Cooking time: 40 minutes

Easy

500 g (1 lb) beetroot, trimmed
60 ml (¼ cup) olive oil
1 large onion, chopped
1 tablespoon ground cumin
400 g (13 oz) can chickpeas, drained
1 tablespoon tahini
90 g (⅓ cup) low-fat plain yoghurt
3 cloves garlic, crushed
60 ml (¼ cup) lemon juice
125 ml (½ cup) vegetable stock

BEETROOT HUMMUS

Beetroot adds colour, flavour, carotene and folate to this delicious, fibre-rich dip.

NUTRITION PER SERVE

- Protein 5.5 g;
- Fat 9 g;
- Carbohydrate 13 g;
- Dietary Fibre 4.5 g;
- Cholesterol 0.5 mg;
- 640 kJ (155 Cal)

1 Scrub the beetroot well. Bring a large saucepan of water to the boil and cook the beetroot for 35–40 minutes over high heat, or until soft and cooked through. Drain and cool slightly before peeling.

2 Meanwhile, heat 1 tablespoon of the oil in a frying pan over medium heat and cook the onion for 2–3 minutes, or until soft. Add the cumin and cook for a further 1 minute, or until fragrant.

3 Chop the beetroot and place in a food processor or blender with the onion mixture, chickpeas, tahini, yoghurt, garlic, lemon juice and stock, and process until smooth. With the motor running, add the remaining oil in a thin steady stream. Process until the mixture is thoroughly combined, adding a little water if it is too thick. Serve the hummus with Lebanese or Turkish bread.

VARIATION: You can use 500 g (1 lb) of any vegetable to make the hummus. Try carrot or pumpkin.

Serves 4

Preparation time: 5 minutes

Cooking time: 12 minutes

Easy

45 g (1½ cups) cornflakes
400 g (14 oz) chicken breast fillets cut
  into bite-sized pieces
seasoned flour
1 lightly beaten egg white
canola spray
1½ tablespoons honey
2 tablespoons Dijon mustard

OVEN-BAKED CHICKEN NUGGETS with
honey mustard sauce

These oven-baked snacks are the perfect healthy option for a mid-morning party.

1 Preheat the oven to 200°C (400°F/
Gas 6). Process the cornflakes in a
food processor to make fine crumbs

2 Cut the chicken breast fillets into
bite-sized pieces. Toss in seasoned
flour then in lightly beaten egg
white. Roll each piece in crumbs
until well coated.

3 Lightly spray a baking tray with
canola spray and place the nuggets
on it. Bake for 10–12 minutes.

3 Combine the honey and Dijon
mustard and serve with the nuggets.

NUTRITION PER SERVE

- Protein 24.5 g;
- Fat 4 g;
- Carbohydrate 17.5 g;
- Dietary Fibre 0.5 g;
- Cholesterol 50 mg;
- 850 kJ (205 Cal)

Serves 4

Preparation time: 5 minutes

Cooking time: 5 minutes

Easy

1 teaspoon dashi granules
2½ tablespoons white or red miso
50 g (1¾ oz) diced silken firm tofu
shredded wakame seaweed
finely sliced spring onion for garnish

NUTRITION PER SERVE

- Protein 3.5 g;
- Fat 2 g;
- Carbohydrate 3.5 g;
- Dietary Fibre 1 g;
- Cholesterol 0 mg;
- 185 kJ (45 Cal)

MISO SOUP

Reseach shows that soup can help you feel full and may decrease your calorie intake through the rest of the day. A water-based broth style soup, such as this miso soup, is far healthier than a high-fat cream option. The tofu in this soup contains valuable protein to enhance the filling effects.

1   Bring dashi granules and 800 ml (3¼ cups) of water to the boil. Dissolve miso in a little boiling water. Add to the stock. Place tofu and some shredded wakame seaweed in each bowl. Pour on stock. Garnish with finely sliced spring onion.

Serves 4

Preparation time: 15 minutes

Cooking time: 5–7 minutes

Easy

½ telegraph (long) cucumber
½ teaspoon salt
100 g (3½ oz) low-fat natural yoghurt
¼ teaspoon lemon juice
1 tablespoon chopped mint
4 skinless and trimmed chicken
    thigh fillets
paprika
4 sheets of Lavash or other flat bread
1 butter lettuce

CHICKEN AND TZATZIKI WRAP

These wraps provide calcium and protein, not to mention plenty of crunch from the cucumber and fresh flavour from the mint and lemon.

1   To make the tzatziki, seed and grate the cucumber into a bowl, then sprinkle with a teaspoon of salt. Leave for 10 minutes. Drain, then mix with the low-fat natural yoghurt, lemon juice and chopped mint. Season. Flatten the chicken thigh fillets, season and sprinkle with spicy paprika. Grill for 5–7 minutes on each side.

2   Place a large butter lettuce leaf on each piece of bread and spread with the tzatziki. Top with a sliced chicken fillet. Roll up, folding one end closed. Repeat. Wrap in baking paper to serve.

NUTRITION PER SERVE

- Protein 40 g;
- Fat 13 g;
- Carbohydrate 38 g;
- Dietary Fibre 3 g;
- Cholesterol 149 g;
- 1830 kJ (435 Cal)

Serves 2

Preparation time: 10 minutes

Cooking time: Nil

Easy

10–12 carrots, quartered lengthways
125 ml (½ cup) pineapple juice
125 ml (½ cup) orange juice
1–2 teaspoons honey, to taste
8 ice cubes

NUTRITION PER SERVE

- Protein 3 g;
- Fat 0.5 g;
- Carbohydrate 34 g;
- Dietary Fibre 10 g;
- Cholesterol 0 g;
- 640 kJ (150 Cal)

CARROT COCKTAIL

This drink is rich in vitamin C and beta-carotene, and also provides some folate and niacin.

1 Using the plunger, push the carrot pieces through a juicer.

2 Combine the carrot juice with the pineapple juice, orange juice, honey and ice cubes in a jug and serve.

NOTE: This drink is delicious served the next day as all the flavours will have time to infuse.

Serves 4

Preparation time:
20 minutes + 10 minutes soaking
+ 30 minutes refrigeration

Cooking time: 40 minutes

Easy

1 litre (4 cups) vegetable stock
150 g (1 cup) polenta
40 g (1 oz) low-fat margarine
1 tablespoon grated fresh Parmesan
rocket, to serve
Parmesan shavings, to serve

MUSHROOM SAUCE
10 g (¼ oz) dried porcini mushrooms
1 tablespoon olive oil
800 g (1lb 9 oz) mixed mushrooms,
    thickly sliced
4 cloves garlic, finely chopped
2 teaspoons chopped fresh thyme
185 ml (¾ cup) dry white wine
125 ml (½ cup) vegetable stock
30 g (½ cup) chopped fresh parsley

NUTRITION PER SERVE

- Protein 14.5 g;
- Fat 11 g;
- Carbohydrate 31.5 g;
- Dietary Fibre 7 g;
- Cholesterol 1.5 mg;
- 1335 kJ (320 Cal)

POLENTA with mushrooms

This dish contains mostly monounsaturated fat and good amounts of fibre, B vitamins and folate.

1 Bring the stock to the boil in a large saucepan. Add the polenta in a thin stream, stirring constantly. Simmer for 20 minutes over very low heat, stirring frequently, until the mixture starts to leave the side of the pan. Add the margarine and Parmesan, and season with salt and ground black pepper. Grease a shallow 20 cm (8 in) square cake tin. Pour in the polenta, smooth the surface and refrigerate for 30 minutes, or until set.

2 To make the mushroom sauce, soak the porcini mushrooms in 125 ml (½ cup) boiling water for 10 minutes, or until softened. Drain, reserving ⅓ cup (80 ml) of the liquid.

3 Heat the oil in a large frying pan. Add the mixed mushrooms and cook over high heat for 4–5 minutes, or until softened. Add the porcini, garlic and thyme, then season and cook for 2–3 minutes. Add the wine and cook until it has evaporated. Add the vegetable stock, then reduce the heat and cook for a further 3–4 minutes, or until the stock has reduced and thickened. Add the parsley.

4 Cut the polenta into 4 squares and grill until golden on both sides. Place one square on each serving plate and top with the mushrooms. Garnish with rocket and Parmesan shavings.

Serves 4

Preparation time: 10 minutes

Cooking time: 40 minutes

Easy

4 large potatoes
2 vine-ripened tomatoes, chopped
125 g (4 oz) can corn kernels,
2 spring onions (scallions), chopped
1 tablespoon lime juice
½ teaspoon sugar
1 avocado, diced
15 g (2 oz) coriander (cilantro) leaves,
   chopped
1 tablespoon low-fat sour cream

BAKED POTATO with avocado, tomato and corn salsa

This is a very sustaining snack that will give you more nutrients than potato crisps. It is a great source of B vitamins, vitamin C, beta-carotene, potassium and phosphorus.

NUTRITION PER SERVE

- Protein 7 g;
- Fat 15 g;
- Carbohydrate 33 g;
- Dietary Fibre 7.5 g;
- Cholesterol 0 mg;
- 1245 kJ (300 Cal)

1 Preheat the oven to 210°C (415°F/Gas 6–7). Scrub 4 large potatoes clean, dry and pierce all over with a fork. Bake directly on the oven rack for 1 hour, or until tender when tested with a skewer. Leave to stand for about 2 minutes. Cut a cross in the top of each cooked potato and squeeze gently from the base to open (if the potato is still too hot, hold the potato in a clean tea towel).

2 Remove the seeds from the tomatoes and chop roughly. Place the tomato in a bowl with the corn kernels, spring onions, lime juice and sugar and mix well. Add the avocado and coriander leaves. Season. Spoon mixture onto each potato and, if desired, dollop with low-fat sour cream.

Serves 6

Preparation time:
45 minutes + overnight refrigeration

Cooking time: 30 minutes

Medium

1 red pepper (capsicum), cut into
    large pieces
1 large courgette (zucchini), thinly sliced
    on the diagonal
2 slender aubergine (eggplant), thinly
    sliced on the diagonal
70 g (2 oz) English spinach leaves
100 g (3½ oz) ricotta
6 round bread rolls
1 tablespoon olive oil
1 clove garlic, crushed
1 tablespoon snipped fresh chives
90 g (3 oz) sliced light leg ham, cut
    into quarters

LAYERED COBS

NUTRITION PER COB

- Protein 15 g;
- Fat 8 g;
- Carbohydrate 45 g;
- Dietary Fibre 4.5 g;
- Cholesterol 16 mg;
- 1330 kJ (320 Cal)

These filling rolls provide carbohydrate, B vitamins, folate and minerals.

1 Cook the pepper (capsicum), skin side up, under a hot grill until blackened and blistered. Place in a plastic bag, cool, then remove the skin. Cut into strips.

2 Lightly spray a non-stick frying pan with oil. Cook the courgette (zucchini) and aubergine (eggplant) in batches until golden. Steam the spinach until just wilted. Cool, squeeze and chop. Combine with the ricotta, and season.

3 Cut the tops from the rolls and remove the bread inside, leaving a 1 cm (½ in) border. Combine the oil, garlic and chives, and brush inside each roll. Add a layer of pepper (capsicum) and courgette (zucchini), spread with the ricotta mixture, then top with the ham and aubergine (eggplant). Lightly press down, then replace the lids.

4 Cover with plastic wrap and place tightly in a baking dish. Place a tray on top and weigh down with heavy cans or weights. Refrigerate overnight.

5 Preheat the oven to hot 220°C (425°F/Gas 7). Remove the plastic wrap from the rolls, place on a baking tray and bake for 10–15 minutes, or until crisp.

Makes 8

Prep time: 10 minutes

Cooking time: 20 minutes

Easy

300 g (2 cups) wholemeal (whole-wheat)
    plain (all-purpose) flour
1 tablespoon canola oil
60 g (¼ cup) low-fat natural yoghurt
½ teaspoon salt
400 g (13 oz) new potatoes cut into
    5 mm (¼ in) cubes
½ teaspoon ground cumin,
½ teaspoon ground coriander
½ teaspoon garam masala
pinch of chilli powder.
2 finely sliced spring onions (scallions)
75 g (2½ oz) fresh peas
2 teaspoons lemon juice
1 tablespoon chopped coriander (cilantro)
    leaves
low-fat natural yoghurt, to serve

OVEN-BAKED SAMOSAS

These samosas make a great healthy snack at any time of the day

1 Place in a bowl flour, canola oil,
   low-fat natural yoghurt and salt. Rub
   the mixture with your fingertips until
   it resembles breadcrumbs. Add
   2 tablespoons cold water and mix to
   bring together, adding a little more
   water if needed. Turn out dough
   onto a lightly floured surface. Knead
   for 1 minute, or until smooth. Wrap
   and set aside to rest.

2 Rinse potatoes. Steam until tender.
   Transfer to a large bowl. Add cumin,
   coriander, garam masala and a pinch
   of chilli powder. Add spring onions,

peas, lemon juice and chopped
coriander leaves and mix. Season.

3 Preheat oven to 180ºC (350°F/Gas
   4). Divide dough into 8 portions.
   Roll out on a lightly floured surface
   into a rough triangle about 2 mm
   (⅛ in) thick. Place
   1 tablespoon of filling in the centre.
   Bring each of the 3 points to the
   centre. Press edges together to seal.
   Remove any excess pastry.

4 Place on a baking tray lined with
   baking paper. Lightly spray with

canola oil spray. Bake for 10 minutes
or until golden and crispy. Serve hot
with low-fat natural yoghurt.

NUTRITION PER SERVE

- Protein 3 g;
- Fat 1.5 g;
- Carbohydrate 11 g;
- Dietary Fibre 2 g;
- Cholesterol 0.5 g;
- 280 kJ (65 Cal)

Serves 4

Preparation time: 5 minutes

Cooking time: 30 minutes

Easy

2 whole aubergines (eggplants)
1 crushed garlic clove
½ teaspoon Indian curry powder
½ teaspoon ground cumin
olive oil, to blend
lemon juice and chopped coriander
    (cilantro) to taste
fresh vegetable sticks, to serve

AUBERGINE DIP

This deliciously exotic dip is both low in fat and packed full of flavour.

1   Grill the aubergines (eggplants), turning occasionally, until the flesh is soft
    and the skin black and charred. Alternatively, roast in an oven heated to
    200°C (400°F/Gas 6) for 50 minutes. Cool and peel off the skin. Drain the
    flesh in a colander for 20 minutes.

2   Transfer to a food processor with garlic clove, curry powder and cumin.
    Slowly add enough olive oil to blend until smooth. Season with salt and
    freshly ground pepper. Add lemon juice and chopped coriander to taste.
    Serve with fresh vegetable sticks.

NUTRITION PER SERVE

- Protein 2 g;
- Fat 0.5 g;
- Carbohydrate 57 g;
- Dietary Fibre 0 g;
- Cholesterol 0 g;
- 980 kJ (235 Cal)

Serves 4

Preparation time: 5 minutes

Easy

250 g (1 cup) low-fat strawberry yoghurt
125 ml (½ cup) chilled cranberry juice
250 g (8 oz) hulled, quartered
    strawberries
260 g (8 oz) frozen raspberries

NUTRITION PER SERVE

- Protein 4 g;
- Fat 0.5 g;
- Carbohydrate 10 g;
- Dietary Fibre 3.5 g;
- Cholesterol 1.5 g;
- 295 kJ (70 Cal)

WILD BERRIES

1 Combine strawberry yoghurt and cranberry juice in a blender. Add strawberries and raspberries (reserving a handful of raspberries to use as a garnish). Blend until smooth. Pour into chilled glasses and top each with the reserved frozen raspberries. Serve with a spoon.

Serves 4

Preparation time: 5 minutes

Cooking time: Nil

Easy

100 g (½ cup) fat-free natural yoghurt
2 passionfruit, pulped
2 bananas
6 strawberries
100g (3½ oz) frozen raspberries
250 ml (1 cup) apple juice
2 ice cubes

NUTRITION PER SERVE

- Protein 3 g;
- Fat 0.25 g;
- Carbohydrate 21 g;
- Dietary Fibre 4 g;
- Cholesterol 1.5 g;
- 415 kJ (100 Cal)

FRUITASIA SMOOTHIE

This fruity drink will satisfy your thirst whatever the time of the day.

1 Blend the yoghurt, passionfruit, bananas, strawberries, raspberries, apple juice and ice cubes in a blender until smooth.

2 Serve in chilled glasses.

Serves 4

Preparation time: 20 minutes

Cooking time: 25 minutes

Medium

1 tablespoon light olive oil
1 onion, thinly sliced
3 cloves garlic, crushed
1 bird's eye chilli, finely chopped
2 teaspoons ground cumin
125 ml (½ cup) vegetable stock
3 tomatoes, peeled, seeded and chopped
1 tablespoon tomato paste
2 x 430 g (14 oz) cans three-bean mix
2 tablespoons chopped fresh coriander
  leaves
8 flour tortillas
1 avocado, peeled and chopped
185 g (¾ cup) light sour cream
10 g (½ cup) fresh coriander sprigs
160 g (2 cups) shredded lettuce

NUTRITION PER SERVE

• Protein 20 g;
• Fat 26 g;
• Carbohydrate 53 g;
• Dietary Fibre 16 g;
• Cholesterol 29.5 mg;
• 2190 kJ (525 Cal)

BEAN ENCHILADAS

Although relatively high in fat, this filling snack is a great choice for vegetarians, providing soluble fibre, slow-release carbohydrate, B vitamins, folate, iron and zinc.

1 Heat the oil in a deep frying pan over medium heat. Add the onion and cook for 3–4 minutes, or until just soft. Add the garlic and chilli and cook for a further 30 seconds. Add the cumin, vegetable stock, tomato and tomato paste and cook for 6–8 minutes, or until the mixture is quite thick and pulpy. Season with salt and ground black pepper.

2 Preheat the oven to warm 170°C (325°F/Gas 3). Drain and rinse the beans, add to the sauce and cook for 5 minutes to heat through, then add the chopped coriander.

3 Meanwhile, wrap the tortillas in foil and warm in the oven for 3–4 minutes.

4 Place a tortilla on a plate and spread with ¼ cup of the bean mixture. Top with some avocado, sour cream, coriander sprigs and lettuce. Roll the enchiladas up, tucking in the ends. Cut each one in half to serve.

Serves 4

Preparation time: 25 minutes

Cooking time: 35 minutes

Easy

100 g (3½ oz) thickly sliced white bread,
  crusts removed
8 rashers lean bacon, rind removed
  (about 90 g/3¼ oz)
500 g (1 lb) chicken breast fillet
¾ teaspoon garlic salt
1 cos lettuce (reserve some leaves for
  serving and tear the remaining leaves
  into small pieces)
2 tablespoons grated fresh Parmesan
4 anchovies, drained and chopped

DRESSING
2 cloves garlic, crushed
2 teaspoons Worcestershire sauce
1 tablespoon Dijon mustard
1½ tablespoons lemon juice
2 anchovies, drained and finely chopped
2 tablespoons olive oil
½ teaspoon caster sugar
Tabasco sauce, to taste

LOW-FAT CHICKEN CAESAR SALAD

A lower-fat version of a popular salad, this dish provides good amounts of B vitamins and minerals.

1 Preheat the oven to moderate 180°C (350°F/Gas 4). Cut the bread slices into 1.5 cm cubes then spread evenly on a baking tray. Bake for 12–15 minutes, or until golden brown. Allow to cool.

2 Cut the bacon into 5 mm (¼ in) strips and place on a foil-lined baking tray. Cook for 10–12 minutes, or until lightly browned. Drain on paper towels and cool.

3 Cut the chicken breast in half lengthways to form two thin

schnitzels. Coat the chicken in the garlic salt, pressing firmly into the flesh. Cook under a hot grill for 3–4 minutes each side, or until just cooked. Remove and cool slightly.

4 To make the dressing, whisk all the ingredients until combined.

5 Arrange the reserved lettuce leaves in serving bowls, then divide the torn leaves among them. Slice the chicken breast on the diagonal and arrange on top of the lettuce. Pour the dressing over the chicken, then

scatter the croutons and bacon on top. Sprinkle with the Parmesan and garnish with the chopped anchovy.

NUTRITION PER SERVE

- Protein 37 g;
- Fat 20 g;
- Carbohydrate 14 g;
- Dietary Fibre 2 g;
- Cholesterol 102 mg;
- 1590 kJ (380 Cal)

Serves 2

Preparation time:
10 minutes + infusing + chilling

Easy

2 peppermint tea bags
6 strips (2 x 5 cm/$\frac{2}{3}$ x 2 in) lemon rind
1 tablespoon sugar
ice cubes, to serve
fresh mint leaves, to garnish

NUTRITION PER SERVE

- Protein 0.5 g;
- Fat 0.5 g;
- Carbohydrate 8.5 g;
- Dietary Fibre 0 g;
- Cholesterol 0 g;
- 165 kJ (40 Cal)

ICED LEMON AND PEPPERMINT TEA

Enjoy this refreshing tea with few calories and small amounts of many vitamins and minerals.

1   Place the tea bags and lemon rind strips in a large bowl. Cover with 830 ml (3$\frac{1}{3}$ cups) boiling water and leave to infuse for 5 minutes.

2   Squeeze out the tea bags and discard. Stir in the sugar to taste.

3   Pour into a jug and chill. Serve in chilled glasses with the ice cubes and fresh mint leaves.

Serves 2

Preparation time: 5 minutes + chilling

Easy

6 Granny Smith apples, quartered
150 g (5 oz) fresh raspberries
ice cubes, to serve
mint sprigs, to garnish

NUTRITION PER SERVE

- Protein 1.5 g;
- Fat 0.5 g;
- Carbohydrate 30 g;
- Dietary Fibre 8 g;
- Cholesterol 0 g;
- 515 kJ (125 Cal)

RASPBERRY AND APPLE JUICE

This drink will satisfy your thirst and your daily vitamin C needs.

1 Using the plunger, push the apple pieces and raspberries through a juicer and into a jug. Chill.

2 Stir well before serving. Add ice and garnish with mint sprigs.

Serves 4

Preparation time: 5 minutes + freezing

Easy

500 g (1 lb) rockmelon
500 g (1 lb) honeydew melon
1 cup ice (12 ice cubes)
2 cups (500 ml) orange juice

NUTRITION PER SERVE

- Protein 2 g;
- Fat 0.5 g;
- Carbohydrate 21.5 g;
- Dietary Fibre 2.5 g;
- Cholesterol 0 g;
- 415 kJ (100 Cal)

MELON FREEZIE

1 Remove the rind and seeds from the melons. Cut the flesh into pieces and mix in a blender for 1 minute, or until smooth.

2 Add the ice and orange juice and blend for a further 30 seconds. Transfer to a large shallow plastic dish and freeze for 3 hours.

3 Return the mixture to the blender and blend quickly until smooth. Serve immediately with straws and long spoons.

Serves 4

Preparation time: 10 minutes

Easy

250 g (1 cup) thick plain low-fat yoghurt
3 tablespoons honey
250 ml (1 cup) reduced-fat milk
3 scoops low-fat vanilla ice cream

YOGHURT AND HONEY SMOOTHIE

NUTRITION PER SERVE

- Protein 7 g;
- Fat 1.5 g;
- Carbohydrate 28 g;
- Dietary Fibre 0 g;
- Cholesterol 9.5 g;
- 640 kJ (155 Cal)

A soothing, sweet drink, this smoothie is rich in calcium, potassium and phosphorus, with a little vitamin A and B2.

1 Blend the yoghurt and honey in a blender for 10 seconds, or until well combined. Add the milk and ice cream and blend until smooth.

2 Serve in chilled glasses.

Serves 6

Preparation time: 25 minutes

Cooking time: 50 minutes

Medium

1.5 kg (3 lb 5 oz) English spinach,
    trimmed and washed
2 teaspoons olive oil
1 onion, chopped
4 spring onions, chopped
750 g (1 lb 8 oz) reduced-fat
    cottage cheese
2 eggs, lightly beaten
2 cloves garlic, crushed
pinch of ground nutmeg
15 g (1/4 cup) chopped fresh mint
8 sheets filo pastry
30 g (1 oz) butter, melted
40 g (1/2 cup) fresh breadcrumbs

NUTRITION PER SERVE

- Protein 33.5 g;
- Fat 10 g;
- Carbohydrate 20.5 g;
- Dietary Fibre 8 g;
- Cholesterol 91.5 mg;
- 1295 kJ (310 Cal)

SPINACH PIE

Lower in fat than many commercial varieties, this pie also contains B vitamins, fibre and iron.

1 Preheat the oven to moderate 180°C (350°F/Gas 4). Lightly spray a square 1.5 litre (6 cup) ovenproof dish with oil. Place the spinach in a large pan. Cover and cook for 2–3 minutes, or until just wilted. Drain, cool, then squeeze dry and chop.

2 Heat the oil in a small pan. Cook the onion and spring onion for 2–3 minutes, or until softened. Combine with the spinach. Stir in the cheese, egg, garlic, nutmeg and mint. Season, and mix thoroughly.

3 Brush a sheet of filo pastry with a little butter. Fold in half widthways and line the base and sides of the dish. Repeat with three more sheets. Keep the unused sheets moist by covering with a damp tea towel.

4 Sprinkle the breadcrumbs over the pastry. Spread the filling in the dish. Fold over any overlapping pastry. Brush and fold another sheet and place on top. Repeat with three more sheets. Tuck the pastry in. Brush the top with any leftover butter. Score squares on top. Bake for 40 minutes, or until golden.

SOUPS

SOUPS

Soups are a wonderful option for a healthy diet, and are a versatile way of incorporating the freshest seasonal ingredients into a one-pot meal that can be as simple or elaborate as you like.

There are many different types of soups that can be made to suit every occasion and season. Many traditional soups are naturally very healthy, or with a few simple changes can be made with relatively little fat, but still plenty of flavour.

Soup may be served as a starter, a light meal with some crusty bread and a green salad, or a hearty vegetable and bean soup can be a complete meal on a chilly winter evening.

Every cuisine around the world embraces soup, whether it be chunky Mediterranean soups flavoured with fresh basil or rosemary, the delicate miso of Japan, or the spicy noodle soups so popular in Southeast Asian cooking.

STOCKS
The making of a delicious soup begins with a flavoursome stock base. Stocks are readily available from the supermarket in waxed cardboard packs, and as stock cubes and powders, and these are great to keep in the pantry, although some brands are high in salt. However, it's very economical and simple to prepare your own stocks at home. Home-made stocks are full of

flavour and contain very little fat and salt. They can be made and then frozen until you are ready to use them.

BEEF STOCK
Roast 1.5 kg (3 lb 5 oz) beef bones on a rack over a large roasting tin in a 220°C (425°F/ Gas 7) oven for 20 minutes. Add a quartered onion, 2 chopped carrots, 1 chopped leek and 1 chopped celery stick and roast for 20 minutes. Transfer to a stockpot with 10 peppercorns, a bouquet garni (a sprig of parsley, a sprig of thyme and a bay leaf wrapped together in a small piece of muslin) and 4 litres (16 cups) water. Bring to the boil, then reduce the heat and simmer

for 6–8 hours, skimming regularly to remove any scum. Strain the stock and leave it to cool in the fridge. Lift off any fat that congeals on the top.

CHICKEN STOCK
Put 1 kg (2 lb) chicken carcasses in a stockpot with a bouquet garni, a quartered onion, 1 chopped carrot and 10 peppercorns. Add 4 litres (16 cups) water and bring to the boil, then reduce the heat and simmer, skimming regularly to remove any scum. Strain the stock, and remove any fat by dragging a piece of paper towel over the surface. Cool in the fridge. When cool, lift off any congealed fat.

FISH STOCK
Put 2 kg (4 lb) fish bones and heads, a bouquet garni, 1 chopped onion and 10 peppercorns in a stockpot. Add 2.5 litres (10 cups) water, bring to the boil, then reduce the heat and simmer the mixture for 20–30 minutes. Skim off any scum. Strain the stock, then cool in the fridge. When cool, lift off any congealed fat. (When making a fish stock, it is better to use the bones from a white-fleshed fish such as cod, snapper or flounder rather than an oily fish such as salmon, tuna or mackerel.)

VEGETABLE STOCK

Put 500 g (1 lb) mixed chopped carrots, celery, onions and leeks in a stockpot with a bouquet garni and 10 pepper-corns. Add 2.5 litres (10 cups) water and bring to the boil. Skim off any scum. Simmer for 1–2 hours, pressing the solids to extract all the flavour, then strain and cool in the fridge.

MAKING LOW-FAT SOUPS

When it comes to preparing soup, it is quite easy to reduce the amount of fat without sacrificing texture or flavour.

- Instead of sautéing any vegetables in butter and oil, combine the vegetables with water or stock, and gently simmer until they are tender.
- While the soup is gently simmering away on the stove, use a metal spoon to skim any fat that rises to the surface.
- Many vegetable purée soups contain cream, but you can reduce their fat content simply by omitting the cream or using low-fat yoghurt. If you purée the soup in a blender, it will be so smooth and creamy that you won't miss the cream.
- If you are looking for a rich, creamy flavour, stir through a spoonful of low-fat sour cream before serving. Don't boil the soup after the sour cream has been added or the soup may curdle. Sour cream is especially delicious in chunky bean soups or spicy Mexican-style soups.
- Add a spoonful of low-fat plain yoghurt to add a delicious tang to Indian spiced bean and lentil soups. Don't boil the soup after adding yoghurt or it will curdle.
- Make croutons for soup by simply dicing a sourdough loaf and baking the bread on a baking tray until crisp, instead of frying the bread in oil or butter. Croutons add a crunchy texture to puréed vegetables soups.

HEALTHY TIPS FOR TASTY SOUPS

- If you are making a stock for an Asian-style soup, add some grated ginger, garlic, star anise, coriander roots and lemon grass.
- Add a spoonful of finely diced tomato and cucumber on top of gazpacho or chilled cucumber soup.
- Gremolata, a mixture of finely chopped fresh parsley, garlic and lemon rind, is a simple and tasty garnish to use on tomato-based soups.
- Use chopped fresh herbs to add flavour.
- Adding dried legumes to chunky soups is an easy way to add more fibre and minerals.
- Turn a simple chicken broth into a meal by adding egg noodles, fresh herbs and shredded poached chicken breast.
- Add some Chinese greens to a ginger-flavoured chicken broth. Try some baby bok choy, Chinese broccoli or Chinese cabbage, which are all very nutritious.
- Clear soups or broths are suitable if you are unwell, as they are easily digested and are an excellent way of getting nourishment when you can't eat solid foods.

Serves 8

Preparation time:
15 minutes + overnight soaking

Cooking time: 2 hours 10 minutes

Easy

500 g (1 lb) yellow or green split peas
1 leek
1 tablespoon oil
2 carrots, chopped
1 celery stick, chopped
2 cloves garlic, crushed
750 g (1 lb 8 oz) meaty ham bone

NUTRITION PER SERVE

- Protein 17 g;
- Fat 8 g;
- Carbohydrate 8.5 g;
- Dietary Fibre 4 g;
- Cholesterol 30 mg;
- 725 kJ (175 Cal)

PEA AND HAM SOUP

The combination of slowly digested carbohydrate, fibre and protein makes this an extremely filling soup, which also contains B vitamins, folate and vitamin A.

1   Put the split peas in a large bowl, cover with water and soak overnight.

2   Cut the leek in half lengthways and wash thoroughly to remove any dirt. Slice thickly. Heat the oil in a large heavy-based pan and add the leek, carrot, celery and garlic. Cook, stirring, for 2–3 minutes, then add the drained peas, the ham bone and 2.5 litres (10 cups) water. Bring to the boil, then reduce the heat and simmer for 2 hours, stirring occasionally.

3   Remove the ham bone and set it aside to cool. Cool the soup a little, then purée in batches in a blender or food processor and return to the pan. Remove the meat from the bone, chop and return the meat to the soup. Season to taste with salt and cracked black pepper, reheat gently and serve hot.

NOTE: If you forget to soak the split peas overnight, rinse them and cook the soup for longer until the peas are tender.

Serves 6

Preparation time: 20 minutes

Cooking time: 55 minutes

Easy

1.25 kg (2 lb 8 oz) pumpkin, peeled and
    cut into chunks
2 tablespoons olive oil
1 large onion, chopped
2 teaspoons ground cumin
1 large carrot, chopped
1 celery stick, chopped
1 litre (4 cups) chicken or vegetable stock
sour cream, to serve
finely chopped fresh parsley, to serve
ground nutmeg, to serve

ROAST PUMPKIN SOUP

Roasted pumpkin gives a stronger flavour to this classic soup—rich in
beta-carotene and potassium, with a little folate and vitamin C.

1 Preheat the oven to moderate
180°C (350°F/Gas 4). Put the
pumpkin on a greased baking tray
and lightly brush with half the olive
oil. Bake for 25 minutes, or until
softened and slightly browned.

2 Heat the remaining oil in a large
pan. Cook the onion and cumin for
2 minutes, then add the carrot and
celery and cook for 3 minutes more,
stirring frequently. Add the roasted
pumpkin and stock. Bring to the
boil, then reduce the heat and
simmer for 20 minutes.

3 Allow to cool a little, then purée
in batches in a blender or food
processor. Return the soup to the pan
and gently reheat without boiling.
Season to taste with salt and cracked
black pepper. Top with sour cream
and sprinkle with chopped parsley
and ground nutmeg before serving.

NUTRITION PER SERVE

- Protein 5 g;
- Fat 8.5 g;
- Carbohydrate 15 g;
- Dietary Fibre 3.5 g;
- Cholesterol 4.5 mg;
- 665 kJ (160 Cal)

NOTE: Butternut pumpkin is often used
in soups as it has a sweeter flavour than
other varieties.

HINT: If the soup is too thick, thin it
down with a little stock.

Serves 6

Preparation time: 15 minutes

Cooking time: 20 minutes

Easy

3 corn cobs
1 tablespoon vegetable oil
4 spring onions, finely chopped
2 teaspoons grated fresh ginger
1 litre (4 cups) chicken stock
1 tablespoon rice wine, mirin or sherry
1 tablespoon light soy sauce
1/2 small barbecued chicken, shredded
1 tablespoon cornflour
1 teaspoon sesame oil
420 g (14 oz) can creamed corn
fresh thyme sprigs, to garnish

NUTRITION PER SERVE

- Protein 14 g;
- Fat 8 g;
- Carbohydrate 30 g;
- Dietary Fibre 5 g;
- Cholesterol 45 mg;
- 1075 kJ (255 Cal)

CHICKEN AND CORN SOUP

This soup is quick to prepare—great for a meal or snack. It provides niacin, vitamin B6 and a little folate and iron.

1 Cut the corn kernels from the cobs—you will need about 400 g (2 cups). Heat the oil in a large pan, and add the spring onion and ginger. Cook for 1 minute, or until softened, then add the corn, stock, rice wine and soy sauce. Bring slowly to the boil, then reduce the heat and simmer for 10 minutes, or until the kernels are cooked through. Add the chicken.

2 In a bowl, blend the cornflour with 60 ml (1/4 cup) water or stock to make a smooth paste. Add to the soup with the sesame oil and simmer, stirring continuously, until slightly thickened. Stir in the creamed corn and heat for 2–3 minutes without allowing to boil. Season with salt and pepper, and serve hot, garnished with thyme sprigs.

NOTE: If fresh corn is unavailable, use a 440 g (14 oz) can of drained corn kernels.

Serves 6

Preparation time: 25 minutes

Cooking time: 1 hour 30 minutes

Easy

50 g (1½ oz) butter
1 leek, chopped
1 celery stick, chopped
1 large carrot, peeled and chopped
1 large potato, peeled and chopped
1 parsnip, peeled and chopped
1 swede or turnip, peeled and chopped
225 g (7 oz) sweet potato, peeled
    and chopped
115 g (½ cup) soup mix (see Note)
2 litres (8 cups) vegetable stock or water
155 g (5½ oz) frozen peas
125 g (4 oz) green beans, chopped
¼ cup (15 g) chopped fresh mint
⅓ cup (20 g) chopped fresh parsley

CHUNKY VEGETABLE SOUP

An easy way to eat a variety of healthy vegetables, this soup provides a range of phytochemicals, folate, beta-carotene and carbohydrate.

1 Heat the butter in a large heavy-based pan, and cook the leek, celery, carrot, potato, parsnip, swede or turnip and sweet potato, stirring, for 5 minutes.

2 Add the soup mix and stock or water. Bring slowly to the boil, then reduce the heat and simmer, covered, for 1¼ hours, or until the soup mix has softened.

3 Add the peas and beans, and cook for a further 10 minutes, or until tender. Stir in the chopped mint and parsley. Season with salt and cracked black pepper. Serve hot. Delicious with crusty bread.

NOTE: Soup mix is a combination of dried beans and pulses.

NUTRITION PER SERVE

- Protein 3 g;
- Fat 7 g;
- Carbohydrate 15 g;
- Dietary Fibre 4 g;
- Cholesterol 20 mg;
- 555 kJ (135 Cal)

Serves 6

Preparation time: 25 minutes

Cooking time: 50 minutes

Easy

500 g (1 lb) veal shanks with bones (osso
   buco), cut into 5 cm (2 in) pieces (ask
   your butcher to do this)
2 tablespoons olive oil
1 onion, diced
1–2 cloves garlic, crushed
425 g (14 oz) can chopped tomatoes
1 tablespoon tomato paste
1/2 teaspoon dried oregano
1.5 litres (6 cups) beef stock
300 g (10 oz) potatoes, cubed
300 g (10 oz) pumpkin, cubed
165 g (3/4 cup) pearl barley
200 g (7 oz) courgette (zucchini), sliced

NUTRITION PER SERVE

- Protein 25 g;
- Fat 10 g;
- Carbohydrate 30 g;
- Dietary Fibre 6 g;
- Cholesterol 70 mg;
- 1310 kJ (315 Cal)

OSSO BUCO AND VEGETABLE SOUP

This is a very filling soup, providing protein, slow-release carbohydrate,
B vitamins, soluble fibre and beta-carotene.

1 Trim the meat from the bones and
   cut it into cubes. Scrape out the
   marrow from the bones, if you want
   to use it, and discard the bones.
   Heat the oil in a heavy-based pan
   and brown the meat and marrow,
   in batches if necessary, until rich
   brown. Remove and drain on paper
   towels. Set the fried marrow aside.

2 Add the onion to the pan and cook
   for 4–5 minutes over low heat, then
   add the garlic and cook for 1 minute
   longer. Add the meat, tomato,
   tomato paste, oregano, stock,
   potato and pumpkin.

3 Wash the barley in a sieve until the
   water runs clean, then drain and
   add to the soup. Bring to the boil,
   reduce the heat to low and simmer,
   covered, for 20 minutes. Add the
   courgette (zucchini) and cook,
   covered, for 10 minutes, or until the
   barley is cooked. Serve topped with
   the fried marrow.

Serves 4–6

Preparation time: 30 minutes

Cooking time: 30 minutes

Easy

60 g (2 oz) butter
3 rashers bacon, chopped
2 onions, chopped
2 cloves garlic, finely chopped
2 celery sticks, sliced
3 potatoes, diced
1.25 litres (5 cups) fish or chicken stock
3 teaspoons chopped fresh thyme
1 tablespoon tomato paste
425 g (14 oz) can chopped tomatoes
375 g (12 oz) boneless white fish fillets,
    cut into chunks
12 large raw prawns, peeled, deveined
    and halved
310 g (10 oz) can baby clams, undrained
2 tablespoons chopped fresh parsley
grated orange rind, to garnish

SEAFOOD CHOWDER

This nutritious broth is full of flavour and is a great source of protein, vitamin A and minerals, including selenium and iron.

NUTRITION PER SERVE (6)

- Protein 35 g;
- Fat 10 g;
- Carbohydrate 15.5 g;
- Dietary Fibre 3 g;
- Cholesterol 166 mg;
- 1270 kJ (300 Cal)

1 Melt the butter in a large pan and cook the bacon, onion, garlic and celery over low heat, stirring occasionally, for 5 minutes, or until soft but not brown. Add the potato, stock and thyme and bring to the boil.

2 Reduce the heat and simmer, covered, for 15 minutes. Stir in the tomato paste and tomato and return to the boil. Add the fish pieces, prawns and clams, and simmer for 3 minutes.

3 Season with salt and ground black pepper, and stir in the parsley. Serve garnished with grated orange rind.

Serves 4

Preparation time: 30 minutes

Cooking time: 25 minutes

Easy

500 g (1 lb) chicken breast fillets
1 large onion, roughly chopped
5 cm (2 in) piece ginger, chopped
8 cm (3 in) piece galangal, peeled and
   chopped
1 stem lemon grass, white part only,
   roughly chopped
2 cloves garlic
1 fresh red chilli, seeded and chopped
2 teaspoons vegetable oil
2 tablespoons mild curry paste
2 cups (500 ml) chicken stock
60 g (2 oz) rice vermicelli
50 g (1½ oz) dried egg noodles
400 ml (1⅔ cups) light coconut milk
10 snow peas (mangetout), halved
3 spring onions, finely chopped
90 g (1 cup) bean sprouts
15 g (½ cup) fresh coriander leaves

NUTRITION PER SERVE

* Protein 30 g;
* Fat 8 g;
* Carbohydrate 4.5 g;
* Dietary Fibre 3 g;
* Cholesterol 65 mg;
* 945 kJ (225 Cal)

CHICKEN LAKSA

This laksa is easy to make and provides niacin, potassium, phosphorus, iron and folate.

1 Cut the chicken into bite-sized cubes. Process the onion, ginger, galangal, lemon grass, garlic and chilli in a food processor until finely chopped. Add the oil and process until the mixture has a paste-like consistency. Spoon into a large wok, add the curry paste and stir over low heat for 1–2 minutes, or until aromatic. Take care not to burn.

2 Increase the heat to medium, add the chicken and stir for 2 minutes, or until the chicken is well coated. Stir in the chicken stock and mix well. Bring slowly to the boil, then simmer for 10 minutes, or until the chicken is cooked through.

3 Meanwhile, cut the vermicelli into shorter lengths using scissors. Cook the vermicelli and egg noodles separately in large pans of boiling water for 5 minutes each. Drain and rinse under cold water.

4 Just prior to serving, add the light coconut milk and snow peas (mange tout) to the chicken and heat through. To serve, divide the vermicelli and noodles among four warmed serving bowls. Pour the hot laksa over the top and garnish with the spring onion, bean sprouts and coriander leaves.

Serves 4

Preparation time: 25 minutes

Cooking time: 25 minutes

Medium

70 g (2 oz) raw prawns
70 g (2 oz) veal mince
60 ml (¼ cup) soy sauce
1 tablespoon finely chopped spring onion
1 tablespoon finely chopped water
   chestnuts
1 teaspoon finely chopped ginger
2 cloves garlic, finely chopped
24 gow gee wrappers
1.25 litres (5 cups) chicken stock
2 tablespoons mirin
500 g (1 lb) baby bok choy,
   finely shredded
8 spring onions, sliced

WON TON SOUP

Low in fat, with plenty of taste, this Asian soup is a great source of folate, calcium, iron, niacin and vitamin C.

1 Peel, devein and finely chop the prawns. Mix with the veal mince, 2 teaspoons soy sauce, spring onion, water chestnuts, ginger and garlic. Lay the round wrappers out on a work surface and place a teaspoon of mixture in the middle of each.

2 Moisten the edges of the wrappers and bring up the sides to form a pouch. Pinch together to seal. Cook in batches in a large pan of rapidly boiling water for 4–5 minutes. Drain and divide among soup bowls.

3 Bring the stock, remaining soy sauce and mirin to the boil in a pan. Add the bok choy, cover and simmer for 2 minutes, or until the bok choy has just wilted. Add the sliced spring onion and season with salt and pepper. Ladle the stock, bok choy and spring onion over the won tons.

NUTRITION PER SERVE

- Protein 18.5 g;
- Fat 3.5 g;
- Carbohydrate 34 g;
- Dietary Fibre 3.5 g;
- Cholesterol 44.5 mg;
- 1075 kJ (255 Cal)

Serves 6

Preparation time: 20 minutes

Cooking time: 40 minutes

Easy

2 teaspoons olive oil
1 onion, chopped
1 carrot, chopped
2 celery sticks, chopped
350 g (11½ oz) sweet potato, chopped
400 g (14 oz) can corn kernels, drained
1 litre (4 cups) vegetable stock
90 g (1 cup) pasta spirals

NUTRITION PER SERVE

- Protein 7.5 g;
- Fat 3 g;
- Carbohydrate 34.5 g;
- Dietary Fibre 4.5 g;
- Cholesterol 0 mg;
- 825 kJ (200 Cal)

VEGETABLE AND PASTA SOUP

This low-fat soup is a good source of fibre, beta-carotene and potassium.

1 Heat the oil in a large pan and add the onion, carrot and celery. Cook over low heat, stirring regularly, for 10 minutes, or until soft.

2 Add the sweet potato, corn kernels and stock. Bring to the boil, reduce the heat and simmer for 20 minutes, or until the vegetables are tender.

3 Add the pasta to the pan and return to the boil. Reduce the heat and simmer for 10 minutes, or until the pasta is tender. Serve immediately.

Serves 4

Preparation time: 5 minutes

Cooking time: 15 minutes

2 teaspoons oil
4 roughly chopped spring onions
200 g (6½ oz) English spinach leaves
390 g (3 cups) minted peas
1 litre (4 cups) chicken stock
low-fat plain yoghurt, to serve

NUTRITION PER SERVE

- Protein 7.5 g;
- Fat 3 g;
- Carbohydrate 7.5 g;
- Dietary Fibre 7.5 g;
- Cholesterol 0.5 mg;
- 365 kJ (85 Cal)

SPINACH AND PEA SOUP

1 Heat oil in a large saucepan, add spring onions and cook, stirring, over medium heat for 2 minutes, or until soft. Add spinach leaves, minted peas and chicken stock. Bring to the boil and cook for 10 minutes, or until the spinach and peas are soft. Transfer to a blender or food processor and blend until smooth. Season and serve with a dollop of low-fat plain yoghurt.

Serves 8

Preparation time: 30 minutes

Cooking time: 2 hours 30 minutes

Easy

1 tablespoon olive oil
1 onion, finely chopped
2 cloves garlic, crushed
2 carrots, diced
2 potatoes, diced
2 celery sticks, finely chopped
2 courgettes (zucchini), finely chopped
125 g (4½ oz) green beans, chopped
150 g (2 cups) shredded cabbage
2 litres (8 cups) beef stock
425 g (14 oz) can chopped tomatoes
80 g (½ cup) macaroni
440 g (14 ½ oz) can borlotti or red
    kidney beans, drained
fresh thyme sprigs, to serve
grated Parmesan, to serve

NUTRITION PER SERVE

- Protein 9 g;
- Fat 3.5 g;
- Carbohydrate 22.5 g;
- Dietary Fibre 6.5 g;
- Cholesterol 0 mg;
- 660 kJ (160 Cal)

MINESTRONE

This nourishing meal is rich in carbohydrate, fibre, folate and beta-carotene.

1 Heat the oil in a large heavy-based saucepan. Add the onion and garlic, and cook over low heat for 5 minutes. Add the carrot, potato and celery, and cook, stirring, for a further 5 minutes.

2 Add the zucchini, green beans and cabbage to the pan and cook, stirring, for 5 minutes. Add the stock and chopped tomatoes. Bring slowly to the boil, then reduce the heat, cover and leave to simmer for 2 hours.

3 Add the macaroni and beans, and cook for 15 minutes, or until the pasta is tender. Serve hot, sprinkled with the thyme sprigs and Parmesan.

NOTE: Any type of pasta can be used for minestrone, although smaller shapes are easier to manage on a soup spoon. The Milanese version uses rice.

Serves 4–6

Preparation time:
15 minutes + 3 hours refrigeration

Cooking time: 50 minutes

Easy

2 tablespoons olive oil
1 onion, chopped
1 leek, sliced
1 celery stick, chopped
2 cloves garlic, crushed
2 rashers bacon, trimmed of fat, chopped
1 litre (4 cups) chicken or vegetable stock
500 g (1 lb) frozen peas
2 tablespoons chopped fresh mint
1½ tablespoons lemon juice
90 g (⅓ cup) low-fat plain yoghurt

CHILLED MINTED PEA SOUP

This cool soup provides a boost of vitamin C, folate, phosphorus, potassium and some B vitamins.

1   Heat the oil in a large saucepan and add the onion, leek, celery, garlic and bacon. Cook, stirring, over medium heat for 4–5 minutes, or until the vegetables are softened.

2   Add the stock, bring to the boil, then reduce the heat and simmer for 25 minutes. Stir in the frozen peas and mint, return to the boil over high heat, then reduce the heat and simmer for a further 15 minutes.

3   Leave the soup to cool slightly (for safety reasons) before transferring to a blender and blending until smooth. Season to taste with salt and cracked black pepper, then stir in the lemon juice. Refrigerate for at least 3 hours, or until well chilled.

4   Serve the chilled pea soup in individual soup bowls with a generous dollop of plain yoghurt and some crusty bread.

NUTRITION PER SERVE (6)

- Protein 11 g;
- Fat 8.5 g;
- Carbohydrate 12.5 g;
- Dietary Fibre 6 g;
- Cholesterol 10 mg;
- 720 kJ (170 Cal)

Serves 4–6

Preparation time:
40 minutes + 3 hours refrigeration

Easy

750 g (1 lb 8 oz) ripe tomatoes
1 short cucumber, chopped
1 green pepper (capsicum), chopped
2–3 cloves garlic, crushed
1–2 tablespoons finely chopped black
    olives (optional)
80 ml (⅓ cup) red or white wine vinegar
60 ml (¼ cup) olive oil
1 tablespoon tomato paste

ACCOMPANIMENTS
1 onion, finely chopped
1 red pepper (capsicum), finely chopped
2 spring onions, finely chopped
1 short cucumber, finely chopped
2 hard-boiled eggs, chopped
chopped mint or parsley

NUTRITION PER SERVE (6)

- Protein 4.5 g;
- Fat 11 g;
- Carbohydrate 6.5 g;
- Dietary Fibre 3 g;
- Cholesterol 73 mg;
- 610 kJ (145 Cal)

GAZPACHO

A refreshingly cold summer soup originally from Spain, Gazpacho contains monounsaturated fat, vitamin C and beta-carotene.

1 Score a cross in the base of each tomato. Cover with boiling water for 1 minute, plunge into cold water, drain and peel away the skins. Chop the flesh so finely that it is almost a purée.

2 Mix together the tomato, cucumber, pepper (capsicum), garlic, olives, vinegar, oil and tomato paste, and season with salt and ground black pepper. Cover and refrigerate for 2–3 hours.

3 Use 750 ml (2–3 cups) of chilled water to thin the soup to your taste. Serve chilled, with the chopped onion, capsicum, spring onion, cucumber, boiled egg and herbs served separately for diners to add to their own bowls.

Serves 4

Preparation time: 30 minutes

Cooking time: 45 minutes

Easy

½ teaspoon saffron threads
3 teaspoons oil
2 large onions, thinly sliced
1 leek, white part only, chopped
4 cloves garlic, finely chopped
1 bay leaf, torn
½ teaspoon dried marjoram
1 teaspoon grated orange rind
2 tablespoons dry white wine
1 red pepper (capsicum), cut into chunks
500 g (1 lb) tomatoes, chopped
125 ml (½ cup) tomato purée
500 ml (2 cups) fish stock
2 tablespoons tomato paste
2 teaspoons soft brown sugar
500 g (1 lb) firm white fish, cut into
   bite-sized pieces
15 g (¼ cup) chopped fresh parsley

NUTRITION PER SERVE

- Protein 31 g;
- Fat 7 g;
- Carbohydrate 14.5 g;
- Dietary Fibre 5 g;
- Cholesterol 74 mg;
- 1065 kJ (255 Cal)

MEDITERRANEAN FISH SOUP

This nutritious soup contains a mix of filling fish protein, fibre and good amounts
of niacin, vitamin C, potassium and lycopene.

1 Soak the saffron in 2 tablespoons boiling water; set
aside. Heat the oil in a large heavy-based pan, over
low heat. Add the onion, leek, garlic, bay leaf and
marjoram. Cover and cook for 10 minutes, shaking
the pan occasionally, until the onion is soft. Add the
rind, wine, capsicum and tomato. Cover and cook for
10 minutes.

2 Stir in the purée, stock, tomato paste, sugar and saffron
(with liquid). Bring to the boil, reduce the heat and
simmer, uncovered, for 15 minutes.

3 Add the fish to the soup, cover and cook for 8 minutes,
or until tender. Add salt and pepper and half the parsley.
Garnish with the remaining parsley.

Serves 6–8

Preparation time: 20 minutes

Cooking time: 1 hour 20 minutes

Easy

2 tablespoons olive oil
1 large brown onion, chopped
1 large carrot, cut into 1 cm cubes
1 large celery stick, cut into 1 cm cubes
2 bay leaves
1 tablespoon fresh thyme, finely chopped
6 cloves garlic, finely chopped
440 g (2 cups) yellow split peas
1 litre (4 cups) chicken stock
60 ml (¼ cup) lemon juice
olive oil, extra

NUTRITION PER SERVE (8)

- Protein 14.5 g;
- Fat 6.5 g;
- Carbohydrate 29 g;
- Dietary Fibre 6.5 g;
- Cholesterol 0 mg;
- 960 kJ (230 Cal)

SPLIT PEA SOUP

A great way to include legumes in your diet, this delicious soup provides carbohydrate energy, soluble fibre, folate, B vitamins and minerals.

1 Heat the oil in a large saucepan over medium heat. Add the onion, carrot and celery, and cook for 4–5 minutes, or until starting to brown. Add the bay leaves, thyme and garlic, and cook for 1 minute.

2 Stir in the split peas, then add the chicken stock and 1 litre (4 cups) water. Cook for 1 hour 15 minutes, or until the split peas and vegetables are soft. Stir often during cooking to prevent the soup from sticking to the bottom of the pan, and skim any scum from the surface. Add a little extra water if the soup is too thick.

3 Remove the soup from the heat and discard the bay leaves. Stir in the lemon juice and season with salt and ground black pepper. Drizzle with a little olive oil before serving.

Serves 4

Preparation time:
40 minutes + 1 hour refrigeration

Cooking time: 2 hours

Medium

2 tablespoons olive oil
8 lamb shanks
2 onions, sliced
4 cloves garlic, finely chopped
3 bay leaves, torn in half
1–2 teaspoons hot paprika
2 teaspoons sweet paprika
1 tablespoon plain flour
60 g (1/4 cup) tomato paste
1.5 litres (6 cups) vegetable stock
4 potatoes, chopped
4 carrots, sliced
3 celery sticks, thickly sliced
3 tomatoes, seeded and chopped

LAMB HOT POT

This thick vegetable and lamb soup is rich in vitamins A, B and C, folate and minerals.

1 Heat 1 tablespoon of the oil in a large, heavy-based pan over medium heat. Brown the lamb shanks well in two batches and drain on paper towels.

2 Add the remaining oil to the pan and cook the onion, garlic and bay leaves over low heat for 10 minutes, stirring regularly. Add the paprika and flour, and cook, stirring continuously, for 2 minutes. Gradually add the combined tomato paste and stock. Bring to the boil, stirring continuously, and return the shanks to the pan. Reduce the heat to low and simmer, covered, for 1½ hours, stirring occasionally.

3 Remove and discard the bay leaves. Remove the shanks, allow to cool slightly and then cut the meat from the bone. Discard the bones. Cut the meat into pieces and refrigerate. Refrigerate the stock for about 1 hour, or until fat forms on the surface and can be spooned off.

4 Return the meat to the soup along with the potato, carrot and celery and bring to the boil. Reduce the heat and simmer for 15 minutes. Season with salt and pepper, and add the chopped tomato to serve.

NUTRITION PER SERVE

• Protein 70 g;
• Fat 15 g;
• Carbohydrate 30 g;
• Dietary Fibre 8 g;
• Cholesterol 170 mg;
• 2200 kJ (525 Cal)

Serves 6

Preparation time: 30 minutes

Cooking time: 40 minutes

Easy

2 tablespoons olive oil
1 small leek (white part only), chopped
2 cloves garlic, crushed
2 teaspoons curry powder
1 teaspoon ground cumin
1 teaspoon garam masala
1 litre vegetable stock
1 fresh bay leaf
185 g (1 cup) brown lentils
450 g (14½ oz) butternut pumpkin,
   peeled and cut into 1 cm (½ in) cubes
400 g (13 oz) can chopped tomatoes
2 courgettes (zucchini), cut in half
   lengthways and sliced
200 g (6½ oz) broccoli, cut into
   small florets
1 small carrot, diced
80 g (½ cup) peas
1 tablespoon chopped fresh mint

SPICED YOGHURT
250 g (1 cup) low-fat thick plain yoghurt
1 tablespoon chopped fresh coriander
   leaves
1 clove garlic, crushed
3 dashes Tabasco sauce

NUTRITION PER SERVE

- Protein 17 g;
- Fat 9 g;
- Carbohydrate 26.5 g;
- Dietary Fibre 9.5 g;
- Cholesterol 4 mg;
- 1055 kJ (255 Cal)

LENTIL AND VEGETABLE SOUP

This flavoursome, aromatic soup provides a great range of nutrients, including carbohydrate, soluble fibre, vitamins A, B and C, calcium and iron.

1 Heat the oil in a saucepan over medium heat. Add the leek and garlic and cook for 4–5 minutes, or until soft and golden. Add the curry powder, cumin and garam masala, and cook for 1 minute.

2 Add the stock, bay leaf, lentils and pumpkin. Bring to the boil, then reduce the heat and simmer for 10–15 minutes, or until the lentils are tender. Season.

3 Add the tomato, zucchini, broccoli, carrot and 500 ml (2 cups) water,

and simmer for 10 minutes, or until the vegetables are tender. Add the peas and simmer for 2–3 minutes.

4 Combine the yoghurt, coriander, garlic and Tabasco. Serve the soup with the yoghurt and mint.

Serves 8

Preparation time:
40 minutes + 1 hour soaking
+ overnight refrigeration

Cooking time: 4 hours

Medium

1 kg (2 lb) lamb shanks, cut in half
   through the bone (ask your butcher to
   do this)
3 onions, chopped
3 turnips, chopped
2 carrots, chopped
1 tablespoon black peppercorns
110 g (½ cup) pearl barley
1 carrot, diced, extra
2 onions, finely chopped, extra
2 turnips, diced, extra
1 leek, chopped
1 celery stick, diced
chopped fresh flat-leaf parsley

SCOTCH BROTH

This broth is a good source of soluble fibre, B vitamins, beta-carotene,
iron and zinc.

1 To make the stock, put the lamb
   shanks, onion, turnip, carrot,
   peppercorns and 2 litres (8 cups) of
   water in a large pan. Bring to the
   boil, reduce the heat and simmer,
   covered, for 3 hours. Skim the
   surface as required.

2 Remove the shanks and any meat
   that has fallen off the bones and
   cool slightly. Remove the meat from
   the bones and finely chop, then

cover and refrigerate. Strain the
stock, discarding the vegetables.
Cool the stock and refrigerate
overnight, or until the fat has set on
top and can be spooned off. Cover
the barley with water and soak for
1 hour, then drain.

3 Put the stock in a large pan and
   gently reheat. Add the barley, extra
   carrot, onion and turnip, and the
   leek and celery. Bring to the boil,

reduce the heat and simmer for
30 minutes, or until the barley and
vegetables are just cooked. Return
the meat to the pan and simmer for
5 minutes. Season well and serve
with the parsley.

NUTRITION PER SERVE

- Protein 35 g;
- Fat 3 g;
- Carbohydrate 20 g;
- Dietary Fibre 6 g;
- Cholesterol 80 mg;
- 970 kJ (230 Cal)

Serves 4

Preparation time: 15 minutes

Cooking time: 30 minutes

Easy

4 leeks, trimmed and quartered
   lengthways
30 g (1 oz) butter
3 floury potatoes, chopped
750 ml (3 cups) chicken or vegetable stock
250 ml (1 cup) reduced-fat milk
¼ teaspoon ground nutmeg
cream and chopped fresh spring onions,
   to serve

NUTRITION PER SERVE

- Protein 9 g;
- Fat 8 g;
- Carbohydrate 21.5 g;
- Dietary Fibre 4 g;
- Cholesterol 23.5 mg;
- 815 kJ (195 Cal)

NOTE: Old floury potatoes such as sebago will give the best results for this dish.

LEEK AND POTATO SOUP

Leeks add a delicate flavour to this nourishing soup, which is a good source of calcium, potassium, niacin, vitamin C and folate.

1   Wash the leeks thoroughly in cold water to remove any dirt, then cut into small chunks. Heat the butter in a large heavy-based pan. Add the leek and cook for 3–4 minutes, stirring frequently, until softened. Add the potato and stock. Bring slowly to the boil, then reduce the heat and simmer for 20 minutes, or until the vegetables are tender.

2   Cool the mixture slightly then transfer to a blender or food processor and purée in batches. Return to the pan, stir in the milk and nutmeg, and season well with salt and cracked black pepper. Reheat gently and serve garnished with a swirl of cream and a scattering of spring onion.

Serves 4

Preparation time: 20 minutes

Cooking time: 30 minutes

1 litre (4 cups) beef stock
2 stems lemon grass (white part only),
   halved
3 cloves garlic, halved
2.5 cm x 2.5 cm (1 in x 1 in) piece fresh
   ginger, sliced
95 g (3 cups) cariander (cilantro) leaves
   and stalks separated
4 spring onions tinly sliced on the
   diagonal
2 strips 1.5 cm x 4 cm ($^5/_8$ in x $^5/_8$ in)
   lime zest
2 star anise
3 small red chilles, seeded and
   finely chopped
500 g (1 lb 2 oz) fillet steak, trimmed
2 tablespoons fish sauce
1 tablespoon grated palm sugar
2 tablespoons lime juice
extra coriander (cilantro) leaves to garnish

NUTRITION PER SERVE

- Protein 31 g;
- Fat 7 g;
- Carbohydrate 7 g;
- Dietary Fibre 0.5 g;
- Cholesterol 84 mg;
- 900 kJ (215 cal)

HOT AND SOUR LIME SOUP WITH BEEF

1 Place the stock, lemon grass, garlic, ginger, coriander (cilantro) stalks, 2 spring onions, lime zest, star anise, 1 teaspoon chopped chilli and 1 litre (4 cups) water in a saucepan. Bring to the boil and simmer, covered, for 25 minutes. Strain and return the liquid to the pan.

2 Heat a ridged chargrill pan until very hot. Brush lightly with olive oil. Sear the steak on both sides until browned on the outside, but very rare in the centre.

3 Reheat the soup, adding the fish sauce and palm sugar. Season with salt and black pepper. Add the lime juice to taste (you may want more than 2 tablespoons)—you should achieve a hot and sour flavour.

4 Add the remaining spring onion and chopped coriander (cilantro) leaves to the soup. Slice the beef across the grain into thin strips. Curl the strips into a decorative pattern, then place in the centre of four deep wide serving bowls. Pour the soup over the beef and garnish with the remaining chilli and extra coriander (cilantro) leaves.

SALADS & VEGETABLES

Vegetables are an important part of a healthy diet, and with such a wide variety and different ways of serving them, they need never be boring or bland.

SALADS

Salads are a naturally healthy and versatile way of incorporating many vegetables and fruits into your diet, either as a complete meal or an accompaniment. Almost any raw or cooked ingredient can be made into a salad, ranging from vegetables and fruits to seafood, poultry, meat, noodles, legumes and pasta.

Salads should make use of the best seasonal ingredients available, and many variations of flavour, texture and temperature are possible by simply using a different dressing, different herbs, cooked rather than raw, and warm rather than cold ingredients.

A salad can be a light starter, or a complex combination of ingredients that provides all the nutrients you need, in one bowl. It can be as simple as some dressed green leaves, or as complicated as a tuna niçoise, which includes a variety of raw and cooked ingredients.

When choosing salad greens, buy them as fresh and green as possible, wash them well in cold water, then dry them with paper towel or in a salad spinner. To create interesting flavours and texture, use a combination of leaves:

- raddichio is colourful and crisp, and has quite a bitter flavour
- rocket has peppery leaves
- watercress is small and delicate looking, but has a mustardy bite
- cos lettuce is crisp, with a sweet flavour
- snow pea (mange tout) sprouts are crunchy and sweet.

Dressings add flavour to salads, but be aware that many salad dressings contain lots of hidden fat. Different salad leaves are suited to different dressings. Leaves that are full flavoured and crisp are ideal for strong, thick dressings, such as cos lettuce with Caesar dressing, while more delicate leaves are better with light dressings, such as butter lettuce with a simple lemon vinaigrette.

SIMPLE, HEALTHY SALADS

- When tomatoes are at the peak of their season, they are best treated simply—sliced, seasoned and drizzled with some balsamic vinegar and extra virgin olive oil.
- Use a Thai-style dressing of chilli, garlic, ginger, lime juice and fish sauce on a coleslaw salad as a low-fat alternative to the traditional mayonnaise dressing.
- Mix some salad vegetables with pasta and canned tuna for a complete meal.
- A low-fat yoghurt dressing flavoured with fresh herbs and a little honey, thinned slightly with lemon juice or warm water, is a tasty alternative dressing, and goes well with legumes such as chickpeas, lentils, cannellini beans, new potatoes, green beans, roasted beetroot, and chargrilled sweet potatoes.
- Asian-style dressings tend to be lower in fat because they contain a minimum of oil or no oil, but the delicate balance of flavours makes them tasty and delicious.
- Dress warm potatoes with a zesty herb vinaigrette rather than mayonnaise.

- Save the juices from roasting red peppers (capsicums), lightly season and use to dress the skinned peppers (capsicums).
- If you marinate seafood, poultry or meat before you cook it, you will only need a very light dressing or squeeze of lemon for a delicious salad.
- Toss leftover diced meats or legumes with a spicy salsa of diced tomato, avocado, chilli, corn and lime juice.
- Use a slightly sweeter vinegar such as balsamic, or rice wine vinegar, or sherry for a more mellow dressing that will require less oil to balance the flavours.

VEGETABLES

Vegetables can be eaten raw or cooked, made into salads, soups, starters, main meals, accompaniments or snacks. They may be steamed, grilled, roasted, braised, boiled or barbecued.

Vegetables provide carbohydrates, dietary fibre, vitamins and minerals. The most delicious, economical and nutritious way of enjoying fresh vegetables is to use them at the peak of their season.

Modern storage methods mean that there is an abundance of fresh vegetables available all year round, but often they are at their peak to complement the season. For example, hearty root vegetables that are perfect for soups or roasting are autumn or winter vegetables, while tomatoes and salad greens are perfect in spring and summer.

When vegetables are at the peak of their season, they are so full of flavour and texture that they need little preparation or dressings.

HEALTHY TIPS FOR COOKING VEGETABLES

- Steam rather than boil vegetables, so that they retain nutrients that may otherwise be leached out into the cooking water.
- Leave the skin on boiled potatoes for a potato salad, for maximum fibre.
- Cook vegetables for the minimum time so they retain more nutrients.

- For flavour and variety, a stir-fry is a great way of incorporating a healthy variety of vegetables into your diet.
- Salting aubergine (eggplant) before cooking will draw out excess moisture, leaching away any bitterness, and less oil will be needed for cooking.
- Spinach and silverbeet need only minimum cooking. Simply wash the leaves and then put them in a saucepan with only the water clinging to the leaves. Place the pan over heat and toss gently until wilted.
- Dress steamed green leafy vegetables with an Asian-style soy and ginger dressing for a highly nutritious dish.
- When roasting vegetables, lightly spray them with olive oil before cooking rather than filling the dish with oil.
- Leave the skin on when roasting pumpkin, carrots, parsnips and potatoes. Wash them thoroughly first.
- Bake a layered potato dish using vegetable or chicken stock rather than cream.

Serves 4

Preparation time:
10 minutes + 10 minutes standing

Cooking time: Nil

Easy

6 ripe Roma tomatoes
1 red onion
1 clove garlic, crushed
60 g (1 cup) finely shredded basil leaves
1–2 tablespoons balsamic vinegar

NUTRITION PER SERVE

- Protein 1.5 g;
- Fat 0.2 g;
- Carbohydrate 3 g;
- Dietary Fibre 2 g;
- Cholesterol 0 mg;
- 90 kJ (20 Cal)

TOMATO AND BASIL SALAD

This fragrant, healthy side salad provides vitamin C, beta-carotene and other antioxidants, with some potassium and folate.

1   Cut the tomatoes into quarters, and thinly slice the red onion. If you find raw onion too strong, put it in a bowl and cover it with boiling water for 5 minutes. Drain well.

2   Combine the tomato, red onion, garlic, basil and balsamic vinegar, and toss to combine. Season with salt and ground black pepper, then set aside for 10 minutes to allow the flavours to develop. Transfer the salad to a shallow dish.

Serves 4–6

Preparation time:
30 minutes + 10 minutes standing
+ 30 minutes refrigeration

Easy

200 g (6½ oz) dried rice vermicelli
140 g (1 cup) crushed peanuts
10 g (½ cup) fresh Vietnamese mint
  leaves, torn
15 g (½ cup) firmly packed fresh
  coriander leaves
½ red onion, cut into thin wedges
1 green mango, cut into julienne strips
1 Lebanese (short) cucumber, halved
  lengthways and thinly sliced on the
  diagonal

LEMON GRASS DRESSING
125 ml (½ cup) lime juice
1 tablespoon shaved palm sugar
60 ml (½ cup) seasoned rice vinegar
2 stems lemon grass, finely chopped
2 red chillies, seeded and finely chopped
3 kaffir lime leaves, shredded

VIETNAMESE SALAD

NUTRITION PER SERVE

- Protein 6.5 g;
- Fat 13 g;
- Carbohydrate 19 g;
- Dietary Fibre 3 g;
- Cholesterol 0 mg;
- 926 kJ (221 Cal)

1 Place the rice vermicelli in a bowl and cover with boiling water. Leave for 10 minutes, or until soft, then drain, rinse under cold water and cut into short lengths.

2 Place the vermicelli, three-quarters of the peanuts, the mint, coriander, onion, mango and cucumber in a large bowl and toss together.

3 To make the dressing, place all the ingredients in a jar with a lid and shake together.

4 Toss the salad and dressing and refrigerate for 30 minutes. Sprinkle with the remaining nuts to serve.

Serves 8

Preparation time:
15 minutes + overnight soaking

Cooking time: 1 hour 15 minutes

Easy

100 g (3½ oz) dried chickpeas
100 g (3½ oz) dried pinto beans
100 g (3½ oz) dried red kidney beans
100 g (3½ oz) dried black-eyed beans
2 onions, sliced
2 teaspoons ground cumin
1 teaspoon ground coriander
420 g (14 oz) can corn kernels, drained
2 tomatoes, chopped
80 ml (⅓ cup) lemon juice
15 g (¼ cup) chopped fresh
    coriander leaves
1 Lebanese (short) cucumber, grated
250 g (1 cup) low-fat plain yoghurt

HOT BEAN SALAD

A satisfying combination of high-fibre beans and nutritious vegetables and herbs, rich in slow-release carbohydrate and soluble fibre, this salad is ideal if you are watching your blood sugar and cholesterol levels.

NUTRITION PER SERVE

- Protein 10 g;
- Fat 2 g;
- Carbohydrate 25 g;
- Dietary Fibre 8.5 g;
- Cholesterol 1.5 mg;
- 745 kJ (180 Cal)

1 Combine the chickpeas, pinto beans, red kidney beans and black-eyed beans in a large bowl. Cover with water and soak overnight. Drain, place in a large saucepan and cover with water. Bring to the boil, then reduce the heat and simmer for 45 minutes, or until tender. Don't overcook or the beans will be mushy.

2 Meanwhile, in a large, deep non-stick frying pan, cook the onion over low heat for 25 minutes, or until golden. Add the cumin and coriander with the beans, and toss to combine. Add the corn kernels, tomato, lemon juice and coriander. Season with salt and black pepper, and stir.

3 Squeeze out the moisture from the cucumber. Combine the cucumber with the yoghurt, and season. Stir to combine.

4 Put the hot bean mixture on a serving plate, and top with the yoghurt mixture.

Serves 6

Preparation time: 20 minutes

Cooking time: Nil

Easy

1 grapefruit
2 small red grapefruit
4 oranges
1 red onion, sliced
10 g (⅓ cup) fresh coriander leaves
2 tablespoons honey
80 ml (⅓ cup) raspberry vinegar
rocket leaves, to serve

CITRUS SALAD with honey dressing

This tangy salad is rich in vitamin C, with some folate, fibre and potassium.
Eat it with red meat to increase iron absorption.

1   Remove the rind from the grapefruit and oranges. Remove and discard all the pith from a few slices of the rind from each fruit and cut the rind into long thin strips. Remove any remaining pith from the fruit and slice between each section. Segment the fruits over a bowl to catch any juice; set the juice aside. Put the citrus segments and rind in a bowl with the onion and coriander.

2   Add the honey and raspberry vinegar to the reserved fruit juice and whisk to combine. Pour over the salad and toss. Serve on a bed of rocket.

NUTRITION PER SERVE

- Protein 2 g;
- Fat 0.5 g;
- Carbohydrate 20 g;
- Dietary Fibre 2.5 g;
- Cholesterol 0 mg;
- 395 kJ (95 Cal)

Serves 4

Preparation time: 20 minutes

Cooking time: 30 minutes

Easy

375 g (12 oz) fresh spinach and ricotta
   ravioli
200 g (6½ oz) cauliflower, cut into florets
200 g (6½ oz) broccoli, cut into florets
155 g (5 oz) asparagus, cut into
   5 cm (2 in) lengths
1 cup (155 g) fresh peas
100 g (3½ oz) baby English spinach
   leaves

DRESSING
2 cloves garlic, finely chopped
1 tablespoon sugar
80 ml (⅓ cup) lime juice
60 ml (¼ cup) raspberry vinegar
50 g (1 cup) chopped fresh coriander

NUTRITION PER SERVE

- Protein 15 g;
- Fat 5 g;
- Carbohydrate 25 g;
- Dietary Fibre 8.5 g;
- Cholesterol 19 mg;
- 960 kJ (230 Cal)

RAVIOLI SALAD
with spring vegetables

The vegetables in this dish provide many beneficial phytochemicals and fibre. The regular intake of cruciferous vegetables, such as broccoli, is associated with a reduced risk of bowel cancer.

1   Bring a large saucepan of lightly salted water to the boil. Add the ravioli and cook until al dente. Drain well.

2   Steam or microwave the cauliflower, broccoli, asparagus and peas separately until just tender and bright. Rinse under cold water and drain well.

3   Place the ravioli, blanched vegetables and spinach in a bowl, and toss to combine.

4   To make the dressing, place the garlic, sugar, lime juice and vinegar in a bowl, and whisk together. Stir in the coriander, pour over the salad and toss to coat.

Serves 4

Preparation time: 20 minutes

Cooking time: 5 minutes

Easy

450 g (14½ oz) Hokkien noodles
200 g (6½ oz) broccoli, cut into florets
4 spring onions, sliced
1 red pepper (capsicum), thinly sliced
1 green pepper (capsicum), thinly sliced
1 carrot, diagonally sliced
100 g (3½ oz) snow peas
   (mange tout), sliced
100 g (3½ oz) fresh baby corn, halved
   lengthways
15 g (¼ cup) chopped fresh coriander
   (cilantro) leaves
1 teaspoon sesame oil
60 ml (¼ cup) sweet chilli sauce
60 ml (¼ cup) light soy sauce
2 tablespoons lime juice

HOKKIEN NOODLE SALAD

NUTRITION PER SERVE

- Protein 12.5 g;
- Fat 5.5 g;
- Carbohydrate 40.5 g;
- Dietary Fibre 8 g;
- Cholesterol 1 mg;
- 1100 kJ (265 Cal)

The noodles and marinade add a zesty Asian flavour to this nutritious salad, bursting with vitamin C, folate, fibre, beta-carotene and potassium. It is also low in fat.

1 Gently separate the noodles, place in a heatproof bowl and cover with boiling water. Leave to stand for 2 minutes, then rinse under cold water and drain well.

2 Boil or steam the broccoli for 3 minutes, or until bright green and tender. Rinse under cold water and drain.

3 Place the noodles, vegetables and coriander in a large bowl, and mix well.

4 Combine the sesame oil, sweet chilli sauce, soy sauce and lime juice. Pour over the salad and toss to coat.

Serves 6–8

Preparation time:
20 minutes + soaking

Easy

150 g (5 oz) fresh flat-leaf parsley
180 g (1 cup) soy grits
2 tablespoons chopped fresh mint
1 small red onion, cut into thin wedges
3 ripe tomatoes, chopped
400 g (13 oz) can chickpeas, rinsed
    and drained
60 ml (¼ cup) lemon juice
2 tablespoons extra virgin olive oil
Lebanese or pitta bread, to serve

NUTRITION PER SERVE (8)

- Protein 12 g;
- Fat 11 g;
- Carbohydrate 13 g;
- Dietary Fibre 6.5 g;
- Cholesterol 0 mg;
- 820 kJ (195 Cal)

TABBOULEH with soy grits

Soy grits and chickpeas add protein, fibre and isoflavones to this version of the traditional Middle-Eastern salad, which provides vitamin C, beta-carotene, folate and potassium.

1 Remove all the parsley leaves from the stalks, roughly chop and place in a large serving bowl.

2 Place the soy grits in a heatproof bowl and pour in 170 ml (⅔ cup) boiling water. Leave to soak for 3 minutes, or until all the water has been absorbed.

3 Add the soy grits to the parsley, along with the mint, onion, tomato and chickpeas. Drizzle with the lemon juice and olive oil. Season well with salt and ground black pepper and toss together. Serve with Lebanese or pitta bread or as an accompaniment to barbecued meat, chicken or fish.

Serves 6

Preparation time: 30 minutes

Cooking time: 40 minutes

Easy

4 Roma tomatoes, quartered lengthways
300 g (10 oz) aubergine (eggplant),
 quartered lengthways, thickly sliced
olive oil spray
500 g (1 lb) orange sweet potato, cut into
 2 cm (3/4 in) slices
1 large red onion, sliced into thin wedges
1 barbecued chicken
2 tablespoons chopped fresh coriander
 leaves
2–3 tablespoons balsamic vinegar
100 g (3 1/2 oz) rocket (arugula) leaves

CHICKEN AND SWEET POTATO SALAD

Tender pieces of chicken are mixed with nutritious vegetables in this light meal, providing good amounts of protein, B vitamins, vitamin E, folate and beta-carotene.

NUTRITION PER SERVE

- Protein 19.5 g;
- Fat 6 g;
- Carbohydrate 15 g;
- Dietary Fibre 3.5 g;
- Cholesterol 62.5 mg;
- 825 kJ (195 Cal)

1 Preheat the oven to moderately hot 200°C (400°F/Gas 6). Place the tomato and aubergine (eggplant) on a non-stick baking tray, spray with a little oil and season with salt and ground black pepper. Bake, turning the aubergine (eggplant) halfway through, for 25–30 minutes.

2 Meanwhile, steam the sweet potato for 15 minutes, or until just tender. Place in a large bowl with the tomato and aubergine (eggplant).

3 Lightly spray a small non-stick frying pan with oil, add the onion and cook over low heat for 6 minutes, or until golden. Set aside.

4 Remove and discard the skin and bones from the chicken. Cut the chicken into bite-sized pieces and add to the vegetables with the coriander and 1 tablespoon balsamic vinegar. Toss gently.

5 Place the rocket (arugula) on a platter, then the chicken mixture, and top with the onion. Drizzle with the remaining balsamic vinegar to taste. Serve.

Serves 4

Preparation time:
20 minutes + 5 minutes standing

Cooking time: 10 minutes

Easy

300 g (10 oz) orange sweet potato, cubed
100 g (3½ oz) green beans, halved
350 g (11½ oz) instant couscous
500 ml (2 cups) boiling chicken stock
200 g (6½ oz) cherry tomatoes, halved
150 g (1 cup) frozen corn kernels, thawed
155 g (1 cup) frozen peas, thawed
1 red pepper (capsicum), chopped
60 g (1 cup) chopped fresh parsley
25 g (½ cup) chopped fresh mint

DRESSING
2 cloves garlic, crushed
60 ml (¼ cup) lemon juice
1 tablespoon oil
1 tablespoon white wine vinegar
1 teaspoon honey mustard

NUTRITION PER SERVE

• Protein 20 g;
• Fat 6.5 g;
• Carbohydrate 92 g;
• Dietary Fibre 9 g;
• Cholesterol 0 mg;
• 2155 kJ (515 Cal)

COUSCOUS SALAD

This salad is a good source of carbohydrate energy, fibre, B vitamins and folate.

1 Boil or steam the sweet potato and beans in separate saucepans until tender, then drain. Place the couscous in a large bowl and pour on the boiling stock. Cover and leave for 5 minutes, or until all the liquid has been absorbed. Fluff with a fork to separate the grains.

2 Add the sweet potato, beans, tomato, corn, peas, pepper (capsicum) and herbs to the couscous, and mix together well.

3 Place the garlic, lemon juice, oil, vinegar and mustard in a bowl, and whisk together. Pour the dressing over the salad and toss well.

Serves 4

Preparation time: 15 minutes

Cooking time: 10 minutes

Easy

400 g (13 oz) lean beef fillet steaks
75 g (2½ oz) mixed salad leaves
½ small red onion, thinly sliced
100 g (3½ oz) cherry tomatoes, halved
1 small Lebanese (short) cucumber,
　thinly sliced
20 g (⅓ cup) chopped fresh coriander
　(cilantro) leaves
20 g (⅓ cup) chopped fresh mint

DRESSING
1½ tablespoons fish sauce
2 tablespoons lime juice
1 tablespoon soft brown sugar
1 small fresh red chilli, seeded and
　finely chopped

NUTRITION PER SERVE

- Protein 22.5 g;
- Fat 5 g;
- Carbohydrate 6 g;
- Dietary Fibre 2 g;
- Cholesterol 67 mg;
- 670 kJ (160 Cal)

THAI BEEF SALAD

Tender strips of lean meat mixed with herbs, vegetables and a tangy aromatic dressing provide good amounts of complete protein, iron, zinc and B vitamins.

1　Season the beef well on both sides with salt and ground black pepper. Spray a chargrill or hotplate with oil spray and, when very hot, sear the beef fillets on each side for 3–4 minutes. Remove and leave to rest for 10 minutes before slicing thinly—the meat should still be quite pink in the middle.

2　While the meat is resting, combine the fish sauce, lime juice, brown sugar, chilli and 2 tablespoons water in a small saucepan. Stir over low heat until the sugar has dissolved. Remove from the heat and keep warm.

3　Place the mixed salad leaves, onion, tomato, cucumber, coriander (cilantro) leaves and mint in a large bowl and toss together. Arrange the salad on a large platter, top with the beef slices and pour the warm dressing on top. Serve immediately.

Serves 4

Preparation time: 20 minutes

Cooking time: 30 minutes

Easy

1.5 kg (3 lb 8 oz) thickly sliced vegetables
    (such as pumpkin, potato, parsnip,
    aubergine (eggplant) and courgette
    (zucchini))
2 tablespoons olive oil
4 cloves garlic, finely chopped
cooking oil spray
300 g (10 oz) baby spinach leaves
½ red pepper (capsicum), thinly sliced
2 tablespoons balsamic vinegar
snipped fresh chives

NUTRITION PER SERVE

- Protein 9 g;
- Fat 10 g;
- Carbohydrate 25 g;
- Dietary Fibre 10 g;
- Cholesterol 0 mg;
- 1000 kJ (240 Cal)

GRILLED VEGETABLES

The nutrients you get from this recipe will depend on which combination of vegetables you choose, but you'll obtain folate, vitamin C and beta-carotene from the other ingredients.

1   Preheat the oven to moderate 180°C (350°F/Gas 4). Place the vegetables in a baking dish with the olive oil and garlic. Toss to combine.

2   Heat a large flat grill or barbecue plate and spray lightly with cooking oil. Grill the vegetables separately (they will cook at different rates), turning until charred.

3   Place the vegetables on a lightly greased baking tray and bake for 15 minutes, or until cooked.

4   Arrange the baby spinach leaves on a platter and top with the vegetables and capsicum. Drizzle with the balsamic vinegar and chives.

Serves 4

Preparation time:
20 minutes + overnight marinating

Cooking time: 15 minutes

Easy

250 g (1 cup) low-fat natural yoghurt
2 cloves garlic, crushed
2 teaspoons grated ginger
2 teaspoons ground turmeric
2 teaspoons garam masala
¼ teaspoon paprika
2 teaspoons ground coriander (cilantro)
red food colouring, optional
500 g (1 lb) lean lamb fillets
80 ml (⅓ cup) lemon juice
1½ teaspoons chopped fresh
    coriander (cilantro)
1 teaspoon chopped fresh mint
150 g (5 oz) mixed salad leaves
1 large mango, cut into strips
2 cucumbers, cut into matchsticks

NUTRITION PER SERVE

- Protein 31 g;
- Fat 5 g;
- Carbohydrate 12 g;
- Dietary Fibre 2.5 g;
- Cholesterol 84.5 mg;
- 935 kJ (225 Cal)

TANDOORI LAMB SALAD

The tender pieces of lean lamb marinated in yoghurt and spices make a nutritious meal that is rich in iron, zinc, B vitamins and potassium.

1   Mix the yoghurt, garlic, ginger and spices in a bowl, add a little colouring and toss with the lamb to thoroughly coat. Cover and refrigerate overnight.

2   Grill the lamb on a foil-lined baking tray under a hot grill for 7 minutes each side, or until the marinade starts to brown. Set aside for 5 minutes before serving.

3   Mix the lemon juice, coriander and mint, then season. Toss with the salad leaves, mango and cucumber, then arrange on plates. Slice the lamb and serve over the salad.

Serves 4

Preparation time: 10 minutes

Cooking time: 5 minutes

Easy

300 g (10 oz) fresh scallops, without roe
100 g (2 cups) baby English spinach
    leaves
1 small red pepper (capsicum), cut into
    very thin strips
50 g (1½ oz) bean sprouts
5 teaspoons sake
1 tablespoon lime juice
2 teaspoons shaved palm sugar
1 teaspoon fish sauce

NUTRITION PER SERVE

- Protein 10 g;
- Fat 0.5 g;
- Carbohydrate 3.5 g;
- Dietary Fibre 1.5 g;
- Cholesterol 25 mg;
- 275 kJ (65 Cal)

SCALLOP AND SPINACH SALAD

Serve this recipe as a light meal or with rice or noodles for a main course. It is a good source of selenium, sulphur, chromium, iodine and vitamin C.

1   Remove any veins, membrane or hard white muscle from the scallops. Lightly brush a chargrill plate with oil. Cook the scallops in batches on the chargrill plate for 1 minute each side, or until cooked.

2   Divide the English spinach leaves, capsicum and bean sprouts among four serving plates. Arrange the scallops over the top.

3   To make the dressing, place the sake, lime juice, palm sugar and fish sauce in a small bowl, and mix together well. Pour over the salad and serve immediately.

NOTE: Sprinkle with toasted sesame seeds, for extra minerals.

Serves 4

Preparation time:
30 minutes + overnight marinating

Cooking time: 20 minutes

Easy

500 g (1 lb) chicken thigh fillets,
 fat removed
2 teaspoons Thai red curry paste
1 teaspoon chopped red chilli
1 clove garlic, crushed
1 stem lemon grass, white part only,
 finely chopped
cooking oil spray
1 red onion, thinly sliced
2 tomatoes, cut in wedges
25 g (½ cup) chopped fresh mint
15 g (¼ cup) chopped fresh
 coriander (cilantro)
400 g (13 oz) mixed salad leaves
2 tablespoons dry-roasted peanuts

DRESSING
1½ tablespoons soft brown sugar
2 tablespoons fish sauce
2 tablespoons lime juice
2 kaffir lime leaves, shredded
2 teaspoons oil

WARM CHICKEN SALAD

This aromatic salad provides good amounts of B vitamins, vitamins A and E, folate and iron.

1 Cut the chicken into thin strips and mix with the curry paste, chilli, garlic and lemon grass. Cover and refrigerate for several hours or overnight.

2 Lightly spray a non-stick frying pan with oil and cook the chicken in batches until tender and lightly browned; set aside. Add the onion to the pan and cook for 1 minute,

or until just soft. Return the chicken and any juices to the pan, and add the tomato, mint and coriander, stirring until heated. Set aside until just warm.

3 To make the dressing, thoroughly mix the ingredients in a jug. In a large bowl, toss the chicken mixture with the salad leaves and dressing, and serve sprinkled with the peanuts.

NUTRITION PER SERVE

- Protein 28.5 g;
- Fat 17 g;
- Carbohydrate 10.5 g;
- Dietary Fibre 5 g;
- Cholesterol 109 mg;
- 1300 kJ (310 Cal)

Serves 4

Preparation time: 15 minutes

Cooking time: 35 minutes

Easy

800 g (1lb 9 oz) jap pumpkin, peeled
2 small red onions
2 cloves garlic, finely chopped
150 g (5 oz) rocket (aragula) leaves
1–2 tablespoons balsamic vinegar

ROAST PUMPKIN AND ONION
with rocket

NUTRITION PER SERVE

- Protein 5.5 g;
- Fat 1 g;
- Carbohydrate 15 g;
- Dietary Fibre 3.5 g;
- Cholesterol 0 mg;
- 395 kJ (95 Cal)

This quick recipe is an excellent source of beta-carotene. One serve provides your daily requirement of vitamin A, and also delivers good amounts of folate, vitamin C and potassium.

1 Preheat the oven to moderately hot 200°C (400°F/Gas 6). Cut the pumpkin into 3 cm (1 in) cubes. Cut the onions into small wedges.

2 Line a small baking dish with baking paper, add the vegetables and sprinkle with the garlic. Lightly spray with oil. Season with salt and ground black pepper.

3 Bake for 30–35 minutes, or until the pumpkin is just tender. Set aside.

4 Tear the rocket leaves into pieces. Arrange on a platter, then top with the pumpkin and onion. Drizzle all over with the balsamic vinegar. Serve warm.

Serves 4

Preparation time: 20 minutes

Cooking time: 10 minutes

Easy

155 g (5 oz) asparagus spears
1 tablespoon wholegrain mustard
60 ml (¼ cup) orange juice
2 tablespoons lemon juice
1 tablespoon lime juice
1 tablespoon orange zest
2 teaspoons lemon zest
2 teaspoons lime zest
2 cloves garlic, crushed
90 g (¼ cup) honey
400 g (13 oz) button mushrooms, halved
150 g (5 oz) rocket (arugula)
1 red pepper (capsicum), cut into strips

ASPARAGUS AND MUSHROOM SALAD

This tangy combination delivers a good dose of vitamin C, folate and potassium.

1 Trim the woody ends from the asparagus spears and cut in half on the diagonal. Place the asparagus in a saucepan of boiling water and cook for 1 minute, or until just tender. Drain, plunge into cold water and set aside.

2 Place the mustard, citrus juice and zest, garlic and honey in a large saucepan and season with pepper. Bring to the boil, then reduce the heat and add the mushrooms, tossing for 2 minutes. Cool.

3 Remove the mushrooms from the sauce with a slotted spoon. Return the sauce to the heat, bring to the boil, then reduce the heat and simmer for 3–5 minutes, or until reduced and syrupy. Cool slightly.

4 Toss the mushrooms, rocket leaves, pepper (capsicum) and asparagus. Place on a plate and drizzle with the sauce.

NUTRITION PER SERVE

- Protein 6.5 g;
- Fat 1 g;
- Carbohydrate 24 g;
- Dietary Fibre 4.5 g;
- Cholesterol 0 mg;
- 555 kJ (130 Cal)

Serves 4

Preparation time:
20 minutes + 10 minutes refrigeration

Cooking time: 5 minutes

Easy

100 g (3½ oz) green beans, chopped
400 g (13 oz) can butter beans, rinsed
and drained
425 g (14 oz) can tuna in brine, drained
200 g (6½ oz) cherry tomatoes, quartered
1 red onion, thinly sliced
100 g (3½ oz) mixed salad leaves
100 g (3½ oz) baby rocket
(aragula) leaves

DRESSING
1 tablespoon extra virgin olive oil
60 ml (¼ cup) lemon juice
1 teaspoon honey
2 cloves garlic, crushed
2 tablespoons chopped fresh dill

NUTRITION PER SERVE

- Protein 24.5 g;
- Fat 7 g;
- Carbohydrate 7.5 g;
- Dietary Fibre 4.5 g;
- Cholesterol 43 mg;
- 815 kJ (195 Cal)

TUNA AND BEAN SALAD

Based on fish and beans, this salad contains filling protein, slow-release carbohydrate and fibre, with good amounts of B vitamins, folate, vitamin C, potassium and some beneficial fish oils.

1 Steam the green beans until tender, rinse under cold water and drain. Place the green and butter beans, tuna, tomato and onion in a bowl, and toss well.

2 To make the dressing, whisk all the ingredients together. Pour the dressing over the tuna mixture, cover and refrigerate for 10 minutes.

3 Combine the salad leaves and rocket (arugula), and arrange on a salad platter. Top with the tuna mixture and serve.

Serves 4

Preparation time: 30 minutes

Cooking time: 25 minutes

Easy

1 large yellow pepper (capsicum),
  quartered
1 large red pepper (capsicum), quartered
cooking oil spray
100 g (3½ oz) lean beef fillet steak
135 g (4½ oz) penne
100 g (3½ oz) button mushrooms,
  quartered

PESTO
50 g (1 cup) fresh basil leaves
2 cloves garlic, chopped
2 tablespoons pepitas
1 tablespoon olive oil
2 tablespoons orange juice
1 tablespoon lemon juice

PESTO BEEF SALAD

The pesto sauce and pepper (capsicum) provide vitamin C, which will increase
the amount of iron you'll absorb from the beef.

1 Grill the pepper (capsicum), skin
side up, until the skin blackens and
blisters. Cool under a damp tea
towel, then peel and dice the flesh.

2 Spray a non-stick frying pan with oil
and cook the steak over high heat for
3–4 minutes each side. Remove and
leave for 5 minutes before cutting into
thin slices. Season with a little salt.

3 To make the pesto, finely chop the
basil leaves, garlic and pepitas in a
food processor. With the motor
running, add the oil, orange and
lemon juice. Season with salt
and pepper.

4 Meanwhile, cook the penne in a
large pan of rapidly boiling salted
water until al dente. Drain, then toss
with the pesto in a large bowl.

NUTRITION PER SERVE

- Protein 12.5 g;
- Fat 10 g;
- Carbohydrate 27.5 g;
- Dietary Fibre 3.5 g;
- Cholesterol 17 mg;
- 1065 kJ (255 Cal)

5 Add the pepper (capsicum) pieces,
steak slices and mushroom quarters
to the penne and toss to distribute
evenly. Serve immediately.

Serves 6–8

Preparation time: 20 minutes

Cooking time: Nil

Easy

6 tomatoes, cut into thin wedges
1 red onion, cut into thin rings
2 Lebanese (short) cucumbers, sliced
185 g (6 oz) Kalamata olives
200 g (13 oz) reduced-fat feta
1 tablespoon extra virgin olive oil
dried oregano, to garnish

GREEK SALAD

This Mediterranean side dish provides monounsaturated fat, some B vitamins, calcium and phosphorus.

NUTRITION PER SERVE (8)

- Protein 8 g;
- Fat 6.5 g;
- Carbohydrate 9 g;
- Dietary Fibre 2 g;
- Cholesterol 15 mg;
- 520 kJ (125 Cal)

1 Combine the tomato, onion, cucumber and olives in a bowl. Season to taste.

2 Break the feta into large pieces and scatter over the top. Drizzle with the olive oil and sprinkle with the oregano.

NOTE: What is widely known as Greek salad is but one of the numerous salads served in Greece. Its Greek name, salata horiatiki, translates as Greek country or village salad. It is a rustic salad with tomato, cucumber, feta cheese and olives as its staple ingredients, although cos lettuce, peppers (capsicums), anchovy fillets, flat-leaf parsley, capers and a sprinkle of oregano are not unusual additions.

Serves 4

Preparation time: 15 minutes

Cooking time: 40 minutes

Easy

2 carrots
2 parsnips
2 large potatoes
300 g (10 oz) pumpkin
cooking oil spray
2 finger aubergines (eggplants)
chopped fresh parsley, to serve

BAKED VEGETABLES

With less fat than regular roast vegetables, this healthy combination provides carbohydrate energy, fibre, beta-carotene, folate and potassium.

1 Preheat the oven to moderately hot 200°C (400°F/Gas 6). Cut the carrots and parsnips in half lengthways, then crossways. Quarter the potatoes. Cut the pumpkin into chunks.

2 Put the carrot, parsnip, potato and pumpkin in a baking dish and spray lightly with cooking oil. Sprinkle with salt and ground black pepper. Bake for 20 minutes, turning occasionally.

3 Meanwhile, cut the aubergines (eggplants) in half lengthways and make thin shallow cuts through the skin. Add to the baking dish and cook, turning occasionally, for 20 minutes, or until all of the vegetables are tender. Sprinkle with the parsley.

NUTRITION PER SERVE

- Protein 5.5 g;
- Fat 1 g;
- Carbohydrate 25 g;
- Dietary Fibre 6 g;
- Cholesterol 0 mg;
- 535 kJ (130 Cal)

Serves 4

Preparation time: 10 minutes

Cooking time: 10 minutes

Easy

15 g (½ oz) butter
3 spring onions, chopped
2 teaspoons chopped fresh thyme
2 cloves garlic, crushed
270 g (9 oz) Swiss brown mushrooms,
   sliced
1 tablespoon red wine vinegar

NUTRITION PER SERVE

- Protein 3 g;
- Fat 3.5 g;
- Carbohydrate 1.5 g;
- Dietary Fibre 2 g;
- Cholesterol 9.5 mg;
- 205 kJ (50 Cal)

SAUTEED MUSHROOMS

Fresh thyme adds some flavour and flavonoids to this delicious side dish, which also provides some B vitamins, potassium and a little vitamin A, but few calories.

1 Heat the butter in a large saucepan. Add the spring onion, thyme and garlic, and cook for 2 minutes. Add the mushrooms and cook, stirring frequently, until the mushrooms are very soft and most of the liquid has evaporated.

2 Add the red wine vinegar to the saucepan, and season well with salt and ground black pepper. Cook for another 2 minutes, then serve. Delicious with grilled meats.

Serves 4

Preparation time: 5 minutes

Cooking time: 20 minutes

Easy

750 g (1 lb 8 oz) desiree potatoes,
 peeled, chopped
500 ml (2 cups) chicken stock
1 clove garlic, crushed
2 tablespoons low-fat sour cream

LOW-FAT POTATO MASH

1 Place potatoes in a large saucepan with chicken stock and enough water to cover. Bring to the boil and cook for 15 minutes, or until tender. Remove from the heat and drain, reserving 80 ml (⅓ cup) of the liquid. Mash the potatoes with a potato masher, then add garlic, the reserved cooking liquid and sour cream. Season well with salt and white pepper, and serve with chicken, steak or fish.

NUTRITION PER SERVE

- Protein 5 g;
- Fat 2.5 g;
- Carbohydrate 24.5 g;
- Dietary Fibre 3 g;
- Cholesterol 6.5 mg;
- 595 kJ (140 Cal)

Serves 4

Preparation time: 10 minutes

Cooking time: 10 minutes

Easy

1 lime, thinly sliced
3 x 3 cm (1¼ x 1¼ in) piece fresh ginger,
   chopped
400 g (13 oz) trimmed mixed Asian
   greens (bok choy, choy sum, Chinese
   broccoli)
2 tablespoons oyster sauce
1 tablespoon Chinese rice wine
1 teaspoon sesame oil
1 clove garlic, crushed
1 teaspoon toasted sesame seeds

STEAMED ASIAN GREENS

This recipe is an excellent way to include nutritious greens in your diet. It is an
excellent source of folate, protective phytochemicals and vitamin C.

1 Bring 750 ml (3 cups) water to the boil in a wok or large saucepan. Add the
lime slices and ginger. Place a bamboo steamer lined with baking paper over the
wok or saucepan, and add the vegetables. Steam, covered, for 2–3 minutes, or
until tender.

2 Combine the oyster sauce, rice wine, sesame oil and garlic in a small saucepan.
Bring to the boil, then reduce the heat and simmer for 1–2 minutes.

3 Place the steamed greens on a large plate, drizzle the sauce over the top
and sprinkle with the sesame seeds. Serve immediately.

NUTRITION PER SERVE

- Protein 2.5 g;
- Fat 2 g;
- Carbohydrate 4 g;
- Dietary Fibre 2.5 g;
- Cholesterol 0 mg;
- 195 kJ (45 Cal)

Serves 4–6

Preparation time: 35 minutes

Cooking time: 1 hour

Easy

1 kg (2 lb) potatoes, peeled and very
   thinly sliced
2 cloves garlic, crushed
400 ml (1⅔ cups) chicken or
   vegetable stock

BOULANGERE POTATOES

Chicken stock and garlic add flavour but no fat to this delicious potato dish.
It is a good source of potassium and carbohydrate energy, with some B vitamins,
vitamin C and folate.

1 Preheat the oven to moderately
hot 200°C (400°F/Gas 6).

2 Thoroughly grease a 1 litre (4 cups)
gratin dish and arrange a layer of
overlapping potato slices in the
base of the dish. Add a little of the
crushed garlic and season with salt
and pepper. Repeat the layers with
the remaining potatoes.

3 Pour the stock over the potato and
bake for 1 hour, uncovered, or until
the potato is tender and the top
crisp and brown.

NOTE: This is a French name meaning
'baker's potatoes'. Last century, when
many didn't have an oven, women
prepared it and left it to be cooked
at the local bakery during the day.

NUTRITION PER SERVE (6)

- Protein 5 g;
- Fat 0.5 g;
- Carbohydrate 22.5 g;
- Dietary Fibre 3 g;
- Cholesterol 0 mg;
- 490 kJ (115 Cal)

Serves 4

Preparation time: 10 minutes

Cooking time: 5 minutes

Easy

150 g (5 oz) young asparagus, trimmed
100 g (3½ oz) baby green beans
2 teaspoons butter
1½ tablespoons toasted flaked almonds

ASPARAGUS AND BEANS with almonds

NUTRITION PER SERVE

- Protein 2.5 g;
- Fat 4 g;
- Carbohydrate 1.5 g;
- Dietary Fibre 1.5 g;
- Cholesterol 6 mg;
- 215 kJ (50 Cal)

Asparagus has a diuretic effect and has been used in traditional medicine to treat arthritis, rheumatism and fluid retention. This variety of ingredients provides a good serve of folate.

1   Add the asparagus and beans to a large saucepan of rapidly boiling water. Cook for 1 minute, or until just tender.

2   Drain the vegetables and toss with the butter and almonds. Season with ground black pepper, and serve immediately.

Serves 4–6

Preparation time: 25 minutes

Cooking time: 55 minutes

Medium

1 kg (2 lb) potatoes
1 tablespoon cream
20 g (¾ oz) butter
1 egg yolk
¼ teaspoon nutmeg

MUSHROOM FILLING
40 g (1 oz) butter
125 g (4 oz) mushrooms, finely chopped
2 spring onions, finely chopped
50 g (1½ oz) ham, finely chopped
60 g (2 oz) Gruyère cheese, grated
80 g (1 cup) fresh breadcrumbs

CREAMY MUSHROOM AND POTATO BAKE

A delicious creamy treat for cold winter nights, this recipe provides folate, vitamin C and potassium.

1   Peel the potatoes and cut them into even pieces. Cook in boiling salted water for 15 minutes, or until tender. Drain the potatoes, then mash thoroughly. Gradually beat in the cream, butter, egg yolk and nutmeg. Season with salt and pepper.

2   To make the filling, melt half the butter in a pan and cook the mushrooms and spring onion for 2–3 minutes, or until softened. Stir in the ham and pepper.

3   Preheat the oven to moderately hot 200°C (400°F/Gas 6). Divide the mashed potato in half. Spread the first half evenly into a well-greased 23 cm ovenproof pie dish. Spread the mushroom filling over the top, sprinkle with the grated cheese, then spread the remaining potato over the top.

4   Melt the remaining butter and stir it through the breadcrumbs, mixing well. Spread the breadcrumbs evenly over the mashed potato, then

bake for 30 minutes, or until lightly browned. Serve at once.

NUTRITION PER SERVE (6)

- Protein 12 g;
- Fat 14.5 g;
- Carbohydrate 33 g;
- Dietary Fibre 4 g;
- Cholesterol 73.5 mg;
- 1315 kJ (315 Cal)

Makes 8

Preparation time: 5 minutes

Easy

4 Roma tomatoes, chopped
2 tablespoons olive oil
1 tablespoon balsamic vinegar
2 tablespoons chopped fresh basil
8 slices of crusty Italian bread
1 clove garlic

NUTRITION PER BRUSCHETTA

- Protein 3.5 g;
- Fat 9 g;
- Carbohydrate 17 g;
- Dietary Fibre 2 g;
- Cholesterol 0 mg;
- 710 kJ (170 Cal)

BRUSCHETTA

1 Combine the tomato with olive oil, vinegar and basil. Season well. Toast 8 slices of crusty Italian bread on one side. Rub the toasted side lightly with a peeled clove of garlic. Top with the tomato mixture and garnish with extra chopped basil. Serve immediately.

Serves 4–6

Preparation time: 30 minutes

Cooking time: 40 minutes

Medium

6 vine-ripened tomatoes
80 ml (⅓ cup) olive oil
500 g (1 lb) aubergine (eggplant),
    cut into 2 cm (¾ in) cubes
375 g (12 oz) zucchini, cut into 2 cm
    (¾ in) slices
1 green pepper (capsicum), cut into
    2 cm (¾ in) cubes
1 red onion, cut into 2 cm (¾ in)
    wedges
3 cloves garlic, finely chopped
¼ teaspoon cayenne pepper
2 teaspoons chopped fresh thyme
2 bay leaves
1 tablespoon red wine vinegar
1 teaspoon caster sugar
15 g (¼ cup) shredded fresh basil

RATATOUILLE

This Mediterranean-style dish provides monounsaturated fat and healthy phytochemicals.

1 Score a cross in the base of each tomato. Place in a bowl of boiling water for 1 minute, then plunge into cold water and peel the skin away from the cross. Roughly chop the flesh.

2 Heat 2 tablespoons oil in a large saucepan and cook the aubergine (eggplant) over medium heat for 4–5 minutes, or until soft but not browned. Remove. Add 1 tablespoon oil to the pan and cook the courette (zucchini) for 3–4 minutes, or until softened. Remove from the pan. Add the capsicum to the pan, cook for 2 minutes, then remove.

3 Heat the remaining oil, add the onion and cook for 2–3 minutes, or until softened. Add the garlic, cayenne, thyme and bay leaves, and cook, stirring, for 1 minute. Return the aubergine (eggplant), cougette (zucchini) and pepper (capsicum) to the pan, and add the tomato, vinegar and sugar. Simmer for 20 minutes, stirring occasionally. Stir in the basil and season with salt and black pepper. Serve hot or cold.

NUTRITION PER SERVE (6)

- Protein 4 g;
- Fat 12.5 g;
- Carbohydrate 8 g;
- Dietary Fibre 5.5 g;
- Cholesterol 0 mg;
- 660 kJ (160 Cal)

Serves 4–6

Preparation time: 10 minutes

Cooking time: 20 minutes

Easy

2 large potatoes
5 large parsnips
30 g (1 oz) butter
1 tablespoon milk
2 tablespoons sour cream
snipped fresh chives

NUTRITION PER SERVE (6)

- Protein 5 g;
- Fat 7 g;
- Carbohydrate 30 g;
- Dietary Fibre 5 g;
- Cholesterol 25 mg;
- 800 kJ (190 Cal)

CREAMY POTATO
and parsnip mash

An easy way to increase the variety of vegetables in your diet, this recipe provides folate, potassium, fibre and some vitamin A and C. Parsnips add a creamy texture without adding extra fat.

1 Peel the potatoes and parsnips, then chop into evenly sized pieces. Cook them in a large pan of lightly salted boiling water for about 20 minutes, or until soft.

2 Drain well, then transfer to a bowl and mash with the butter, milk and sour cream until smooth and fluffy. Season generously with salt and ground black pepper. Sprinkle with chives and serve at once.

NOTE: Sebago, bison, coliban, nicola, pontiac and King Edward are some good all-purpose potatoes that give successful results in this recipe.

Serves 4

Preparation time: 15 minutes

Cooking time: 45 minutes

Easy

800 g (1 lb 9 oz) orange sweet
   potato, peeled
2 teaspoons olive oil
2 tablespoons honey, warmed
2 teaspoons cumin seeds
2 teaspoons coriander (cilantro)
   seeds, crushed
2 tablespoons fresh coriander
   (cilantro) sprigs
½ teaspoon ground cinnamon

SPICY BAKED SWEET POTATO

NUTRITION PER SERVE

- Protein 4 g;
- Fat 2.5 g;
- Carbohydrate 40 g;
- Dietary Fibre 3.5 g;
- Cholesterol 0 mg;
- 820 kJ (195 Cal)

These spicy sweet potatoes provide plenty of carbohydrate energy, beta-carotene, vitamin C and potassium.

1 Preheat the oven to moderately hot 190°C (375°F/Gas 5). Cut the sweet potato into small wedges or rounds, then place in a bowl and toss with the olive oil, honey, cumin seeds, crushed coriander seeds, coriander sprigs and cinnamon.

2 Transfer the sweet potato wedges to a lightly greased baking tray and bake for 45 minutes. Serve immediately. If desired, top the sweet potato wedges with a dollop of low-fat yoghurt.

Serves 6

Preparation time: 20 minutes

Cooking time: 5 minutes

Easy

2 tablespoons oil
4 spring onions, cut into 3 cm lengths
3 cloves garlic, crushed
1 fresh red chilli, seeded and sliced
75 g (2½ oz) button mushrooms,
    quartered
100 g (3½ oz) Chinese cabbage, roughly
    chopped
2 tablespoons soy sauce
1 teaspoon fish sauce
1 tablespoon oyster sauce
60 ml (¼ cup) vegetable stock
½ teaspoon grated palm sugar
150 g (5 oz) snow peas (mange tout)
150 g (5 oz) cauliflower, cut into
    small florets
150 g (5 oz) broccoli, cut into small florets
fresh coriander (cilantro) leaves, chopped,
    to garnish

NUTRITION PER SERVE

- Protein 4.5 g;
- Fat 6.5 g;
- Carbohydrate 5.5 g;
- Dietary Fibre 3.5 g;
- Cholesterol 0 mg;
- 430 kJ (100 Cal)

STIR-FRIED VEGETABLES

Stir-frying preserves the crisp texture and fresh flavour of the vegetables, and helps retain water-soluble vitamins. This combination of vegetables provides vitamin C and phytochemicals.

1   Heat a wok until very hot, add the oil and swirl to coat. Add the spring onion, garlic and chilli. Stir-fry for 20 seconds. Add the mushrooms and cabbage, and stir-fry for 1 minute.

2   Stir in the sauces, stock, palm sugar, snow peas (mange tout) , cauliflower and broccoli. Cook for 2 minutes, or until tender. Garnish with the coriander leaves.

Makes 8

Preparation time: 10 minutes

Cooking time: 5 minutes

8 field mushrooms
95 g (1/2 cup) instant couscous
1 tablespoon extra virgin olive oil
1 teaspoon ground cumin
1/4 teaspoon cayenne pepper
2 teaspoons finely grated lemon rind
125 ml (1/2 cup) boiling chicken stock
1 finely chopped tomato
1 tablespoon lemon juice
2 tablespoons chopped fresh parsley
2 tablespoons chopped fresh mint

NUTRITION PER MUSHROOM

- Protein 3 g;
- Fat 2 g;
- Carbohydrate 11 g;
- Dietary Fibre 1 g;
- Cholesterol 0 mg;
- 317 kJ (75 Cal)

STUFFED MUSHROOMS

1 Peel and remove the stalks from the mushrooms, then grill top side up. Place couscous, olive oil, cumin, pepper and lemon rind in a bowl. Season. Stir the flavourings through the couscous. Stir in chicken stock, and cover. Leave for 5 minutes, then fluff the grains with a fork. Stir in tomato, lemon juice, parsley and mint. Fill each of the mushrooms with the couscous mixture and pack down firmly. Grill until the couscous is golden. Serve hot or cold.

RICE

RICE

For centuries, rice has been an important part of Asian diets, but it is now a popular staple around the world due to its nutritient content and versatility.

Rice is a staple food in Asian countries, but it also features significantly in the cooking of the Middle East and the Mediterranean.

Rice is a cereal grain with a high starch content, and there are thousands of varieties cultivated across the world. It is eaten as an accompaniment to many Asian dishes, but can also be the main ingredient of a meal, flavoured in various ways, such as in a risotto, paella or pilaf.

Rice by itself is quite healthy, being rich in carbohydrate, but some rice dishes may contain large amounts of fat. Brown rice in particular is a good source of vitamins, minerals, protein and fibre. White rice has fewer nutrients than brown rice because the outer bran layer, which includes the embryo of the seed, is removed during the milling process.

There are three broad classifications of rice—long-grain rice, medium-grain rice and short-grain rice. The different types of rice are suited to different styles and methods of cooking.

TYPES OF RICE
- Basmati rice is a fragrant Indian extra-long-grain rice, great for curries.

- Jasmine rice is a long-grain aromatic rice, very popular in Southeast Asia.
- Long-grain rice can be either white or brown.
- Arborio rice is a short-grain Italian rice, grown specifically for making risotto. Its high starch content gives risotto dishes their characteristic creamy texture.
- Short-grain rice has a sticky, plump texture when cooked, making it ideal for paella and sushi. It is also used for making rice desserts.
- Wild rice is not actually a rice at all, but a type of grass. It is cooked in a similar way to brown rice, and has a chewy texture and a nutty flavour.

FLAVOURING RICE
On its own, rice has quite a bland flavour, but it is usually served as an accompaniment to spiced or highly flavoured dishes. To add more flavour to rice, cook it in vegetable or chicken stock instead of water.

There are many ingredients that can be added to rice during cooking that will subtly add flavour and enhance the overall meal (some will need to be removed before serving):
- slices of fresh ginger
- slices of garlic
- pieces of lemon grass
- a cinnamon stick
- whole cloves
- crushed cardamom pods
- star anise
- saffron strands or a little turmeric
- fresh or dried chilli
- fresh thyme
- bay leaves
- lime leaves
- pandanus leaf
- crumbled nori.

HEALTHY RICE HINTS AND TIPS
- When making fried rice, use the same combination of vegetables that you would normally use, but steam or blanch them instead of

frying, and add them to steamed rice with lots of finely chopped garlic chives and spring onion. Scatter with toasted sesame seeds and sprinkle with salt-reduced soy sauce.

- Use dried wild forest mushrooms in a risotto. Soak them in warm water, drain them and set aside to add to the risotto. Reserve the soaking liquid to add to the stock for cooking the risotto. It will have a delicious, earthy flavour.
- Add some drained and rinsed red kidney beans to white rice while it is cooking, along with some crushed garlic and chilli powder. Stir through lots of chopped fresh parsley and chives, and serve as an accompaniment, or rolled up in a tortilla.

- Nori rolls are simple to make and construct, and are a tasty, low-fat and nutritious lunch, snack or hors d'oeuvre. The base is short-grain rice flavoured with rice wine vinegar, sugar and salt (see page 211), and fillings can be added to suit your requirements. Serve the rolls with a salt-reduced soy sauce, wasabi and some pickled ginger. Try these suggestions as individual fillings, or combine them to suit your taste:
  — strips of omelette flavoured with Japanese soy sauce
  — simple combinations of vegetables, such as cucumber, blanched carrot and capsicum
  — the classic sashimi tuna and salmon
  — smoked salmon
  — hot smoked trout

  — avocado
  — cooked prawns (shrimp)
  — Chinese mushrooms sprinkled with sesame seeds
  — Japanese smoked eel.
- Cooked brown or white rice can be seasoned and flavoured with herbs, toasted nuts, lemon zest, onion, garlic and ginger, and then used as a tasty and filling stuffing. Try it as a stuffing for:
  — vine leaves, braised in the oven with stock
  — cabbage leaves, braised with a light tomato and herb sauce
  — red peppers (capsicums)
  — banana chillies
  — a boned leg of lamb for roasting
  — a whole chicken for roasting
  — chicken breast fillets.

Serves 4

Preparation time: 15 minutes

Cooking time: 35 minutes

Easy

1 litre (4 cups) chicken stock
1 tablespoon oil
30 g (1 oz) butter
1 leek, thinly sliced
200 g (6 ½ oz) Swiss brown mushrooms,
   sliced
200 g (6 ½ oz) button mushrooms, sliced
60 ml (¼ cup) balsamic vinegar
500 g (1 lb) chicken tenderloins, halved
125 ml (½ cup) white wine
275 g (1¼ cups) arborio rice
2 tablespoons snipped fresh chives

CHICKEN AND MUSHROOM RISOTTO

This creamy Italian risotto provides a light yet satisfying meal with good amounts of B vitamins, pantothenic acid, iron, zinc, folate, potassium and phosphorus.

NUTRITION PER SERVE

- Protein 37 g;
- Fat 15 g;
- Carbohydrate 54 g;
- Dietary Fibre 4 g;
- Cholesterol 82 mg;
- 2090 kJ (500 Cal)

1 Place the stock in a saucepan and heat until the stock is simmering.

2 Heat the oil and butter in a separate saucepan, add the leek and cook over medium heat for 5 minutes, or until golden. Add the mushrooms and 2 tablespoons balsamic vinegar, and cook until tender and the liquid is absorbed.

3 Add the chicken and cook until browned. Stir in the wine and bring to the boil. Add the rice and stir to coat.

4 Add 125 ml (½ cup) stock, stirring constantly over medium heat until all the liquid is absorbed. Continue adding the stock, 125 ml (½ cup) at a time, stirring for 25 minutes, or until all the stock is absorbed and the rice is tender. Stir in the remaining vinegar and chives, and season with salt and ground black pepper.

Serves 6

Preparation time: 40 minutes

Cooking time: 1 hour

Difficult

500 ml (2 cups) vegetable stock
1 tablespoon olive oil
1 onion, chopped
2 cloves garlic, crushed
110 g (½ cup) arborio rice
1 red pepper (capsicum), chopped
250 g (9 oz) mushrooms, chopped
60 g (2 ¼ oz) reduced-fat Cheddar,
   grated
15 g (¼ cup) shredded fresh basil
6 large silverbeet leaves
2 x 400 g (13 oz) cans chopped tomatoes
1 tablespoon balsamic vinegar
1 teaspoon soft brown sugar

NUTRITION PER SERVE

* Protein 8.5 g;
* Fat 6 g;
* Carbohydrate 22.5 g;
* Dietary Fibre 4 g;
* Cholesterol 6 mg;
* 755 kJ (180 Cal)

SILVERBEET PARCELS

A delicious blend of risotto, cheese and vegetables in nutritious silverbeet delivers carbohydrate, B vitamins, folate, vitamin C and potassium.

1 Heat the stock in a pan and maintain at simmering point. Heat the oil in a large pan, add the onion and garlic and cook until softened. Add the rice, capsicum and mushrooms, and stir until well combined. Gradually add 125 ml (½ cup) hot stock, stirring until the liquid is absorbed. Add the stock, a little at a time, until it is all absorbed and the rice is tender (about 20 minutes). Remove from the heat, add the cheese and basil, and season well.

2 Trim the stalks from the silverbeet and cook the leaves, a few at a time, in a large pan of boiling water for 30 seconds, or until wilted. Drain on a tea towel. Cut away any tough white veins from the leaves. Place a portion of mushroom filling in the centre of each leaf, fold in the sides and roll up carefully. Tie with string.

3 Put the tomato, vinegar and sugar in a large, deep non-stick frying pan and stir to combine. Add the silverbeet parcels, cover and simmer for 10 minutes. Remove the string and serve with tomato sauce.

Serves 4

Preparation time: 15 minutes

Cooking time: 30 minutes

Easy

1 tablespoon olive oil
1 large onion, chopped
2 cloves garlic, crushed
1 large green pepper (capsicum), cut into
   2 cm (¾ in) cubes
2 celery sticks, cut into 1 cm (½ in) slices
3 teaspoons paprika
300 g (1½ cups) long-grain rice
750 ml (3 cups) chicken stock
400 g (13 oz) can diced tomatoes
200 g (6½ oz) light ham, chopped
2 bay leaves
7 g (¼ cup) chopped fresh flat-leaf
   parsley
80 g (½ cup) frozen peas

NUTRITION PER SERVE

- Protein 19.5 g;
- Fat 9 g;
- Carbohydrate 69 g;
- Dietary Fibre 5 g;
- Cholesterol 26 mg;
- 1835 kJ (440 Cal)

TOMATO AND HAM PILAF

This quick and easy meal provides carbohydrate energy, B vitamins, folate, vitamin C and iron.

1 Heat the oil in a large saucepan over medium heat, add the onion and cook for 3 minutes, or until soft. Add the garlic, capsicum, celery and paprika, and cook for 3–4 minutes, or until softened.

2 Add the rice and stir to coat. Add the stock, tomato, ham and bay leaves, and bring to the boil. Reduce the heat and simmer, covered, for 15 minutes, or until the rice is tender.

3 Add the parsley and peas, stir well and simmer, uncovered, for 5 minutes. Season with salt and ground black pepper.

Serves 5

Preparation time: 15 minutes

Cooking time: 1 hour 10 minutes

Medium

200 g (6½ oz) baby English
   spinach leaves
100 g (⅔ cup) raw cashew nuts,
   chopped
2 tablespoons olive oil
6 spring onions, chopped
300 g (1½ cups) long-grain brown rice
2 cloves garlic, finely chopped
1 teaspoon fennel seeds
2 tablespoons lemon juice
625 ml (2½ cups) vegetable stock
15 g (¼ cup) chopped fresh mint
7 g (¼ cup) chopped fresh flat-leaf
   parsley

GREEN PILAU with cashews

Cashews complement the rice and improve the amino acid content of this
vegetarian dish. Top it with low-fat yoghurt for extra calcium.

1 Preheat the oven to moderate
180°C (350°F/Gas 4). Wash the
English spinach leaves, then shred
them into 1 cm slices.

2 Place the cashew nuts on a baking
tray and roast for 5–10 minutes, or
until golden brown—watch carefully.

3 Heat the oil in a large frying pan
and cook the spring onion over
medium heat for 2 minutes, or until
soft. Add the rice, garlic and fennel
seeds, and cook, stirring frequently,
for 1–2 minutes, or until the rice is
evenly coated. Increase the heat
to high, add the lemon juice, stock
and 1 teaspoon salt, and bring to
the boil. Reduce to low, cover and
cook for 45 minutes without lifting
the lid. Remove from the heat and
sprinkle with the spinach and herbs.

Stand, covered, for 8 minutes, then
fork the spinach and herbs through
the rice. Season. Serve sprinkled
with the cashews.

NUTRITION PER SERVE

• Protein 9 g;
• Fat 16 g;
• Carbohydrate 43.5 g;
• Dietary Fibre 4 g;
• Cholesterol 0 mg;
• 1490 kJ (355 Cal)

Serves 4

Preparation time: 40 minutes

Cooking time: 50 minutes

Medium

150 g (5 oz) boneless white fish fillet
    such as sea perch
8 black mussels (200 g/7 oz)
8 raw prawns (shrimp) (250 g/9 oz)
1.75 litres (7 cups) chicken stock
cooking oil spray
2 onions, finely chopped
2 cloves garlic, finely chopped
1 celery stick, finely chopped
440 g (2 cups) arborio rice
2 tablespoons chopped fresh parsley
1 tablespoon chopped fresh oregano
1 tablespoon chopped fresh thyme
    leaves
2 tablespoons grated Parmesan

NUTRITION PER SERVE

- Protein 40 g;
- Fat 5 g;
- Carbohydrate 90 g;
- Dietary Fibre 4 g;
- Cholesterol 175 mg;
- 2395 kJ (570 Cal)

SEAFOOD AND HERB RISOTTO

This nutritious and aromatic risotto is an excellent source of lean protein.

1   Cut the fish into small cubes. Scrub
    the mussels and remove the beards.
    Discard any musssels that are open.
    Peel and devein the prawns (shrimp),
    leaving the tails intact. Put the
    seafood in a bowl and refrigerate.

2   Put the stock in a saucepan and
    bring to the boil, then reduce the
    heat until gently simmering.

3   Lightly spray a large saucepan with
    oil and heat over medium heat. Cook
    the onion, garlic and celery for
    2–3 minutes. Add 2 tablespoons
    water, cover and cook for 5 minutes,
    or until the vegetables are beginning
    to soften. Add the rice and 2 table-
    spoons water, cover and cook for
    3–4 minutes, or until the rice is coated.

4   Gradually add 125 ml (½ cup) of
    the hot stock to the rice mixture,
    stirring constantly over low heat,
    until all the stock has been absorbed.
    Repeat the process, adding 125 ml
    (½ cup) of liquid each time until all
    but a small amount of stock is left
    and the rice is just tender.

5   Meanwhile, bring a small amount
    of water to the boil in a saucepan.
    Add the mussels, cover and cook
    for 3 minutes, shaking the pan
    occasionally, until the mussels have
    opened. Drain the mussels and
    discard any that have not opened.

6   Add the fish and prawns and the
    remaining stock to the rice. Stir and
    cook for 5–10 minutes, or until the
    seafood is just cooked and the rice
    is tender and creamy. Remove from
    the heat, add the mussels, cover and
    set aside for 5 minutes. Stir the herbs
    and Parmesan through the risotto,
    then season well with salt and
    cracked pepper. Serve immediately.

Serves 6

Preparation time:
35 minutes + 40 minutes standing

Cooking time: 15 minutes

Easy

400 g (2 cups) long-grain white rice
1 pandan leaf, tied in a knot (see Note)
185 ml (¾ cup) coconut cream

COCONUT RICE

This rice dish is a good source of carbohydrate, with small amounts of niacin and minerals.

1 Rinse the rice and cover with 1 litre (4 cups) water. Set aside for 30 minutes. Drain. Bring 750 ml (3 cups) water to the boil. Add the rice, pandan leaf and salt, to taste. Reduce the heat and cook, covered, for 12 minutes, or until the rice is just cooked.

2 Remove from the heat and add the coconut cream. Stir gently to avoid breaking the grains. Cover and set aside for 10 minutes or until the rice absorbs the coconut cream. Discard the pandan leaf before serving.

NOTE: Pandan leaves, also known as pandanus or screw pine leaves. They are available in Asian grocery stores.

NUTRITION PER SERVE

- Protein 5 g;
- Fat 6.5 g;
- Carbohydrate 54 g;
- Dietary Fibre 1 g;
- Cholesterol 0 mg;
- 1245 kJ (295 Cal)

Serves 4–6

Preparation time: 30 minutes

Cooking time: 50 minutes

Easy

2 tablespoons olive oil
1 large red onion, finely chopped
1 clove garlic, crushed
2 rashers bacon, trimmed of fat,
   finely chopped
300 g (1½ cups) long-grain rice
1 red pepper (capsicum), diced
150 g (5 oz) ham, chopped
425 g (14 oz) can tomatoes, chopped
425 g (14 oz) can tomato purée
1 teaspoon Worcestershire sauce
dash Tabasco sauce
½ teaspoon dried thyme leaves
30 g (½ cup) chopped fresh parsley
50 g (1½ oz) cooked, peeled,
   small prawns
4 spring onions, thinly sliced

NUTRITION PER SERVE (6)

- Protein 14.5 g;
- Fat 9.5 g;
- Carbohydrate 48 g;
- Dietary Fibre 3.5 g;
- Cholesterol 37 mg;
- 1415 kJ (340 Cal)

JAMBALAYA

This thick, stew-like dish contains a wide range of ingredients and delivers many nutrients. It is a good source of carbohydrate, B vitamins, vitamin C and plant antioxidants.

1 Heat the oil in a large saucepan over medium heat. Add the onion, garlic and bacon, and cook, stirring, for 5 minutes, or until soft. Stir in the rice and cook for 2 minutes.

2 Add the red pepper (capsicum), ham, tomato, tomato purée, sauces and thyme. Stir for 1 minute. Bring to the boil, then reduce the heat to low. Cook, covered, for 40 minutes, or until the rice is tender.

3 Stir in the parsley and prawns (shrimp). Season with salt and ground black pepper, and serve, sprinkled with the spring onion.

Serves 4–6

Preparation time: 15 minutes

Cooking time: 25 minutes

Easy

1 tablespoon coriander (cilantro) seeds
1 tablespoon cardamom pods
1 tablespoon cumin seeds
1 teaspoon black peppercorns
1 teaspoon cloves
1 small cinnamon stick, crushed
60 ml (¼ cup) oil
1 onion, chopped
3 cloves garlic, chopped
200 g (1 cup) basmati rice
250 g (1 cup) red lentils
750 ml (3 cups) hot vegetable stock
spring onions, thinly sliced on the
    diagonal, to garnish

RICE AND LENTIL PILAU

Highly aromatic and full of protein and slow-release carbohydrate, this dish will satisfy your energy needs.
It's a good choice for vegetarians.

1 To make the garam masala, place the coriander seeds, cardamom pods, cumin seeds, peppercorns, cloves and cinnamon in a dry frying pan. Shake over medium heat for 1 minute, or until the mixture is fragrant. Blend in a spice grinder or blender until a fine powder.

2 Heat the oil in a large saucepan. Add the onion, garlic and 3 teaspoons of the garam masala. Cook over medium heat for 3 minutes, or until the onion is soft.

3 Stir in the rice and lentils, and cook for 2 minutes. Add the hot stock and stir well. Slowly bring to the boil, then reduce the heat, and simmer, covered, for 15–20 minutes, or until the rice is cooked and all the stock has been absorbed. Gently fluff the rice with a fork. Garnish with spring onion.

NUTRITION PER SERVE (6)

- Protein 14 g;
- Fat 10.5 g;
- Carbohydrate 45 g;
- Dietary Fibre 7 g;
- Cholesterol 0 mg;
- 1370 kJ (330 Cal)

Serves 6

Preparation time:
20 minutes + overnight soaking

Cooking time: 40 minutes

Medium

200 g (1 cup) dried haricot beans
1/4 teaspoon saffron threads
2 tablespoons olive oil
1 onion, diced
1 red pepper (capsicum), cut into 1 cm x
    4 cm (1/3 x 1 1/2 in) strips
5 cloves garlic, crushed
275 g (1 1/4 cups) paella rice or arborio
1 tablespoon sweet paprika
1/2 teaspoon mixed spice
750 ml (3 cups) vegetable stock
400 g (13 oz) can diced tomatoes
1 1/2 tablespoons tomato paste
150 g (1 cup) fresh or frozen soya beans
100 g (3 1/2 oz) silverbeet leaves (no stems),
    shredded
400 g (13 oz) can artichoke hearts,
    drained, quartered
20 g (1/3 cup) chopped fresh coriander
    (cilantro) leaves

VEGETARIAN PAELLA

This vegetarian version of the classic Spanish recipe is an excellent
source of slow-release carbohydrate, fibre, folate and iron.

1   Cover the haricot beans in cold
    water and soak overnight. Drain
    and rinse well.

2   Dry-fry the saffron in a small frying
    pan over medium–low heat for
    1 minute, or until darkened.
    Remove from the heat and
    crumble into a small bowl. Pour
    in 125 ml (1/2 cup) warm water
    and allow to steep.

3   Heat the oil in a large frying pan.
    Cook the onion and capsicum over
    medium–high heat for 4–5 minutes,
    or until soft. Stir in the garlic and
    cook for 1 minute. Reduce the heat
    and stir in the beans, rice, paprika,
    mixed spice and 1/2 teaspoon salt.
    Add the saffron water, stock, tomato
    and tomato paste, and bring to the
    boil. Cover, reduce the heat and
    simmer for 20 minutes.

4   Stir in the soya beans, silverbeet
    and artichokes. Cook, covered,
    for 8 minutes, or until the liquid is
    absorbed and the rice and beans are
    tender. Turn off the heat. Leave for
    5 minutes, then stir in the coriander.

NUTRITION PER SERVE

- Protein 16.5 g;
- Fat 9.5 g;
- Carbohydrate 56.5 g;
- Dietary Fibre 12 g;
- Cholesterol 0 mg;
- 1565 kJ (375 Cal)

Serves 6

Preparation time: 15 minutes

Cooking time: 25 minutes

Easy

300 g (1½ cups) basmati rice
300 g (1½ cups) split mung beans
   (mung lentils)
2 tablespoons oil
1 onion, sliced
3 bay leaves
1 teaspoon cumin seeds
2 pieces cassia bark
1 tablespoon cardamom seeds
6 cloves
¼ teaspoon black peppercorns

KITCHEREE

The combination of rice and lentils in this quick vegetarian dish provides complete protein, slow-release carbohydrate and fibre.

1 Wash the rice and lentils, then drain and set aside.

2 Heat the oil in a frying pan, add the onion, bay leaves and spices, and cook over low heat for 5 minutes, or until the onion is softened and the spices are fragrant. Add the rice and lentils, and cook, stirring, for 2 minutes.

3 Pour in 1.25 litres (5 cups) water and season with salt. Bring to the boil, then reduce the heat and cook, covered, over low heat for 15 minutes. Stir gently to avoid breaking the grains and cook, uncovered, over low heat for 3 minutes, or until all the moisture has evaporated. Serve hot with Indian curries.

NUTRITION PER SERVE

- Protein 15 g;
- Fat 7.5 g;
- Carbohydrate 59 g;
- Dietary Fibre 7.5 g;
- Cholesterol 0 mg;
- 1500 kJ (360 Cal)

Serves 4–6

Preparation time: 25 minutes

Cooking time: 15 minutes

Easy

5–8 long red chillies, seeded and
   chopped
2 teaspoons shrimp paste
8 cloves garlic, finely chopped
oil, for cooking
2 eggs, lightly beaten
350 g (11½ oz) chicken thigh fillets, cut
   into thin strips
200 g (6½ oz) peeled raw prawns
   (shrimp), deveined
1.5 kg (8 cups) cooked rice
80 ml (⅓ cup) kecap manis
80 ml (⅓ cup) soy sauce
2 small Lebanese (short) cucumbers,
   finely chopped
1 large tomato, finely chopped
lime wedges, to serve

NASI GORENG

This recipe will help you on your way to eating the recommended 30 different foods a day.

1 Mix the chilli, shrimp paste and garlic in a food processor to make a paste.

2 Heat 1 tablespoon of the oil in a wok and swirl it around to coat the side. Add the egg and push the egg up the side of the wok to form a large omelette. Cook for 1 minute over medium heat, or until the egg is set, then flip it over and cook the other side for 1 minute. Remove from the wok and cool before slicing into strips.

3 Reheat the wok, add 1 tablespoon of the oil and stir-fry the chicken and half the chilli paste over high heat until just cooked. Remove from the wok.

4 Reheat the wok, add 1 tablespoon of the oil and stir-fry the prawns and remaining chilli paste until the prawns are cooked. Remove from the wok.

5 Reheat the wok, add 1 tablespoon of the oil and the rice, and toss over medium heat for 4–5 minutes, or until the rice is heated through. Add the kecap manis and soy sauce, and toss until the rice is coated in the sauces. Return the chicken and prawns to the wok, and toss until

heated through. Season with salt and pepper. Transfer to a large deep serving bowl and top with the omelette strips, cucumber and tomato. Serve with the lime wedges.

NUTRITION PER SERVE (6)

- Protein 29 g;
- Fat 10.5 g;
- Carbohydrate 74.5 g;
- Dietary Fibre 3.5 g;
- Cholesterol 170.5 mg;
- 2160 kJ (515 Cal)

Makes 8 balls

Preparation time: 35 minutes
+ 30 minutes refrigeration

Cooking time: 55 minutes

Easy

3 potatoes
100 g (½ cup) long-grain rice
50 g (½ cup) rolled oats
415 g (13½ oz) can red salmon,
    drained and flaked
1 egg, lightly beaten
3 spring onions, chopped
2 tablespoons lemon juice
2 tablespoons sweet chilli sauce
80 g (1 cup) fresh breadcrumbs
2 eggs, lightly beaten
200 g (2 cups) dry breadcrumbs
cooking oil spray
lemon juice, to serve

SALMON BALLS

These lightly spiced salmon balls provide protein, slow-release carbohydrate, fibre and B vitamins.

1   Steam or microwave the potatoes until tender. Drain and mash. Boil the rice for 15 minutes, or until tender. Cool.

2   Place the potato, rice, oats, salmon, egg, spring onion, lemon juice, sweet chilli sauce and breadcrumbs in a bowl, and mix together well. Season with salt and pepper.

3   Divide the mixture into eight portions and shape into balls. Dip in the egg, then the dry breadcrumbs. Refrigerate on a lined baking tray for 30 minutes.

4   Preheat the oven to moderately hot 200°C (400°F/Gas 6). Spray the salmon balls lightly with oil and bake for 30 minutes, or until crisp, golden and heated through. Serve with lemon juice.

NUTRITION PER BALL

- Protein 18.5 g;
- Fat 9 g;
- Carbohydrate 44.5 g;
- Dietary Fibre 3 g;
- Cholesterol 102.5 mg;
- 1415 kJ (340 Cal)

Serves 4–6

Preparation time: 15 minutes

Cooking time: 35 minutes

Medium

1 litre (4 cups) chicken, fish or vegetable
   stock
360 g (2¾ cups) fresh or frozen
   baby peas
2 tablespoons light sour cream
2 tablespoons finely shredded fresh mint
1 tablespoon olive oil
1 small onion, finely chopped
2 cloves garlic, finely chopped
150 g (5 oz) arborio rice
16 large scallops (without roe)
1 tablespoon grated Parmesan
4 fresh mint leaves, to garnish
lemon wedges, to serve

RISOTTO with scallops

This dish has a creamy texture without too much fat. It provides carbohydrate, protein, niacin, folate and monounsaturated fat.

NUTRITION PER SERVE (6)

- Protein 12.5 g;
- Fat 6 g;
- Carbohydrate 27.5 g;
- Dietary Fibre 5 g;
- Cholesterol 17 mg;
- 910 kJ (215 Cal)

1 Put the stock in a saucepan and bring to the boil. Simmer the peas for 1–2 minutes, or until tender, then remove with a slotted spoon. Keep the stock at a low simmer. Blend 230 g (1¾ cups) of the peas with the sour cream in a food processor until smooth. Season and stir in half the mint.

2 Heat the oil in a large saucepan. Cook the onion over low heat for 4–5 minutes, or until soft. Add the garlic and cook for 30 seconds. Stir in the rice and increase the heat to medium.

3 Add 250 ml (1 cup) stock to the rice and cook, stirring, until all the liquid has evaporated. Add 125 ml (½ cup) stock at a time, until the rice is cooked and the mixture is creamy (about 20 minutes).

4 Lightly season the scallops. Sear the scallops on both sides in a chargrill pan.

5 Fold the pea purée through the risotto with the whole peas and Parmesan. Serve the risotto topped with the scallops, remaining mint, a fresh mint leaf and a wedge of lemon.

Serves 6

Preparation time: 20 minutes

Cooking time: 15 minutes

Easy

cooking oil spray
4 egg whites, lightly beaten
2 cloves garlic, crushed
350 g (11½ oz) raw prawns (shrimp),
    peeled, deveined and halved
    lengthways
100 g (3½ oz) cooked chicken, shredded
80 g (½ cup) frozen peas
180 g (6 oz) sliced light ham, cut into
    small strips
1 red pepper (capsicum), diced
4 spring onions, sliced
750 g (4 cups) cooked white and wild rice
    blend (see Note)
1½ tablespoons soy sauce
3 teaspoons fish sauce
1½ teaspoons soft brown sugar

FRIED RICE

A reduced-fat fried rice, this version is high in protein and carbohydrate, with
good amounts of vitamin C, B vitamins, potassium and phosphorus.

1 Lightly spray a non-stick wok with
   oil and pour in the egg white. Cook
   over low heat, stirring until the egg is
   just cooked and slightly scrambled,
   then remove and set aside.

2 Add the garlic, prawns, chicken,
   peas, ham and pepper (capsicum) to

the wok, and stir-fry for 3–4 minutes,
or until the prawns are cooked.

3 Add the spring onion, rice, soy
   sauce, fish sauce and sugar, and
   toss for 30 seconds, or until heated
   through. Add the egg, toss lightly
   and serve.

NUTRITION PER SERVE

- Protein 25 g;
- Fat 3.5 g;
- Carbohydrate 39 g;
- Dietary Fibre 2 g;
- Cholesterol 91 mg;
- 1225 kJ (295 Cal)

NOTE: You will need to cook 260 g
(1⅓ cups) white and wild rice blend for
this recipe.

Serves 4

Preparation time:
10 minutes + 15 minutes soaking

Cooking time: 35 minutes

Medium

15 g (1/2 oz) dried sliced mushrooms
500 ml (2 cups) vegetable stock
125 ml (1/2 cup) dry sherry
1 tablespoon oil
3 large French shallots, thinly sliced
2 large cloves garlic, crushed
1 tablespoon grated fresh ginger
1 teaspoon Sichuan peppercorns,
    crushed
330 g (11/2 cups) pearl barley
500 g (16 oz) choy sum, cut into
    5 cm (2 in) lengths
3 teaspoons kecap manis
1 teaspoon sesame oil

NUTRITION PER SERVE

- Protein 9.5 g;
- Fat 8.5 g;
- Carbohydrate 48 g;
- Dietary Fibre 10.5 g;
- Cholesterol 0 mg;
- 1415 kJ (340 Cal)

ASIAN BARLEY PILAU

Once an important dietary staple, barley is often overlooked in modern societies, even though it's a highly nutritious food. This satisfying recipe is a great choice for those trying to control their weight.

1 Place the mushrooms in a bowl and cover with boiling water, then leave for 15 minutes. Strain, reserving 125 ml (1/2 cup) of the liquid.

2 Bring the stock and sherry to the boil in a saucepan, then reduce the heat, cover and simmer until needed.

3 Heat the oil in a large saucepan and cook the shallots over medium heat for 2–3 minutes, or until soft. Add the garlic, ginger and peppercorns, and cook for 1 minute. Add the barley and mushrooms and mix well. Stir in the stock and mushroom liquid, then reduce the heat and simmer, covered, for 25 minutes, or until the liquid evaporates.

4 Meanwhile, steam the choy sum until wilted. Add to the barley mixture. Stir in the kecap manis and sesame oil.

Makes 40

Preparation time:
45 minutes + 20 minutes standing

Cooking time: 15 minutes

Difficult

440 g (2 cups) short-grain white rice
2 tablespoons rice vinegar
2 tablespoons caster sugar
10 g (¼ oz) dried sliced Chinese
   mushrooms
250 g (9 oz) choy sum, shredded and
   blanched
1 tablespoon pickled ginger, shredded
1 tablespoon toasted sesame seeds
1 tablespoon kecap manis
½ teaspoon wasabi paste
2 teaspoons mirin
1 tablespoon salt-reduced soy sauce
10 nori sheets
purchased dipping sauce for sushi,
   to serve

NORI CONES

Add some smoked salmon to these nutritious cones for extra protein, iron and essential fatty acids.

1 Rinse the rice until the water runs clear. Put in a saucepan with 500 ml (2 cups) water. Bring to the boil, then reduce the heat and simmer for 10 minutes. Remove from the heat, and cover for 15 minutes.

2 Spread the rice in a shallow dish. Place the vinegar, sugar, ½ teaspoon salt and 2 tablespoons water in a saucepan, and stir over low heat until the sugar dissolves. Pour over the rice, fork it through and cool.

3 Soak the mushrooms in boiling water for 5 minutes. Drain, squeeze out the excess liquid and roughly chop.

4 Place the rice in a large bowl and stir in the mushrooms, choy sum, ginger, sesame seeds and the combined kecap manis, wasabi, mirin and soy sauce.

5 Place the nori sheets shiny-side down and cut each sheet into four squares. Brush the edge with water and place 1 tablespoon of the mixture in the centre of each square.

Roll up to form a cone and top up with 2 teaspoons of filling. Serve immediately with the dipping sauce.

NUTRITION PER CONE

- Protein 1.5 g;
- Fat 0 g;
- Carbohydrate 20 g;
- Dietary Fibre 1 g;
- Cholesterol 0 mg;
- 390 kJ (95 Cal)

PASTA

PASTA

With over 300 varieties of pasta to choose from, and possibly as many pasta sauces, it's easy to incorporate many nutritious pasta meals into your diet without becoming bored.

Pasta is a simple preparation of flour, water and sometimes eggs. It is readily available in either fresh or dried form, is economical and very easy to cook, even for beginners. On its own, pasta is a healthy source of carbohydrate energy. However, it is the sauce with which the pasta is served that dictates how healthy the dish will be.

There are many delicious rich, creamy and cheesy pasta sauces that are all relatively high in fat. The sauces that are low in fat, but are still very tasty, are mostly tomato-based sauces—a great choice for healthy cooking, or for healthy eating when dining out.

It is generally agreed that chunky, thick pasta sauces are best when served with one of the short pastas such as penne, spirali or farfalle, and that saucy, creamy or oil-based sauces go well with one of the long pastas such as spaghetti, linguine or tagliatelle. Small pasta shapes such as orzo or stelline are a delicious addition to vegetable soups— simply add them to the soup in the last 10 minutes of cooking.

Pasta sauces are another easy way to eat a variety of healthy vegetables. They should be of a consistency and

quantity to coat the pasta, not leave it swimming in excess sauce in the bottom of the bowl.

LOW-FAT PASTA SAUCES
*   If you can't resist a rich, creamy pasta sauce, one way of reducing the fat is to substitute low-fat evaporated milk for cream. To get the desired creamy and saucey consistency, you will need to simmer the sauce until reduced.
*   When making a pasta sauce, instead of using olive oil to sauté the ingredients, give your pan a light spray with cooking oil. If more moisture is needed, add a

tablespoon of water or stock to help soften the ingredients.
*   If you are using bacon as an ingredient in the sauce, be sure to remove as much of the fat as possible before cooking.
*   When purchasing mince for bolognese sauce, choose one of the lean or low-fat varieties that are often available from butchers or supermarkets.
*   Read the labels on filled pastas such as ravioli or tortellini to check for high salt or cheese contents.
*   Crisp prosciutto or pancetta on a grill tray in the oven, so that any excess fat drips off. Drain on paper towels, then crumble over the top of your pasta dish.
*   When draining cooked pasta, reserve a little of the cooking water to stir through the sauce. This will add a little flavour, moisture and starch to the dish and, particularly for pasta dishes with an olive oil sauce, this will reduce the amount of oil needed to moisten the pasta. For example, when tossing pesto through pasta, a tablespoon of the cooking water will help distribute the sauce evenly and smoothly.
*   A simple sauce made with puréed, skinned roasted red pepper

(capsicum), thinned with a little vegetable stock, seasoned and tossed with chopped fresh herbs, is delicious tossed through hot linguine with some roughly chopped rocket. Add any juices that come from the peppers (capsicums) while roasting to the purée for a flavour boost.

- When making lasagne, instead of the béchamel sauce, use a layer of ricotta whisked until smooth with some low-fat evaporated milk and low-fat cream cheese.

SIMPLE AND HEALTHY PASTA SAUCE IDEAS

- Roast pumpkin pieces until they are soft and caramelised, then toss them through pasta with some low-fat ricotta, garlic chives and a little extra virgin olive oil.
- Combine capers, diced fresh tomato flesh, chopped fresh parsley and canned tuna in springwater (with the juices), and stir through hot spaghetti.
- Add some diced bocconcini to pasta that has been dressed with a simple fresh tomato and basil sauce and leave it for 2 minutes so that the bocconcini melts into strands.
- Instead of tossing pasta with pesto, use half pesto and half tomato passata, chicken or vegetable stock to reduce the amount of oil.
- Add chickpeas, lentils or other cooked legumes or pulses to your favourite pasta sauce for added texture and fibre.
- Make a purée with fresh seasonal vegetables, such as pumpkin, sweet potato, asparagus, artichokes, caul-iflower, broccoli, peas, broadbeans, spinach and mushrooms (fresh and dried, using the soaking liquid in the purée for added flavour). Cook the vegetables with some garlic, blend with vegetable or chicken stock until the mixture reaches the required consistency, then season well and add plenty of chopped fresh herbs. Serve the sauce with your favourite pasta shape. If you prefer a richer, slightly creamier sauce, blend the sauce with some low-fat ricotta until smooth.
- Make a risotto-style dish using orzo instead of rice, cooked with stock, and add your favourite seasonings.
- Stir some low-fat ricotta through a tomato and chilli pasta sauce for a creamier taste.
- Take advantage of the best green spring vegetables, blanch them in vegetable stock until just tender in vegetable stock, and then toss with some hot pasta and fresh herbs, and enough of the stock to moisten. A light dust with finely grated Parmesan is all that is needed for the perfect pasta Primavera.

Serves 4–6

Preparation time: 30 minutes

Cooking time: 1 hour 20 minutes

Easy

cooking oil spray
2 onions, finely chopped
2 cloves garlic, finely chopped
2 carrots, finely chopped
2 celery sticks, finely chopped
400 g (13 oz) lean beef mince
1 kg (2 lb) tomatoes, chopped
125 ml (½ cup) red wine
350 g (11½ oz) spaghetti
15 g (¼ cup) finely chopped fresh parsley

SPAGHETTI BOLOGNESE

This low-fat pasta dish is topped with a thick meat and vegetable sauce. It is packed with good-quality protein, slow-release carbohydrate, iron, zinc, vitamin B12 and niacin.

NUTRITION PER SERVE (6)

- Protein 22.5 g;
- Fat 6.5 g;
- Carbohydrate 46.5 g;
- Dietary Fibre 5.5 g;
- Cholesterol 34 mg;
- 1470 kJ (350 Cal)

1   Lightly spray a large saucepan with oil. Heat over medium heat, and add the onion, garlic, carrot and celery. Stir for 5 minutes, or until the vegetables have softened. If you find the vegetables are sticking, add 1 tablespoon water.

2   Increase the heat to high, add the mince and cook for 5 minutes, or until browned. Stir constantly to prevent the meat sticking. Add the tomato, wine and 250 ml (1 cup) water. Bring to the boil, then reduce the heat and simmer, uncovered, for 1 hour, or until the sauce has thickened.

3   Cook the spaghetti in a large pan of rapidly boiling water for 10–12 minutes, or until al dente. Drain, stir the parsley through the sauce and season well with salt and cracked black pepper. Divide the spaghetti among pasta bowls and top with the bolognese sauce. Garnish with a little chopped fresh parsley.

Serves 4

Preparation time: 20 minutes

Cooking time: 25 minutes

Easy

3 rashers bacon
2 teaspoons olive oil
2–3 cloves garlic, crushed
1 red onion, chopped
185 g (6 oz) field mushrooms, sliced
20 g (⅓ cup) chopped fresh parsley
155 g (1 cup) peas
375 ml (1½ cups) low-fat light
   evaporated milk
2 teaspoons cornflour
325 g (11 oz) dried linguine
25 g (1 oz) Parmesan shavings

LINGUINE with bacon, mushrooms and peas

This dish tastes so good you won't even realise it's relatively low in fat. It's also a good source of B vitamins, folate, potassium, phosphorus and calcium.

1 Remove the fat and rind from the bacon and chop roughly. Heat the oil in a medium pan, add the garlic, onion and bacon, and cook over low heat for 5 minutes, stirring frequently, until the onion and bacon are soft. Add the sliced mushrooms and cook, stirring, for another 5 minutes, or until soft.

2 Add the parsley, peas and milk to the pan. Mix the cornflour with 1 tablespoon of water until smooth, add to the mixture and stir over medium heat until slightly thickened.

3 Meanwhile, cook the pasta in a large pan of rapidly boiling water for 8 minutes, or until al dente. Drain and serve with the hot sauce and Parmesan shavings.

NUTRITION PER SERVE

- Protein 31.5 g;
- Fat 9 g;
- Carbohydrate 74.5 g;
- Dietary Fibre 6 g;
- Cholesterol 44.5 mg;
- 2140 kJ (510 Cal)

NOTE: Parmesan adds a nice flavour to this dish, but leave it out if you want to achieve a lower fat content.

Serves 4

Preparation time: 20 minutes

Cooking time: 15 minutes

Easy

160 g (2 cups) spiral pasta
4 thick beef sausages
2 teaspoons olive oil
2 red onions, cut into wedges
340 g (1⅓ cups) ready-made chunky
    tomato pasta sauce
4 small ripe tomatoes, peeled, seeded
    and chopped
20 g (⅓ cup) chopped fresh flat-leaf
    parsley

BEEF SAUSAGE PASTA

This quick-to-prepare meal provides good amounts of iron, zinc, vitamin A, B vitamins and fibre.

NUTRITION PER SERVE

• Protein 12 g;
• Fat 18 g;
• Carbohydrate 44 g;
• Dietary Fibre 7.5 g;
• Cholesterol 17 mg;
• 1605 kJ (385 Cal)

1   Bring a large saucepan of water to the boil and cook the pasta until al dente. Drain, reserving 60 ml (¼ cup) of the cooking water.

2   Meanwhile, prick the sausages all over with a fork. Heat a non-stick frying pan and cook the sausages over medium heat, turning often, for 5 minutes, or until cooked. Cut into thick diagonal slices and set aside.

3   Clean the frying pan and heat the oil. Cook the onion wedges over medium heat for 3 minutes, or until soft. Add the tomato pasta sauce and the tomato. Cook for 3–4 minutes, or until the tomato has softened. Add the sliced sausage and heat through for 1 minute.

4   Toss the pasta through the sauce, adding a little of the reserved pasta water, if necessary. Sprinkle with parsley and serve.

Serves 4

Preparation time: 15 minutes

Cooking time: 15 minutes

Medium

6 red peppers (capsicums)
6 slices prosciutto
625 g (1 lb 6 oz) chicken or
   ricotta ravioli
2 tablespoons olive oil
3 cloves garlic, crushed
2 leeks, white part only, thinly sliced
1 tablespoon chopped fresh oregano
2 teaspoons soft brown sugar
250 ml (1 cup) hot chicken stock

RAVIOLI with pepper sauce

Bright red peppers (capsicums) and leeks add colour and nutritional value to this dish, which is a good source of vitamin C, beta-carotene, folate, B vitamins, potassium, iron and zinc.

NUTRITION PER SERVE

- Protein 25 g;
- Fat 19.5 g;
- Carbohydrate 58.5 g;
- Dietary Fibre 8.5 g;
- Cholesterol 56 mg;
- 2125 kJ (510 Cal)

1 Cut the peppers (capsicums) into large pieces, removing the seeds and membrane. Place, skin-side up, under a hot grill until the skin blackens and blisters. Cool in a plastic bag, then peel away the skin. Place the prosciutto under the hot grill and cook for 1 minute each side, or until crisp. Break into pieces and set aside.

2 Cook the pasta in a large saucepan of boiling water until al dente.

Meanwhile, heat the oil in a frying pan and cook the garlic and leek over medium heat for 3–4 minutes, or until softened. Add the oregano and sugar, and stir for 1 minute.

3 Place the capsicum and leek mixture in a food processor or blender, season with salt and pepper, and process until combined. Add the chicken stock and process until smooth. Drain the pasta and

return to the saucepan. Gently toss the sauce through the ravioli over low heat until warmed through. Divide among four serving bowls and sprinkle with the prosciutto.

Serves 4

Preparation time: 20 minutes

Cooking time: 20 minutes

Medium

BALSAMIC SYRUP
80 ml (⅓ cup) balsamic vinegar
1½ tablespoons brown sugar

1 cup (150 g) fresh or frozen peas
16 asparagus spears, cut into 5 cm (2 in)
  lengths
2 large courgettes (zucchini), cut into
  thin ribbons
2 fresh lasagne sheets (200 g/3½ oz),
  (each sheet 24 cm x 35 cm/
  9½ x 14 in)
100 g (5 oz) rocket (arugula) leaves
30 g (1 cup) fresh basil, torn
2 tablespoons extra virgin olive oil
150 g (5 oz) semi-dried tomatoes
250 g (8 oz) low-fat ricotta
Parmesan shavings, to garnish

VEGETABLE LASAGNE with rocket

With less fat than meat lasagne, this colourful vegetarian dish is packed with vitamin C, beta-carotene, folate, potassium, calcium, iron and zinc. The vitamin C will enhance iron absorption.

NUTRITION PER SERVE

- Protein 18 g;
- Fat 16 g;
- Carbohydrate 36 g;
- Dietary Fibre 6 g;
- Cholesterol 63 mg;
- 1515 kJ (360 Cal)

1   To make the syrup, place the vinegar and brown sugar in a small saucepan and stir over medium heat until the sugar dissolves. Reduce the heat and simmer for 3–4 minutes, or until the sauce becomes syrupy. Remove from the heat.

2   Bring a large saucepan of water to the boil. Blanch the peas, asparagus and courgette (zucchini) in separate batches until just tender, removing each batch with a slotted spoon and refreshing in cold water. Reserve the cooking liquid and return to the boil.

3   Cook the lasagne sheets in the boiling water for 1–2 minutes, or until al dente. Refresh in cold water and drain well. Cut each lasagne sheet in half length-ways 12 cm x 35 cm (4⅔ x 13⅔ in).

4   Toss the vegetables and the rocket (arugula) with the basil and olive oil. Season with salt and black pepper.

5   To assemble, place one strip of pasta on a serving plate—one-third on the centre of the plate and two-thirds overhanging one side. Place a small mound of the salad on the centre third, topped with some tomatoes and ricotta. Season lightly and fold over one-third of the lasagne sheet. Top with another layer of salad, tomato and ricotta. Fold back the final layer of pasta and garnish with salad and tomato. Repeat with the remaining pasta strips, salad, tomato and ricotta to make four individual lasagne. Just before serving, drizzle with the balsamic syrup and garnish with Parmesan.

Serves 4

Preparation time: 5 minutes

Cooking time: 15 minutes

Easy

1 tablespoon oil
1 crushed clove garlic
1 finely chopped onion
6 chopped anchovies
2 tablespoons chopped capers
3 tablespoons chopped marinated
   black olives
2 x 400 g (13 oz) cans chopped tomatoes
1 tablespoon balsamic vinegar
2 teaspoons sugar

NUTRITION PER SERVE

- Protein 17 g;
- Fat 7 g;
- Carbohydrate 97 g;
- Dietary Fibre 9.5 g;
- Cholesterol 3.5 mg;
- 2220 kJ (530 Cal)

PUTTANESCA SAUCE

1 Heat oil in a large frying pan, add garlic and onion. Cook over medium heat for 3 minutes, or until golden. Add anchovies, capers and olives. Cook for 2 minutes, then stir in tomatoes, balsamic vinegar and sugar. Boil, then reduce the heat and simmer for 10 minutes, or until the sauce has reduced and thickened slightly. Toss through spaghetti.

Serves 4

Preparation time: 20 minutes

Cooking time: 25 minutes

Easy

375 g (12 oz) dried (or 500 g/1 lb fresh)
   tagliatelle
250 ml (1 cup) chicken or vegetable stock
2 leeks, white part only, thinly sliced
3 cloves garlic, crushed
235 g (1½ cups) shelled fresh peas
1 tablespoon finely chopped fresh mint
400 g (13 oz) asparagus spears, cut into
   5 cm (2 in) lengths
15 g (¼ cup) finely chopped fresh parsley
30 g (½ cup) shredded fresh basil
80 ml (⅓ cup) light cream
pinch of nutmeg
1 tablespoon grated Parmesan
1½ tablespoons extra virgin olive oil,
   to drizzle

NUTRITION PER SERVE

- Protein 21 g;
- Fat 14 g;
- Carbohydrate 76 g;
- Dietary Fibre 9 g;
- Cholesterol 32 mg;
- 2160 kJ (515 Cal)

TAGLIATELLE with peas and asparagus

Based on a medley of crisp spring vegetables and aromatic herbs, this dish is highly nutritious. It's an excellent source of folate, vitamin C, plant antioxidants, fibre, potassium and carbohydrate.

1 Cook the pasta in a large saucepan of boiling water until al dente. Drain well.

2 Place 125 ml (½ cup) of the stock and the leek in a large, deep frying pan. Cook over low heat, stirring often, for 4–5 minutes. Stir in the garlic, peas and mint, and cook for 1 minute. Add the remaining stock and 125 ml (½ cup) water and bring to the boil. Simmer for 5 minutes. Add the asparagus, parsley and basil, and season well with salt and ground black pepper. Simmer for a further 3–4 minutes, or until the asparagus is just tender. Gradually increase the heat to reduce the sauce to a light coating consistency, if necessary. Stir in the cream, nutmeg and Parmesan, and adjust the seasonings if necessary.

3 Add the tagliatelle to the sauce and toss lightly to coat. Divide among individual serving bowls and drizzle with the extra virgin olive oil. Garnish with extra grated Parmesan, if desired.

Serves 4–6

Preparation time: 40 minutes

Cooking time: 1 hour

Medium

12 black mussels, scrubbed clean, beards removed
125 ml (½ cup) white wine
2 tablespoons olive oil
1 onion, finely chopped
2–3 cloves garlic, finely chopped
2 x 400 g (13 oz) cans peeled tomatoes, chopped
50 g (1¾ oz) tomato paste
500 g (1 lb) spaghetti
250 g (8 oz) raw medium prawns (shrimp), peeled and deveined, tails intact
250 g (8 oz) scallops, with coral intact, cleaned
250 g (8 oz) boneless fish fillets, cubed
12 calamari rings
grated rind and juice of half a lemon
15 g (¼ cup) chopped fresh parsley

SPAGHETTI MARINARA

This low-fat dish is a wonderful way to enjoy the goodness of seafood. It contains filling protein, slow-release carbohydrate, B vitamins, potassium, iron, iodine, selenium and sulphur.

1 Place the mussels (discarding any open ones) in a large saucepan with the wine and 125 ml (½ cup) water. Cook, covered, over high heat for 2–3 minutes, or until the mussels open. Discard any unopened mussels and reserve the liquid.

2 Heat the oil in a large frying pan. Add the onion and garlic, and cook over medium heat for 3 minutes, or until the onion is soft. Add the tomato, tomato paste and reserved liquid. Simmer for 30 minutes, or until the sauce thickens.

3 Cook the pasta in a large saucepan of boiling water until al dente. Drain.

4 Add all the seafood to the sauce. Cook over low heat for 3–4 minutes, or until cooked through. Add the lemon rind, juice and parsley. Toss the sauce and mussels through the pasta and serve immediately.

NUTRITION PER SERVE (6)

- Protein 40 g;
- Fat 9.5 g;
- Carbohydrate 65 g;
- Dietary Fibre 5.5 g;
- Cholesterol 150.5 mg;
- 2200 kJ (525 Cal)

Serves 6

Preparation time: 30 minutes + soaking

Cooking time: 2 hours 10 minutes

Easy

125 g (½ cup) red lentils
2 teaspoons olive oil
2–3 cloves garlic, crushed
1 large onion, chopped
1 small red capsicum (pepper), chopped
2 courgettes (zucchini), sliced
1 celery stick, sliced
2 x 425 g (14 oz) cans chopped tomatoes
2 tablespoons tomato paste
1 teaspoon dried oregano
350 g (11½ oz) ricotta
12 instant or fresh lasagne sheets
60 g (2 oz) reduced-fat cheese, grated

WHITE SAUCE
40 g (⅓ cup) cornflour
750 ml (3 cups) skim milk
¼ onion
½ teaspoon ground nutmeg

RED LENTIL AND RICOTTA LASAGNE

An excellent choice for vegetarians, this recipe provides complete protein and plenty of slow-release carbohydrate energy, fibre and good amounts of vitamins and minerals.

1   Soak the lentils in boiling water to cover, for at least 30 minutes, then drain. Meanwhile, heat the oil in a large pan, add the garlic and onion, and cook for 2 minutes. Add the pepper (capsicum), courgette (zucchini) and celery, and cook for 2–3 minutes.

2   Add the lentils, tomato, tomato paste, oregano and 375 ml (1½ cups) water. Bring slowly to the boil, reduce the heat and simmer for 30 minutes, or until the lentils are tender. Stir occasionally.

3   To make the white sauce, blend the cornflour with 2 tablespoons of the milk in a saucepan until smooth. Add the remaining milk and the onion, and stir over low heat until

the mixture boils and thickens. Add the nutmeg and some ground black pepper, then cook over low heat for 5 minutes. Remove the onion.

4   Beat the ricotta with about 125 ml (½ cup) of the white sauce. Preheat the oven to moderate 180°C (350°F/ Gas 4). Spread one-third of the lentil mixture over the base of a 3 litre (12 cup) ovenproof dish. Cover with a layer of lasagne sheets. Spread another third of the lentil mixture over the pasta, then spread the ricotta evenly over the top. Follow with another layer of lasagne, then the remaining lentils. Pour the white

sauce evenly over the top and sprinkle with the grated cheese. Bake for 1 hour, covering loosely with foil if the top starts to brown too much. Leave for 5 minutes before cutting.

NUTRITION PER SERVE

- Protein 24.5 g;
- Fat 11 g;
- Carbohydrate 54 g;
- Dietary Fibre 7 g;
- Cholesterol 37 mg;
- 1725 kJ (410 Cal)

Serves 4

Preparation time: 5 minutes

Cooking time: 20 minutes

Easy

1 tablespoon oil
1 crushed clove garlic
7 sliced spring onions
100 g (3½ oz) chopped light ham
100 g (3½ oz) sliced cap mushrooms
60 ml (1¼ cup) chicken stock
125 ml (½ cup) light cream

NUTRITION PER SERVE

- Protein 20 g;
- Fat 14 g;
- Carbohydrate 90 g;
- Dietary Fibre 7.5 g;
- Cholesterol 34 mg;
- 2405 kJ (575 Cal)

BOSCAIOLA SAUCE

1 Heat oil in a non-stick frying pan, add garlic and spring onions. Cook over medium heat for 3 minutes, stir in ham, mushrooms and chicken stock. Bring to the boil and boil until the liquid has evaporated. Add another 250 ml (1 cup) chicken stock and cream, and bring to the boil. Boil for 5 minutes, or until thickened slightly. Season to taste with salt and ground black pepper, and serve tossed through farfalle. Garnish with extra sliced spring onions.

Serves 6

Preparation time: 40 minutes

Cooking time: 1 hour 45 minutes

Easy

500 g (1 lb) lean veal mince
1 onion, very finely chopped
4 cloves garlic, finely chopped
1 egg white, lightly beaten
80 g (1 cup) fresh breadcrumbs
30 g (½ cup) finely chopped fresh parsley
7 g (¼ cup) finely chopped fresh oregano
cooking oil spray
1.5 kg (3 lb) ripe tomatoes, peeled,
    roughly chopped
2 onions, thinly sliced
125 g (½ cup) tomato paste
½ teaspoon sugar
350 g (12 oz) penne

PENNE with meatballs

This delicious dish is rich in slow-release carbohydrate and complete protein.

1 Combine the veal mince, onion, half the garlic, the egg white, breadcrumbs, two-thirds of the parsley and 1 tablespoon of the oregano. Season well. Mix with your hands until well combined. Shape into small balls. Spray a large non-stick frying pan with oil. Cook the meatballs in three batches over high heat for 4–5 minutes, or until browned, turning constantly. Remove from the pan.

2 Lightly spray the base of a large, deep non-stick saucepan with oil. Add the sliced onion and remaining garlic. Cook over low heat for 2–3 minutes, stirring. Add 2 tablespoons water, cover and cook for 5 minutes. Stir in the tomato and tomato paste. Simmer, covered, for 10 minutes, then uncover and simmer gently for 40 minutes. Add the meatballs, and simmer, covered, for 15–20 minutes, or until just cooked. Add the sugar, remaining parsley and oregano, and season.

3 Cook the penne in a large saucepan of rapidly boiling water until al dente, then drain. Serve with the hot meatballs.

NUTRITION PER SERVE

- Protein 31 g;
- Fat 8 g;
- Carbohydrate 57.5 g;
- Dietary Fibre 7.5 g;
- Cholesterol 68.5 mg;
- 1805 kJ (430 Cal)

Serves 6

Preparation time: 15 minutes

Cooking time: 35 minutes

Easy

1 kg (2 lb) pumpkin, cut into 2 cm
   (¾ in) cubes
80 ml (⅓ cup) olive oil
500 g (1 lb) orecchiette
2 cloves garlic, crushed
1 teaspoon dried chilli flakes
1 teaspoon coriander (cilantro)
   seeds, crushed
1 tablespoon cumin seeds, crushed
200 g (6 ½ oz) Greek-style natural
   yoghurt
15 g (¼ cup) chopped fresh coriander
   (cilantro) leaves

ORECCHIETTE with pumpkin and yoghurt

Pumpkin and yoghurt give this dish a creamy texture. It is rich in beta-carotene, potassium, calcium and B vitamins.

1 Preheat the oven to moderately hot 200°C (400°F/Gas 6). Toss the pumpkin in 2 tablespoons of the oil, place in a roasting tin and bake for 30 minutes, or until golden, tossing halfway through.

2 Meanwhile, cook the pasta in a large saucepan of boiling water until al dente. Drain, then return to the saucepan.

3 Heat the remaining oil in a saucepan. Add the garlic, chilli, coriander and cumin, and cook for 30 seconds, or until fragrant. Toss the spice mix and pumpkin through the pasta, then stir in the yoghurt and fresh coriander. Season with salt and cracked black pepper. Divide among serving bowls and serve.

NUTRITION PER SERVE

- Protein 15 g;
- Fat 13.5 g;
- Carbohydrate 71.5 g;
- Dietary Fibre 5.5 g;
- Cholesterol 9.5 mg;
- 1960 kJ (470 Cal)

Serves 8

Preparation time: 40 minutes

Cooking time: 1 hour 35 minutes

Easy

2 teaspoons olive oil
1 large onion, chopped
2 carrots, finely chopped
2 celery sticks, finely chopped
2 courgettes (zucchini), finely chopped
2 cloves garlic, crushed
500 g (1 lb) lean beef mince
2 x 400 g (13 oz) cans crushed
   tomatoes
125 ml (½ cup) beef stock
2 tablespoons tomato paste
2 teaspoons dried oregano
375 g (12 oz) instant or fresh
   lasagne sheets

CHEESE SAUCE
750 ml (3 cups) skim milk
40 g (⅓ cup) cornflour
100 g (3½ oz) reduced-fat
   Cheddar, grated

NUTRITION PER SERVE

- Protein 27.5 g;
- Fat 8.5 g;
- Carbohydrate 48.5 g;
- Dietary Fibre 5 g;
- Cholesterol 41.5 mg;
- 1585 kJ (380 Cal)

LASAGNE

This reduced-fat version of the traditional recipe makes a healthy family meal. One serve provides good amounts of protein, B vitamins, vitamin A, potassium, phosphorus, calcium, iron and zinc.

1 Heat the olive oil in a large non-stick frying pan. Add the onion and cook for 5 minutes, or until soft. Add the carrot, celery and courgette (zucchini), and cook, stirring constantly, for 5 minutes, or until the vegetables are soft. Add the crushed garlic and cook for another minute. Add the beef mince and cook over high heat, stirring, until well browned. Break up any lumps of meat with a wooden spoon.

2 Add the crushed tomato, beef stock, tomato paste and dried oregano to the pan and stir to thoroughly combine. Bring the mixture to the boil, then reduce the heat and simmer gently, partially covered, for 20 minutes, stirring occasionally to prevent the mixture sticking to the pan.

3 Preheat the oven to moderate 180°C (350°F/Gas 4). Spread a little of the meat sauce into the base of a 23 x 30 cm (9 x 11½ in) ovenproof dish. Arrange a layer of lasagne sheets in the dish, breaking some of the sheets, if necessary, to fit in neatly.

4 Spread half the meat sauce over the top to cover evenly. Cover with another layer of lasagne sheets, a layer of meat sauce, then a final layer of lasagne sheets.

5 To make the cheese sauce, blend a little of the milk with the cornflour, to form a smooth paste, in a small pan. Gradually blend in the remaining milk and stir constantly over low heat until the mixture boils and thickens. Remove from the heat and stir in the grated cheese until melted. Spread evenly over the top of the lasagne and bake for 1 hour.

6 Check the lasagne after 25 minutes. If the top is browning too quickly, cover loosely with non-stick baking paper or foil. Take care when removing the baking paper or foil that the topping does not come away with the paper. For serving, cut the lasagne into eight portions and garnish with fresh herbs.

Serves 4

Preparation time: 15 minutes

Cooking time: 25 minutes

Easy

1 tsp olive oil
2 cloves garlic, chopped
1 small red chilli, seeded and chopped
2 x 400 g (14 oz) tins chopped tomatoes
125 g (¾ cup) black olives in brine,
   pitted and chopped
2 tbs capers, rinsed and drained
1 large handful basil, shredded
1 tsp sugar
200 g (7 oz) tin herring fillets in
   tomato sauce
500 g (1 lb) spaghetti
shredded basil, extra, to serve
grated Parmesan, to serve

HERRINGS IN TOMATO SAUCE PASTA

The zesty tomato sauce combines well with the pasta and herrings to make this a nutritious, low-GI meal. The olives contain monounsaturated fat and the fish provides omega-3 fat. The tomato sauce is a good source of antioxidants.

1 Heat the oil in a heavy-based saucepan. Add the garlic and chilli and cook briefly for 1 minute without browning. Add the tomatoes, olives, capers, basil and sugar. Stir well and simmer, uncovered, for 20 minutes, or until thick and reduced. Stir through the fish to break up a little. Season with pepper to taste.

2 Meanwhile, cook the pasta in a large saucepan of boiling salted water for 10 minutes, or until just tender. Drain and return to the saucepan. Toss through the sauce. Divide between 4 plates, top with basil and Parmesan and, if you like, serve with a salad.

NUTRITION PER SERVE

- Protein 18 g;
- Fat 2 g;
- Carbohydrate 98 g;
- Dietary Fibre 8.5 g;
- Cholesterol 0.5 mg;
- 2055 kJ (490 Cal)

Serves 4

Preparation time: 20 minutes

Cooking time: 15 minutes

Easy

2 teaspoons olive oil
2 rashers bacon, chopped,
    rind and fat removed
2–3 cloves garlic, crushed
1 onion, finely chopped
2 spring onions, finely chopped
250 g (8 oz) ricotta
30 g (½ cup) finely chopped fresh basil
325 g (11 oz) penne
8 cherry tomatoes, halved

PENNE with ricotta and basil sauce

An aromatic and creamy sauce, this recipe contains less fat than most cheesy sauces. It provides plenty
of carbohydrate energy, with some B vitamins, potassium, phosphorus, calcium and vitamin A.

NUTRITION PER SERVE

- Protein 22 g;
- Fat 12.5 g;
- Carbohydrate 60.5 g;
- Dietary Fibre 3.5 g;
- Cholesterol 56 mg;
- 1865 kJ (445 Cal)

1   Heat the oil in a pan, add the bacon, garlic, onion and spring onion, and stir over medium heat for 5 minutes, or until cooked. Remove from the heat, stir in the ricotta and chopped basil, and beat until smooth.

2   Meanwhile, cook the pasta in a large saucepan of rapidly boiling water for 10 minutes, or until al dente. Just prior to draining the pasta, add 250 ml (1 cup) of the pasta water to the ricotta mixture to thin the sauce. Add more water if you prefer an even thinner sauce. Season well with salt and ground black pepper.

3   Drain the pasta and stir the sauce through with the tomato halves. Garnish with small basil leaves, if desired.

Serves 4–6

Preparation time: 15 minutes

Cooking time: 35 minutes

Easy

2 tablespoons olive oil
1 onion, finely chopped
2 cloves garlic, finely chopped
2 tablespoons finely chopped fresh
    flat-leaf parsley
2 x 400 g (13 oz) cans peeled
    tomatoes, chopped, or 1 kg (2 lb)
    ripe tomatoes, peeled and chopped
1 tablespoon tomato paste
1 teaspoon caster sugar
500 g (1 lb) bucatini
15 g (¼ cup) shredded fresh basil

BUCATINI POMODORO

This low-fat dish is quick and easy to prepare. It is packed with carbohydrate energy and good amounts of fibre, potassium and some plant antioxidants.

1   Heat the oil in a large frying pan. Cook the onion, garlic and parsley over low heat for 3 minutes, or until the onion is soft.

2   Add the canned or fresh tomato, tomato paste and sugar. Partially cover and simmer for 30 minutes, or until the sauce thickens. Season with salt and ground black pepper.

3   Cook the pasta in a large saucepan of boiling water until al dente. Drain.

4   Toss the sauce through the pasta and garnish with shredded basil. Serve with grated Parmesan, if desired.

NUTRITION PER SERVE (6)

*   Protein 11 g;
*   Fat 3 g;
*   Carbohydrate 63 g;
*   Dietary Fibre 5 g;
*   Cholesterol 0 mg;
*   1365 kJ (325 Cal)

PAN-FRIES & BARBECUES

PAN-FRIES & BARBECUES

Pan-fries and barbecues are ideal for quick, healthy cooking, particularly if you are entertaining guests.
It's easy to add extra flavour and interest with a simple marinade or rub.

Because pan-frying and barbecuing are relatively quick cooking methods using an intense application of heat, they are well suited to cooking tender and smaller cuts of meat. Steaks, chops, sausages, chicken pieces or fillets, rissoles or patties, and skewers are all suitable for these methods of cooking.

Pan-frying and barbecuing are also excellent methods for cooking fish and other seafood, as they provide the high heat necessary to cook it quickly. Try fish fillets, fish cutlets, fish steaks, prawns (in or out of the shell), octopus and scallops. Shellfish such as oysters, mussels or clams can be placed directly on the barbecue and will be ready when the shells open.

Vegetables are also ideal for pan-frying and barbecuing. The surface of the vegetables will caramelise as they cook, and the inside will be moist and tender. Slice the vegetables so that they will cook through quickly, then brush or spray them with olive oil before cooking. Vegetables suited to this method of cooking include: courgette (zucchini), aubergine (eggplant), pepper (capsicum), pumpkin, mushrooms, sweet potato, cauliflower, fennel and squash.

After cooking the vegetables, lightly season them with salt and cracked black pepper, a drizzle of balsamic vinegar or a splash of lemon juice, and sprinkle with some finely chopped fresh herbs.

PAN-FRIES

The benefit of pan-frying is that the food is cooked over a relatively high heat, so the outside browns, forming a delicious caramelised crust, and the inside can be cooked to whatever stage you desire.

To make your pan-fried dishes as healthy as possible, use a non-stick frying pan sprayed with a light spray of olive oil rather than oil or butter.

When pan-frying meats that naturally contain a lot of fat, such as lamb chops, pork chops or bacon, it is unnecessary to add any fat while cooking. The fat that is contained within the meat will melt on heating and be sufficient to cook with.

After pan-frying foods, drain them on crumpled paper towels to remove any excess fat.

Ridged chargrill pans are also perfect for giving a barbecued appearance and smoky barbecue flavour.

BARBECUES

Barbecuing is also a healthy method of cooking. The grill bars simply need a light spray of oil to make sure the food doesn't stick. If the food is cooked on the grill bars rather than on the barbecue plate, any fat that comes out of the food while cooking will simply drip away.

An alternative method of barbecuing is cooking in a kettle barbecue, which is a covered barbecue. This type of cooking is more suited to larger joints of meat and vegetables. It will give the meat a delicious crust while helping the internal flesh to stay moist and tender.

RUBS AND MARINADES

Rubs and marinades are simple ways of adding flavour, tenderising and in some cases even preserving foods.

Rubs are mixtures of dry spices that can be used to 'rub' onto meat, chicken or fish for flavour and variety. You can make up your own combination or they can be purchased already blended from the supermarket. When purchasing prepared mixes, try to avoid brands that have a high salt content. Rub the spice mixture all over the food, then pan-fry or barbecue it.

Marinades are usually liquid, and may contain ingredients such as oil, wine, vinegar, citrus juices, herbs, spices, aromatics (such as garlic, chilli and ginger), and vegetables such as carrot and celery. Different types of marinades are suitable for different types of ingredients. They are not only used to add flavour to the cooked dish, but marinades that contain an acidic ingredient such as citrus juice or vinegar

also aid in tenderising. While this may be desirable for some tougher cuts of meat, the same marinade would start to 'cook' the flesh of fish, altering the texture. It is important to drain marinated food before cooking or the excess liquid will cause the food to stew.

RUBS

- Cajun spice mix is a spicy blend from the south of the USA, ideal for chicken.
- Garam masala is a mixture of Indian spices, which is great with lamb.
- Lemon pepper is a subtle, spiced pepper blend, perfect for coating fish or chicken.
- Sumac is a lemony North African crushed berry, which goes well with red meats.
- Smoked paprika is made from dried and crushed smoked peppers, and also goes well with red meats.

MARINADES

- Combine some chopped fresh parsley, crushed garlic and finely grated lemon rind, moisten the mixture with a little olive oil, and use it to marinate fish fillets or chicken pieces or fillets before pan-frying or barbecuing.
- Mix together some Dijon mustard, lemon juice, rosemary and a little olive oil, and use the mixture to marinate lamb or pork chops or whole joints that are to be roasted in a kettle barbecue.
- Use red wine, bay leaves, fresh parsley, and diced onion, carrot and celery to marinate beef steak and more robust gamey meats.
- Soy, ginger and garlic can be used to marinate chicken pieces, skewers of lamb and beef steaks for an Asian-style flavour.
- Blend chopped coriander with garlic, ginger, finely chopped chilli and ground turmeric to marinate chicken pieces, lamb loins or salmon steaks.
- Low-fat natural yoghurt mixed with tandoori spices is delicious with lamb.

Serves 4

Preparation time: 30 minutes

Cooking time: 1 hour

Medium

1 red pepper (capsicum), quartered
1 yellow pepper (capsicum), quartered
1 green pepper (capsicum), quartered
400 g (13 oz) baking potatoes (pontiac
   or desiree)
garlic oil spray
300 g (10 oz) lean lamb mince
2 teaspoons chopped fresh thyme
2 tablespoons chopped fresh parsley
2 tomatoes, seeded and finely chopped
1 large onion, finely chopped
25 g (⅓ cup) fresh breadcrumbs
1 egg white, lightly beaten
1 teaspoon ground black pepper
4 slices low-fat cheese
1 large red onion, thinly sliced
2 teaspoons olive oil
4 hamburger buns, toasted
40 g (1 oz) rocket

NUTRITION PER SERVE

- Protein 34.5 g;
- Fat 14 g;
- Carbohydrate 52 g;
- Dietary Fibre 5.5 g;
- Cholesterol 65.5 mg;
- 1995 kJ (475 Cal)

LAMB BURGER

This burger provides good-quality protein and well-absorbed iron and zinc.

1 Grill the pepper (capsicum), skin side up, until the skin blackens and blisters. Place it in a plastic bag until cool enough to handle, then peel off the skin and cut the flesh into strips.

2 Preheat the oven to moderately hot 200°C (400°F/Gas 6). Line a baking tray with foil. Cut the potatoes into wedges. Spray with the oil, then season. Spread out on the tray. Bake for 40 minutes, or until crisp and golden, turning once.

3 Meanwhile, combine the mince, thyme, parsley, tomato, onion, breadcrumbs, egg white and pepper. Form into four patties. Heat a non-stick frying pan over medium heat and cook the patties for 5 minutes on each side, or until cooked.

Remove from the pan and put a slice of cheese on top. Cook the onion in the olive oil for 4–5 minutes over medium heat until the onion is softened.

4 To assemble, layer the buns with rocket, the patty with cheese, onion, a strip each of red, yellow and green pepper (capsicum), and top with rocket and the top of the bun. Cut in half and serve with the wedges.

Serves 4

Preparation time:
20 minutes + 2 hours marinating

Cooking time: 50 minutes

Easy

4 chicken breast fillets
2 tablespoons honey
1 tablespoon wholegrain mustard
1 tablespoon soy sauce
2 red onions, cut into wedges
8 Roma tomatoes, halved lengthways
2 tablespoons soft brown sugar
2 tablespoons balsamic vinegar
cooking oil spray
snow pea (mange tout) sprouts, to serve

HONEY AND MUSTARD CHICKEN

A low-fat recipe, this chicken provides lots of lean protein, phosphorus and potassium, as well as some iron and zinc. The tomatoes add extra vitamin A and C, and the antioxidant lycopene.

NUTRITION PER SERVE

- Protein 25 g;
- Fat 2.5 g;
- Carbohydrate 30 g;
- Dietary Fibre 3 g;
- Cholesterol 50 mg;
- 990 kJ (235 Cal)

1 Preheat the oven to moderate 180°C (350°F/Gas 4). Trim the chicken of any excess fat and place in a shallow dish. Combine the honey, mustard and soy sauce, and pour over the chicken, tossing to coat. Cover and refrigerate for 2 hours, turning once.

2 Place the onion wedges and tomato halves on a baking tray covered with baking paper. Sprinkle with the sugar and drizzle with the balsamic vinegar. Bake for 40 minutes.

3 Heat a chargrill pan and lightly spray it with oil. Remove the chicken from the marinade and cook for 4–5 minutes on each side, or until cooked through. Slice the chicken and serve it with the mange tout (snow pea) sprouts, tomato halves and onion wedges.

Serves 4

Preparation time:
30 minutes + overnight marinating

Cooking time: 40 minutes

Medium

250 g (1 cup) low-fat plain yoghurt
2 cloves garlic, crushed
2 tablespoons tandoori paste
1 tablespoon lemon juice
2 tablespoons chopped fresh coriander
  leaves
600 g (1lb 4 oz) pork fillet, cubed
1 teaspoon olive oil
1 onion, chopped
2 cloves garlic, crushed
2 teaspoons ground cumin
1/2 teaspoon paprika
1 teaspoon ground coriander (cilantro)
380 g (2 cups) basmati and wild rice blend
1 litre (4 cups) vegetable stock
185 g (3/4 cup) low-fat plain yoghurt, extra
1 tablespoon chopped fresh coriander,
  extra

NUTRITION PER SERVE

- Protein 48 g;
- Fat 9 g;
- Carbohydrate 88 g;
- Dietary Fibre 3 g;
- Cholesterol 75 mg;
- 2670 kJ (640 Cal)

TANDOORI PORK KEBABS

The pork in this meal is an excellent source of niacin, thiamin, zinc and iron, while the rice provides slowly digested carbohydrate, fibre and niacin.

1 Combine the yoghurt, garlic, tandoori paste, lemon juice and coriander. Add the pork and stir to coat. Refrigerate, covered, overnight.

2 Heat the oil in a saucepan, add the onion, garlic and spices, and cook for 5 minutes, or until golden. Add the rice and stir to coat. Add the stock, bring to the boil, then simmer for 10 minutes, or until tunnels appear in the rice. Reduce the heat to low, cover and cook for 10 minutes.

3 Thread the pork onto eight skewers. Heat a chargrill plate and cook for 3–5 minutes on each side, or until tender.

4 Combine the extra yoghurt and coriander, and serve with the pork and spiced rice.

Serves 4

Preparation time:
10 minutes + overnight soaking
+ 30 minutes marinating

Cooking time: 1 hour 25 minutes

Medium

220 g (1 cup) dried chickpeas
6 Roma tomatoes, quartered lengthways
2 tablespoons olive oil
4 tuna steaks (about 150 g/5 oz each)
2 tablespoons lemon juice
1 red onion, chopped
1 clove garlic, crushed
1 teaspoon ground cumin
30 g (1 cup) chopped fresh flat-leaf parsley
fresh flat-leaf parsley, extra, to garnish

TUNA with chickpea salad

This is a highly filling mix of fish protein, fibre and slowly digested carbohydrate.

1 Cover the chickpeas with water and soak overnight, then drain. Place the chickpeas in a saucepan with enough water to cover them and bring to the boil. Cook for 25–30 minutes, or until tender. Drain, then rinse well under cold water.

2 Preheat the oven to moderate 180°C (350°F/Gas 4). Combine the tomato, 2 teaspoons of the oil, salt and pepper. Bake on a baking tray for 35–40 minutes.

3 Brush the tuna with 2 teaspoons of the oil and 1 tablespoon of the lemon juice, and season. Refrigerate for 30 minutes.

4 Heat the remaining olive oil in a frying pan over medium heat. Add the onion and garlic and cook, stirring, for 4–5 minutes, or until softened. Add the ground cumin and cook for 1 minute, then add the chickpeas. Cook for 5 minutes, stirring occasionally. Add the tomato, parsley and remaining lemon juice. Season to taste.

5 Heat a non-stick chargrill plate to high. Cook the tuna steaks on each side for 1–2 minutes. Serve on top of the warm salad and garnish with parsley.

NUTRITION PER SERVE

- Protein 47.5 g;
- Fat 20 g;
- Carbohydrate 21 g;
- Dietary Fibre 8 g;
- Cholesterol 54 mg;
- 1930 kJ (460 Cal)

Serves 4

Preparation time:
50 minutes + 3 hours marinating

Cooking time: 10 minutes

Medium

500 g (1 lb) calamari tubes, cleaned
2 stems lemon grass, white part only,
    chopped
3 teaspoons grated ginger
3 cloves garlic, finely chopped
½ teaspoon chopped red chilli
1 tablespoon vegetable oil
2 very ripe tomatoes
150 g (5 oz) mixed lettuce
7 g (¼ cup) fresh coriander (cilantro) leaves
2 tablespoons lime juice
1 teaspoon finely grated lime rind
1 red pepper (capsicum), cut into strips

LIME, CHILLI AND GARLIC SAUCE
60 ml (¼ cup) lime juice
1 tablespoon lemon juice
2 tablespoons fish sauce
1 tablespoon caster sugar
2 teaspoons chopped red chilli
2 cloves garlic, finely chopped
1 tablespoon finely chopped fresh
    coriander (cilantro)

NUTRITION PER SERVE

* Protein 25 g;
* Fat 6.5 g;
* Carbohydrate 5 g;
* Dietary Fibre 3 g;
* Cholesterol 250 mg;
* 755 kJ (180 Cal)

CALAMARI with spicy sauce

Although high in cholesterol, this meal is relatively low in fat. It is an excellent source of vitamin C, beta-carotene, potassium and phosphorus.

1 Cut the calamari tubes open, wash and pat dry. Cut shallow slashes about 5 mm (⅙ in) apart on the soft inside, in a diamond pattern, then cut into 3 cm (1¼ in) strips. Mix in a bowl with the lemon grass, ginger, garlic, chilli and oil. Cover and refrigerate for 3 hours.

2 Cut the tomatoes in half, scoop out the seeds and finely chop them, retaining the juice. Cut the flesh into cubes. Arrange the lettuce and coriander in serving bowls.

3 Just before serving, lightly grease and heat a solid barbecue plate or large, heavy non-stick pan until very hot. Quickly cook the calamari in batches, tossing for 2–3 minutes,

until just tender and curled, sprinkling the lime juice and rind over the top. Remove the calamari, toss with the chopped tomato seeds and arrange on the salad. Scatter the tomato and capsicum over the top. Season well.

4 Stir the sauce ingredients together until the sugar dissolves. Drizzle the sauce over the calamari.

Serves 4

Preparation time: 40 minutes

Cooking time: 30 minutes

Medium

SAUCE
185 ml (3/4 cup) beef stock
2 teaspoons soy sauce
2 tablespoons red wine
2 teaspoons wholegrain mustard
2 teaspoons cornflour

1 red pepper (capsicum), quartered
4 x 150 g (5 oz) lean pork leg steaks
90 g (1/3 cup) ricotta
2 spring onions, finely chopped
1 clove garlic, crushed
75 g (2½ oz) rocket
4 small lean slices prosciutto
cooking oil spray

PORK ROLLS with capsicum

This dish provides a delicious blend of flavours, and is an excellent source of potassium, vitamin C, niacin and thiamin.

NUTRITION PER SERVE

- Protein 40 g;
- Fat 5 g;
- Carbohydrate 3.5 g;
- Dietary Fibre 1 g;
- Cholesterol 95 mg;
- 925 kJ (220 Cal)

1 To make the sauce, put the beef stock, soy sauce, red wine and mustard in a pan. Blend the cornflour with 1 tablespoon water and add to the pan. Stir until the mixture boils and thickens.

2 Grill the pepper (capsicum) until the skin blisters and blackens. Place in a plastic bag until cool enough to handle, then peel and cut the flesh into thin strips.

3 Flatten the steaks with a mallet. Combine the ricotta, onion and garlic, then spread over the pork. Top with a layer of rocket and prosciutto. Place some pepper (capsicum) at one end and roll up to enclose the capsicum. Tie with string at even intervals.

4 Lightly spray a non-stick pan with oil and fry the pork rolls over medium heat for 5 minutes, or until well browned. Add the sauce and simmer over low heat for 10–15 minutes, or until the rolls are cooked through. Serve sliced with the sauce.

Serves 4

Preparation time:
20 minutes + overnight marinating

Cooking time: 15 minutes

Easy

4 chicken thigh fillets
1½ tablespoons soft brown sugar
1½ tablespoons lime juice
2 teaspoons green curry paste
18 kaffir lime leaves
2 stems lemon grass

MANGO SALSA
1 small mango, finely diced
1 teaspoon grated lime rind
2 teaspoons lime juice
1 teaspoon soft brown sugar
½ teaspoon fish sauce

LEMON GRASS CHICKEN SKEWERS

This is a high-protein dish, and a good source of monounsaturated fat, niacin, potassium and some vitamin A.

NUTRITION PER SERVE

- Protein 19.5 g;
- Fat 8 g;
- Carbohydrate 11 g;
- Dietary Fibre 1 g;
- Cholesterol 87 mg;
- 810 kJ (195 Cal)

1 Discard any excess fat from the chicken fillets and cut them in half lengthways. Combine the brown sugar, lime juice, curry paste and two of the kaffir lime leaves, shredded, in a bowl. Add the chicken and mix well. Cover and refrigerate for several hours or overnight.

2 Trim the lemon grass to measure about 20 cm (8 in), leaving the root end intact. Cut each stem lengthways into four pieces. Cut a slit in each of the remaining lime leaves and thread one onto each skewer. Cut two slits in each piece of chicken and thread onto a piece of lemon grass, followed by another lime leaf. Pan-fry or barbecue the skewers until the chicken is cooked through.

3 To make the mango salsa, put all the ingredients in a bowl and stir gently to combine. Serve with the chicken skewers.

Serves 4

Preparation time:
20 minutes + 10 minutes standing

Cooking time: 55 minutes

Easy

4 potatoes, thinly sliced
1 onion, thinly sliced
250 ml (1 cup) chicken stock
60 ml (¼ cup) light cream
ground nutmeg, to taste
4 lean beef eye-fillet steaks
90 g (⅓ cup) wholegrain mustard
olive oil spray

MUSTARD-CRUSTED STEAKS

Many beef-based meals are easy to prepare, and are a valuable addition to healthy diets. This meal provides well-absorbed iron and zinc, as well as plenty of protein, potassium, niacin and Vitamin C.

1 Preheat the oven to moderately hot 200°C (400°F/Gas 6). Layer the slices of potato and onion in four 250 ml (1 cup) ramekins.

2 Combine the stock and cream in a jug. Season with salt, ground black pepper and nutmeg. Pour over the potato and leave for 10 minutes. Place the ramekins on a baking tray and bake for 55 minutes, or until the potato is tender.

3 Meanwhile, spread each side of the steaks with the mustard. Lightly spray a large non-stick frying pan with the oil and heat over high heat. Add the steaks and cook for 3–4 minutes each side, or until cooked to your liking.

4 Remove the gratin from the dishes and serve with the steaks and some steamed green vegetables.

NUTRITION PER SERVE

- Protein 24.5 g;
- Fat 8.5 g;
- Carbohydrate 20 g;
- Dietary Fibre 3 g;
- Cholesterol 72.5 mg;
- 1080 kJ (260 Cal)

Serves 4

Preparation time: 20 minutes

Cooking time: 1 hour

Medium

60 g (⅓ cup) brown lentils
2 large aubergine (eggplants)
cooking oil spray
1 red onion, chopped
2 cloves garlic, crushed
1 red pepper (capsicum), finely chopped
40 g (¼ cup) pine nuts, toasted
440 g (14½ oz) can chopped tomatoes
140 g (¾ cup) cooked short-grain rice
2 tablespoons chopped fresh coriander
1 tablespoon chopped fresh parsley
2 tablespoons grated Parmesan

STUFFED AUBERGINES

Aubergines (eggplants) have been used in traditional medicine for thousands of years. This is an excellent meal for vegetarians, with slowly digested carbohydrate, protein, vitamin C, B vitamins and antioxidants.

NUTRITION PER SERVE

- Protein 15 g;
- Fat 10 g;
- Carbohydrate 50 g;
- Dietary Fibre 8.5 g;
- Cholesterol 9.5 mg;
- 1490 kJ (355 Cal)

1 Simmer the brown lentils in a pan of water for 25 minutes, or until soft; drain. Slice the aubergines (eggplants) in half lengthways and scoop out the flesh, leaving a 1 cm (½ in) shell. Chop the flesh finely.

2 Spray a deep, large non-stick frying pan with oil, add 1 tablespoon water to the pan, then add the onion and garlic, and stir until softened. Add the cooked lentils to the pan with the pepper (capsicum), pine nuts,

tomato, rice and aubergine (eggplant) flesh. Stir over medium heat for 10 minutes, or until the aubergine (eggplant) has softened. Add the fresh coriander and parsley. Season, then toss until well mixed.

3 Cook the aubergine (eggplant) shells in boiling water for 4–5 minutes, or until tender. Spoon the filling into the aubergine (eggplant) shells and sprinkle with the Parmesan. Grill until golden. Serve immediately.

Serves 4

Preparation time:
30 minutes + refrigeration

Cooking time: 25 minutes

Easy

500 g (1 lb) white fish fillets
2 tablespoons finely chopped fresh parsley
2 tablespoons finely chopped fresh dill
2 tablespoons lemon juice
1 tablespoon capers, finely chopped
2 fincly chopped gherkins
350 g (11½ oz) potatoes, cooked and
    mashed
plain flour, for dusting
2 teaspoons olive oil
4 hamburger buns, toasted
lettuce leaves
2 Roma tomatoes, sliced

TARTARE SAUCE
90 g (⅓ cup) low-fat mayonnaise
½ gherkin, finely chopped
2 teaspoons capers, finely chopped
½ teaspoon malt vinegar
2 teaspoons finely chopped fresh parsley
2 teaspoons lemon juice

FISH BURGERS

These burgers are a great source of iron, B vitamins, vitamin C, potassium and good-quality protein.

1 Place the fish in a frying pan and cover with water. Slowly heat the water, without boiling. Cover and cook over low heat until just cooked. Drain, transfer to a bowl and flake with a fork. Add the parsley, dill, lemon juice, capers, gherkin and potato, season, and combine well. Divide into four portions and shape into patties. Dust with flour, then refrigerate for 1 hour.

2 Meanwhile, make the tartare sauce by mixing all the ingredients in a bowl.

3 Heat the oil in a large non-stick frying pan. Cook the patties for 5–6 minutes on each side, or until well browned.

4 Place some lettuce leaves, tomato slices, a fish patty and a quarter of the tartare sauce on each bun.

NUTRITION PER SERVE

* Protein 33.5 g;
* Fat 10.5 g;
* Carbohydrate 46.5 g;
* Dietary Fibre 4.5 g;
* Cholesterol 78.5 mg;
* 1745 kJ (415 Cal)

Serves 4

Preparation time:
20 minutes + 30 minutes refrigeration
+ 10 minutes resting

Cooking time: 20 minutes

Easy

4 scotch fillet steaks
80 ml (1/3 cup) soy sauce
2 tablespoons mirin
1 tablespoon sake (optional)
1 clove garlic, crushed
1 teaspoon grated ginger
1 teaspoon sugar
1 teaspoon toasted sesame seeds

CUCUMBER SALAD
1 large Lebanese (short) cucumber,
    peeled, seeded and diced
1/2 red pepper (capsicum), diced
2 spring onions, sliced thinly on the
    diagonal
2 teaspoons sugar
1 tablespoon rice wine vinegar

BEEF TERIYAKI

The salad turns this dish into a light and nutritious meal, providing high-quality protein, iron and zinc, with vitamin C and potassium.

1 Place the steaks in a non-metallic dish. Combine the soy, mirin, sake, garlic and ginger, and pour over the steaks. Cover and refrigerate for at least 30 minutes.

2 To make the salad, place the cucumber, pepper (capsicum) and spring onion in a bowl. Place the sugar, rice wine vinegar and 60 ml (1/4 cup) water in a small saucepan and stir over medium heat until the sugar dissolves. Simmer rapidly for 3–4 minutes, or until thickened.

Pour over the salad, stir to combine and leave to cool completely.

3 Spray a chargrill plate with oil and heat until very hot. Drain the steaks, reserving the marinade. Cook for 3–4 minutes on each side. Remove and rest before slicing.

4 Place the sugar and reserved marinade in a small saucepan and heat, stirring, until the sugar has dissolved. Bring to the boil, then simmer for 2–3 minutes.

5 Slice each steak and arrange on serving plates. Spoon on some of the marinade and salad, and sprinkle with sesame seeds.

NUTRITION PER SERVE

- Protein 23 g;
- Fat 5 g;
- Carbohydrate 6 g;
- Dietary Fibre 1 g;
- Cholesterol 67 mg;
- 720 kJ (170 Cal)

Serves 4

Preparation time:
20 minutes + 30 minutes refrigeration

Cooking time: 15 minutes

Medium

1 kg (2 lb) lean minced lamb
60 g (1 cup) finely chopped fresh parsley
25 g (½ cup) finely chopped fresh mint
1 onion, finely chopped
1 clove garlic, crushed
1 egg
1 teaspoon chilli sauce
4 small wholemeal pitta pockets

MINT SALAD
3 small tomatoes
1 small red onion, thinly sliced
20 g (1 cup) fresh mint
1 tablespoon olive oil
2 tablespoons lemon juice

GRILLED LAMB PITTAS

This is a refreshing and satisfying lunch or dinner, rich in protein, iron, zinc, potassium and B vitamins. The soothing mint enhances the lamb's flavour, and adds some vitamin C and minerals.

1 Place the lamb, parsley, mint, onion, garlic, egg and chilli sauce in a large bowl and mix together. Shape into eight patties. Chill for 30 minutes. Preheat the oven to warm 160°C (315°F/Gas 2–3).

2 To make the mint salad, slice the tomatoes into thin rings and place in a bowl with the onion, mint, olive oil and lemon juice. Season well with salt and pepper. Gently toss to coat.

3 Wrap the pitta breads in foil and warm in the oven for 5–10 minutes.

4 Heat a chargrill or hot plate and brush with a little oil. When very hot, cook the patties for 3 minutes on each side. Do not turn until a crust has formed on the base or they will fall apart.

5 Remove the pitta breads from the oven. Cut the pockets in half, fill each half with some mint salad and a lamb patty. Serve with some low-fat yoghurt, if desired.

NUTRITION PER SERVE

- Protein 59 g;
- Fat 24 g;
- Carbohydrate 29 g;
- Dietary Fibre 8 g;
- Cholesterol 211 mg;
- 2390 kJ (570 Cal)

Serves 8

Preparation time:
20 minutes + 30 minutes soaking

Cooking time: 40 minutes

Easy

SALSA VERDE
1 clove garlic
1 tablespoon drained capers
20 g (1 cup) fresh flat-leaf parsley
15 g (½ cup) fresh basil
10 g (½ cup) fresh mint
80 ml (⅓ cup) olive oil
1 teaspoon Dijon mustard
1 tablespoon red wine vinegar

16 small yellow squash
16 French shallots, peeled
16 baby courgettes (zucchini)
16 baby carrots, peeled
1 large red pepper (capsicum), halved
    and cut into 2 cm (⅔ in) thick slices
2 cloves garlic, crushed
1 teaspoon chopped fresh thyme
1 tablespoon olive oil
16 fresh bay or sage leaves

NUTRITION PER SERVE

* Protein 3 g;
* Fat 11 g;
* Carbohydrate 5 g;
* Dietary Fibre 3.5 g;
* Cholesterol 0 mg;
* 525 kJ (125 Cal)

VEGETABLE SKEWERS
with salsa verde

Just one serve of this recipe meets your daily vitamin A needs,
and provides potassium.

1 Soak 16 wooden skewers in cold water for 30 minutes.

2 To make the salsa verde, combine the garlic, capers and herbs in a food processor until roughly chopped. With the motor running, slowly pour in the olive oil until incorporated. Combine the mustard with the red wine vinegar and stir through the salsa verde. Season. Cover and refrigerate.

3 Blanch the vegetables separately in a large pot of boiling, salted water until just tender. Drain in a colander, then toss with the garlic, thyme and oil. Season well.

4 Thread the vegetables onto the skewers starting with a squash, then a shallot, a bay leaf, courgette (zucchini), carrot and pepper (capsicum).

5 Cook the skewers on a hot barbecue grill for 3 minutes on each side, or until cooked and browned. Arrange on couscous or rice and serve with the salsa verde.

Serves 4

Preparation time: 20 minutes

Cooking time: 15 minutes

Easy

2 x 185 g (6 oz) cans lemon pepper tuna, drained
1 large onion, chopped
65 g (2/3 cup) dry breadcrumbs
1 egg, lightly beaten
2 tablespoons chopped fresh lemon thyme
1 tablespoon chopped fresh parsley
2 teaspoons grated lemon rind
1 tablespoon oil
1 loaf Turkish bread
80 g (1/3 cup) fat-free mayonnaise
150 g (5 oz) rocket
4 slices low-fat cheese
2 tomatoes, sliced
1 cucumber, sliced
1/2 red onion, sliced

NUTRITION PER SERVE

- Protein 30.5 g;
- Fat 9.5 g;
- Carbohydrate 56 g;
- Dietary Fibre 5.5 g;
- Cholesterol 73 mg;
- 1825 kJ (435 Cal)

LEMON PEPPER TUNA BURGER

This delicious fish recipe provides some omega-3 and monounsaturated fats, with good amounts of fibre, niacin, thiamin, folate, calcium and vitamin C. It is a good choice for women who are trying to fall pregnant.

1   Combine the tuna, onion, breadcrumbs, egg, thyme, parsley and lemon rind in a bowl and mix well. Form into four patties and flatten slightly. Heat the oil in a non-stick frying pan. Cook the patties over medium heat for 5 minutes on each side, or until browned.

2   Cut the bread into 4 portions. Split each portion in half horizontally and place under a grill to lightly brown.

3   Spread both cut sides of the bread with mayonnaise. Top with some rocket and layer with a patty, a slice of cheese and slices of tomato, cucumber and onion. Place the other half of the Turkish bread on top, cut in half and serve.

Serves 4

Preparation time:
20 minutes + 10 minutes marinating

Cooking time: 30 minutes

Easy

4 salmon fillets
1 tablespoon oil
1 clove garlic, crushed
2 tablespoons white wine vinegar
1 teaspoon finely grated lime rind
2 tablespoons chopped fresh dill
600 g (1 lb 4 oz) can cannellini beans,
 rinsed and drained
1 bay leaf
250 ml (1 cup) chicken stock
100 g (3½ oz) baby English
 spinach leaves

NUTRITION PER SERVE

- Protein 28 g;
- Fat 14 g;
- Carbohydrate 16 g;
- Dietary Fibre 10 g;
- Cholesterol 70 mg;
- 1405 kJ (335 Cal)

SALMON with bean puree

This nourishing meal is an easy and delicious way to include fish in your diet. It provides slowly released carbohydrate energy, filling protein and fibre, monounsaturated fat, niacin, folate, potassium and iron.

1 Place the salmon in a non-metallic dish. Combine the oil, garlic, vinegar, lime and dill, pour over the fish, then cover and leave for 10 minutes.

2 Place the beans, bay leaf and stock in a saucepan, and simmer for 10 minutes. Remove the bay leaf. Place in a food processor and purée. Season.

3 Drain the salmon, reserving the marinade. Cook in a non-stick frying pan over high heat for 3–5 minutes each side, or until crisp and golden. Remove, add the marinade to the pan and bring to the boil.

4 Steam the spinach until wilted. Serve the salmon on the purée and spinach, and drizzle with the marinade.

Serves 4

Preparation time:
20 minutes + 30 minutes soaking
+ overnight marinating

Cooking time: 30 minutes

Medium

1 kg (2 lb) pork fillet, cut into 2 cm
   (2/3 in) cubes
8 spring onions, cut into 3 cm
   (1¼ in) lengths
2 tablespoons rice wine vinegar
2 teaspoons chilli bean paste
60 ml (¼ cup) char siu sauce
400 g (14 oz) fresh flat rice noodles
30 g (1 cup) fresh coriander (cilantro)
   leaves, chopped
3 spring onions, extra, sliced
1 tablespoon vegetable oil
fresh coriander (cilantro) sprigs, to garnish

PORK SKEWERS
on rice noodle cakes

This spicy pork dish will supply you with your daily niacin and thiamin needs.

1 Soak eight bamboo skewers in water for 30 minutes. Thread the pork and spring onion alternately on the skewers. Combine the vinegar, bean paste and char siu sauce in a shallow non-metallic dish. Add the skewers and coat. Refrigerate overnight.

2 Drain the skewers, reserving the marinade. Heat a grill plate until very hot. Cook the skewers for 1–2 minutes on each side, or until brown and cooked through. Remove and keep warm. Place the marinade in a saucepan and bring to the boil.

3 Separate the noodles with your hands, and toss with the coriander and extra spring onion. Divide into four portions. Heat the oil in a non-stick frying pan over medium heat. Place one portion in the pan, pressing down with a spatula to form a pancake. Cook for 3–4 minutes on each side, or until golden. Remove and keep warm. Repeat with the remaining noodles.

4 Place each noodle cake on a plate and top with two skewers. Drizzle with the marinade and garnish with the coriander (cilantro).

NUTRITION PER SERVE

- Protein 59.5 g;
- Fat 11.5 g;
- Carbohydrate 46.5 g;
- Dietary Fibre 3 g;
- Cholesterol 237.5 mg;
- 2240 kJ (535 Cal)

Serves 4

Preparation time:
25 minutes + 30 minutes soaking
+ 30 minutes marinating

Cooking time: 20 minutes

Easy

1 kg (2 lb) swordfish steaks, cut into
    3 cm (1¼ in) cubes
1 tablespoon olive oil
2 tablespoons lemon juice
1 clove garlic, crushed
1 tablespoon chopped fresh rosemary
1 tablespoon chopped fresh thyme
2 tablespoons chopped fresh flat-leaf
    parsley

BEAN PURÉE
2 x 400 g (14 oz) cans cannellini beans,
    rinsed
375 ml (1½ cups) chicken stock
2 fresh bay leaves
2 cloves garlic, crushed
1 teaspoon chopped fresh thyme
½ teaspoon finely grated lemon rind
60 ml (¼ cup) extra virgin olive oil

NUTRITION PER SERVE

- Protein 62 g;
- Fat 21 g;
- Carbohydrate 18 g;
- Dietary Fibre 9 g;
- Cholesterol 147 mg;
- 2115 kJ (505 Cal)

SWORDFISH SKEWERS
with bean puree

This recipe is rich in potassium, phosphorus, niacin, fibre and protein.

1   Soak eight wooden skewers in water for 30 minutes. Thread the swordfish cubes onto the skewers. Place in a large non-metallic dish and pour on the combined oil, lemon juice, garlic, rosemary and thyme; season. Refrigerate for 30 minutes.

2   To make the bean purée, place the beans in a large saucepan. Add the stock, bay leaves and 125 ml (½ cup) water. Bring to the boil, then reduce the heat and simmer for 10 minutes. Remove from the heat and drain, reserving 2 tablespoons of liquid.

3   Place the beans and liquid in a food processor with the garlic, thyme and rind. Season, and process until

smooth. With the motor running, gradually pour in the oil. Process until well combined; keep warm.

4   Cook the skewers on a very hot chargrill or hot plate, turning regularly and basting with the marinade, for 3–4 minutes, or until cooked through and golden. Serve with parsley and a spoonful of the purée.

Serves 4

Preparation time:
25 minutes + 30 minutes refrigeration

Cooking time: 15 minutes

Easy

400 g (13 oz) lean chicken mince
80 g (1 cup) fresh breadcrumbs
1 clove garlic, crushed
15 g (½ cup) chopped fresh
   coriander leaves
60 ml (¼ cup) sweet chilli sauce
1 teaspoon ground coriander (cilantro)
3 spring onions, finely chopped
60 g (¼ cup) sugar
2 tablespoons white vinegar
2 tablespoons finely chopped peanuts
1 tablespoon chopped fresh coriander
   (cilantro) leaves, extra
1 large carrot
1 large Lebanese (short) cucumber
4 hamburger buns
70 g (2 oz) mixed lettuce leaves
1 large vine-ripened tomato, sliced

THAI CHICKEN BURGERS

A lower-fat chicken burger, this dish provides flavonoids, potassium, vitamin A, fibre and monounsaturated fat.

1 Place the mince, breadcrumbs, garlic, fresh coriander, sweet chilli sauce, ground coriander and spring onion in a large bowl, and mix together with your hands. Shape into four patties. Refrigerate, covered, for 30 minutes.

2 Place the sugar, vinegar and 60 ml (¼ cup) water in a small saucepan, and stir over low heat until the sugar dissolves. Simmer for 5 minutes, or until slightly thickened. Cool and stir in the peanuts and extra coriander. Peel strips of carrot and cucumber to make 'ribbons'.

3 Heat a chargrill plate and grill the burgers for 4 minutes each side, or until tender. Serve on hamburger buns, with the dressing, lettuce leaves, tomato, carrot and cucumber.

NUTRITION PER SERVE

- Protein 28 g;
- Fat 5 g;
- Carbohydrate 63 g;
- Dietary Fibre 5.5 g;
- Cholesterol 40 mg;
- 1710 kJ (410 Cal)

STIR-FRIES & STEAMED DISHES

STIR-FRIES & STEAMED DISHES

When it comes to simple, quick and healthy cooking, stir-fried and steamed meals are hard to beat.
All you need is a wok or steamer basket, your favourite ingredients, and a little imagination.

STIR-FRYING

Stir-frying is a fast, easy and healthy cooking method, which combines the best of fresh produce with exotic flavours. Stir-frying is Asian in origin, but recipes can be varied to suit your individual tastes or the ingredients you have.

It is important that all the preparation of ingredients is done before you begin cooking, because once the cooking starts, there's no time to stop. For the best tasting stir-fries, the ingredients should be added at various stages of the process, according to how long they take to cook.

Stir-frying involves cooking in a wok over high heat. It needs only a minimum of oil, and if you use a non-stick wok, you can stir-fry with just a light spray of oil.

A stir-fry served with noodles or rice is a healthy, convenient, complete and filling meal. It can be a simple dish of meat, poultry, seafood or vegetables tossed with a sauce, or a complex combination of flavours and ingredients.

Firm tofu or tofu puffs are a great vegetarian choice for stir-fries, and add protein and minerals to the dish.

PREPARING INGREDIENTS
- Meat and poultry should be from a cut that will be tender after only a short cooking time. Cut the meat into thin, even-sized strips across the grain. Marinating the food before cooking will tenderise it and also add to the flavour of the whole dish.
- Seafood such as prawns, scallops and squid need only the briefest time to cook through. If cooking fish, use firm-fleshed pieces that won't break up, and move them gently around the wok to cook, without breaking up.
- Vegetables are perfect for stir-frying, and the quick cooking helps them to retain texture, colour and nutrients.

Different vegetables require different cooking times, and should be cut and added to the dish accordingly:
— cauliflower, potatoes and carrots will take longer to cook, so slice them thinly and add them at the beginning of cooking
— peas, asparagus and mushrooms should be added towards the end of cooking
— bean sprouts, herbs and leafy vegetables such as bok choy and spinach should be tossed through at the end, because they need only to be heated through until they are just wilted.

STIR-FRYING TIPS
- Make sure that the wok is very hot before you begin. Add a minimum of oil and swirl to coat the bottom and side of the wok, or give a light spray of oil.
- Drain any marinade from the ingredients before you begin to stir-fry, otherwise they will tend to steam or stew in the juices.
- Cook meat in batches over high heat. This will allow each batch to cook evenly and quickly, and will help to maintain the heat through-out cooking. Reheat the wok after cooking each batch.

- Set the cooked meat aside, then cook the aromatics such as garlic, ginger, onion and chilli, followed by the slower-cooking ingredients. Return the meat to the wok just before adding the sauce ingredients, and then any leafy greens and herbs.
- Keep all the ingredients moving constantly around the wok to make sure they cook evenly.
- If the stir-fry looks a little dry, add a little water or stock to moisten and prevent sticking.
- Serve the stir-fry immediately so the ingredients don't go soggy.

STEAMING

Steaming is an efficient and extremely healthy cooking method. It is particularly suitable for cooking most types of vegetables and seafood. The ingredient is placed in a bamboo or metal steamer basket, covered and then placed directly above simmering water in a wok or saucepan. The rising steam becomes trapped by the steamer basket and cooks the food.

Steaming allows food to cook without any fat and, because it doesn't come into contact with the water, more water-soluble nutrients are retained. Several steamer baskets may be stacked on top of each other to cook large quantities of food, or for cooking different types of food that require different cooking times.

Aromatics can be added to the steaming liquid, which will impart a subtle flavour to the food being steamed. Try:
- garlic
- ginger
- lemon grass
- lemon or lime zest
- lime leaves
- coriander (cilantro) roots
- star anise.

STEAMING IDEAS
- Lightly marinate skinless chicken breast fillets with garlic, ginger and soy sauce, and steam until cooked through. Serve sliced with sweet chilli dipping sauce over jasmine rice.
- Steam baby bok choy or Chinese broccoli until tender, then drizzle with oyster sauce.
- Top an Atlantic salmon steak with finely shredded spring onion and coriander leaves, steam until cooked to your liking, and serve with lemon wedges and a green salad.
- Steam mussels in a spicy Thai-flavoured broth until they just open, and serve with crusty bread.
- Leave scallops in their half shell, pour over a little miso broth, top with a few thinly sliced spring onions and steam on the shell until they are just cooked.
- Steam prawns (shrimp) in their shells until they are pink and cooked through, and serve with a Vietnamese lime and chilli dipping sauce.
- Steam fresh summer sweet corn chunks, asparagus and sugar snap peas, and serve as a delicious side dish.

Serves 4

Preparation time: 20 minutes

Cooking time: 15 minutes

Easy

600 g (1 lb 4 oz) Shanghai noodles
1 tablespoon olive oil
1 tablespoon julienned fresh ginger
1 long red chilli, seeded and finely
    chopped
500 g (1 lb) chicken breast fillets, cut
    crossways into 1 cm (¼ in) slices
2 cloves garlic, crushed
60 ml (¼ cup) salt-reduced soy sauce
3 teaspoons sesame oil
700 g (1 lb 7 oz) baby bok choy, sliced
    lengthways into eighths
2 tablespoons sesame seeds, toasted

SESAME CHICKEN AND NOODLE STIR-FRY

This high-protein dish is an excellent source of B vitamins, fibre, potassium, phosphorus and iron.

1   Cook the noodles in a saucepan of boiling water for 4–5 minutes, or until tender. Drain and rinse under cold water. Drain again.

2   Heat the oil in a wok and swirl to coat. Add the ginger and chilli, and stir-fry for 1 minute. Add the chicken and stir-fry for a further 3–5 minutes, or until browned and almost cooked.

3   Add the garlic and cook for 1 minute. Pour in the soy sauce and sesame oil, and toss to coat. Add the bok choy and noodles, and stir-fry until the bok choy is tender and the noodles are warmed through. Place in individual serving bowls, sprinkle with sesame seeds and serve.

NUTRITION PER SERVE

- Protein 45 g;
- Fat 19 g;
- Carbohydrate 80 g;
- Dietary Fibre 6 g;
- Cholesterol 102 mg;
- 2850 kJ (680 Cal)

Serves 4

Preparation time:
15 minutes + 10 minutes soaking

Cooking time: 15 minutes

Easy

350 g (12 oz) lean beef fillet, partially
  frozen
100 g (3½ oz) mange tout (snow peas)
600 g (1 lb 4 oz) fresh Hokkien noodles
1 tablespoon peanut oil
1 large onion, cut into thin wedges
1 large carrot, sliced thinly on the
  diagonal
1 medium red pepper (capsicum), cut into
  thin strips
2 cloves garlic, crushed
1 teaspoon grated fresh ginger
200 g (6½ oz) fresh shiitake mushrooms,
  sliced
60 ml (¼ cup) oyster sauce
2 tablespoons light soy sauce
1 tablespoon soft brown sugar
½ teaspoon five-spice powder

NUTRITION PER SERVE

- Protein 37.5 g;
- Fat 10 g;
- Carbohydrate 91.5 g;
- Dietary Fibre 6.5 g;
- Cholesterol 78 mg;
- 2555 kJ (610 Cal)

BEEF AND NOODLE STIR-FRY

High in top-quality protein and B vitamins, this dish also provides significant
amounts of fibre, iron, zinc, potassium and vitamin A.

1 Cut the steak into thin slices. Top and tail the snow peas
(mange tout) and slice in half diagonally. Soak the noodles in
a large bowl with enough boiling water to cover for 10 minutes.

2 Spray a large wok with oil spray and, when very hot, cook
the steak in batches until brown. Remove and keep warm.

3 Heat the oil in the wok and, when very hot, stir-fry the
onion, carrot and pepper (capsicum) for 2–3 minutes, or
until tender. Add the garlic, ginger, snow peas
(mange tout) and shiitake mushrooms, and cook for
another minute before returning the steak to the wok.

4 Separate the noodles with a fork, then drain. Add to the
wok, tossing well. Combine the oyster sauce with the soy
sauce, brown sugar, five-spice powder and 1 tablespoon
water, and pour over the noodles. Toss until warmed
through, then serve immediately.

Serves 4

Preparation time:
15 minutes + 10 minutes marinating

Cooking time: 15 minutes

Easy

3 teaspoons cornflour
2 teaspoons soy sauce
1 teaspoon oyster sauce
1 clove garlic, finely chopped
250 g (8 oz) pork mince
1 tablespoon oil
3 teaspoons red bean chilli paste
3 teaspoons preserved bean curd
750 g (1 lb 8 oz) firm tofu, drained,
   cubed
2 spring onions, sliced
3 teaspoons oyster sauce, extra
2 teaspoons soy sauce, extra
1½ teaspoons sugar

NUTRITION PER SERVE

- Protein 26 g;
- Fat 12 g;
- Carbohydrate 5 g;
- Dietary Fibre 0 g;
- Cholesterol 30 mg;
- 1090 kJ (260 Cal)

MA POR TOFU

This dish is a great choice for people who don't eat dairy products as it contains calcium, magnesium, phosphorus, protein and potassium.

1   Put the cornflour, soy sauce, oyster sauce and garlic in a bowl, and mix well. Add the mince and toss to coat. Set aside for 10 minutes.

2   Heat a wok until very hot, add the oil and swirl to coat. Add the mince and stir-fry for 5 minutes, or until browned. Add the chilli paste and bean curd, and cook for 2 minutes, or until fragrant.

3   Add the remaining ingredients and stir for 3–5 minutes, or until the tofu is heated through. Serve with rice.

Serves 4–6

Preparation time:
30 minutes + 20 minutes soaking

Cooking time: 15 minutes

Easy

25 g (¾ oz) dried Chinese mushrooms
1 tablespoon oil
½ teaspoon sesame oil
1 tablespoon finely chopped fresh ginger
4 cloves garlic, crushed
100 g (3½ oz) fresh shiitake mushrooms, trimmed, sliced
150 g (5 oz) oyster mushrooms, sliced
150 g (5 oz) shimeji mushrooms, trimmed, pulled apart
185 ml (¾ cup) dashi (see Note)
60 ml (¼ cup) soy sauce
60 ml (¼ cup) mirin
¼ teaspoon white pepper
25 g (1 oz) butter
2 tablespoons lemon juice
100 g (3½ oz) enoki mushrooms, trimmed, pulled apart
500 g (1 lb) thin Hokkien noodles, separated
1 tablespoon chopped fresh chives

MUSHROOM NOODLES

Suitable for vegetarians, this dish provides fibre, some minerals, B vitamins and folate.

1 Soak the dried Chinese mushrooms in 375 ml (1½ cups) boiling water for 20 minutes, or until soft. Drain, reserving the liquid. Discard the stems. Slice the caps.

2 Heat a wok until very hot, add the oils and swirl to coat. Add the ginger, garlic, shiitake, oyster and shimeji mushrooms, and stir-fry for 1–2 minutes, or until the mushrooms have wilted. Remove.

3 Combine the dashi, soy sauce, mirin, white pepper and 185 ml (¾ cup) of the reserved liquid, add to the wok and cook for 3 minutes. Add the butter, juice and 1 teaspoon salt, and cook for 1 minute, or until thickened. Return the mushrooms to the wok, cook for 2 minutes, then stir in the enoki and Chinese mushrooms.

4 Add the noodles and stir for 3 minutes, or until heated through.

NUTRITION PER SERVE (6)

- Protein 15 g;
- Fat 8.5 g;
- Carbohydrate 60 g;
- Dietary Fibre 5 g;
- Cholesterol 25 mg;
- 1610 kJ (385 Cal)

Sprinkle with the chives and serve immediately.

NOTE: Dissolve 1½ teaspoons dashi powder in 185 ml (¾ cup) water to make the dashi.

Serves 4

Preparation time:
10 minutes + 20 minutes soaking
+ 1 hour marinating

Cooking time: 20 minutes

Medium

8–10 g (1/4 oz) dried Chinese mushrooms
2 tablespoons light soy sauce
2 tablespoons rice wine
1/2 teaspoon sesame oil
1 tablespoon thinly sliced fresh ginger
4 chicken breast fillets (about 200 g/
    61/2 oz each), trimmed
450 g (141/2 oz) bok choy, ends removed,
    cut lengthways into quarters
125 ml (1/2 cup) chicken stock
1 tablespoon cornflour

STEAMED CHICKEN
with Asian greens

This light, low-fat chicken dish provides good-quality protein, potassium and niacin.

1 Soak the dried mushrooms in 60 ml (1/4 cup) boiling water for 20 minutes. Drain and reserve the liquid. Discard the stalks and thinly slice the caps.

2 Combine the soy sauce, wine, sesame oil and ginger in a non-metallic dish. Add the chicken to the marinade and turn to coat. Cover and marinate for 1 hour.

3 Line a bamboo steamer with baking paper. Place the chicken on top, reserving the marinade. Bring water to the boil in a wok, then place the steamer in the wok. Cover and steam for 6 minutes, then turn the chicken over and steam for a further 6 minutes. Place the bok choy on top of the chicken and steam for 2–3 minutes.

4 Meanwhile, place the reserved marinade, mushrooms and liquid in a small saucepan and bring to the boil. Add enough stock to the cornflour to make a smooth paste. Add the cornflour paste and remaining stock, and stir for 2 minutes over medium heat, or until the sauce thickens.

5 Place some bok choy and a chicken fillet on each plate, then pour on some sauce. Serve with rice.

NUTRITION PER SERVE

- Protein 45.5 g;
- Fat 5.5 g;
- Carbohydrate 4.5 g;
- Dietary Fibre 2 g;
- Cholesterol 95 mg;
- 1085 kJ (260 Cal)

Serves 4

Preparation time: 20 minutes

Cooking time: 15 minutes

Easy

400 g (13 oz) lean pork leg steaks
1 tablespoon canned salted
    black beans, rinsed
500 g (1 lb) baby bok choy
2 teaspoons sesame oil
2 onions, thinly sliced
2 cloves garlic, finely chopped
2–3 teaspoons chopped fresh ginger
1 red pepper (capsicum), cut into strips
80 g (½ cup) water chestnuts,
    thinly sliced
2 tablespoons oyster sauce
1 tablespoon soy sauce
2 teaspoons fish sauce

PORK AND BOK CHOY STIR-FRY

NUTRITION PER SERVE

- Protein 30 g;
- Fat 3 g;
- Carbohydrate 20 g;
- Dietary Fibre 3.5 g;
- Cholesterol 55 mg;
- 910 kJ (215 Cal)

This dish is bursting with potassium, vitamin C and niacin, and provides good amounts of thiamin, iron and folate.

1 Slice the pork steaks into strips, cutting across the grain. Roughly chop the beans. Cut the ends off the bok choy, separate the leaves and shred.

2 Heat half the sesame oil in a large non-stick frying pan or wok. Cook the onion, garlic and ginger over high heat for 3–4 minutes, add the

pepper (capsicum), and cook for 2–3 minutes. Remove from the pan. Heat the remaining sesame oil and stir-fry the pork in batches over high heat.

3 Return the pork to the pan along with the onion mixture, black beans, shredded bok choy, water chestnuts and oyster, soy and fish sauces. Toss

quickly to combine the ingredients, lower the heat, cover and steam for 3–4 minutes, or until the bok choy is just wilted. Serve immediately.

Serves 4–6

Preparation time:
35 minutes + 20 minutes soaking

Cooking time: 15 minutes

Medium

4 dried Chinese mushrooms
oil, for deep-frying
100 g (3½ oz) dried rice vermicelli
100 g (3½ oz) fried tofu, cut into
  matchsticks
4 cloves garlic, crushed
1 onion, chopped
200 g (6½ oz) lean pork fillet,
  thinly sliced
1 chicken breast fillet, thinly sliced
8 green beans, sliced on the diagonal
6 spring onions, thinly sliced on the diagonal
8 raw prawns (shrimp), peeled, deveined
30 g (1 oz) bean sprouts
fresh coriander (cilantro) leaves, to garnish

SAUCE
1 tablespoon soy sauce
60 ml (¼ cup) white vinegar
60 g (¼ cup) sugar
60 ml (¼ cup) fish sauce
1 tablespoon chilli sauce

NUTRITION PER SERVE (6)

- Protein 25 g;
- Fat 10 g;
- Carbohydrate 17 g;
- Dietary Fibre 2.5 g;
- Cholesterol 72 mg;
- 1055 kJ (255 Cal)

MEE GROB

This noodle dish is a delicious combination of nutritious foods,
providing good amounts of niacin, potassium and protein.

1 Cover the mushrooms with hot
   water and soak for 20 minutes.
   Drain, discard the stems and
   thinly slice.

2 Fill a wok one-third full of oil and
   heat to 180°C (350°F), or until a
   cube of bread dropped into the oil
   browns in 15 seconds. Cook the
   vermicelli in batches for 20 seconds,
   or until puffed and crispy. Drain
   and cool.

3 Add the tofu to the wok in batches
   and cook for 1 minute, or until
   crisp. Drain. Carefully ladle out
   all but 2 tablespoons of the oil.

4 Reheat the wok until very hot. Stir-
   fry the garlic and onion for 1 minute.
   Add the pork and stir-fry for
   3 minutes. Add the chicken, beans,
   mushrooms and half the spring
   onion, and stir-fry for 2 minutes, or
   until the chicken has almost cooked
   through. Add the prawns (shrimp)
   and stir-fry for 2 minutes, or until
   just tender.

5 Combine the sauce ingredients, add to
   the wok and stir-fry for 2 minutes, or
   until the meat and prawns are tender.

6 Remove from the heat and stir in
   the bean sprouts, tofu and noodles.
   Garnish with the coriander (cilantro)
   and the remaining spring onion.

Serves 4

Preparation time: 10 minutes

Cooking time: 10 minutes

Easy

1.6 kg (3 lb) Chinese broccoli, cut into
    5 cm (2 in) lengths
1 tablespoon peanut oil
2 cm (¾ in) piece fresh ginger, julienned
2 cloves garlic, crushed
500 g (1 lb) Chinese barbecue pork,
    thinly sliced
60 ml (¼ cup) chicken or vegetable stock
60 ml (¼ cup) oyster sauce
1 tablespoon kecap manis

NUTRITION PER SERVE

- Protein 30 g;
- Fat 7 g;
- Carbohydrate 4.5 g;
- Dietary Fibre 6 g;
- Cholesterol 60 mg;
- 885 kJ (210 Cal)

BARBECUE PORK
with Asian greens

Very simple, but highly nutritious, this dish is loaded with vitamin C, folate,
niacin, potassium, iron and zinc—even before you add rice or noodles.

1   Place the broccoli in a steamer over a saucepan or wok of
    simmering water and cook for 5 minutes, or until just
    tender but still crisp.

2   Heat a wok until very hot, add the oil and swirl to coat.
    Add the ginger and garlic, and stir-fry for 30 seconds, or

until fragrant. Add the broccoli and pork, and toss
to coat.

3   Pour in the combined stock, oyster sauce and kecap
    manis, and stir-fry until heated through. Serve with rice
    or noodles.

Serves 4–6

Preparation time: 20 minutes

Cooking time: 15 minutes

Easy

60 ml (¼ cup) peanut oil
800 g (1 lb 8 oz) aubergine (eggplant), cut
    into 2 cm (¾ in) cubes
4 spring onions, chopped
3 cloves garlic, crushed
1 tablespoon finely chopped fresh ginger
1 tablespoon hot bean paste
125 ml (½ cup) vegetable stock
60 ml (¼ cup) Chinese rice wine
2 tablespoons rice vinegar
1 tablespoon tomato paste
2 teaspoons soft brown sugar
2 tablespoons soy sauce
1 teaspoon cornflour
2 tablespoons shredded fresh basil

AUBERGINE with hot bean sauce

NUTRITION PER SERVE (6)

- Protein 2 g;
- Fat 10 g;
- Carbohydrate 5.5 g;
- Dietary Fibre 3.5 g;
- Cholesterol 0 mg;
- 550 kJ (130 Cal)

The eggplant in this spicy vegetarian dish provides a number
of protective compounds.

1   Heat a wok until very hot, add
    1 tablespoon of the oil and swirl
    to coat. Stir-fry the aubergine
    (eggplant) in batches for 3–4 minutes,
    or until browned. Remove.

2   Reheat the wok, add the remaining
    oil and swirl to coat. Stir-fry the
    spring onion, garlic, ginger and bean
    paste for 30 seconds. Add the stock,
    rice wine, rice vinegar, tomato paste,
    sugar and soy sauce, and stir-fry
    for 1 minute.

3   Blend the cornflour with 1 table-
    spoon water, add to the wok and
    bring to the boil. Return the
    eggplant to the wok and stir-fry
    for 2–3 minutes, or until cooked
    through. Sprinkle with basil.

Serves 4

Preparation time: 30 minutes

Cooking time: 15 minutes

Easy

2 tablespoons peanut oil
350 g (11½ oz) beef fillet, thinly sliced
1 large onion, cut into thin wedges
1 large carrot, thinly sliced on the diagonal
1 red pepper (capsicum), cut into thin strips
100 g (3½ oz) snow peas (mange tout), halved diagonally
150 g (5½ oz) baby corn, halved diagonally
200 g (6½ oz) can straw mushrooms, drained
2 tablespoons oyster sauce
1 clove garlic, crushed
1 teaspoon grated fresh ginger
2 tablespoons light soy sauce
2 tablespoons medium sherry
1 tablespoon honey
1 teaspoon sesame oil
2 teaspoons cornflour

BEEF AND VEGETABLE STIR-FRY

This beef stir-fry features an array of different coloured vegetables and healthy elements, including vitamin C, beta-carotene, fibre, phytochemicals, iron and zinc.

NUTRITION PER SERVE

- Protein 25 g;
- Fat 16 g;
- Carbohydrate 24 g;
- Dietary Fibre 5 g;
- Cholesterol 59 mg;
- 1445 kJ (345 Cal)

1 Heat a wok over high heat, add 1 tablespoon of the peanut oil and swirl it around to coat the side of the wok. Cook the meat in batches for 2–3 minutes, or until nicely browned. Remove the meat from the wok and keep warm.

2 Heat the remaining peanut oil in the wok, add the onion, carrot and pepper (capsicum), and cook, stirring, for 2–3 minutes, or until the vegetables are just tender. Add the snow peas (mange tout), corn and straw mushrooms, cook for a further minute, then return all the meat to the wok.

3 Combine the oyster sauce with the garlic, ginger, soy sauce, sherry, honey, sesame oil and 1 tablespoon water in a small bowl, then add the mixture to the wok. Mix the cornflour with 1 tablespoon of water, add to the wok and cook for 1 minute, or until the sauce thickens. Season with salt and ground black pepper. Serve immediately with rice or thin egg noodles.

Serves 4–6

Preparation time:
20 minutes + 30 minutes soaking
+ 30 minutes marinating

Cooking time: 10 minutes

Easy

400 g (13 oz) dried rice vermicelli
2 cloves garlic, crushed
2 teaspoons grated fresh ginger
60 ml (¼ cup) oyster sauce
¼ cup (60 ml) soy sauce
250 g (8 oz) chicken breast fillet,
    thinly sliced
2 tablespoons oil
2 celery sticks, julienned
1 large carrot, julienned
3 spring onions, diagonally sliced
1½ tablespoons Asian curry powder
½ teaspoon sesame oil
65 g (2 oz) bean sprouts

NUTRITION PER SERVE (6)

- Protein 14.5 g;
- Fat 9.5 g;
- Carbohydrate 47.5 g;
- Dietary Fibre 2.5 g;
- Cholesterol 28.5 mg;
- 1405 kJ (335 Cal)

SINGAPORE NOODLES

This popular dish is tasty as well as being healthy. It contains good amounts of monounsaturated fat, protein, niacin, potassium and phosphorus.

1 Cover the vermicelli with cold water and leave for 30 minutes, or until soft. Drain.

2 Place the garlic, ginger, 1 tablespoon oyster sauce and 2 teaspoons soy sauce in a bowl and mix well. Add the chicken, toss to coat and marinate for 30 minutes.

3 Heat a wok until very hot, add the oil and swirl to coat. Stir-fry the chicken until browned. Add the celery, carrot and half the spring onion, and stir-fry for 2–3 minutes, or until slightly softened. Add the curry powder and stir-fry for 2 minutes, or until aromatic.

4 Add the noodles and mix well to coat and heat through. Stir in the remaining oyster sauce, soy sauce, spring onion, sesame oil and bean sprouts. Serve hot.

Serves 4

Preparation time: 30 minutes

Cooking time: 10 minutes

Easy

1 tablespoon peanut oil
2 cloves garlic, crushed
1 tablespoon finely grated fresh ginger
2 tablespoons finely chopped lemon grass
8 spring onions, cut into 4 cm (1½ in)
   pieces
1 kg (2 lb) raw prawns (shrimp), peeled,
   deveined, tails intact
2 tablespoons lime juice
1 tablespoon soft brown sugar
2 teaspoons fish sauce
60 ml (¼ cup) chicken stock
1 teaspoon cornflour
500 g (1 lb) baby bok choy, halved
   lengthways
15 g (¼ cup) chopped fresh mint

LEMON GRASS PRAWNS

This quick-cooking, aromatic prawn dish gives you valuable selenium and iodine, with good amounts of vitamin C, folate, niacin and potassium.

1 Heat a wok until very hot, add the oil and swirl to coat. Add the garlic, ginger, lemon grass and spring onion, and stir-fry for 1 minute, or until fragrant. Add the prawns (shrimp) and stir-fry for 2 minutes.

2 Place the lime juice, sugar, fish sauce, chicken stock and cornflour

in a small bowl. Mix well, then add to the wok and stir until the sauce boils and thickens. Cook for a further 1–2 minutes, or until the prawns are pink and just tender.

3 Add the bok choy and stir-fry for 1 minute, or until wilted. Stir in the mint and serve.

NUTRITION PER SERVE

- Protein 60 g;
- Fat 8.5 g;
- Carbohydrate 8 g;
- Dietary Fibre 1.6 g;
- Cholesterol 373 mg;
- 1435 kJ (340 Cal)

STEWS & CURRIES

STEWS & CURRIES

Nothing is more welcoming on a cold winter's night than a steaming stew or spicy curry, and it's not difficult to transform your old favourites into healthy meals with some simple substitutions.

STEWS

A stew is a meal that is simmered on the stove top in an enclosed dish, unlike a casserole, which is cooked in the oven. It is cooked with very little fat, in a liquid usually consisting of a stock base seasoned with aromatics, and is cooked until the ingredients are tender. It is best to use tougher cuts of meat for stews because the long, slow cooking process will break down the connective tissue of these cuts, and develop a deep, succulent flavour.

A stew can be mainly meat based; it may be a combination of meat, poultry, seafood, and vegetables; or perhaps vegetables with spices and legumes. It may simply have a stock base, or include wine (red or white), tomatoes or cream.

One of the most important steps to creating a full-flavoured stew is the initial browning of the ingredients. It is at this stage that you may need to use fat to caramelise the ingredients. This, however, can be kept to a minimum if you use a non-stick frying pan, sprayed with a little oil. Make sure the pan is very hot before you add the ingredients to brown so that they will sear, and develop colour without cooking in their

own juices. Once the ingredients are browned, the liquid is added and the dish is covered, the stew simply simmers gently until dinner time. It may be necessary to skim the surface of the stew as it cooks to remove any fat that rises to the surface during cooking.

TIPS FOR HEALTHY STEWS
- Add some soaked dried beans or legumes to a vegetable stew to add fibre, minerals and complete protein.
- When simmering your stew, be sure to have the heat as low as possible, so that the bubbles are gentle and barely break the surface. This will

ensure that the stew cooks without any of the ingredients breaking up.
- For extra flavour, add finely chopped fresh herbs at the very end of cooking. Either stir them through before serving, or scatter them over the dish. This way, they will retain their colour and fresh flavour.
- If your stew still has a lot of liquid towards the end of cooking, instead of thickening the sauce, add some uncooked pasta 10 minutes before the end of the cooking time, or rice 20 minutes before the end. The pasta or rice will absorb the delicious flavours of the stew and become a one-pot meal.
- If the stew needs thickening, dissolve 1 teaspoon of cornflour in 1 tablespoon of cold water. Add a little at a time to the hot stew, stirring well, until the stew begins to thicken.
- The flavours of a stew will develop if it is allowed to sit overnight. Crockpots are good for this.

STEW ACCOMPANIMENTS
- Serve rich red wine beef stews with garlic mashed potato or soft polenta.
- Couscous is traditionally served with North African-style tagines and stews.

- Serve Asian-flavoured stews with steamed jasmine or basmati rice.
- Risotto is delicious with osso bucco and rich, meaty stews.
- Try short pasta such as penne or maccheroni for added carbohydrate.
- Serve meaty stews with a green salad.

CURRIES

The main distinction between a curry and a stew is in the use of curry paste or spices that are used to give curries their distinctive flavour. Curries can be either wet or quite dry in texture.

Curries may be made from virtually any kind of meat, poultry, seafood or vegetable. They are usually Indian or Southeast Asian in origin, and the spices and heat will vary according to the region they are from.

Indian curries generally use a blend of dry spices. Traditionally, the whole spices are dry-roasted to enhance the flavour, and then ground to a powder. There are many spice blends available in supermarkets that are simple to use and make a fragrant and authentically flavoured curry.

The spices that are used in Indian spice blends are chilli powder, cumin, cardamom, cinnamon, mustard seeds, turmeric, fenugreek, coriander seeds, curry leaves, cloves and black pepper.

Curries that are Southeast Asian in origin use a curry paste as a base, and may include red or green chillies, garlic, ginger, coriander (cilantro) root, shrimp paste, lemon grass, galangal, kaffir lime leaves, tamarind, palm sugar and basil.

TIPS FOR HEALTHY CURRIES

- Use a heavy-based non-stick deep frying pan or saucepan. When you are browning the meat, use a light spray of oil in the pan. Add the dry spice mix to the meat so that any fat in the meat will help to sauté the spices, reducing the need to add any fat.
- Use stock or tomatoes as the liquid base for the curry instead of coconut milk or cream. For a little creaminess, stir through some low-fat yoghurt just before serving. Alternatively, use low-fat evaporated milk in place of coconut milk.
- Skim off any fat that rises to the surface during cooking.
- If you use a curry paste, don't add any oil for frying the ingredients, as the paste itself contains enough oil.

Serves 4

Preparation time: 25 minutes

Cooking time: 40 minutes

Easy

500 g (1 lb) chicken breast fillets
plain flour, for dusting
2 teaspoons olive oil
2 onions, thinly sliced
2 cloves garlic, finely chopped
2 anchovy fillets, chopped
440 g (14½ oz) can chopped tomatoes
125 ml (½ cup) dry white wine
60 g (¼ cup) tomato paste
1 teaspoon soft brown sugar
6 Kalamata olives, pitted and chopped
chopped fresh parsley, to garnish

NUTRITION PER SERVE

- Protein 31 g;
- Fat 5.5 g;
- Carbohydrate 3 g;
- Dietary Fibre 3 g;
- Cholesterol 64 mg;
- 1000 kJ (240 Cal)

CHICKEN CACCIATORE

This popular Italian dish provides protein, monounsaturated fat, potassium, niacin mixed with vitamin C, and antioxidants.

1 Trim the fat from the chicken and lightly dust the chicken in plain flour. Heat the oil in a large, heavy-based non-stick frying pan and cook the chicken over high heat for 10 minutes, turning until golden and almost cooked. (If the chicken begins to stick, sprinkle with water and reduce the heat.) Remove, cover and set aside.

2 Add the onion to the pan with the garlic, anchovies and 1 tablespoon of water. Cover and cook for 5 minutes, stirring. Add the tomato, wine, tomato paste, sugar and 200 ml (¾ cup) water. Bring to the boil, then reduce the heat and simmer for 20 minutes. Season with salt and pepper.

3 Return the chicken and juices to the pan. Add the olives and simmer for 5 minutes, or until the chicken is heated through. Garnish with parsley. Delicious with fusilli or other pasta.

Serves 6

Preparation time: 30 minutes

Cooking time: 45 minutes

Easy

2 teaspoons olive oil
1 onion, chopped
2 cloves garlic, crushed
2 teaspoons ground cumin
2 teaspoons ground coriander (cilantro)
3 teaspoons Madras curry powder
500 g (1 lb) potatoes, cut into bite-sized
    pieces
500 g (1 lb) pumpkin, cut into bite-sized
    pieces
2 large courgettes (zucchini), thickly sliced
2 large carrots, thickly sliced
400 g (13 oz) can chopped tomatoes
250 ml (1 cup) vegetable stock
100 g (3½ oz) broccoli florets
150 g (5 oz) green beans, cut into
    short lengths
15 g (¼ cup) chopped fresh
    coriander (cilantro)
250 g (1 cup) low-fat natural yoghurt

VEGETABLE CURRY

NUTRITION PER SERVE

- Protein 8.5 g;
- Fat 4 g;
- Carbohydrate 25 g;
- Dietary Fibre 6 g;
- Cholesterol 7 mg;
- 715 kJ (170 Cal)

This is a nutritious vegetarian meal that is low in fat, but loaded with protective plant compounds, fibre, vitamin A, vitamin C and potassium. Serve the curry with rice and extra yoghurt for a complete protein meal.

1 Heat the oil in a large deep pan, add the onion and garlic, and cook until softened. Add the ground cumin, coriander (cilantro) and curry powder, and cook for 1–2 minutes, or until fragrant. Add the potato, pumpkin, zucchini and carrot, and toss to coat in the spices.

2 Stir in the tomato and stock, bring to the boil, then reduce the heat and simmer, covered, for 30 minutes, or until the vegetables are tender, stirring frequently. Add the broccoli florets and chopped beans, and simmer, uncovered, for 5 minutes, or until all the vegetables are tender. Stir in the chopped coriander and serve with yoghurt. Can be served with steamed rice.

Serves 4

Preparation time: 25 minutes

Cooking time: 35 minutes

Medium

500 g (1 lb) minced lean lamb
1 onion, finely chopped
1 clove garlic, finely chopped
1 teaspoon grated fresh ginger
1 small red chilli, finely chopped
1 teaspoon garam masala
1 teaspoon ground coriander (cilantro)
25 g (¼ cup) ground almonds
2 tablespoons chopped fresh
    coriander (cilantro) leaves

SAUCE
1 tablespoon oil
1 onion, finely chopped
3 tablespoons Korma curry paste
400 g (13 oz) can chopped tomatoes
125 g (½ cup) low-fat plain yoghurt
1 teaspoon lemon juice

NUTRITION PER SERVE

- Protein 32.5 g;
- Fat 25.5 g;
- Carbohydrate 10.5 g;
- Dietary Fibre 5.5 g;
- Cholesterol 88 mg;
- 1675 kJ (400 Cal)

LAMB KOFTA CURRY

Although higher in fat than other recipes, most of the fat in this curry is monounsaturated. The lamb provides top-quality protein.

1 Combine the lamb, onion, garlic, ginger, chilli, garam masala, ground coriander (cilantro) , ground almonds and 1 teaspoon salt in a bowl. Shape into walnut-sized balls with your hands.

2 Heat a large non-stick frying pan and cook the koftas in batches until brown on both sides—they don't have to be cooked all the way through.

3 Meanwhile, to make the sauce, heat the oil in a saucepan over low heat. Add the onion and cook for 6–8 minutes, or until soft and golden. Add the curry paste and cook until fragrant. Add the chopped tomatoes and simmer for 5 minutes. Stir in the yoghurt (1 tablespoon at a time) and the lemon juice until combined.

4 Place the lamb koftas in the tomato sauce. Cook, covered, over low heat for 20 minutes. Serve over steamed rice and garnish with the chopped coriander (cilantro).

Serves 6

Preparation time: 25 minutes

Cooking time: 50 minutes

Easy

¼ teaspoon saffron threads
100 ml (½ cup) olive oil
2 onions, thinly sliced
3 cloves garlic, crushed
2 thin carrots, cut into 5 mm (⅙ in) slices
1 cinnamon stick
2 teaspoons ground cumin
1 teaspoon ground ginger
½ teaspoon ground turmeric
½ teaspoon cayenne pepper
300 g (10 oz) pumpkin, cut into 2 cm (¾ in) cubes
4 ripe tomatoes, peeled, seeded and quartered
400 g (13 oz) can chickpeas, rinsed and drained
1 litre (4 cups) vegetable stock
1 courgette (zucchini), halved lengthways and sliced
55 g (⅓ cup) raisins
50 g (1 cup) chopped fresh coriander (cilantro) leaves
500 g (1 lb) instant couscous
1 tablespoon olive oil
2 teaspoons low-fat margarine
2 tablespoons flaked almonds, toasted

VEGETABLE TAGINE

A high-carbohydrate vegetarian recipe, this tagine provides good quantities of potassium and fibre.

1 Place the saffron threads in a frying pan over low heat. Dry-fry for 1 minute, or until darkened. Remove from the heat.

2 Heat 80 ml (⅓ cup) of the oil in a large flameproof casserole. Add the onion, garlic, carrot, cinnamon, cumin, ginger, turmeric, cayenne and saffron. Cook over medium–low heat, stirring often, for 10 minutes. Add the pumpkin, tomato and chickpeas, and stir to coat. Add half the stock, bring to the boil, then reduce the heat and simmer, covered, for 10 minutes. Stir in the courgette (zucchini), raisins and half the coriander. Cover and simmer for 20 minutes.

3 Bring the remaining stock to the boil in a large saucepan. Place the couscous in a heatproof bowl and add the remaining oil and hot stock. Cover and leave for 5 minutes, then fluff the grains with a fork. Stir in the margarine and season.

4 Spoon the couscous onto a large serving platter. Spoon the vegetables and sauce on top and sprinkle with the almonds and the remaining coriander. Serve at once.

NUTRITION PER SERVE

- Protein 19.5 g;
- Fat 20 g;
- Carbohydrate 86.5 g;
- Dietary Fibre 7 g;
- Cholesterol 0 mg;
- 2525 kJ (605 Cal)

Serves 4–6

Preparation time: 10 minutes

Cooking time: 2 hours

Easy

1 kg (2 lb) topside or round steak
plain flour, seasoned with salt and pepper
3 rashers bacon, rind removed
oil, for cooking
12 pickling onions
250 ml (1 cup) red wine
500 ml (2 cups) beef stock
1 teaspoon dried thyme
200 g (7 oz) button mushrooms
2 bay leaves

BEEF BOURGUIGNON

This nourishing and comforting meal is perfect for cold winter nights. It is an excellent source of protein, iron, zinc and niacin.

1 Trim the steak of fat and sinew, and cut it into 2 cm (3/4 in) cubes. Lightly toss the beef in the seasoned flour, shaking off the excess.

2 Cut the bacon into 2 cm (3/4 in) squares. Heat some oil in a large pan and quickly cook the bacon over medium heat. Remove the bacon from the pan, then add the meat and brown well in batches.

Remove and set aside. Add the onions to the pan and cook until golden.

3 Return the bacon and meat to the pan with the remaining ingredients. Bring to the boil, then reduce the heat and simmer, covered, for 1½ hours, or until the meat is very tender, stirring occasionally. Remove the bay leaves to serve. Serve with mashed potato and steamed green beans.

NUTRITION PER SERVE (6)

- Protein 40 g;
- Fat 7 g;
- Carbohydrate 5 g;
- Dietary Fibre 1 g;
- Cholesterol 90 mg;
- 1150 kJ (275 Cal)

Serves 4–6

Preparation time: 15 minutes

Cooking time: 35 minutes

Easy

200 g (6½ oz) red lentils
4 cm (1½ in) piece fresh ginger, cut
    into 3 slices
½ teaspoon ground turmeric
1 tablespoon ghee or oil
2 cloves garlic, crushed
1 onion, finely chopped
½ teaspoon yellow mustard seeds
pinch of asafoetida, optional
1 teaspoon cumin seeds
1 teaspoon ground coriander (cilantro)
2 green chillies, halved lengthways
2 tablespoons lemon juice
1 tablespoon chopped fresh coriander
    (cilantro) leaves

DHAL

This well-known vegetarian dish is based on highly nutritious lentils, combining them with aromatic herbs and spices for a filling meal that provides protein, slow-release starch, fibre, flavonoids and iron. Dhal is a great choice for people with diabetes or high blood cholesterol.

1 Place the lentils and 750 ml (3 cups) water in a saucepan, and bring to the boil. Reduce the heat, add the ginger and turmeric, and simmer, covered, for 20 minutes, or until the lentils are tender. Stir occasionally to prevent the lentils sticking to the pan. Remove the ginger and stir in ½ teaspoon salt.

2 Heat the ghee in a frying pan, add the garlic, onion and mustard seeds, and cook over medium heat for 5 minutes, or until the onion is golden. Add the asafoetida, cumin seeds, ground coriander (cilantro) and chilli, and cook for 2 minutes.

3 Add the onion mixture to the lentils and stir gently to combine. Add 125 ml (½ cup) water, reduce the heat to low and cook for 5 minutes. Stir in the lemon juice and season with salt and pepper. Sprinkle with the coriander.

NUTRITION PER SERVE (6)

- Protein 8.5 g;
- Fat 3.5 g;
- Carbohydrate 13 g;
- Dietary Fibre 5 g;
- Cholesterol 8 mg;
- 505 kJ (120 Cal)

Serves 6–8

Preparation time:
40 minutes + 1 hour soaking

Cooking time: 1 hour 10 minutes

Easy

18 dried apricots
1 tablespoon ghee
2 x 1.5 kg (3 lb) chickens, jointed
3 onions, thinly sliced
1 teaspoon grated fresh ginger
3 cloves garlic, crushed
3 large green chillies, seeded and finely
   chopped
1 teaspoon cumin seeds
1 teaspoon chilli powder
½ teaspoon ground turmeric
4 cardamom pods, bruised
4 large tomatoes, peeled and cut into
   eighths

CHICKEN AND APRICOT CURRY

The apricots add fibre, beta-carotene and a sweet taste to enrich the flavour
of this aromatic curry.

1 Soak the dried apricots in 250 ml
(1 cup) hot water for 1 hour.

2 Melt the ghee in a large saucepan,
add the chicken in batches and
cook over high heat for 5–6 minutes,
or until browned. Remove from
the pan. Add the onion and cook,
stirring often, for 10 minutes,
or until the onion is soft and
golden brown.

3 Add the ginger, garlic and green
chilli, and cook, stirring, for
2 minutes. Stir in the cumin seeds,
chilli powder and ground turmeric,
and cook for a further 1 minute.

4 Return the chicken to the pan, add
the cardamom, tomato and apricots,
with any remaining liquid, and mix
well. Simmer, covered, for 35 minutes,
or until the chicken is tender.

5 Remove the chicken, cover and keep
warm. Bring the liquid to the boil
and boil rapidly, uncovered, for
5 minutes, or until it has thickened
slightly. To serve, spoon the liquid
over the chicken. Serve with steamed
rice mixed with raisins, grated carrot
and toasted flaked almonds.

NUTRITION PER SERVE (8)

• Protein 43 g;
• Fat 19.5 g;
• Carbohydrate 11.5 g;
• Dietary Fibre 3.5 g;
• Cholesterol 197.5 mg;
• 1655 kJ (395 Cal)

Serves 6

Preparation time: 15 minutes

Cooking time: 1 hour 10 minutes

Easy

2 teaspoons olive oil
1 large onion, chopped
1 clove garlic, crushed
1 teaspoon cayenne pepper
2 teaspoons paprika
1 teaspoon dried oregano
2 teaspoons ground cumin
750 g (1 lb 8 oz) extra lean beef mince
375 ml (1½ cups) beef stock
400 g (13 oz) can diced tomatoes
125 g (½ cup) tomato paste
300 g (10½ oz) can kidney beans,
   drained and rinsed
fresh parsley sprigs, to garnish

NUTRITION PER SERVE

- Protein 30 g;
- Fat 11 g;
- Carbohydrate 12 g;
- Dietary Fibre 4.5 g;
- Cholesterol 63.5 mg;
- 1125 kJ (270 Cal)

CHILLI CON CARNE

The kidney beans in this dish add phytochemicals, starch and fibre to a meal rich in protein and iron.

1 Heat the oil in a saucepan over low heat. Add the onion and cook for 4–5 minutes, or until soft. Stir in the garlic, cayenne pepper, paprika, oregano, cumin and ½ teaspoon salt. Increase the heat to medium, add the minced beef and cook for 5–8 minutes, or until just browned.

2 Reduce the heat to low and add the stock, tomato and tomato paste. Cook for 35–45 minutes, stirring frequently.

3 Stir in the kidney beans and simmer for 10 minutes. Serve the chilli con carne on its own in small bowls or over rice. Garnish with a sprig of parsley.

Serves 6

Preparation time: 20 minutes

Cooking time: 45 minutes

Easy

420 g (14 oz) can creamed corn
375 ml (1½ cups) vegetable stock
75 g (½ cup) instant polenta
310 g (10 oz) can corn kernels, drained
40 g (⅓ cup) grated low-fat vintage
   Cheddar
15 g (¼ cup) chopped fresh coriander
   (cilantro) leaves
1 tablespoon olive oil
1 red onion, sliced
2 cloves garlic, crushed
1 teaspoon chilli powder
1 teaspoon paprika
1 tablespoon ground cumin
1 teaspoon ground coriander (cilantro)
400 g (13 oz) can kidney beans,
   rinsed and drained
400 g (13 oz) can borlotti beans,
   rinsed and drained
800 g can tomatoes
2 tablespoons tomato paste

NUTRITION PER SERVE

- Protein 16 g;
- Fat 7 g;
- Carbohydrate 43 g;
- Dietary Fibre 16 g;
- Cholesterol 5 mg;
- 1255 kJ (300 Cal)

CHILLI BEANS with polenta

This vegetarian recipe contains ingredients from four different food groups to provide complete protein. It is also rich in filling fibre and starch, with good amounts of most minerals, niacin, folate and vitamin A.

1 Line a 20 cm (8 in) round cake tin with plastic wrap. Place the creamed corn and stock in a saucepan, and bring to the boil. Stir in the polenta and corn kernels, and cook over medium heat until it comes away from the side of the pan. Stir in the cheese and 1 tablespoon of the coriander, and place the polenta in the tin. Cool, then cut into wedges.

2 Heat the oil in a large saucepan, add the onion, garlic and spices, and cook until soft. Stir in the beans, tomato and tomato paste. Simmer for 20 minutes. Stir in the remaining coriander leaves. Serve with the polenta wedges.

Serves 4

Preparation time: 20 minutes

Cooking time: 25 minutes

Easy

500 g (1 lb) rump steak
cooking oil spray
1 onion, sliced
1/4 teaspoon paprika
250 g (8 oz) button mushrooms, halved
2 tablespoons tomato paste
125 ml (1/2 cup) beef stock
125 ml (1/2 cup) low-fat light
    evaporated milk
3 teaspoons cornflour
chopped fresh parsley, for serving

NUTRITION PER SERVE

- Protein 35 g;
- Fat 4 g;
- Carbohydrate 8 g;
- Dietary Fibre 2.5 g;
- Cholesterol 85 mg;
- 900 kJ (215 Cal)

BEEF STROGANOFF

A reduced-fat version of the traditional favourite, this dish has less fat but all the flavour. It is an excellent source of protein, potassium, iron and zinc.

1   Remove any excess fat from the steak and slice into thin strips. Cook in batches in a large, lightly greased non-stick frying pan over high heat, until just cooked. Remove from the pan.

2   Lightly spray the pan and cook the onion, paprika and mushrooms over medium heat until the onion has softened. Add the meat, tomato paste, stock and 125 ml (1/2 cup) water. Bring to the boil, then reduce the heat and simmer for 10 minutes.

3   In a small bowl, mix the evaporated milk with the cornflour. Add to the pan and stir until the sauce boils and thickens. Season well and sprinkle with parsley. Delicious over pasta.

Serves 6

Preparation time: 30 minutes

Cooking time: 1 hour

Easy

2 stems lemon grass, white part only,
    sliced
1 red onion, chopped
1 clove garlic
1 teaspoon grated fresh ginger
2 large dried red chillies
1 teaspoon fenugreek seeds, roasted
    and ground
1 teaspoon yellow mustard seeds,
    roasted and ground
2 teaspoons paprika
2 tablespoons Worcestershire sauce
750 g (1 lb 8 oz) lean boneless
    shoulder pork, cut into
    2.5 cm (1 in) cubes
2 tablespoons fish sauce
6 new potatoes, peeled and sliced
2 small red onions, diced
2 tablespoons oil
2 tablespoons mango chutney

BURMESE PORK CURRY

NUTRITION PER SERVE

• Protein 28 g;
• Fat 11.5 g;
• Carbohydrate 14.5 g;
• Dietary Fibre 2 g;
• Cholesterol 74 mg;
• 1160 kJ (275 Cal)

This dish is a good source of iron, zinc and B vitamins, particularly niacin.
The spices add flavour and some minerals, but few calories.

1 Place the lemon grass, onion, garlic,
ginger, chillies, fenugreek seeds,
yellow mustard seeds, paprika
and Worcestershire sauce in a food
processor or blender, and process
to a thick paste.

2 Place the pork in a bowl, sprinkle
with the fish sauce and ¼ teaspoon
ground black pepper, and toss
to coat.

3 Place the potato and onion in
another bowl, add 70 g (¼ cup)
of the paste and toss to coat. Add
the remaining paste to the pork
mixture and mix well.

4 Heat 1 tablespoon oil in a saucepan
or wok over medium heat. Add the
pork mixture and cook in batches,
stirring, for 8 minutes, or until the
meat begins to brown. Add more oil
as necessary. Remove from the pan.
Add the potato and onion, and
cook, stirring, for 5 minutes, or
until soft and starting to brown.

5 Return the meat to the saucepan
and add 750 ml (3 cups) water,
250 ml (1 cup) at a time, stirring
after each addition. Stir in the mango
chutney, then reduce the heat and
simmer for 30 minutes, or until the
meat and potatoes are tender.

Serves 6

Preparation time: 20 minutes

Cooking time: 1 hour 45 minutes

Easy

1 tablespoon vegetable oil
2 onions, finely chopped
3 cloves garlic, finely chopped
1 tablespoon grated fresh ginger
4 tablespoons madras curry paste
1 kg (2 lb) lean chuck steak, trimmed and
    cut into 3 cm (1¼ in) cubes
60 g (¼ cup) tomato paste
250 ml (1 cup) beef stock
6 new potatoes, halved
155 g (1 cup) frozen peas

NUTRITION PER SERVE

- Protein 39.5 g;
- Fat 13 g;
- Carbohydrate 15 g;
- Dietary Fibre 5.5 g;
- Cholesterol 112 mg;
- 1410 kJ (335 Cal)

MADRAS BEEF CURRY

This popular Indian curry is rich in protein, zinc, niacin, potassium and phosphorus.

1   Preheat the oven to moderate 180°C (350°F/Gas 4). Heat the oil in a large heavy-based 3 litre (12 cup) flameproof casserole dish. Cook the onion over medium heat for 4–5 minutes. Add the garlic and ginger, and cook, stirring, for a further 5 minutes, or until the onion is lightly golden, taking care not to burn it.

2   Add the curry paste and cook, stirring, for 2 minutes, or until fragrant. Increase the heat to high, add the meat and stir constantly for 2–3 minutes, or until the meat is well coated. Add the tomato paste and stock, and stir well.

3   Bake, covered, for 50 minutes, stirring 2–3 times during cooking, and add a little water if necessary. Reduce the oven to warm 160°C (315°F/Gas 2–3). Add the potato and cook for 30 minutes, then add the peas and cook for another 10 minutes, or until the potato is tender. Serve hot with steamed jasmine rice.

Serves 4–6

Preparation time: 25 minutes

Cooking time: 1 hour 40 minutes

Easy

1 tablespoon or oil
2 onions, chopped
½ cup (125 g) low-fat plain yoghurt
1 teaspoon chilli powder
1 tablespoon ground coriander (cilantro)
2 teaspoons ground cumin
1 teaspoon ground cardamom
½ teaspoon ground cloves
1 teaspoon ground turmeric
3 cloves garlic, crushed
1 tablespoon grated fresh ginger
400 g (13 oz) can chopped tomatoes
1 kg (2 lb) boned leg of lamb,
    trimmed, cubed
30 g (¼ cup) slivered almonds
1 teaspoon garam masala
chopped fresh coriander (cilantro) leaves,
    to garnish

The exotic blend of spices and herbs in this dish adds some minerals and phytochemicals, while the lamb provides protein, niacin, iron and zinc.

NUTRITION PER SERVE (6)

- Protein 58.5 g;
- Fat 22 g;
- Carbohydrate 7 g;
- Dietary Fibre 2.5 g;
- Cholesterol 172.5 mg;
- 1915 kJ (460 Cal)

ROGAN JOSH

1 Heat the oil in a large saucepan, add the onion and cook, stirring, for 5 minutes, or until soft. Stir in the yoghurt, chilli powder, coriander (cilantro), cumin, cardamom, cloves, turmeric, garlic and ginger. Add the tomato and 1 teaspoon salt, and simmer for 5 minutes.

2 Add the lamb and stir until coated. Cover and cook over low heat, stirring occasionally, for 1–1½ hours, or until the lamb is tender. Uncover and simmer until the liquid thickens.

3 Meanwhile, dry-fry the almonds over medium heat for 3–4 minutes, shaking the pan gently, until the nuts are golden brown. Remove from the pan at once.

4 Add the garam masala to the curry and mix through well. Sprinkle the slivered almonds and coriander (cilantro) leaves over the top.

Serves 4–6

Preparation time: 25 minutes

Cooking time: 15 minutes

Easy

50 g (1½ oz) butter
1 onion, finely chopped
1 clove garlic, crushed
1½ tablespoons curry powder
2 tablespoons plain flour
2 cups (500 ml) reduced-fat milk
1 kg (2 lb) raw medium prawns, peeled
  and deveined
1½ tablespoons lemon juice
2 teaspoons sherry, optional
1 tablespoon finely chopped fresh parsley

PRAWN CURRY

This quickly prepared seafood dish provides niacin and small to moderate amounts of most minerals, including selenium and iodine. Serve the curry with rice for extra carbohydrate, fibre and B vitamins.

1 Heat the butter in a large saucepan. Add the onion and garlic, and cook for 5 minutes, or until softened. Add the curry powder and cook for 1 minute, then stir in the flour and cook for a further 1 minute.

2 Remove from the heat and stir in the milk until smooth. Return to the heat and stir constantly until the sauce has thickened. Simmer for 2 minutes and then stir in the prawns. Continue to simmer for 5 minutes, or until the prawns are just cooked.

NUTRITION PER SERVE (6)

- Protein 38 g;
- Fat 12 g;
- Carbohydrate 9 g;
- Dietary Fibre 1.5 g;
- Cholesterol 280 mg;
- 1245 kJ (300 Cal)

3 Stir in the lemon juice, sherry and parsley, and serve immediately with rice.

CASSEROLES & BAKES

CASSEROLES & BAKES

Some of the simplest meals are the ones you pop into the oven and forget about until dinner time.
This chapter contains some healthier versions of traditional favourites.

CASEROLES

A casserole is very similar to a stew, the main difference being that a casserole is cooked in a covered dish in the oven, while a stew is cooked on the stove. Types of casseroles include Asian-style claypot dishes, braised dishes and hotpots. Casseroling can be a healthy method of cooking as the ingredients are slowly cooked in a liquid, which helps retain more vitamins and minerals than frying or boiling.

Casseroles usually contain a number of ingredients, including meat, poultry, seafood, vegetables and herbs, and are a great way to increase the variety of healthy foods you eat. The only fat that is needed in the cooking process is for the initial sautéing and browning.

HEALTHY CASSEROLE TIPS

- Use a casserole dish with a non-stick surface or, if you don't have one of these, first sauté the ingredients to brown them in a heavy-based non-stick frying pan, then transfer them to your casserole dish. Use only a light spray of olive or canola oil when sautéing.
- Make sure the pan is hot before you add the ingredients. This will ensure

that the meat browns quickly and evenly, rather than stewing in its own juices.

- If you are browning vegetables for a casserole and think you may need more oil, add a little water or vegetable stock instead. It will help the vegetables to soften as they cook, without burning.
- When the casserole is ready, remove it from the oven and leave it for 10 minutes; then, using a metal spoon, carefully skim any fat that may have risen to the surface during cooking.
- Add soaked dried legumes such as chickpeas, cannellini beans or lentils

to your casserole for extra fibre and minerals.

- Pot roasting is suitable for slowly cooking large cuts of meat until tender. It is suitable for beef topside or bolar blade. First brown the meat over high heat, then add some stock, cover and cook at a low to moderate heat in the oven. An hour before the meat is ready, add some vegetables to the casserole. The vegetables will complement all the delicious meat flavours, and you will have a simple, aromatic and healthy one-pot meal.
- Casseroles with smaller pieces of meat will usually take between 1 and 2 hours to cook.
- The oven temperature should be low enough for the casserole to cook at a gentle simmer.

CUTS OF MEAT SUITABLE FOR CASSEROLING

- beef round
- beef topside
- beef blade
- beef bolar blade
- beef brisket
- beef skirt steak
- beef chuck
- beef spareribs
- beef silverside

Serves 6

Preparation time: 25 minutes

Cooking time: 1 hour 5 minutes

Easy

250 g (8 oz) orange sweet potato, cut into
  2 cm (¾ in) cubes
2 tablespoons olive oil
3 cloves garlic, unpeeled
250 g (8 oz) English spinach, blanched
  and excess moisture squeezed
  out, roughly chopped
40 g (¼ cup) pine nuts, toasted
125 g (4 oz) low-fat feta, crumbled
3 spring onions, including green part,
  chopped
50 g (1½ oz) black olives, pitted and
  sliced
15 g (¼ cup) chopped fresh basil
1 tablespoon chopped fresh rosemary
8 sheets filo pastry
2 tablespoons sesame seeds

NUTRITION PER SERVE

- Protein 11 g;
- Fat 15.5 g;
- Carbohydrate 19 g;
- Dietary Fibre 3.5 g;
- Cholesterol 12.5 mg;
- 1080 kJ (260 Cal)

SWEET POTATO STRUDEL

The variety of ingredients in this easy dish delivers good amounts
of monounsaturated fat and fibre.

1 Preheat the oven to moderate 180°C (350°F/Gas 4). Place the sweet potato in a roasting tin and brush lightly with oil. Add the garlic and roast for 30 minutes, or until the sweet potato is soft. Cool slightly.

2 Combine the sweet potato, spinach, pine nuts, feta, spring onion, olives, basil and rosemary. Peel the garlic cloves and roughly chop the flesh, then add to the sweet potato mixture, and season.

3 Cover the pastry with a damp tea towel to prevent it drying out. Lay the pastry out in front of you, in a stack, and brush every second layer with the remaining oil. Spread the filling in the centre of the pastry, covering an area 10 x 30 cm (4 x 11⅔ in). Fold in the shorter ends of the pastry. Fold the long side closest to you over the filling, then carefully roll up. Place the strudel on a greased baking tray, seam-side down. Brush with any remaining oil and sprinkle with sesame seeds. Bake for 35 minutes, or until crisp and golden. Serve warm.

Serves 6

Preparation time:
30 minutes + 20 minutes standing

Cooking time: 1 hour 30 minutes

Medium

1 kg (2 lb) aubergines (eggplants)
cooking oil spray
400 g (13 oz) lean lamb mince
2 onions, finely chopped
2 cloves garlic, crushed
400 g (13 oz) can tomatoes
1 tablespoon chopped fresh thyme
1 teaspoon chopped fresh oregano
1 tablespoon tomato paste
80 ml (1/3 cup) dry white wine
1 bay leaf
1 teaspoon sugar

CHEESE SAUCE
315 ml (1¼ cups) skim milk
2 tablespoons plain flour
30 g (¼ cup) grated reduced-fat
   Cheddar
250 g (1 cup) ricotta
pinch of cayenne pepper
¼ teaspoon ground nutmeg

MOUSSAKA

This reduced-fat version of a popular Mediterranean dish contains good amounts of many nutrients, including B vitamins, folate, vitamin A, fibre, potassium, calcium, iron and zinc. Serve the moussaka with crusty grain bread and salad for a complete meal.

NUTRITION PER SERVE

- Protein 25 g;
- Fat 11 g;
- Carbohydrate 15 g;
- Dietary Fibre 5 g;
- Cholesterol 70 mg;
- 1110 kJ (265 Cal)

1   Cut the aubergine (eggplant) into 1 cm (1/3 in) thick slices, place in a colander over a large bowl, layering with a generous sprinkling of salt, and leave to stand for 20 minutes. This is to draw out the bitter juices.

2   Lightly spray a non-stick frying pan with oil and brown the lamb mince, in batches if necessary, over medium-high heat. Remove the meat from the pan.

3   Spray the pan again with oil, add the onion and stir continuously for 2 minutes. Add 1 tablespoon water to the pan to prevent sticking. Add the garlic and cook for about 3 minutes, or until the onion is golden brown.

4   Push the undrained tomatoes through a sieve, then discard the solids.

5   Return the meat to the pan with the onion. Add the herbs, tomato pulp, tomato paste, wine, bay leaf and sugar. Cover and simmer over low heat for 20 minutes. Preheat a grill.

6   Thoroughly rinse and pat dry the aubergine (eggplant), place on a grill tray, spray lightly with oil and grill under a hot grill until golden brown. Turn over, spray lightly with oil and grill until golden brown. Arrange half the eggplant (aubergine) slices over the base of a 1.5 litre (6 cup) baking dish. Top with half the meat mixture and then repeat the layers.

7   Preheat the oven to moderate 180°C (350°F/Gas 4). To make the cheese sauce, blend a little of the milk with the flour to form a paste in a small pan. Gradually blend in the remaining milk, stirring constantly over low heat until the milk starts to simmer and thicken. Remove from the heat and stir in the Cheddar, ricotta, cayenne and nutmeg. Pour the sauce over the moussaka and bake for 35–40 minutes, or until the cheese is golden brown and the moussaka is heated through.

NOTE: The moussaka can be frozen for up to 2 months. Thaw it in the fridge, then reheat it in a moderate oven for 30–45 minutes.

Serves 6

Preparation time:
45 minutes + 25 minutes refrigeration

Cooking time: 2 hours 30 minutes

Easy

1 large potato
400 g (13 oz) pumpkin
200 g (6½ oz) orange sweet potato
2 large parsnips
1 red pepper (capsicum)
2 onions, cut into wedges
6 cloves garlic, halved
2 teaspoons olive oil
155 g (1¼ cups) plain flour
40 g (1 oz) butter
45 g (1½ oz) ricotta
250 ml (1 cup) skim milk
3 eggs, lightly beaten
30 g (¼ cup) grated reduced-fat Cheddar
2 tablespoons chopped fresh basil

NUTRITION PER SERVE

- Protein 14.5 g;
- Fat 11.5 g;
- Carbohydrate 40.5 g;
- Dietary Fibre 5 g;
- Cholesterol 126 mg;
- 1360 kJ (325 Cal)

VEGETABLE QUICHE

This colourful, reduced-fat quiche provides vitamin A, B vitamins, potassium and calcium.

1 Preheat the oven to moderate 180°C (350°F/Gas 4). Lightly spray a 23 cm (9 in) loose-based flan tin with oil. Cut the vegetables into chunks, place in a baking dish with the onion and garlic, and drizzle with the oil. Season and bake for 1 hour, or until tender. Leave to cool.

2 Mix the flour, butter and ricotta in a food processor, then gradually add up to 3 tablespoons of the milk to form a soft dough. Turn out onto a lightly floured surface and gather together into a smooth ball. Cover and refrigerate for 15 minutes.

3 Roll the pastry out on a lightly floured surface, then ease it into the tin. Trim the edge and refrigerate for 10 minutes. Increase the oven to 200°C (400°F/Gas 6). Cover the

pastry with crumpled baking paper and fill with baking beads or rice. Bake for 10 minutes, remove the beads and paper, then bake for 10 minutes.

4 Place the vegetables in the pastry and pour in the combined remaining milk, egg, cheese and basil. Reduce the oven to 180°C (350°F/Gas 4). Bake for 1 hour 10 minutes, or until set. Leave in the tin for 5 minutes.

Serves 6

Preparation time: 20 minutes

Cooking time: 15 minutes

Easy

250 g (8 oz) ricotta
6 small oval pitta breads
125 g (4 oz) sliced smoked salmon
1 small red onion, sliced
1 tablespoon baby capers
small fresh dill sprigs, to garnish
1 lemon, cut into thin wedges, to serve

NUTRITION PER SERVE

- Protein 13 g;
- Fat 6.5 g;
- Carbohydrate 24 g;
- Dietary Fibre 1.5 g;
- Cholesterol 30 mg;
- 875 kJ (110 Cal)

SMOKED SALMON PIZZAS

Topped with cheese and salmon, these reduced-fat pizzas provide calcium, zinc, iodine, some vitamin A and B vitamins.

1 Preheat the oven to moderate 180°C (350°F/Gas 4). Put the ricotta in a bowl, season well with salt and cracked pepper, and stir until smooth. Spread the ricotta over the breads, leaving a border.

2 Top each pizza with some smoked salmon slices, then some onion pieces. Scatter baby capers over the top and bake on a baking tray for 15 minutes, or until the bases are slightly crispy around the edges. Garnish with a few dill sprigs and serve with lemon wedges.

Serves 4

Preparation time: 30 minutes

Cooking time: 1 hour 30 minutes

Easy

1 red pepper (capsicum)
1 aubergine (eggplant)
3 tomatoes, cut into quarters
200 g (6½ oz) Large button mushrooms, halved
1 onion, cut into thin wedges
cooking oil spray
1½ tablespoons tomato paste
125 ml (½ cup) chicken stock
60 ml (¼ cup) white wine
2 lean bacon rashers
4 chicken breast fillets (500 g/1 lb), trimmed
4 small sprigs fresh rosemary

CHICKEN with baked eggplant and tomato

This colourful, hearty meal provides protein, B vitamins and antioxidants.

1 Preheat the oven to moderately hot 200°C (400°F/Gas 6). Cut the pepper (capsicum) and aubergine (eggplant) into bite-sized pieces and combine with the tomato, mushrooms and onion in a baking dish. Spray with oil and bake for 1 hour, or until starting to brown and soften, stirring once.

2 Pour the combined tomato paste, chicken stock and wine into the dish, and bake for 10 minutes, or until thickened.

3 Meanwhile, discard the fat and rind from the bacon and cut in half. Wrap a strip around each chicken breast and secure it underneath with a toothpick. Poke a sprig of fresh rosemary underneath the bacon. Pan-fry in a non-stick frying pan sprayed with oil, over medium heat, until golden on both sides. Cover and cook for 10–15 minutes, or until the chicken is tender and cooked through. Remove the toothpicks. Serve the chicken on the vegetable mixture, surrounded with the sauce.

NUTRITION PER SERVE

- Protein 36 g;
- Fat 10.5 g;
- Carbohydrate 8 g;
- Dietary Fibre 5 g;
- Cholesterol 95 mg;
- 1190 kJ (285 Cal)

Serves 4

Preparation time: 15 minutes

Cooking time: 30 minutes

Easy

2 baby fennel bulbs (about 300 g/
    10½ oz), trimmed and thinly sliced
1 clove garlic, thinly sliced
1 tablespoon chopped fresh dill
60 ml (¼ cup) olive oil
2 tablespoons lemon juice
1 large flathead (about 1.25 kg/2 lb 8 oz),
    gutted and head removed
small fresh dill sprigs, to garnish
small fresh parsley sprigs, to garnish
lemon wedges, to serve

NUTRITION PER SERVE

* Protein 40.5 g;
* Fat 12 g;
* Carbohydrate 3 g;
* Dietary Fibre 2.5 g;
* Cholesterol 107 mg;
* 1190 kJ (285 Cal)

BAKED FLATHEAD

Flathead is relatively low in calories, yet with its high protein content it makes a filling meal. The combination of fish and olive oil provides monounsaturated fat and essential fatty acids.

1 Place the fennel in a bowl with the garlic, dill, oil and lemon juice. Season well with salt and ground black pepper.

2 Preheat the oven to moderate 180°C (350°F/Gas 4). Cut a piece of baking paper 5 cm (2 in) longer than the fish. Cut a large strip of baking paper wide enough to support the main body of the fish and long enough to wrap around it. Place the strip vertically down the centre of a large baking tray, then place the other piece horizontally over the top, forming a cross. Place the fish in the centre of the baking paper and spoon the fennel mixture into its cavity and over the top. Fold the top and bottom ends of paper over the fish, then fold the sides in about 2 cm (¾ in), securing with staples. Fold the side ends over the top of the fish and secure with staples. Bake for 30 minutes, or until the flesh flakes easily when tested with a fork.

3 Place the parcel on a warm serving platter and cut a hole in the top. Fold the edges back to expose the fish. Sprinkle with the sprigs of dill and parsley and serve with lemon wedges.

Serves 4

Preparation time: 30 minutes

Cooking time: 1 hour 30 minutes

Medium

100 g (½ cup) long-grain rice
1 tablespoon olive oil
4 spring onions, chopped
4 cloves garlic, crushed
40 g (¼ cup) pine nuts
50 g (1½ oz) currants
2 tablespoons chopped fresh parsley
2 teaspoons finely grated lemon rind
2 teaspoons lemon juice
1 onion, sliced
1 bird's eye chilli, chopped
2 teaspoons paprika
½ cup (125 ml) white wine
2 x 420 g (14 oz) cans crushed tomatoes
1 fresh bay leaf
7 g (¼ cup) chopped fresh flat-leaf
   parsley
8 small–medium (450 g/1 lb) cleaned
   squid hoods

NUTRITION PER SERVE

- Protein 25 g;
- Fat 12.5 g;
- Carbohydrate 38 g;
- Dietary Fibre 6 g;
- Cholesterol 224 mg;
- 1615 kJ (385 Cal)

STUFFED SQUID

This seafood dish provides unsaturated fat, essential fatty acids and vitamins A, B, C and E.

1 Cook the rice in a large saucepan of boiling water for 12 minutes, stirring occasionally. Drain and cool.

2 Heat 1 teaspoon of the oil in a saucepan. Cook the spring onion and half the garlic over low heat for 1–2 minutes, or until softened. Add the rice, pine nuts, currants, parsley, lemon rind and juice, and season. Remove from the pan and cool.

3 Heat the remaining oil in a heavy-based saucepan. Cook the onion over low heat for 6–8 minutes, or until soft and golden. Add the chilli and remaining garlic, and cook for 1 minute. Add the paprika and cook for 1 minute. Add the wine and cook for 2 minutes, or until reduced by half. Add the tomato and bay leaf, bring to the boil, then reduce the heat and simmer for 30 minutes, stirring occasionally. Stir in the parsley, and season. Discard the bay leaf.

4 Preheat the oven to moderate 180°C (350°F/Gas 4). Spoon the rice into the squid hoods and secure with a toothpick. Place in an ovenproof ceramic dish and pour the sauce on top. Bake for 30 minutes.

Serves 4

Preparation time: 40 minutes

Cooking time: 40 minutes

Easy

cooking oil spray
2 onions, thinly sliced
1 large carrot, finely chopped
2 celery sticks, finely chopped
500 g (1 lb) lean lamb mince
2 tablespoons plain flour
2 tablespoons tomato paste
2 tablespoons Worcestershire sauce
1 beef or chicken stock cube
1.25 kg (2 lb 8 oz) potatoes, chopped
125 ml (½ cup) skim milk
20 g (⅓ cup) finely chopped fresh parsley
paprika, to sprinkle

NUTRITION PER SERVE

- Protein 36.5 g;
- Fat 9.5 g;
- Carbohydrate 54.5 g;
- Dietary Fibre 7.5 g;
- Cholesterol 87.5 mg;
- 1895 kJ (450 Cal)

SHEPHERD'S PIE

This pie is an excellent way to feed children meat and potatoes. It provides plenty of carbohydrate, B vitamins, folate, beta-carotene, potassium, iron and zinc.

1   Lightly spray a large non-stick frying pan with oil and heat over medium heat. Stir the onion, carrot and celery constantly for 5 minutes, or until the vegetables begin to soften. Add 1 tablespoon water to prevent sticking. Remove from the pan and set aside. Spray the pan with a little more oil, add the lamb mince and cook over high heat until well browned.

2   Add the flour and stir for 2–3 minutes. Add the vegetables with the tomato paste, Worcestershire sauce, stock cube and 500 ml (2 cups) water. Slowly bring to the boil. Reduce the heat, cover and simmer for 20 minutes, stirring occasionally.

3   Meanwhile, steam or microwave the potatoes until tender. Drain and mash until smooth. Add the milk, season with salt and black pepper, then beat well.

4   Stir the parsley through the mince and season. Preheat a grill. Pour the mince into a 1.5 litre (6 cup) baking dish. Spoon the potato over the top, spreading evenly with the back of the spoon. Use a fork to roughen up the potato. Sprinkle with paprika and grill until golden, watching carefully because the potato browns quickly.

Serves 4

Preparation time: 50 minutes

Cooking time: 1 hour

Difficult

300 g (10½ oz) chicken breast fillet, trimmed of fat
1 bay leaf
500 ml (2 cups) chicken stock
2 large potatoes, chopped
250 g (8 oz) orange sweet potato, chopped
2 celery sticks, chopped
2 carrots, chopped
1 onion, chopped
1 parsnip, chopped
1 clove garlic, crushed
1 tablespoon cornflour
250 ml (1 cup) skim milk
155 g (1 cup) frozen peas, thawed
1 tablespoon chopped fresh chives
1 tablespoon chopped fresh parsley
185 g (1½ cups) self-raising flour
20 g (¾ oz) butter
80 ml (⅓ cup) milk
1 egg, lightly beaten
½ teaspoon sesame seeds

CHICKEN PIES

With less fat than commercial pies, these are rich in beta-carotene, folate, potassium, phosphorus and protein.

1 Combine the chicken, bay leaf and stock in a large, deep non-stick frying pan and simmer over low heat for 10 minutes, or until the chicken is cooked through. Remove the chicken, set aside and, when cool, cut into small pieces. Add the chopped potato, orange sweet potato, celery and carrot to the pan and simmer, covered, for about 10 minutes, until just tender. Remove the vegetables from the pan with a slotted spoon.

2 Add the onion, parsnip and garlic to the pan and simmer, uncovered, for about 10 minutes, or until very soft. Discard the bay leaf. Purée in the stock mixture in a food processor until smooth.

3 Stir the cornflour into 2 tablespoons of the skim milk until it forms a smooth paste, stir into the puréed mixture with the remaining milk and then return to the pan. Stir over low heat until the mixture boils and thickens. Preheat the oven to moderately hot 200°C (400°F/Gas 6).

4 Combine the puréed mixture with the cooked vegetables, peas, chicken and herbs. Season with salt and pepper. Spoon into four 440 ml (1¾ cup) ovenproof dishes.

5 To make the pastry, sift the flour into a large bowl, rub in the butter with your fingertips, then make a well in the centre. Combine the milk with 80 ml (⅓ cup) water and add enough to the dry ingredients to make a soft dough. Turn out onto a lightly floured surface and knead until just smooth. Cut the dough into four portions and roll each out so that it is l cm larger than the top of the dish. Brush the edge of the dough with some of the egg and fit it over the top of each dish, pressing the edge firmly to seal.

6 Brush the pastry tops lightly with beaten egg and sprinkle with the sesame seeds. Bake for 30 minutes, or until the tops are golden and the filling is heated through.

NUTRITION PER SERVE

- Protein 33 g;
- Fat 12 g;
- Carbohydrate 68.5 g;
- Dietary Fibre 8.5 g;
- Cholesterol 117.5 mg;
- 2170 kJ (520 Cal)

Serves 4

Preparation time: 30 minutes

Cooking time: 50 minutes

Easy

1 tablespoon olive oil
1 large onion, chopped
2 cloves garlic, crushed
2 teaspoons sweet paprika
1 large potato, chopped
1 large carrot, sliced
400 g (13 oz) can chopped tomatoes
375 ml (1½ cups) vegetable stock
400 g (13 oz) orange sweet potato, cut
   into 1.5 cm (½ in) cubes
150 g (5 oz) broccoli, cut into florets
2 courgettes (zucchini), thickly sliced
125 g (1 cup) self-raising flour
20 g (¾ oz) chilled butter, cut into
   small cubes
2 teaspoons chopped fresh flat-leaf
   parsley
1 teaspoon fresh thyme
1 teaspoon chopped fresh rosemary
80 ml (⅓ cup) milk
2 tablespoons reduced-fat sour cream

NUTRITION PER SERVE

- Protein 12 g;
- Fat 13 g;
- Carbohydrate 51 g;
- Dietary Fibre 8.5 g;
- Cholesterol 22 mg;
- 1560 kJ (375 Cal)

VEGETABLE CASSEROLE
with dumplings

This casserole is suitable for vegetarians. It is an excellent source of fibre, B vitamins and folate.

1 Heat the oil in a large saucepan and cook the onion over low heat, stirring occasionally, for 5 minutes, or until soft. Add the garlic and paprika, and cook, stirring, for 1 minute.

2 Add the potato, carrot, tomato and stock. Bring to the boil, then reduce the heat and simmer, covered, for 10 minutes. Add the sweet potato, broccoli and courgette (zucchini), and simmer for 10 minutes, or until tender. Preheat the oven to moderately hot 200°C (400°F/Gas 6).

3 Sift the flour and a pinch of salt into a bowl. Rub the butter into the flour with your fingertips until it resembles fine breadcrumbs. Stir in the herbs and make a well in the centre. Add the milk and mix with a flat-bladed knife, using a cutting action, until the mixture comes together in beads. Gather the dough and lift onto a lightly floured surface, then divide into 8 portions. Shape each portion into a ball.

4 Add the sour cream to the casserole and transfer to a 2 litre (8 cup) ovenproof dish. Top with the dumplings. Bake for 20 minutes, or until the dumplings are golden and a skewer comes out clean when inserted in the centre.

Serves 6

Preparation time:
30 minutes + proving

Cooking time: 1 hour

Medium

4 Roma tomatoes, quartered
3/4 teaspoon caster sugar
7 g (1/4 oz) dry yeast or 15 g (1/2 oz)
  fresh yeast
215 g (1 3/4 cups) plain flour
125 ml (1/2 cup) skim milk, warmed
2 teaspoons olive oil
2 cloves garlic, crushed
1 onion, thinly sliced
750 g (1 lb 8 oz) cap mushrooms, sliced
250 g (1 cup) ricotta
2 tablespoons sliced black olives
small fresh basil leaves

MUSHROOM, RICOTTA AND OLIVE PIZZA

NUTRITION PER SERVE

- Protein 14.5 g;
- Fat 7 g;
- Carbohydrate 33.5 g;
- Dietary Fibre 5.5 g;
- Cholesterol 20.5 mg;
- 1085 kJ (260 Cal)

A lower-fat gourmet pizza, this recipe provides good amounts of fibre, B vitamins and folate.

1 Preheat the oven to hot 210°C (415°F/Gas 6–7). Put the tomato on a baking tray covered with baking paper, sprinkle with salt, cracked black pepper and 1/2 teaspoon sugar, and bake for 20 minutes, or until the edges are starting to darken.

2 Stir the yeast and remaining sugar with 60 ml (1/4 cup) warm water until the yeast dissolves. Cover and leave in a warm place until foamy. Sift the flour into a large bowl and stir in the yeast and warm milk. Mix to a soft dough, then turn onto a lightly floured surface. Knead for 5 minutes, cover and leave in a lightly oiled bowl in a warm place for 40 minutes, or until doubled.

3 Heat the oil in a pan and fry the garlic and onion until soft. Add the mushrooms and stir until they are soft and the liquid has evaporated. Cool.

4 Lightly knead the dough on a lightly floured surface. Roll out to a 36 cm (14 in) circle and transfer to a lightly greased baking or pizza tray. Spread with the ricotta, leaving a border to turn over the filling. Top with the mushroom mixture, leaving a circle in the centre, and arrange the tomato and olives in the circle. Fold the dough edge over onto the mushroom mixture and dust with flour. Bake for 25 minutes, or until the crust is golden. Garnish with basil.

Serves 4

Preparation time:
25 minutes + 15 minutes refrigeration

Cooking time: 20 minutes

Easy

60 g (¾ cup) fresh breadcrumbs
25 g (¾ cup) cornflakes
1 sheet nori, torn roughly (see Note)
¼ teaspoon paprika
4 x 150 g (5 oz) pieces firm white
    fish fillets
plain flour, for dusting
1 egg white
1 tablespoon skim milk
1 spring onion, thinly sliced

WASABI CREAM
125 g (½ cup) low-fat plain yoghurt
1 teaspoon wasabi (see Note)
1 tablespoon light mayonnaise
1 teaspoon lime juice

CRUMBED FISH
with wasabi cream

NUTRITION PER SERVE

- Protein 36.5 g;
- Fat 5 g;
- Carbohydrate 19 g;
- Dietary Fibre 2 g;
- Cholesterol 91.5 mg;
- 1125 kJ (270 Cal)

Satisfy a craving for fried fish using this healthier recipe. This meal is high in protein and provides good amounts of B vitamins, folate and minerals.

1 Preheat the oven to moderate 180°C (350°F/Gas 4). Combine the bread-crumbs, cornflakes, nori and paprika in a food processor and process until the nori is finely chopped.

2 Dust the fish lightly with flour, dip into the combined egg white and milk, then into the breadcrumb mixture. Press the crumb mixture on firmly, then refrigerate the fish for 15 minutes.

3 Line a baking tray with non-stick baking paper and put the fish on the paper. Bake for 15–20 minutes, or until the fish flakes easily when tested with a fork.

4 To make the wasabi cream, mix the ingredients thoroughly. Serve a spoonful with the fish. Sprinkle with spring onion.

NOTE: Nori (sheets of paper-thin dried seaweed) and wasabi paste (a pungent paste, also known as Japanese horseradish) are available from Japanese food stores.

Serves 4

Preparation time: 25 minutes

Cooking time: 35 minutes

Easy

2 large red peppers (capsicums),
    quartered and seeded
cooking oil spray
4 finger aubergines (eggplants), quartered
    lengthways
16 fresh sardines, butterflied (about
    300 g/10½ oz)
1 slice white bread, crusts removed
10 g (⅓ cup) fresh parsley
1 clove garlic, crushed
1 teaspoon grated lemon rind

DRESSING
1 tablespoon olive oil
1 tablespoon balsamic vinegar
½ teaspoon soft brown sugar
1 clove garlic, crushed
1 tablespoon chopped fresh chives

NUTRITION PER SERVE

• Protein 16 g;
• Fat 7 g;
• Carbohydrate 7.5 g;
• Dietary Fibre 2 g;
• Cholesterol 40 mg;
• 665 kJ (160 Cal)

SARDINES with chargrilled pepper and aubergine

The nutritious ingredients of this easy-to-prepare fish meal provide good amounts of protein, and monounsaturated fat.

1   Preheat the oven to moderate 180°C (350°F/Gas 4). Lightly grease a large baking dish with oil. Preheat the grill and line with foil.

2   Grill the pepper (capsicum) until the skin is blistered and blackened. Cool in a plastic bag or under a damp tea towel, then peel and slice thickly lengthways. Lightly spray the aubergine (eggplant) with oil and grill each side for 3–5 minutes, or until softened.

3   Combine the dressing ingredients in a jar and shake well. Put the pepper (capsicum) and aubergine (eggplant) in a bowl, pour the dressing over, toss well and set aside.

4   Place the sardines on a baking tray in a single layer, well spaced. Finely chop the bread, parsley, garlic and lemon rind together in a food processor. Sprinkle over each sardine. Bake for 10–15 minutes, until cooked through. Serve the pepper (capsicum) and eggplant (aubergine) topped with sardines.

DESSERTS

Serves 10–12

Preparation time:
20 minutes + freezing

Cooking time: Nil

Medium

30 g (1 oz) crystallised ginger, finely chopped
50 g (1½ oz) red glacé cherries, roughly chopped or sliced
300 g (10½ oz) low-fat vanilla ice cream, softened
250 g (8 oz) frozen strawberry fruit dessert, softened
300 g (10½ oz) low-fat chocolate ice cream, softened

CASSATA

This low-fat ice cream dessert will satisfy sweet cravings with fewer calories than traditional cassata. The fruit and ginger provide some extra vitamins and minerals.

1 Line a 1.25 litre (5 cup) rectangular tin with plastic wrap, leaving an overhang on the sides.

2 Stir the ginger and glacé cherries into the vanilla ice cream until well combined. Spoon into the prepared tin and smooth down. Freeze for 1 hour, or until firm.

3 Spoon the strawberry fruit dessert over the ice cream mixture, smooth the surface and freeze for another hour.

4 Spoon the chocolate ice cream over the strawberry, smoothing the surface. Cover with plastic wrap, and freeze for at least 3 hours or overnight. To serve, plunge the bottom of the tin into warm water for 10 seconds to loosen and lift out using the plastic wrap. Cut into slices and serve.

NUTRITION PER SERVE (12)

- Protein 3 g;
- Fat 2 g;
- Carbohydrate 18 g;
- Dietary Fibre 0.5 g;
- Cholesterol 5 mg;
- 375 kJ (90 Cal)

Serves 6

Preparation time:
15 minutes + overnight refrigeration

Cooking time: 5 minutes

Easy

30 g (¼ cup) custard powder
250 ml (1 cup) skim milk
2 tablespoons caster sugar
2 teaspoons vanilla essence
2 x 130 g (4½ oz) tubs low-fat French
    vanilla fromage frais
2 egg whites
410 ml (1⅔ cups) strong coffee, cooled
2 tablespoons amaretto
250 g (8 oz) savoiardi (sponge finger)
    biscuits
2 tablespoons unsweetened dark
    cocoa powder

NUTRITION PER SERVE

- Protein 5 g;
- Fat 5.5 g;
- Carbohydrate 26 g;
- Dietary Fibre 1 g;
- Cholesterol 7.5 mg;
- 755 kJ (180 Cal)

TIRAMISU

You won't miss the fat in this healthier version of the traditional favourite.
This recipe is a great source of calcium, phosphorus and potassium.

1   Stir the custard powder in a small
    pan with 2 tablespoons of the milk
    until dissolved. Add the remaining
    milk, sugar and vanilla, and stir over
    medium heat until the mixture boils
    and thickens. Remove from the
    heat. Transfer to a bowl, cover the
    surface with plastic wrap and leave
    to cool.

2   Using electric beaters, beat the
    custard and the fromage frais for
    2 minutes. Whip the egg whites
    until soft peaks form, then fold
    into the custard mixture.

3   Pour the coffee and amaretto into a
    dish. Quickly dip the biscuits, one at
    a time, into the coffee mixture, just
    enough to cover (don't leave them
    in the liquid or they will go soggy)
    and arrange in a single layer over the
    base of a 2.75 litre (9 cup) dish.

4   Smooth half the custard mixture
    evenly over the biscuits. Dust half the
    cocoa over the top and then repeat
    the layers with the biscuits and cream.
    Cover and refrigerate overnight, or
    for at least 6 hours. Dust with the
    remaining cocoa to serve.

Serves 4

Preparation time:
30 minutes + refrigeration

Cooking time: Nil

Easy

3 teaspoons gelatine
250 g (1 cup) low-fat vanilla yoghurt
2 x 200 g (6½ oz) tubs low-fat French
 vanilla fromage frais
4 egg whites
150 g (5 oz) fresh or frozen, thawed,
 raspberries, mashed
fresh raspberries and mint leaves, for
 serving

RASPBERRY MOUSSE

This refreshing and nutritious low-fat mousse is a great source of bone-building nutrients.

NUTRITION PER SERVE

- Protein 18 g;
- Fat 0.5 g;
- Carbohydrate 21 g;
- Dietary Fibre 2 g;
- Cholesterol 8.5 mg;
- 730 kJ (175 Cal)

1 Sprinkle the gelatine in an even layer over 1 tablespoon water in a small bowl and leave to go spongy. Bring a small pan of water to the boil, remove from the heat and place the bowl in the pan. Stir until clear and dissolved.

2 In a large bowl, stir the vanilla yoghurt and fromage frais together, then add the gelatine and mix well.

3 Using electric beaters, beat the egg whites until stiff peaks form, then fold through the yoghurt mixture. Transfer half to a separate bowl and fold the mashed raspberries through.

4 Divide the raspberry mixture into the bases of 4 long glasses or serving bowls. Top with the vanilla mixture. Refrigerate for several hours, or until set. Decorate with fresh raspberries and mint leaves.

Serves 8

Preparation time:
25 minutes + 30 minutes refrigeration

Cooking time: 1 hour

Easy

90 g (¾ cup) plain flour
2 tablespoons icing (confectioners') sugar
2 tablespoons custard powder
30 g (1 oz) butter
3 tablespoons light evaporated milk

FILLING
125 g (½ cup) ricotta
1 teaspoon vanilla essence
30 g (¼ cup) icing (confectioners') sugar
2 eggs, lightly beaten
90 g (⅓ cup) passionfruit pulp (about
    8 passionfruit)
185 ml (¾ cup) light evaporated milk

NUTRITION PER SERVE

- Protein 8 g;
- Fat 6.5 g;
- Carbohydrate 21.5 g;
- Dietary Fibre 3 g;
- Cholesterol 65.5 mg;
- 730 kJ (175 Cal)

PASSIONFRUIT TART

Amaze your guests with this low-fat treat, which provides calcium,
potassium and phosphorus.

1   Preheat the oven to moderately hot
    200°C (400°F/Gas 6). Lightly spray a
    22 cm loose-based flan tin with oil
    spray. Sift the flour, icing sugar and
    custard powder into a bowl and
    rub in the butter until the mixture
    resembles fine breadcrumbs. Add
    enough evaporated milk to form a
    soft dough. Bring together on a lightly
    floured surface until just smooth.
    Gather into a ball, wrap in plastic
    and refrigerate for 15 minutes.

2   Roll the pastry out on a floured
    surface, use it to fit the tin, then
    refrigerate for 15 minutes. Cover
    with baking paper and fill with
    uncooked rice or beans. Bake for
    10 minutes, remove the rice or beans
    and paper, and bake for another
    5–8 minutes, or until golden. Allow
    to cool. Reduce the oven to warm
    160°C (315°F/Gas 2–3).

3   Beat the ricotta with the vanilla
    essence and icing sugar until
    smooth. Add the eggs, passionfruit
    pulp and milk, then beat well. Put
    the tin with the pastry case on a
    baking tray and gently pour in the
    mixture. Bake for 40 minutes, or
    until set. Allow to cool in the tin.
    Dust lightly with icing sugar just
    before serving.

Serves 4

Preparation time:
10 minutes + overnight refrigeration

Cooking time: 45 minutes

Medium

canola oil spray
90 g (⅓ cup) caster sugar
375 ml (1½ cups) skim milk
2 eggs
1½ tablespoons caster (superfine)
    sugar, extra
½ teaspoon vanilla essence
1 teaspoon maple syrup

CREME CARAMEL

NUTRITION PER SERVE

- Protein 7 g;
- Fat 2.5 g;
- Carbohydrate 33 g;
- Dietary Fibre 0 g;
- Cholesterol 93 mg;
- 730 kJ (175 Cal)

Fans of traditional crème caramel won't realise that this recipe contains much less fat. It is a good choice for those watching their weight.

1 Preheat the oven to warm 160°C (315°F/Gas 2–3). Lightly spray four 125 ml (½ cup) ovenproof ramekins (7.5 cm/3 in diameter) with canola oil. Place the caster sugar and 1½ tablespoons water in a small heavy-based saucepan. Stir over low heat until the sugar is dissolved. Bring to the boil, then reduce the heat and simmer until the syrup turns straw coloured and begins to caramelise. Remove from the heat and divide among the ramekins, coating the bases evenly.

2 Heat the milk in a small saucepan with a pinch of salt over low heat until almost boiling. Place the eggs and extra sugar in a bowl and whisk together for 2 minutes. Stir in the warm milk, vanilla and maple syrup. Strain into a jug and divide evenly among the ramekins.

3 Place the ramekins in a baking dish and add enough boiling water to reach halfway up the sides of the ramekins. Bake for 35 minutes, or until the custards are set. Remove from the baking tray and leave to cool completely. Refrigerate for at least 2 hours, or overnight.

4 To serve, carefully run a knife around the edge of each custard. Invert the ramekins onto serving plates and lift off, giving them a gentle shake if necessary to dislodge the custard.

Serves 4–6

Preparation time: 20 minutes

Cooking time: 40 minutes

Easy

30 g (1 oz) butter
250 g (1 cup) sugar
1 tablespoon grated lime rind
2 eggs, separated
40 g (1/3 cup) self-raising flour
150 ml (2/3 cup) skim milk
125 ml (1/2 cup) lime juice

LIME DELICIOUS

One serve of this tangy dessert gives you more than a quarter of your daily vitamin C requirement and small to moderate amounts of most other vitamins and minerals.

1 Preheat the oven to moderate 180°C (350°F/Gas 4). Lightly grease a 1 litre (4 cup) ovenproof dish. Beat the butter, sugar and lime rind together until light and creamy. Gradually add the egg yolks, beating well after each addition. Fold in the flour, milk and lime juice alternately.

2 Place the egg whites in a clean, dry bowl and beat until soft peaks form. Gently fold into the butter and sugar mixture, then pour into the prepared dish and bake for 40 minutes, or until golden brown. Serve with low-fat ice cream, if desired.

NUTRITION PER SERVE (6)

- Protein 3.5 g;
- Fat 6 g;
- Carbohydrate 48 g;
- Dietary Fibre 0 g;
- Cholesterol 75 mg;
- 1070 kJ (255 Cal)

BAKING

BAKING

If you can't resist the aroma of a freshly baked cake or loaf of bread, look among this selection of delicious baking recipes for healthier versions of your favourite treats.

Baking your own cakes, pastries or bread is not only a very satisfying experience, it also ensures that you're in control of the ingredients that go into them, so you can make them as healthy as you wish.

Baking is one of the most technical cooking methods. It relies on a series of chemical reactions among the ingredients to cause the food to rise and develop a delicious taste and texture. Although this may sound daunting, if you follow the recipes through step by step, you will achieve the results you are looking for. Once you have become familiar with the process and comfortable with the recipe, you can make slight alterations to flavours to suit your own tastes.

SUGAR
Sugar is an essential ingredient in most baked goods. It increases the shelf-life of cakes and biscuits, adds texture and colour to most baked goods, and also gives yeast the energy it requires for bread to rise. Although moderate amounts of refined sugar won't cause health problems or weight gain, it's better to obtain sweetness from foods that contain natural sugars, so you will also be getting other valuable nutrients.

Honey is often used as a substitute for sugar, and while it may contain slightly more nutrients than sugar, it should still be used in moderation.

TIPS FOR USING LESS SUGAR IN BAKING
- Use fruit purées as a liquid alternative to sugar in cake and biscuit mixtures.
- Use low-fat fruit yoghurts or low-fat vanilla fromage frais to sweeten and moisten cake and biscuit batters.
- When fruit is fully ripe, it will be at its sweetest, and can often be used to totally replace any refined sugar in a recipe.

- Add dried fruits such as sultanas, raisins, currants, apricots or dates, which are naturally very sweet, to cake and biscuit mixtures, and add less sugar.

SALT
Not a lot of salt is used in baking—just a pinch in sweet and savoury products to enhance the flavours. If you are trying to reduce your salt intake, you can leave it out of the recipe altogether without adversely affecting the texture or appearance of the finished baked food. You can also use unsalted butter instead of regular butter for all baking.

FAT
Usually the fat content of baked goods needs to be reduced, in order to make them healthier. Most baked goods will contain fat in some form—usually butter, margarine or oil, but sometimes cream, sour cream, cream cheese or even chocolate. It is possible to reduce the amount of fat in most bakery recipes to some extent, but not completely, as some fat is needed to achieve the colour, taste and texture you expect from bakery products. Most home-baked breads don't contain fat, but check the labels on bread purchased from the supermarket.

TIPS FOR REDUCING FAT IN BAKING
- Use skim milk in place of full-fat milk.
- Use light or reduced-fat sour cream instead of regular sour cream.
- Instead of using chocolate in a recipe, choose a recipe that uses cocoa powder.
- Use buttermilk in place of milk or sour cream. Buttermilk is a low-fat milk product that has been thickened with a bacterial culture to make it slightly sour.
- Use low-fat cream cheese instead of regular cream cheese in cream cheese icings.
- Use low-fat ricotta instead of butter for making icings.
- Use low-fat natural or fruit yoghurt instead of full-fat yoghurt.
- Substitute a fruit juice for milk.
- Use a fruit purée instead of oil or sour cream. Try apple or pear, or soaked dried apricots.
- Use filo pastry for pies and tarts, brush every third layer with oil, or even with apple juice if you are very concerned about your fat intake.
- Use low-fat margarine in place of regular margarine or butter.
- For a sweet pie crust, use finely crushed low-fat plain biscuits, moisten with a fruit purée and refrigerate or bake until set.
- Be sure to use non-stick baking tins—a light spray of oil and lining with baking paper is all that will be needed to ensure that your cakes or biscuits don't stick.
- Use low-fat evaporated milk in custard fillings for a creamy yet light alternative.
- Use canola oil in recipes requiring vegetable oil—it has a neutral flavour, is a monounsaturated fat, and contains no cholesterol.

SOY
Many people are interested in incorporating soy products into their diet. Soy products are an excellent source of protein, and contain phytochemicals and a range of healthy nutrients. Soya beans are a good source of fibre, and as most soy products are dairy free they are a good alternative for those who are lactose intolerant.

TIPS FOR USING SOY PRODUCTS IN BAKING
- Soy milk can generally be substituted for regular milk in most baking, and low-fat soy milk is available.
- Soy butter may be used in baking, but not where melted butter is required.
- Soy margarine is made from soya bean oil, and may be used for cooking. Use this when a recipe calls for melted butter or margarine.
- Soy flour is rich in protein and is gluten free. Because of the lack of gluten, soy flour does not have the same properties as wheat flour, so a direct substitution is not possible. You will need to use a combination of soy flour and wheat flour to get the same texture, particularly for yeast baked goods.

Makes 14 slices

Preparation time: 20 minutes

Cooking time: 1 hour 15 minutes

Easy

310 g (2½ cups) self-raising flour
1 teaspoon bicarbonate of soda
2 teaspoons ground cinnamon
1 teaspoon mixed spice
95 g (½ cup) soft brown sugar
80 g (½ cup) sultanas
2 eggs, lightly beaten
2 tablespoons vegetable oil
80 ml (⅓ cup) low-fat milk
140 g (4½ oz) apple purée
290 g (10 oz) carrot, coarsely grated

RICOTTA TOPPING
125 g (4 oz) ricotta
30 g (¼ cup) icing (confectioners') sugar
½ teaspoon grated lime rind

CARROT CAKE

With less fat but all the flavour of regular carrot cake, this version also provides some beta-carotene, fibre and calcium.

1   Preheat the oven to moderate 180°C (350°F/Gas 4). Lightly grease a 10 x 18 cm (4 x 7 in) loaf tin and cover the base with baking paper. Sift the flour, soda and spices into a large bowl. Stir in the brown sugar and sultanas. Combine the egg, oil, milk and apple purée in a large jug.

2   Stir the egg mixture into the dry ingredients, then stir in the carrot. Spread into the tin and bake for 1¼ hours, or until a skewer comes out clean when inserted in the centre of the cake and the cake comes away slightly from the sides of the tin. Leave in the tin for 5 minutes before turning out to cool on a wire rack.

3   To make the topping, beat the ingredients together until smooth. Spread over the cake.

NUTRITION PER SLICE

- Protein 4.5 g;
- Fat 5 g;
- Carbohydrate 30 g;
- Dietary Fibre 2 g;
- Cholesterol 30 mg;
- 755 kJ (180 Cal)

Serves 8

Preparation time: 20 minutes

Cooking time: 40 minutes

Easy

2 teaspoons baking powder
125 g (1 cup) plain flour
60 g (½ cup) cocoa powder
¼ teaspoon mixed spice
12 egg whites
2 teaspoons cream of tartar
250 g (1 cup) caster (superfine) sugar
1 teaspoon vanilla essence
icing (confectioners') sugar, to dust
250 g (8 oz) fresh or frozen raspberries
1 tablespoon lemon juice
2–4 tablespoons icing (confectioners')
    sugar, to taste, extra

CHOCOLATE ANGEL FOOD CAKE

NUTRITION PER SERVE

- Protein 9 g;
- Fat 1.5 g;
- Carbohydrate 46.5 g;
- Dietary Fibre 2.5 g;
- Cholesterol 0 mg;
- 965 kJ (230 Cal)

This light, airy cake has a chocolate taste, but with relatively little fat and few calories.

1 Preheat the oven to warm 160°C (315°F/ Gas 2–3). Sift together the baking powder, flour, cocoa powder and mixed spice three times.

2 Using electric beaters, beat the egg whites in a clean, dry bowl until foamy, add the cream of tartar and continue to beat until soft peaks form. Add half the sugar and beat on high speed for 10 minutes, or until the meringue is very firm and glossy. Fold in the vanilla, flour mixture and remaining sugar, working quickly and gently until combined.

3 Pour into a very clean, ungreased angel food cake tin and bake for 35–40 minutes, or until the cake is firm to the touch and comes away slightly from the sides of the tin. Turn out onto a wire rack to cool completely. Dust with sugar.

4 Place the raspberries in a blender or food processor, add the lemon juice and extra icing (confectioners') sugar and blend until smooth. Push through a sieve to remove the seeds and serve with the angel food cake.

Serves 8

Preparation time: 15 minutes

Cooking time: 20 minutes

Easy

60 g (½ cup) self-raising flour
30 g (¼ cup) cocoa powder
3 eggs
125 g (½ cup) caster (superfine) sugar

DATE AND ORANGE CREAM
100 g (3½ oz) dried dates
125 ml (½ cup) orange juice
250 g (8 oz) ricotta
1 tablespoon caster (superfine) sugar
125 g (4 oz) light cream cheese
2 tablespoons honey
1 teaspoon grated orange rind

CHOCOLATE SWISS ROLL
with date and orange cream

NUTRITION PER SERVE

- Protein 9 g;
- Fat 8.5 g;
- Carbohydrate 36 g;
- Dietary Fibre 1.5 g;
- Cholesterol 90.5 mg;
- 1045 kJ (250 Cal)

Just like a decadent gateau, this cake has a rich, creamy taste but relatively little fat. It also provides some vitamin A, B vitamins and calcium.

1 Preheat the oven to moderate 180°C (350°F/Gas 4). Line a 30 x 25 cm (11⅔ in) swiss roll tin with baking paper, extending over the two long sides. Sift the flour and cocoa powder together three times. Using electric beaters, beat the eggs in a clean, dry bowl for 4 minutes, or until thick and pale. Gradually add the sugar, beating until the mixture becomes pale yellow and glossy.

2 Using a metal spoon, fold the cocoa, flour and 1 tablespoon hot water into the egg mixture (work quickly and lightly). Pour into the prepared tin, smooth the surface, and bake

for 12–15 minutes, or until golden brown and lightly springy.

3 Meanwhile, to make the date and orange cream, chop the dates and place in a small saucepan with the orange juice. Cover and bring to a simmer over very low heat for 4–5 minutes, or until softened. Remove from the pan and leave to cool completely. Place the ricotta in a small mixing bowl and, using a wooden spoon, beat in the sugar. Add the cream cheese, honey and orange rind, and mix together well. Stir in the dates and all of the juice.

4 Place a large sheet of baking paper on a clean tea towel. Turn the cake out onto the paper and leave for 1 minute. Peel the baking paper off the cake and, working quickly and gently, roll the cake up lengthways using the baking paper underneath as a guide. Leave the cake rolled

like this until it is completely cool. Unroll the cake, spread evenly with the date cream mixture and re-roll, ensuring that the edge rests underneath the cake. Trim the ends of the cake before serving.

NOTES: It is important to roll up the cake as soon as it is removed from the tin and to allow it to cool while rolled. This will prevent it from cracking when it is re-rolled with the filling inside.

This cake can be made a few hours ahead of time and stored, covered, in the refrigerator.

For something a little special, try adding Grand Marnier to the date and orange cream. Decrease the amount of orange juice by the amount of liqueur that you add. Try mixing strawberries, blueberries or your favourite mixed berries through the ricotta mixture, instead of the dates. Replace the orange juice with your favourite berry or other liqueur to complement the berry flavours.

Serves 4–6

Preparation time: 15 minutes

Cooking time: 30 minutes

Easy

95 g (½ cup) soft brown sugar
1 egg
200 g (6½ oz) low-fat vanilla fromage
    frais or whipped yoghurt
2 tablespoons oil
2 ripe bananas, mashed
40 g (¼ cup) sultanas
125 g (1 cup) self-raising flour
35 g (¼ cup) wholemeal self-raising flour
½ teaspoon bicarbonate of soda
2 tablespoons unprocessed bran
1 teaspoon ground cinnamon
½ teaspoon ground nutmeg

WHOLEMEAL BANANA BREAD

This banana bread has less fat and more fibre than regular varieties, and provides unsaturated fat, vitamin B6 and potassium. Serve the bread with yoghurt for a calcium boost.

1 Preheat the oven to warm 160°C (315°F/Gas 2–3). Cover the base of a 20.5 x 10.5 cm (8 x 4 in) non-stick loaf tin with baking paper.

2 Place the sugar, egg, fromage frais and oil in a large bowl, and whisk until well combined. Fold in the banana and sultanas, then fold in the sifted flours, bicarbonate of soda, bran, cinnamon and nutmeg.

3 Spoon the mixture into the prepared tin and bake for 50 minutes, or until cooked through when tested with a skewer. Serve warm or cold with low-fat yoghurt or fromage frais. Delicious toasted.

NUTRITION PER SERVE (6)

- Protein 6.5 g;
- Fat 7 g;
- Carbohydrate 49 g;
- Dietary Fibre 3 g;
- Cholesterol 1.5 mg;
- 1190 kJ (285 Cal)

NOTE: You will need 240 g (1 cup) mashed banana. Bananas are a good source of carbohydrate and fibre.

Makes 18

Preparation time: 15 minutes

Cooking time: 30 minutes

Easy

cooking oil spray
60 g (½ cup) plain flour
60 g (½ cup) self-raising flour
1 teaspoon bicarbonate of soda
90 g (¾ cup) cocoa powder
2 eggs
310 g (1¼ cups) caster (superfine) sugar
2 teaspoons vanilla essence
2 tablespoons oil
200 g (6½ oz) low-fat vanilla fromage
   frais or whipped yoghurt
140 g (4½ oz) apple purée
icing (confectioners') sugar, for dusting

FUDGE BROWNIES

These brownies will prove that reduced-fat foods can be healthy and delicious too. Moist and sweet, they contain carbohydrate and small amounts of most vitamins and minerals.

1 Preheat the oven to moderate 180°C (350°F/Gas 4). Spray a 30 x 20 cm (11⅔ x 8 in) shallow baking tin with oil and line the base with baking paper.

2 Sift the flours, bicarbonate of soda and cocoa powder into a large bowl. Combine the eggs, sugar, vanilla essence, oil, fromage frais and apple purée. Add to the flour and mix well. Spread into the tin and bake for 30 minutes, or until a skewer comes out clean.

3 The brownie will sink slightly in the centre as it cools. Leave in the tin for 5 minutes before turning onto a wire rack to cool. Dust with icing sugar, cut into pieces and serve

NUTRITION PER BROWNIE

- Protein 3.5 g;
- Fat 4 g;
- Carbohydrate 26 g;
- Dietary Fibre 0.5 g;
- Cholesterol 21.5 mg;
- 630 kJ (150 Cal)

Makes 12

Preparation time: 20 minutes

Cooking time: 20 minutes

Easy

155 g (1¼ cups) self-raising flour
110 g (¾ cup) wholemeal self-raising
   flour
1 teaspoon ground cinnamon
75 g (½ cup) oat bran
140 g (¾ cup) soft brown sugar
150 g (5⅓ oz) fresh or frozen blueberries
135 g (½ cup) bottled chunky apple sauce
1 egg, lightly beaten
250 ml (1 cup) skim milk
2 egg whites

APPLE, BLUEBERRY AND BRAN MUFFINS

These fruity muffins are moist and soft, yet relatively low in fat, and also provide fibre, B vitamins and phosphorus.

NUTRITION PER MUFFIN

- Protein 5.5 g;
- Fat 1.5 g;
- Carbohydrate 35 g;
- Dietary Fibre 3 g;
- Cholesterol 17.5 mg;
- 720 kJ (170 Cal)

1 Preheat the oven to moderately hot 200°C (400°F/Gas 6). Sift the flours and cinnamon into a bowl and return the husks to the bowl. Stir in the oat bran, sugar and blueberries.

2 Place the apple sauce, egg, skim milk and egg whites in a jug and mix together well. Pour into the dry ingredients and mix until just combined, but still lumpy. Do not overmix.

3 Spoon the mixture into twelve 125 ml (½ cup) non-stick muffin holes and bake for 20 minutes, or until cooked through. Leave in the tin for 5 minutes before turning out on a wire rack to cool.

Makes 12

Preparation time: 15 minutes

Cooking time: 20 minutes

Easy

110 g (¾ cup) polenta
1 tablespoon sugar
215 g (1¾ cups) plain flour
1 tablespoon baking powder
2 tablespoons oil
1 egg, lightly beaten
315 ml (1¼ cups) skim milk
125 g (4 oz) can creamed corn
4 spring onions, thinly sliced
150 g (5 oz) shaved light ham, chopped
50 g (2 oz) fat-free cheese, grated

HAM, CORN AND POLENTA MUFFINS

NUTRITION PER MUFFIN

- Protein 8 g;
- Fat 4.5 g;
- Carbohydrate 25 g;
- Dietary Fibre 1.5 g;
- Cholesterol 25 mg;
- 730 kJ (175 Cal)

These delicious savoury muffins provide carbohydrate energy, B vitamins and minerals, without too much fat.

1 Preheat the oven to moderately hot 200°C (400°F/Gas 6). Sift the polenta, sugar, flour and baking powder into a bowl. Place the oil, egg and skim milk in a separate bowl, mix together well and pour into the dry ingredients.

2 Add the creamed corn, spring onion, ham and cheese, and stir together with a large metal spoon until just combined. Do not overmix. The mixture should still be lumpy. Spoon the mixture into twelve 125 ml (½ cup) non-stick muffin holes and bake for 20 minutes, or until risen and golden brown. Leave in the tin to cool for 5 minutes before turning out onto a wire rack to cool fully.

Serves 6

Preparation time: 30 minutes

Cooking time: 30 minutes

Easy

cooking oil spray
125 g (1 cup) plain flour
60 g (½ cup) self-raising flour
1 teaspoon ground cinnamon
1 teaspoon ground ginger
40 g butter, chopped
95 g (½ cup) soft brown sugar
125 ml (½ cup) buttermilk
200 g (6½ oz) blueberries
2 bananas
2 teaspoons lemon juice
1 tablespoon demerara sugar

BANANA AND BLUEBERRY TART

NUTRITION PER SERVE

- Protein 5 g;
- Fat 6.5 g;
- Carbohydrate 52 g;
- Dietary Fibre 2.5 g;
- Cholesterol 19 mg;
- 1180 kJ (280 Cal)

A colourful and tasty dessert, this tart delivers carbohydate energy,
some B vitamins and minerals. Serve it with yoghurt for extra calcium.

1 Preheat the oven to moderately hot
   200°C (400°F/Gas 6). Spray a baking
   tray or pizza tray lightly with oil.
   Sift the flours and spices into a
   bowl. Add the butter and sugar and
   rub in until the mixture resembles
   breadcrumbs. Make a well and then
   add enough buttermilk to mix to
   a soft dough.

2 Roll the dough out on a lightly
   floured surface to a 23 cm (9 in)
   diameter round. Place on the tray
   and roll the edge to form a lip to
   hold the fruit in.

3 Spread the blueberries over the
   dough, keeping within the lip. Slice
   the bananas, toss them in the lemon

juice, then arrange over the top.
Sprinkle with the sugar, and bake
for 25 minutes, or until the base
is browned. Serve immediately.

Makes 12

Preparation time: 15 minutes

Cooking time: 15 minutes

Easy

250 g (2 cups) self-raising flour
1 teaspoon baking powder
30 g (1 oz) cold butter, cut into
   small cubes
80 g (1/2 cup) sultanas
250 ml (1 cup) milk
milk, extra, to glaze

SULTANA SCONES

These scones get their sweetness from natural sugars, and are a good source
of carbohydrate.

1 Preheat the oven to hot 220°C
(425°F/Gas 7). Lightly grease a
baking tray, or line with baking
paper. Sift the flour, baking powder
and a pinch of salt into a bowl and
add the butter. Rub the butter into
the flour with your fingertips, then
stir in the sultanas. Make a well in
the centre.

2 Add almost all the milk and mix
with a flat-bladed knife, using a
cutting action, until the dough

comes together in clumps. Use the
remaining milk if necessary.
With floured hands, gently gather
the dough together, lift out onto a
lightly floured surface and pat into a
smooth ball. Do not knead the
dough or the scones will be tough.

3 Pat the dough out to a 2 cm (1 in)
thickness. Using a floured 5 cm
(2 in) cutter, cut into rounds. Gather
the dough trimmings together and,
without handling too much, press

out again to a 2 cm (1 in) thickness
and cut out more rounds. Place the
scones close together on the baking
tray and brush lightly with the extra
milk. Bake for 15 minutes, or until
risen and golden brown on top.
Serve the scones warm or
at room temperature.

NUTRITION PER SCONE

- Protein 3 g;
- Fat 3 g;
- Carbohydrate 21 g;
- Dietary Fibre 1 g;
- Cholesterol 9 mg;
- 520 kJ (125 Cal)

Makes 20

Preparation time: 10 minutes

Cooking time: 40 minutes

Easy

120 g (4 oz) reduced-fat margarine
60 g (⅓ cup) soft brown sugar
115 g (⅓ cup) honey
2 egg whites
1 teaspoon vanilla extract
150 g (1½ cups) quick-cooking oats
90 g (¾ cup) plain flour
½ teaspoon ground cinnamon
½ teaspoon baking powder
¼ teaspoon mixed spice
60 g (⅓ cup) dark chocolate chips

NUTRITION PER COOKIE

- Protein 1.5 g;
- Fat 4 g;
- Carbohydrate 17 g;
- Dietary Fibre 1 g;
- Cholesterol 0 mg;
- 455 kJ (110 Cal)

CHOCOLATE-CHIP COOKIES

These cookies are lower in fat than regular biscuits, but you still need to eat sensible amounts if you're watching your weight.

1 Preheat the oven to moderately hot 190°C (375°F/Gas 5). Line two large baking trays with baking paper.

2 Place the reduced-fat spread, sugar, honey, egg whites and vanilla extract in a bowl and beat with electric beaters until well combined.

3 In a separate bowl, combine the oats, flour, cinnamon, baking powder and mixed spice. Stir the dry ingredients into the wet ingredients, stirring until well mixed. Add the

chocolate chips, making sure they are distributed evenly throughout the mixture.

4 Place tablespoons of the mixture on the lined baking sheets and press down with the back of a spoon until the cookies are about 1 cm (½ in) thick. Allow plenty of room for spreading (you will probably fit about 6 biscuits per tray). Bake for 10–12 minutes, or until crisp at the edges but still a little soft in the centre. Transfer to a wire rack to cool while you cook the remaining biscuits.

Makes 40

Preparation time: 20 minutes

Cooking time: 1 hour

Easy

2 eggs
155 g (²/₃ cup) firmly packed soft
   brown sugar
125 g (1 cup) self-raising flour
90 g (¾ cup) plain flour
125 g (4 oz) almonds
1 tablespoon finely grated orange rind
¼ teaspoon ground cardamom

ALMOND AND ORANGE BISCOTTI

An excellent accompaniment to low-fat puddings, these crisp biscuits provide monounsaturated fat, some niacin and minerals.

1 Preheat the oven to warm 160°C (315°F/Gas 2–3). Line a baking tray with baking paper.

2 Beat the eggs and sugar in a bowl with electric beaters until pale and creamy. Sift the self-raising and plain flours into the bowl, then add the almonds, orange rind and cardamom, and mix to a soft dough.

3 Turn out the dough onto a lightly floured work surface. Divide the mixture into two portions, shaping into two 5 cm x 20 cm (2 x 8 in) loaves.

4 Bake the loaves for 35–40 minutes, or until lightly golden. Transfer to a wire rack to cool. Cut the loaves into 1 cm (½ in) diagonal slices with a large serrated bread knife. The biscotti will be crumbly on the edges so work slowly and, if possible, try to hold the sides as you cut.

5 Arrange the slices on baking trays in a single layer. Return to the oven for 10 minutes on each side. Don't worry if they don't seem fully dry as they will become crisp on cooling.

NUTRITION PER BISCOTTI

- Protein 1 g;
- Fat 2 g;
- Carbohydrate 5.5 g;
- Dietary Fibre 0.5 g;
- Cholesterol 10 mg;
- 185 kJ (45 Cal)

Cool the biscotti completely before serving. Store in an airtight container for 2–3 weeks.

Makes 1 round loaf

Preparation time:
35 minutes + 2 hours rising

Cooking time: 50 minutes

Medium

300 g (10 oz) pumpkin, chopped
7 g (¼ oz) sachet dried yeast
1 teaspoon salt
560 g (4½ cups) white bread flour
1 egg, beaten
pumpkin seeds (pepitas), to decorate

NUTRITION PER SERVE (8)

- Protein 10 g;
- Fat 2.5 g;
- Carbohydrate 53 g;
- Dietary Fibre 3 g;
- Cholesterol 25 mg;
- 1160 kJ (275 Cal)

PUMPKIN BREAD

Delicious served with soups or stews, this bread is a great source of carbohydrate, potassium and beta-carotene.

1 Steam or boil the pumpkin for 10 minutes, or until tender. Drain thoroughly, then mash. Grease a 20 cm (8 in) round cake tin and line the base with baking paper. Place the yeast and 60 ml (¼ cup) warm water in a small bowl and stir well. Leave in a warm, draught-free place for 10 minutes, or until bubbles appear on the surface. The mixture should be frothy and slightly increased in volume. If your yeast doesn't foam it is dead, so you will have to discard it and start again.

2 Sift the salt and 500 g (4 cups) of the flour into a large bowl. Add the pumpkin, yeast mixture and 60 ml (¼ cup) warm water. Mix thoroughly using a wooden spoon, and then your hands, until well combined. The dough will form a rough, slightly sticky ball. Add more liquid if the mixture is too dry—the amount of liquid will depend on the moistness of the pumpkin.

3 Turn the dough out onto a floured surface. Knead for 10 minutes, or until the dough is smooth and elastic. Incorporate enough of the remaining flour to form a smooth dough. Place the dough in a lightly oiled bowl and brush with oil. Cover with plastic wrap or a damp tea towel and leave in a warm place for 1 hour, or until well risen.

4 Punch down the dough, knead for 1 minute, then pull away a golf ball-sized piece of dough. Shape the remaining dough into a smooth round ball and place in the tin. Roll the smaller ball into a rope 35 cm (13⅔ in) long. Tie into a loose knot and place across the top of the dough, then seal with a little water to hold in place. Cover with plastic wrap or a damp tea towel and leave in a warm place for 1 hour, or until risen to the top of the tin.

5 Preheat the oven to hot 210°C (415°F/Gas 6–7). Beat 2 teaspoons water into the egg and brush over the dough. Sprinkle with the pumpkin seeds and bake for 20 minutes. Reduce the oven to moderate 180°C (350°F/Gas 4), then bake for another 20 minutes, or until cooked. Cover with foil during the last 10 minutes of cooking if the bread is browning too much. Transfer to a wire rack to cool.

NOTE: Pumpkin bread is delicious served with butter. It will keep for up to three days in an airtight container, and it also freezes well for up to a month.

Makes 12

Preparation time:
50 minutes + 1 hour 30 minutes rising

Cooking time: 15 minutes

Medium

1 teaspoon dried yeast
¼ teaspoon sugar
150 ml (⅔ cup) warm milk
185 g (1½ cups) white bread flour
¼ teaspoon salt
30 g (1 oz) butter, melted
1 egg yolk, lightly beaten
coarse sea salt, to sprinkle

PRETZELS

These oven-baked pretzels have less fat than many snack foods, and provide some niacin and fibre.

NUTRITION PER PRETZEL

- Protein 2.5 g;
- Fat 3 g;
- Carbohydrate 12 g;
- Dietary Fibre 0.5 g;
- Cholesterol 23 mg;
- 355 kJ (85 Cal)

1 Place the yeast, sugar and milk in a small bowl and stir well. Leave in a warm place for 10 minutes, or until bubbles appear on the surface. The mixture should be frothy and slightly increased in volume. If your yeast doesn't foam it is dead, so you will have to discard it and start again.

2 Place the flour and salt in a large bowl and make a well in the centre. Add the yeast mixture and butter, and mix to a rough dough with a wooden spoon. Turn out onto a floured surface and knead for 10 minutes until smooth and elastic.

3 Place into an oiled bowl, oil the surface of the dough, cover and set aside in a warm place for 1 hour, or until doubled in size.

4 Preheat the oven to moderately hot 190°C (375°F/Gas 5). Line a baking tray with baking paper. Punch down the dough and knead for 2–3 minutes. Divide into 12 pieces. Cover the dough while working. Roll each piece into a long rope 40 cm (16 in) long. Circle and knot into a pretzel shape. Place well spaced on the tray. Cover with a tea towel. Leave to rise in a warm, draught-free place for 20–30 minutes.

5 Lightly brush the pretzels with the beaten egg yolk and sprinkle with sea salt. Place the pretzels in the oven and spray them twice with water before baking for 12–15 minutes, or until crisp and golden brown. Transfer to a wire rack to cool.

Makes 1 loaf

Preparation time: 30 minutes + rising

Cooking time: 50 minutes

Medium

110 g (½ cup) pearl barley
7 g (¼ oz) sachet dried yeast
1 teaspoon caster sugar
1 teaspoon salt
1 tablespoon linseeds
2 tablespoons soy flour
2 tablespoons gluten flour
150 g (1 cup) wholemeal bread flour
310 g (2½ cups) white bread flour
2 tablespoons olive oil

SOY AND LINSEED LOAF

This highly nutritious bread contains phytochemicals, carbohydrate and different fibres.

1 Brush a 26 x 10 cm (10½ x 4 in) bread tin with oil. Put the barley in a saucepan with 500 ml (2 cups) water, bring to the boil and boil for 20 minutes, or until softened. Drain.

2 Mix the yeast, sugar and 155 ml (⅔ cup) warm water in a small bowl. Leave in a warm place for 10 minutes, or until bubbles appear on the surface. The mixture should be frothy and slightly increased in volume.

3 Place the barley, salt, linseeds, soy and gluten flours, wholemeal flour and 250 g (2 cups) of the white flour in a large bowl. Make a well and add the yeast mixture, oil and 155 ml (⅔ cup) warm water. Mix with a wooden spoon to a soft dough. Turn out onto a floured surface and knead for 10 minutes, or until smooth and elastic. Incorporate enough of the remaining flour until the dough is no longer sticky.

4 Place the dough in an oiled bowl and brush with oil. Cover and leave in a warm place for 45 minutes, or until doubled in size. Punch down and knead for 3 minutes.

5 Pat the dough to a 24 x 20 cm (9½ x 8 in) rectangle. Roll up from the long side and place in the tin, seam side down. Cover and set aside in a warm place for 1 hour, or until risen to the top of the tin.

NUTRITION PER SERVE (10)

- Protein 8 g;
- Fat 5 g;
- Carbohydrate 41 g;
- Dietary Fibre 5 g;
- Cholesterol 0 mg;
- 1025 kJ (245 Cal)

Preheat the oven to moderately hot 200°C (400°F/Gas 6).

6 Brush the dough with water and make two slits on top. Bake for 30 minutes, or until golden. Cool on a wire rack.

Makes 1 loaf

Preparation time:
25 minutes + 1 hour rising

Cooking time: 45 minutes

Medium

7 g (1/4 oz) sachet dried yeast
2 teaspoons sugar
400 g (2 1/4 cups) gluten-free plain flour
1/2 teaspoon salt
50 g (1/2 cup) milk powder
1 tablespoon xanthan gum
2 eggs, lightly beaten
60 ml (1/4 cup) oil
1 tablespoon sesame seeds

NUTRITION PER SERVE (10)

- Protein 5 g;
- Fat 7.5 g;
- Carbohydrate 32 g;
- Dietary Fibre 0.8 g;
- Cholesterol 40.5 mg;
- 915 kJ (220 Cal)

GLUTEN-FREE BREAD

This bread contains mostly unsaturated fat, and is a good source
of carbohydrate and B vitamins.

1 Lightly grease a 22 x 9 x 5.5 cm (8 1/4 x 3 1/2 x 2 1/4 in) loaf tin. Place the yeast, sugar and 440 ml warm water in a small bowl and stir well. Leave in a warm place for 10 minutes, or until bubbles appear on the surface. The mixture should be frothy and slightly increased in volume. If the yeast doesn't foam you will have to discard it and start again.

2 Sift the flour, salt, milk powder and xanthan gum into a large bowl. Make a well in the centre and add the yeast mixture, egg and oil. Using a wooden spoon, stir together well until it forms a soft moist mixture. Beat for 1 minute.

3 Spoon the mixture into the loaf tin and smooth the surface with moist hands. Sprinkle the sesame seeds over the top. Cover with lightly greased plastic wrap and leave in a warm place for 1 hour, or until nearly risen to the top of the tin. Preheat the oven to moderately hot 190°C (375°F/Gas 5). Bake the bread for 40–45 minutes, or until it is golden and sounds hollow when tapped. Leave in the tin for 5 minutes before transferring to a wire rack to cool. Allow the bread to cool completely before cutting.

Serves 6–8

Preparation time:
25 minutes + 1 hour 40 minutes rising

Cooking time: 30 minutes

Medium

7 g (¼ oz) dried yeast
1 teaspoon sugar
500 g (4 cups) plain flour
1½ teaspoons salt
2 tablespoons chopped fresh parsley
2 tablespoons chopped fresh chives
1 tablespoon chopped fresh thyme
60 g (½ cup) grated reduced-fat Cheddar
milk, to glaze

CHEESE AND HERB PULL-APART LOAF

Lower in fat than regular garlic bread, this loaf provides carbohydrate,
fibre and B vitamins.

1 Combine the yeast, sugar and 125 ml (½ cup) of warm water in a small bowl. Cover and set aside in a warm place for 10 minutes, or until frothy.

2 Sift the flour and salt into a bowl. Make a well in the centre and pour in 250 ml (1 cup) warm water and the yeast. Mix to a soft dough. Knead on a lightly floured surface for 10 minutes, or until smooth. Put the dough in an oiled bowl, cover and leave for 1 hour, or until doubled in size.

3 Punch down the dough and knead for 1 minute. Divide in half and shape each half into 10 flat, 6 cm (2½ in) discs. Mix the herbs with the Cheddar and put 2 teaspoons on a disc. Press another disc on top. Repeat with the remaining discs and herb mixture.

4 Grease a 21 x 10.5 x 6.5 cm (8¼ x 4 x 2½ in) loaf tin. Stand the filled discs upright in the prepared tin, squashing them together. Cover the tin and set aside in a warm place

for 30 minutes, or until well risen. Preheat the oven to hot 210°C (415°F/Gas 6–7). Glaze the bread with milk and bake for 30 minutes, or until brown and crusty.

NUTRITION PER SERVE (8)

- Protein 9.5 g;
- Fat 2 g;
- Carbohydrate 45.5 g;
- Dietary Fibre 2.5 g;
- Cholesterol 4 mg;
- 1005 kJ (240 Cal)

HOW TO USE THIS SECTION

The food composition chart shows the fibre, carbohydrate and energy values for most commonly available foods. The figure next to each food represents the average serving, but if the food has no typical serving, as is the case with flour, a 100 g amount is given. In the fibre column, N denotes that the figure has not been calculated, + that amounts have been detected but not accurately calculated and Tr means that only a trace (less than 0.1g) has been found.

The notes next to the chart focus on particular foods, providing useful information about different varieties, healthy recipe variations, and hints and tips for making the foods part of a balanced diet. Essential tips on the best choices for everyday shopping are combined with notes on how to opt for lower-fat versions, and how taste needn't be compromised for health.

CARBOHYDRATE, FIBRE & CALORIE COUNTER

ALCOHOL Drinking alcohol in moderate amounts (no more than 2 to 3 units a day for women, or 3 to 4 units for men), does not appear to have any adverse health effects in adults of a healthy weight. However, do have at least one or two alcohol-free days a week and avoid binge drinking. Try to limit alcohol to meal times.

BEER A drink made by the fermentation of cereals (usually barley), beer can be high in calories and may also weaken resolve when it comes to reaching for high-fat snacks.

WHITE WINE Mix with ice-cold soda water to make a wine spritzer with half the calories of a glass of wine.

	CARB g	FIBRE g	FAT g	ENERGY kcal	ENERGY kJ
ALCOHOL					
Beers					
ale, brown, bottled – small, 275ml	8.3	0	0	82	346
ale, pale, bottled – small, 275ml	5.5	0	0	77	325
ale, strong – small, 275ml	17	0	0	182	756
beer, average, 1 pint, 574ml	13	0	0	182	756
beer, bitter, canned, 440ml	10.3	0	0	143	586
beer, bitter, canned, large, 500ml	11.6	0	0	161	660
beer, bitter, low alcohol, 1 pint, 574ml	12	0	0	75	310
beer, draught, 1 pint, 574ml	13.3	0	0	184	755
beer, keg, 1 pint, 574ml	13.2	0	0	178	741
beer, mild, draught, 1 pint, 574ml	9.3	0	0	145	597
lager, average, canned and draught, 500ml	Tr	0	0	145	605
lager, bottled, large, 500ml	7.5	0	0	146	598
lager, reduced-alcohol, 1 pint, 574ml	8.6	0	0	57.4	235
lager, premium, strong, 500ml	Tr	0	0	295	1220
shandy, canned, large, 500ml	15	0	0	55	240
stout, bottled, small, 275ml	11.4	0	0	100	429
stout, strong, large, 500ml	10.5	0	0	195	817
stout, strong, small, 275ml	5.8	0	0	107	449
Ciders					
cider, dry, 1 pint, 574ml	15	0	0	208	873
cider, sweet, 1 pint, 574ml	24.4	0	0	244	1011
cider, vintage, strong, 1 pint, 574ml	42	0	0	578	2417
Cocktails					
cocktail, Bloody Mary, 165ml	5.5	0.5	0	124	520
cocktail, Daiquiri, 60ml	4	0	0	111	465
cocktail, Tequila Sunrise, 60ml	7	0	0	66	275
Liqueurs					
liqueur, egg-based, 25ml	7	0	1.6	65	273
liqueur, cherry brandy/coffee, 25ml	8.2	0	0	65.5	275
liqueur, cream, 25ml	6	0	4	81	338
liqueur, drambuie, 25ml	6.1	0	0	78.5	330
Spirits					
spirits, average, 40% volume – brandy, gin, rum, vodka, whiskey, 25ml	0	0	0	55	230
spirits, average, 37.5% volume, 25ml	0	0	0	51	214
Wines					
wine, red, small glass, 120ml	0.4	0	0	85	356
wine, rose, 120ml	3.1	0	0	89	367
wine, white, dry, 120ml	0.7	0	0	82	343
wine, white, medium, 120ml	4.3	0	0	94	388
wine, white, sweet, 120ml	7.4	0	0	118	493
wine, fortified, port, 50ml	6	0	0	80	327
wine, fortified, sherry, dry, 50ml	0.7	0	0	58	240
wine, fortified, sherry, medium, 50ml	3	0	0	60	252
wine, fortified, sherry, sweet, 50ml	3.5	0	0	68	284
wine, fortified, vermouth, dry, 50ml	1.5	0	0	55	227
wine, fortified, vermouth, sweet, 50ml	7.6	0	0	75	315
champagne, 125ml	1.7	0	0	95	394
APPLE					
chutney, 1 serving, 35g	18	0.6	0	68	288
cooking, stewed with sugar, 4oz, 100g	19	1.8	0	74	314

	CARB g	FIBRE g	FAT g	ENERGY kcal	ENERGY kJ
APPLE cont.					
cooking, stewed without sugar, 4oz, 100g	8	2	0	33	138
eating, raw, unpeeled, 1 average, 5oz, 125g	13	2.2	0	52.5	224
eating, raw, peeled, 1 average, 4oz, 100g	11	0	0	45	190
dried, 1oz, 25g	15	2.4	0	60	254
juice, unsweeted, small glass, 4fl oz, 100ml	10	Tr	0	38	164
juice, concentrated, 1fl oz, 25g	14	Tr	0	57	243
APRICOT					
canned in juice, 6 halves, 120g	9.6	1.2	0	41	176
canned in syrup, 6 halves, 120g	19	1.2	0	76	321
raw, 3, 110g	6.8	2	0	28	119
stewed with sugar, 4oz serving, 100g	18	2	0	72	308
stewed without sugar, 4oz serving, 100g	6	2	0	27	115
dried, 3 whole, 50g	22	4	0	94	401
ready to eat – semi-dried, 4oz, 100g	36	6.3	0	158	674
juice drink, 35% juice, 1 glass, 250ml	20	1	0	18	75
nectar, 50% juice, glass, 250ml	32	0	0	129	540
ARTICHOKE					
globe, boiled, 1 medium, 220g	2.6	1	0	17	70
hearts, canned in brine, drained, 1 heart, 50g	1	1.5	0	8	35
Jerusalem, peeled, boiled, 1 medium, 100g	10	3.5	0	41	207
ASPARAGUS					
canned, drained, 8 spears, 100g	1.5	2.9	0	24	100
fresh, boiled, 4 spears, 120g	1	1	0	15	63
AUBERGINE (see also EGGPLANT)					
fried in corn oil, 100g	2.8	2.3	32	302	1262
raw, 100g	2.2	2	0.4	15	64
AVOCADO					
medium, 1 raw 100g	1.9	3.4	19.5	190	784
BABY FOOD					
baby rusk, plain, average, 100g	82.8	N	7.9	408	1729
rusk, flavoured, 100g	78.1	N	9	401	1698
rusk, low sugar, 100g	77.8	N	9.7	414	1751
rusk, wholemeal, 100g	76.5	N	10.1	411	1739
cereal, ground muesli, 100g	70	N	8	400	1690
cereal, creamed porridge,100g	58	N	5.5	360	1510
cereal, mixed, powder, 100g	71	N	5	377	1599
cereal, fruit, banana & apple, powder, 100g	70	N	3.8	359	1527
cereal, apple & blackberry, powder, 100g	77	N	4	365	1552
baby rice, powder, 100g	78	N	3	365	1553
baby rice, mixed, 100g	78	N	2	372	1565
dessert, creamed rice, jar, 128g	8	0	0.5	40	155
dessert, fruit, powder, 100g	90	1.3	0.6	383	1635
dessert, caramel custard, 100g	13	N	2.5	82	345
dessert, fruit custard, 100g	17	N	0.5	74	310
dinner, beef, junior, 100g	10	1	0.5	60	240
dinner, chicken & vegetable, 100g	8	1.5	1.5	60	250
dinner, chicken, junior, 100g	9	0.5	1	55	230
dinner, chicken noodle, junior, 100g	9.5	0.5	1	57	240
egg/cheese based meal, canned, 100g	10	1	3.4	82	344
meat based meal, average, canned, 100g	8.6	1.1	3	73	306
dinner, lamb casserole, jar 200g	18	N	2	121	510
dinner, lamb, junior, 100g	7	1	2.5	62	260

BABY FOOD Most babies are ready for 'solid' foods by about the age of 4 months. Keep things simple to start with, by offering puréed fruit or vegetables, with no added salt or sugar. Try to keep commercially produced baby foods to a minimum, and always check labels to ensure that the food is suitable for your child.

FAT There's no need to limit the calorie intake of your baby – some fats are important for a child's development.

FIBRE Babies only have small stomachs and need to obtain a lot of nutrients from small portions. Foods high in fibre such as wholewheat cereals and/or wholemeal bread can be filling, without providing sufficient energy, so avoid offering them every day.

BEANS Rich in protein, dietary fibre and complex carbohydrates, and low in fat, beans should be an essential part of our diet, especially for people who don't eat any or much meat. The canned varieties are great if you don't have time to soak dried beans overnight.

KIDNEY BEANS Next time you make chilli con carne, try using more kidney beans and less beef mince, as kidney beans are high in fibre and supply all the protein of meat without the fat.

CHICKPEAS Readily available in tins, chickpeas are a great source of fibre and a cheap, low-fat alternative to meat.

	CARB g	FIBRE g	FAT g	ENERGY kcal	kJ
BABY FOOD cont.					
dinner, lentil hot-pot, jar, 200g	20	N	0.5	114	480
dinner, fish based, average, canned, 100g	9	0.6	3	76	321
dinner, garden vegetable, jar, 200g	24	N	0.5	124	520
dinner, mixed vegetable, strained, 100g	8.5	N	1	46	195
dinner, pasta & vegetable, jar, 200g	27	N	1	138	580
dinner, pasta based, average, canned, 100g	8.5	0.7	3	71	300
dinner, vegetable based, canned, 100g	10	2	2	67	284
BACON					
bits, 2tsp	0	0	1.5	30	125
fried & 2 fried eggs	0	0	18	215	905
middle rasher, fried, 1 slice, 10g	0	0	3	37	155
middle rasher, trimmed, fried, 1, 10g	0	0	1	23	95
middle rasher, grilled, 1, 10g	0	0	2	32	135
middle rasher, trimmed, grilled, 1, 10g	0	0	1	24	100
BAGEL					
plain, average, 1, 60g	29	+	0.5	137	575
BAKLAVA					
bought, average piece, 100g	40	+	17.5	322	1349
BAMBOO SHOOTS					
canned or bottled, drained, 1 cup, 140g	1.5	2.2	0	11	45
raw, 50g	3	N	0	14.3	60
BANANA					
chips, crystallised, 1oz, approx. 25 chips, 25g	15	0.5	7.8	128	534
dried, 100g	28	3	0	119	500
raw, peeled, 140g	32.5	1	Tr	133	564
BARLEY					
bran, raw, 40g	30	+	1	131	550
cooked, 1 portion, 180g	38	+	1.5	190	800
pearl, cooked, 100g	27.7	+	1	120	510
wholegrain, raw, 100g	64	15	2	301	1282
BEANS & LENTILS					
aduki, cooked, 4oz portion, 100g	22.5	5.5	0.2	123	525
baked, canned in tomato sauce, 100g	15	3.5	0.6	81	345
balor, canned in salted water, 100g	2.8	2.7	0.1	19	83
black-eyed, cooked, 100g	20	3.5	0.7	116	494
black gram, cooked, 100g	13.5	N	0.4	89	379
black kidney, cooked, 100g	24.5	N	0.5	130	545
borlotti, canned, drained, 100g	25	N	0.5	112	470
borlotti, cooked, 100g	28.5	N	0.5	146	612
broad, fresh, cooked, 100g	5.6	5.4	0.8	48	204
butter (cannellini), canned, 100g	13	4.6	0.5	77	327
chickpeas, canned, drained, 100g portion	16	4.1	2.9	115	487
green, fresh, cooked, 100g	3	2.4	0	22	92
green, frozen, cooked, 100g	4.7	4.1	0	25	108
haricot, cooked, 100g	17.2	6.1	0.5	95	406
kidney, red, canned, drained, cooked, 100g	12.2	4.1	0.5	70	380
lentils, canned in tomato sauce, 100g	9.3	1.7	0.2	55	236
lentils, red, split, cooked, 100g	17.5	2	0.4	100	424
lentils, whole, dried, cooked, 100g	17	3.8	0.7	105	446
lima, dried, cooked, 100g	10	5.5	Tr	70	295
mung, cooked, 100g	15.3	10	0.4	91	389
pinto, cooked, 100g	24	N	0.7	137	583

	CARB g	FIBRE g	FAT g	ENERGY kcal	ENERGY kJ
BEANS AND LENTILS cont.					
red kidney bean, cooked, 100g	17.4	6.7	0.5	103	440
red kidney beans, in chilli sauce,100g	13.1	3.6	2.6	91	383
runner, fresh, cooked, 100g	2.3	1.9	0.5	18	76
soya, canned, drained, 100g	5.1	6.1	7.3	141	590
soya, canned in tomato sauce, 100g	7	3	3	90	380
soya, dried, cooked, 100g	1.5	6.1	7.5	128	540
three-bean mix, canned, drained, 100g	14	N	0.5	86	360
tofu, soya bean, steamed, 100g	0.7	N	4.2	73	304
BEEF					
steak, lean, grilled, 1 medium, 117g	0	0	10.5	224	940
steak, untrimmed, grilled, 1, 120g	0	0	12.5	250	1040
chuck steak, untrimmed, simmered, 1, 190g	0	0	26	486	2040
corned, canned, 100g	0	0	12.5	217	905
corned, sliced, 100g	0	0	9	150	625
fillet steak, lean, grilled, 1, small, 85g	0	0	7	167	700
fillet steak, untrimmed, grilled, 1 small, 85g	0	0	11	198	830
Beef burgers, grilled, 100g	0.1	0	24.4	326	1355
homemade, 100g	1	0	20	287	1194
takeaway, in bun with salad, 100g	18	N	12.7	238	996
economy, frozen, grilled, 100g	9.7	0.8	19.3	273	1138
heart, simmered, 100g	0	0	5.9	179	752
kidney, simmered, 100g	0	0	6.1	153	641
liver, simmered, 100g	0	0	9.5	198	831
mince, simmered, drained, 170g	0	0	20.5	390	1623
mince, lean, simmered, drained, 170g	0	0	16.5	309	1300
oxtail, simmered, 100g	0	0	13.5	243	1014
pepper steak with cream sauce, 1 serving, 200g	0	0	35	536	2250
pie, bought, family size, 1 serving, 250g	38.5	+	36.5	560	2355
pie, bought, individual, 250g	45	+	34.5	564	2370
pie, bought, party size, 1, 40g	7.5	+	7.5	111	465
rib steak, lean, grilled, 100g	0	0	5.5	176	740
rissoles, fried, 2, 340g	0	+	30	662	2780
round steak, lean, grilled, 100g	0	0	6	176	740
round steak, untrimmed, grilled, 100g	0	0	9.5	202	850
rump steak, lean, grilled, 175g	0	0	11.5	334	1405
rump steak, untrimmed, grilled, 200g	0	0	33.5	538	2260
silverside, lean, baked, 2 slices, 80g	0	0	3.5	131	550
silverside, untrimmed, baked, 2 slices, 85g	0	0	10	189	795
sirloin steak, lean, grilled, 110g	0	0	9.5	192	806
sirloin steak, untrimmed, grilled, 127g	0	0	24	348	1460
skirt steak, lean, simmered, 100g	0	0	5	188	790
skirt steak, untrimmed, simmered, 100g	0	0	6	196	825
steak, lean, grilled, 1 small, 110g	0	0	9	216	910
steak, untrimmed, grilled, 1 small, 130g	0	0	20.5	330	1390
T-bone, lean, grilled, 100g	0	0	5.5	134	565
T-bone, untrimmed, grilled, 100g	0	0	8	164	690
tongue, simmered, 100g	0	0	25	307	1290
topside roast, lean, baked, 2 slices. 80g	0	0	4	124	520
topside roast, untrimmed, baked, 2 slices, 90g	0	0	9	171	720
topside steak, lean, grilled,1 small, 100g	0	0	5	151	635
topside steak, untrimmed, grilled, 1 small,100g	0	0	6.5	162	680
tripe, simmered, 100g	0	0	3	83	350

BEEF Lean beef, cooked without any added fat, can contain as little as 5% fat. Moderate amounts of red meat, such as beef, can be part of a healthy balanced diet and is an excellent source of iron and other minerals. Choose lean cuts that have had all visible fat removed and use low-fat marinades, such as lemon juice, mustard, soy sauce and herbs.

RECIPE To give a fillet steak extra flavour when you are grilling or frying it without fat, baste with a little marinade of soy sauce, spread both sides with wholegrain mustard or coat in cracked black pepper.

MINCE To make really lean mince, buy lean steak and mince it yourself in a food processor. Alternatively, buy extra lean mince, cook without fat and drain off all juices.

BISCUITS Sweet biscuits are often high in sugar and saturated fat, but they can be useful as a quick source of carbohydrate. If you want something lower in fat to snack on, reach for fresh or dried fruit, or a crispbread or rice cake with cottage cheese.

COOKIES Chewy ones get their texture from the high amount of butter and sugar. Don't be fooled into thinking oatmeal biscuits are lower in fat, though they do contain more fibre.

CREAM-FILLED High in fat and sugar, the centre is usually a mix of icing sugar, butter and water, and in most cases the biscuit is sweet and buttery.

	CARB g	FIBRE g	FAT g	ENERGY kcal	ENERGY kJ
BEETROOT					
fresh, peeled, boiled, 2 slices	5	0.4	0	25	105
pickled, 5 slices, 100g	14	1.7	0	64	270
raw, grated, 30g	2.5	0.6	0	12	50
BISCUITS					
assorted creams, 1, 15g	12.5	N	4	75	315
brandy snaps, 1, 10g	6.4	Tr	2	44	183
bourbon, 1, 12.5g	8.5	N	3.2	64	270
chocolate, full coated, 1 small, 25g	17	0.6	7	131	549
chocolate coated, 2, 30g	20	0.9	7.2	148	621
chocolate chip cookies, 1	4.5	N	2	36	150
chocolate shortbreads, 1	5	N	2.5	35	147
choc-chip, 1, 10g	8	N	2	51	215
cookies, 1, 10g	9	N	2.5	62	260
coconut ice, 1	9.5	+	3.5	71	300
cream biscuit, 1, 10g	6.4	N	2	46	194
custard cream, 1, 12.5g	8	N	3	64	270
digestive biscuits, plain, 2, 30g	20	0.7	6.3	141	593
digestive biscuit, chocolate, 1, 15g	10	0.3	3.6	74	311
flapjacks, 1, 25g	15	0.7	6.5	121	552
ginger nuts, 2, 20g	16	0.4	3	91	385
gingernut biscuits, homemade, 1, 20g	13	0.3	3.4	90	377
golden oat, 1, 15g	9.5	0.5	1.5	54	225
jaffa cake, 2	7	N	1	36	153
melting moments, 1, 10g	5.5	0.1	3.6	55	229
oatcakes, homemade, 1, 10g	6.3	0.6	1.8	44.5	187
oatcakes, retail, 1, 10g	6.3	N	1.8	44	185
fruit slice, 1, 15g	8	+	0.5	37	155
sandwich biscuit, 2, 25g	17.3	N	6.5	128	538
semi-sweet, 2, 15g	11.2	0.3	2.5	69	289
semi-sweet, coconut type, 1, 10g	9	0.1	2	56	23
semi-sweet, morning coffee type, 1, 12g	4.5	0.1	1	30	126
semi-sweet, rich tea type, 1, 7.5g	5.6	0.1	1.2	35	145
short-sweet biscuit, 2, 20g	12.4	0.3	4.7	94	393
shortbread, 2 fingers, 35g	22	0.8	9	174	730
shortbread, cream, 1	10.5	0	4.5	87	365
shortbread, scotch finger, 1	12	0.5	4	88	370
shortcake, 2, 20g	12	0.3	5	94	393
wafers, filled, 3, 18g	12	N	5.4	96	404
savoury, biscuit, 1	2	N	0.5	14	60
savoury, crackers, cream, 3, 21g	14.3	0.6	3.4	92	390
savoury, crackers, wholemeal, 3, 21g	15	1	2.4	87	366
crispbread, cracotte type, 3, 15g	9.4	0.4	2.3	61	256
crispbread, rye, 3, 24g	17	2.8	0.5	77	328
matzos, 1, 30g	26	1	0.6	115	490
oatcakes, 2, 26g	16.4	1.2	4.8	115	482
water biscuits, 3, 21g	16	0.6	2.6	92	390
BLACKBERRIES					
canned, sweetened, 100g	23	+	0	92	385
fresh, raw, 1/2 punnet, 100g	12.5	3.1	0.5	52	220
frozen, 100g	15.5	+	0.5	64	270
BLACKCURRANT JUICE					
prepared, diluted, 250ml	28	0	0	107	450

	CARB g	FIBRE g	FAT g	ENERGY kcal	ENERGY kJ
BLUEBERRIES					
canned in syrup, drained, 100g	17	+	0	69	290
frozen, 100g	12	+	0.5	51	215
raw, 1/2 punnet, 100g	14	1.8	0.5	56	235
BOYSENBERRIES					
canned in heavy syrup, 100g	22.5	2.6	0	88	370
canned, no added sugar, 100g	4	+	0	27	115
raw, 1/2 punnet, 100g	6	+	0	13	55
BRAN (see CEREAL)					
BRANDY BUTTER					
1tbsp, 30g	16	0	8	146	615
BRAWN					
2 slices, 70g	0	0	12	151	635
BREAD					
bagel, plain, average, 1, 60g	29	+	0.5	137	575
breadcrumbs, homemade, 100g	77.5	2.2	1.9	354	1508
breadcrumbs, manufactured, 100g	78.5	N	2.1	354	1505
brown bread, average, 38g	16.8	1.3	0.8	83	352
brown roll, crusty, 48g	24.2	1.7	1.3	122	521
brown roll, soft, 48g	24.9	1.7	1.8	129	547
chapatis, made with fat, 1, 100g	48.3	N	12.8	328	1383
chapatis, made without fat, 1, 100g	43.7	N	1	202	860
corn, 90g	20	+	7	178	750
croissant, 60g	23	1	12.2	216	903
crumpet, wholemeal, toasted, 1, 44g	17	1.5	0.5	84	355
currant bread, 1 slice, 25g	12.7	+	1.9	72	305
focaccia, 1, 50g	30	2	1.5	139	585
focaccia, herb & garlic, 1, 70g	32	2	1.5	170	715
granary, 1 slice, 38g	17.6	1.6	1	89	380
hamburger roll, 85g	41.5	1.3	4.3	224	953
loaf, average, white, 2 slices	35	3.5	2	189	795
loaf, fruit, fruit & spice, 2 slices	34.5	+	2	177	745
loaf, fruit, raisin toast, 2 slices	26	+	1.5	134	565
loaf, fruit, spicy fruit, 2 slices	33.5	+	2	174	730
loaf, gluten/wheat free, 2 slices	12	+	2	64	270
loaf, mixed grain, 2 slices	33.5	+	3.5	196	825
loaf, multi-grains, 2 slices	35	+	2	187	785
loaf, pumpernickel, 2 slices	18	3.7	1	92	385
loaf, rice bran, 2 slices	2	+	10	69	290
loaf, black rye, 1 slice	42	+	2	214	900
loaf, rye, 2 slices	30	2.2	3	176	740
loaf, soya & linseed, 2 slices	40	++	6	259	1090
malt bread, 1 slice, 35g	19.9	+	0.8	94	399
naan, 1, 160g	80	3	20	538	2264
papadum, fried, 1, 13g	5.1	N	2.2	48	201
pitta, white, 1, 95g	55	2.1	1.1	252	1071
rye bread, 25g	11.4	1.1	0.4	55	233
soda bread, yeast-free, 1, 60g	35	1.2	1.5	178	750
toasted, regular, 1, 45g	19.5	1	0.5	93	390
tortillas made with wheat flour, 1, 30g	15	0.8	2	86	360
wheatgerm bread, I slice, 25g	10.9	0.8	0.8	57	244
white bread, average, 35g	17.3	0.5	0.7	82	357
white bread med. slice, large loaf, 36g	16.8	0.5	0.5	78	333

BREAD Let's dispel the myth once and for all that bread is fattening—it is the spreads that we cover it with that can be. Bread provides us with dietary fibre, energy and valuable vitamins and minerals, and even white bread is nutritious. One pitfall is that commercial bread can be high in sodium— check the label for details.

WATER CRACKERS Relatively fat-free, these crackers are a good source of carbohydrate. Serve them with low-fat soft cheese or yogurt dips, salad vegetables or reduced fat hummus.

WHITE A good source of carbohydrate, fibre, vitamins and minerals. It contains less fibre than wholemeal varities, but is still low in fat and an important part of a healthy diet.

BUTTER & MARGARINE

Which is healthier? In fact, they both have the same fat and calorie content, though margarines are usually lower in saturated fat than butter. Replacing butter, for example, with a polyunsaturated fat or monounsaturated spread may help reduce cholesterol levels in the blood. However, try to use all spreads sparingly.

BUTTER By law, butter must contain over 80% fat. This fat is predominantly saturated and high in cholesterol.

REDUCED-FAT SPREADS
A blend of milk fat or vegetable oil and water, with about 50% of the fat of butter or margarine.

	CARB g	FIBRE g	FAT g	ENERGY kcal	kJ
white bread roll, crusty, 1, 50g	28.8	0.8	1.1	140	596
white bread roll, soft, 1, 45g	23.2	0.7	1.9	121	512
white bread, fried in oil, 45g	21.8	0.7	14.3	226	946
white bread, with added fibre, 1 slice, 38g	17.4	1.1	0.5	81	342
wholemeal bread, average, 38g	15.8	2.2	0.9	82	347
wholemeal roll, 1 average, 48g	23.2	2.8	1.4	116	492
wholemeal, roll, 1 large, 105g	46	6	2.5	250	1050
stick, French (baguette), white, 1, 50g	22.5	0.7	1.5	128	540
stick, French (baguette), wholemeal, 1, 50g	21	+	1.5	119	500
toast, French, 2 slices	20	+	8.5	182	765
BROCCOLI					
raw, 100g	0	2.6	0	24	100
BRUSSELS SPROUTS					
raw, 100g	2	4.1	0	24	100
BUCKWHEAT KERNELS					
boiled, 100g	73	2.1	2.5	334	1400
BULGUR (CRACKED WHEAT)					
cooked, 100g	68.5	+	2.5	319	1340
BUN					
brioche, 1	N	N	16	278	1170
cinnamon, 1, 100g	45	1.5	15	263	1105
chelsea, 78g	43.8	1.3	10.8	285	1203
cream, 1 small, 60g	15.5	0.5	21.5	261	1082
finger, iced, 1, 65g	30	N	5	192	805
fruit, iced, 1, 90g	42	N	7	265	1115
hot cross, 1, 50g	29.3	1	3.5	155	657
BUTTER (see also FAT and MARGARINE)					
clarified (ghee), 1tbsp	0	0	17	150	630
garlic, 1tbsp	0	0	16.5	145	610
regular, average, 1tbsp	0	0	16.5	145	610
reduced-fat average, 1tbsp	0	0	8	76	320
CABBAGE					
chinese, raw, 40g	0	0.6	0	3	14
chinese, flowering (pak choi), raw, 40g	0	1	0	5	20
mustard (dai gai choi), raw, 75g	0.5	2	0	11	45
red, raw, 40g	1	1.2	0	9.5	40
red, cooked, 60g	2	1	0	12	50
rolls, Lebanese, 3 small, 250g	40	+	10	290	1220
savoy, cooked, 60g	1	1.5	0	10	40
savoy, raw, 40g	1	1.5	0	7	30
CAKE					
angel, average slice	40.5	N	0.5	181	760
apricot crumble tea cake, 100g	44	+	15	324	1360
apple, average slice	40	+	10	252	1060
banana cake, 100g	68	+	16	428	1800
banana madeira, 100g	58	+	13.5	367	1540
banana tea loaf, 100g	57	+	12	351	1475
battenburg, 100g	50	N	17.5	370	1551
Bavarian chocolate, 100g	30	N	22.5	332	1395
black forest, 100g	40	N	17	331	1390
bran loaf, large slice, 100g	58.4	4.6	1.6	254	1081
cake mix, sponge, made up, 50g	27	N	8	280	1220

	CARB g	FIBRE g	FAT g	ENERGY kcal	ENERGY kJ
CAKE cont.					
carrot cake, bought, 100g	44	+	23	402	1690
carrot cake, fingers, 100g	64	+	17	420	1770
cheesecake, 100g	30	0.4	20	320	1350
cherry cake, 100g	61.7	1.1	15.8	384	1657
chinese cakes, 100g	51.9	N	21.5	415	1740
chocolate, 100g	55	N	17	391	1645
christmas, 1 piece, 60g	33.5	+	6	193	810
coconut, 100g	51.2	2.5	23.8	434	1815
crispie cakes, 100g	73.1	0.3	18.6	464	1951
date loaf, 1 piece, 55g	27	+	4.5	158	665
date & walnut loaf, 1 piece, 60g	32	+	6	189	795
eclair, chocolate, bought, 70g	22.5	0.5	18	264	1110
flan, fruit, 100g	28.5	0.7	8	187	785
fruit, plain, 1 piece, 50g	271	+	6	165	695
fruit, retail, 1 piece, 70g	39	0.7	7	225	945
fruit cake, iced, 70g	43.9	1.2	8	249	1053
fruit cake, rich, 1 slice, 70g	41.7	1.2	7.7	239	1007
gateau, 1 slice, 85g	36.9	0.3	143	286	1201
gingerbread, 50g	32.4	0.6	8.3	190	800
hazelnut torte, average slice	N	+	30	402	1690
jam fairy, 100g	58.5	N	18	417	1750
jam sponge, 100g	67.5	1.8	2.5	312	1310
lamington, bought, 1, 75g	36	+	9	233	980
lamington, cream-filled, 1, 60g	30	+	7	187	785
lemon rolls, 100g	60.5	N	15	360	1510
madeira, 1 slice, 40g	23.4	0.4	6.8	157	661
madeira, iced, 100g	58	N	14	369	1550
marble, 100g	60	N	13.5	374	1570
mud, 100g	59	N	20	428	1800
rock, 1 medium, 60g	33	0.8	8	221	930
rum baba, average serving	47	N	10	326	1370
sponge cake, average slice, 60g	31.4	0.5	15.8	275	1152
sponge cake, fatless, 1 slice, 58g	30.7	0.5	3.5	171	722
sponge, fairy, 100g	60.5	N	8.5	344	1445
sponge, jam-filled, 1 slice, 60g	38.5	1.1	2.9	181	768
sponge with butter icing, slice, 60g	31.4	0.4	18.4	294	1228
swiss roll, 1 slice, 35g	22.5	0.5	2.5	114	480
swiss roll, chocolate, individual, 25g	14.5	N	2.8	84	355
CAPERS					
1 tbsp	1	+	0	7	30
CAPSICUM (PEPPER)					
green, raw, 100g	2.5	1.6	0	15	65
red, raw, 100g	4	1.6	0	25	105
CAROB					
bar, 1, 45g	18	+	11.5	186	780
coated biscuit 1, 18g	9.5	N	5.5	89	375
powder, 2 tbsp, 40g	15	+	0	59	250
CARROT					
baby, raw, peeled, 50g	3	1.2	0	13	55
canned, 100g	4	1.9	0,	20	85
juice, 125ml	8	+	0	39	165
raw, peeled, boiled, 70g	4	2	0	19	80

CAKE As a general rule, the lighter and whiter the cake, the lower its fat content. Small amounts of any cake, as an occasional treat, can be eaten as part of a healthy diet. However, as a healthier option, go for fat-free sponge and fruit cakes (which contain more fibre) than creamy cakes with jam or butter icing. For increased fibre content, try making cakes with wholemeal flour.

MUFFINS For healthy home-made muffins, use wholemeal self-raising flour to add fibre and replace the fat with half low-fat yoghurt and half orange juice.

SWISS ROLL A jam filling is less fattening than a cream one, though jam will increase the sugar content.

CEREAL BRANS Eating a healthy diet with plenty of fibre may help to prevent cancer of the bowel and constipation, and cereal brans (the husks of grain) are a concentrated source. However, uncooked bran contains phytates that hinder the absorption of minerals. The best way to boost your fibre intake is with wholegrain cereals and breads, legumes, fruit and vegetables.

HIGH-FIBRE BREAKFAST Packed with fibre, baked beans on a piece of wholemeal toast or muffin is a great start to the day.

BRAN CEREALS Processed bran cereals are a good, high-fibre alternative to raw bran, but check the labels for added salt and sugar.

	CARB g	FIBRE g	FAT g	ENERGY kcal	kJ
CASSAVA					
peeled, boiled, 100g	30.5	1.6	0.5	131	550
CAULIFLOWER					
boiled, 100g	2	1.6	0	19	80
cheese, 200g	11	2	20	269	1130
raw, 50g	1	1	0	9	40
CELERIAC					
fresh, Peeled, boiled, 100g	5.5	3.2	0	31	130
fresh, peeled, 120g	5	4.5	0	29	120
CELERY					
chopped, boiled, 63g	1.5	0.7	0	8	35
raw, 2 x 10cm sticks, 40g	1	0.5	0.5	5	20
CEREAL					
bran strands, 40g	18.6	9.8	1.4	104	444
bran with fruit and oats, 45g	34.5	9	1.5	138	580
bran, natural, 12g	7.5	4.5	0.5	33	140
bran, oat, unprocessed, 2 tbsp, 22g	11	3.5	1.5	53	225
bran, rice, 15g	7.5	4	3	70	295
bran, wheat, processed, 45g	31	14	2.5	161	675
bran, wheat, unprocessed, 2 tbsp, 10g	1	4	0.5	15	65
branflakes, 30g	20.8	3.9	0.6	95	406
chocolate flavoured rice pops, 30g	28.3	0.2	0.3	115	491
cornflakes, 30g	25.8	0.3	0.2	108	461
cornflakes, with nuts, 30g	26.6	0.2	1.2	119	507
crispies, rice based, 30g	27	0.2	0.3	111	472
crunchy oat bran flakes with fruit, 45g	31	N	2	160	675
crunchy oat bran flakes, 30g	22.2	3	1.2	107	456
fruit & fibre flakes, 30g	21.6	2.1	1.4	105	444
fruit & nut wheat flakes, 45g	31	3	1.5	157	660
grapenuts, 30g	25.5	+	1	113	475
high-energy multi flakes, 100g	81.7	2	1.7	355	1504
high-energy wheat flakes, 45g	35.5	2	1.5	170	715
high-protein rice flakes, 30g	24.5	0.6	0.3	113	481
honeynut cornflakes, 30g	26.6	0.2	1.2	119	507
honey wheat puffs, 30g	26.6	0.9	0.6	116	493
instant oats, 36g	24.7	2.6	2.8	134	569
muesli, swiss style, 50g	36.1	3.2	3	182	770
muesli with no added sugar, 50g	33.5	3.8	3.9	183	776
muesli, apricot & almond, 60g	35.5	+	4.5	210	880
muesli, apricot toasted, 30g	20	+	3	121	510
muesli, natural, 60g	39.5	2	2.5	208	875
muesli, oat & honey, 45g	31	+	7	188	790
muesli, traditional, 60g	37	2	4	221	930
muesli flakes, 45g	32	+	1	157	660
multigrain flakes, 30g	21.5	1	3	115	485
nut crunchie clusters, 45g	33.5	+	3.5	177	745
oat bran, crunchy, 45g	30	+	2.5	170	710
oat bran & fruit, 40g	30.5	+	3.5	168	705
oat flakes, 30g	23.5	+	1.5	115	485
porridge oats made with water, 200g	18	1.6	2.2	98	418
porridge, made with whole milk, 200g	27.4	1.6	10.2	232	976
puffed wheat, 20g	13.5	1.1	0.3	64	273
puffed wheat with honey, 30g	25.4	1	0.2	104	445

	CARB g	FIBRE g	FAT g	ENERGY kcal	kJ
CEREAL cont.					
puffed wheat, sugar coated, 30g	25.4	1	0.2	104	445
cereal cont.					
rice puffs, 30g	26.9	0.2	0.3	111	472
rice puffs, sugar coated, 30g	28.7	0.1	0.2	114	487
small whole wheat biscuits, 45g	33.3	4.3	0.7	149	635
small whole wheat biscuits with added fruit, 40g	30.2	3.2	0.8	135	573
sugar coated cornflakes, 30g	28.1	0.2	0.2	113	482
sultana bran flakes, 50g	34	5	0.8	150	645
wheat biscuits, 1, 20g	15	1.9	0.5	70	300
wheat flakes, 30g	24	2.6	0.8	108	459
wheat flakes and raisins, 40g	26	4	1.5	140	585
wheat rings, 100g	86.1	N	2.7	372	1581
wheat biscuits, 2, 40g	30	3.8	1	140	600
whole wheat biscuit, 1, 22g	15	2.2	0.7	72	304
CEREAL BAR (see also MUESLI BAR)					
apricot fruity bar, 1 small	18	+	2.5	105	440
low sugar, 1 large	26	+	2.5	136	570
sports, 1	28.5	I	2.5	145	610
CHEESE					
blue brie, 30g	0	0	13.5	126	530
blue castello, 30g	0	0	10	110	465
blue vein, 30g	0	0	9.5	110	465
bocconcini, 20g	0	0	7	76	320
brie, 30g	0	0	8.5	101	425
camembert, 30g	0	0	8	92	385
canola, mild, 30g	0	0	6.5	94	395
cheddar, 30g	0	0	10	122	505
cheddar, low-fat, 30g	0	0	7	99	410
cheddar, processed, 30g	0	0	8	99	415
cheddar, reduced-fat, 30g	0	0	7	98	410
cheddar slices, 20g	1	0	4.5	61	255
cheddar slices, reduced-fat, 20g	1	0	3	48	200
cheddar sticks, 20g	1	0	6	67	280
cheshire, 30g	0	0	10	114	480
cottage, 1tbsp	0	0	2	29	120
cottage, with cheese, 1tbsp	0.5	0	0.5	17	70
cottage, low-fat, 1tbsp	0.5	0	0.5	18	75
cottage with pineapple, low-fat, 1tbsp	3	0.5	0	27	115
creamed cottage, 1tbsp	0.5	0	1	24	100
creamed cottage, low-fat, 1tbsp	1	0	0.5	19	80
cream, 30g	1	0	10	101	425
cream, fruit, 30g	0	0	7.5	83	350
cream, light, 30g	1	0	5	48	200
cream, full fat, 30g	0.5	0	10	102	430
double Gloucester, 30g	0	0	10	120	505
edam, 30g	0	0	8	106	445
emmental, 30g	0	0	9	113	475
fetta, 30g	0	0	7	83	350
goat's, 30g	0.5	0	4.5	58	245
gouda, 30g	0	0	9	113	475
hallourni, 30g	0	0	5	73	305
havarti, 30g	0	0	11	120	505

CHEESE Belonging in the milk and dairy food section of the food pyramidl, cheese should be consumed in moderation. It is an excellent source of calcium—the mineral essential for healthy teeth and bones. Many cheeses are relatively high in fat, although reduced-fat varieties are becoming increasingly available.

MOZZARELLA Pizza-lovers take note, this cheese is relatively high in fat (about 21%). If you're making pizza at home, replace half with low-fat mozzarella, so you get lots of taste, but less fat.

PARMESAN Hard cheeses can contain up to 35% fat, but with Parmesan, the strong flavour means that, though high in fat, a little can go a long way. Grate with the fine side of the grater and you'll end up using less cheese.

CHICKEN A good source of protein and B vitamins. If you are watching the amount of fat in your diet, avoid the skin of the chicken, which makes up about 50% of its fat content (remove it before cooking if possible). Without its skin, chicken is a low-fat source of protein, especially if you poach, steam or grill it.

BBQ CHICKEN Better than deep-fried chicken because fat is lost during cooking on the rotisserie. Avoid the skin, as that is where the fat is hidden.

BREASTS VS THIGHS
Although chicken breast can be 2 or 3g lower in fat than the same amount of thigh meat, it tends to dry out if cooked for too long. Thighs are perfect for slower cooking in curries and casseroles.

	CARB g	FIBRE g	FAT g	ENERGY kcal	ENERGY kJ
CHEESE cont.					
jarisberg, 30g	0	0	9	113	475
jarlsberg lite, 30g	0	0	5	82	346
lancashire, 30g	0	0	9.5	110	465
leicester, 30g	0	0	10	119	500
mozzarella, 30g	0	0	6.5	90	380
mozzarella, reduced-fat, 30g	0	0	5.5	86	360
parmesan, 30g	0	0	9.5	132	555
pizza, grated, 30g	0	0	6.5	93	390
processed, 30g	0	0	7	42	175
quark, 20g	0	0	2.5	26	110
quark, low-fat, 20g	0	0	0.5	15	65
reduced-fat, 20g	0	0	4.5	69	290
ricotta, 20g	0	0	2	30	125
ricotta, reduced-fat, 20g	0.5	0	1.5	25	105
ricotta, smooth, 20g	0	0	2	25	105
sheep's milk, fresh, 30g	0	0	6.5	90	380
soft, 30g	0	0	10	124	520
soya, 30g	0	0	8	93	390
stilton, 30g	0	0	9.5	111	465
swiss, 30g	0	0	9	114	480
wensleydale, 30g	0	0	9.5	112	470
CHERRIES					
canned in syrup, drained, 100g	17	0.6	0	70	295
glace, 6, 30g	20	0.3	0	77	325
raw, weighed with stones, 100g	12	0.7	0.1	53	225
CHEWING GUM					
sugarless, per piece, 10g	0	0	0	4	15
with sugar, per piece, 10g	3	0	0	9.5	40
CHICKEN					
breast, no skin, grilled, 100g	0	0	5	157	660
breast, with skin, grilled, 100g	0	0	12.5	218	915
breast, quarter, no skin, barbecued, 100g	0	0	6	199	835
breast, quarter, with skin, rotisseried, 100g	N	0	12.5	214	900
breast, lean, 100g	0	0	1	40	170
chicken pastrami, 1 serving, 30g	N	N	1	40	170
crispy-skinned, 100g	0	0	3	64	270
drumstick, no skin, baked, 2	0	0	9	179	750
drumstick, with skin, baked, 2	0	0	14.5	229	960
drumstick crumbed, 145g	N	0	17	313	1315
fried chicken (see FAST FOOD)					
nuggets, 1, 20g	2.5	0	3.5	57	240
roll, processed, 1 slice, 38g	4.5	N	9.5	158	665
sausage, cooked, skinless, 2	0	0	10	164	690
thigh, no skin, cooked, 2	0	0	6	126	530
thigh, with skin, cooked, 2	0	0	8	145	610
wing, with skin, cooked, 2	0	0	12	179	750
CHICKPEAS					
canned, drained, 186g	29.9	7.6	5.4	214	906
dried, boiled, 180g	32.8	7.7	3.8	218	922

	CARB g	FIBRE g	FAT g	ENERGY kcal	ENERGY kJ
CHICORY GREENS					
raw, 100g	2.8	1	0.6	11	45
CHILLI					
powder, 1 tsp, 5g	Tr	Tr	0	N	N
green, raw, each, 20g	1	N	0	4	15
red, raw, each, 20g	1	0.3	0	6	25
CHIVES					
fresh, 2 tbsp, 40g	Tr	0.8	0	1	5
CHOCOLATE					
after-dinner mint, 1, 6g	11	0	1.5	87	365
block, 100g	55.5	N	32.5	536	2250
coconut, bar, 1, 57g	33.2	+	14.9	270	1129
caramels, 1, 20g	12	0	5.5	99	415
cherry-flavoured centre, 1, 55g	30.5	0	13.5	248	1040
cream, 100g	43	N	46.5	604	2535
cooking, dark, 100g	56	+	31	505	2120
cooking, milk, 100g	61.5	+	28.5	505	2120
coated waffer biscuits, 1, 45g	27	N	11.5	220	945
coated candies, 1 packet, 55g	40	N	10.5	257	1080
coated peanuts, 1 packet, 55g	34	+	13.5	273	1145
coated malt balls, 1 packet, 45g	30	N	9.5	212	890
coated nougat and toffee bar, 1, medium, 65g	43.2	+	12.3	285	1204
coated nougat bar, 1, 25g	13.5	N	9	137	575
coated whipped bar, 1, 26g	16.5	+	4.1	103	435
coated biscuit fruit and nut bar, 1, 55g	27.5	+	16.5	280	1175
coated peanut bar, 1, 60g	36	+	13.5	283	1190
coated biscuit, 1, 55g	35	+	13.8	264	1128
choc bar, 1, 40g	23	+	11.5	204	855
full cream, milk, 1, 54g	32.1	+	16.4	286	1196
fruit & nut bar, 100g	54	+	34	540	2270
honeycomb bar, 80g	56	0	163	387	1625
in crisp sugar shells, 1 tube, 37g	27.3	+	6.5	169	711
soft centres, 100g	64.5	0	21.5	469	1970
triangular nougat bar, 1, 50g	28.5	N	15	264	1110
CHUTNEY					
fruit, homemade, 1tbsp	8.5	0.4	0	34	145
mango, 1tbsp	9	0.2	0	30	125
COCOA POWDER					
1tbsp	1.5	1.2	1	21	90
COCONUT					
cream, block,100g	7	+	68.8	669	2760
desiccated, dried, 25g	1.6	3.4	15.5	151	623
oil, 1tbsp	0	0	20	176	740
COFFEE					
for each teaspoon of sugar in coffee, add ...	5	0	0	19	80
cappuccino, whole milk, 1 cup, 200ml	N	0	5	89	375
cappuccino, skim milk, 1 cup, 200ml	N	0	0	50	210

CHOCOLATE Good for an occasional energy boost, a chocolate bar is, however, high in fat and sugar and does contain caffeine. Chocolate is made up of about 30% fat, usually in the form of cocoa butter, and this is what gives chocolate its melt-in-the-mouth texture. Carob is also high in fat, although it is caffeine-free.

MILK CHOCOLATE This is usually made by adding milk solids to chocolate. It has the same sugar content as dark and white chocolate.

WHITE CHOCOLATE Not a true chocolate because it doesn't contain cocoa solids. It is, however, still made from cocoa butter, milk and sugar, and is high in fat.

CREAM A concentrated source of saturated fat and calories. However, not all creams have the same fat content; a general rule is the thicker the cream, the higher the fat content. For example, single cream contains about 19% fat whereas clotted cream contains about 63% fat! Consider using low-fat yoghurt as a dessert alternative.

IMITATION CREAMS These are not necessarily lower in fat than 'real' creams. The saturated fat content tends to be lower because they are often made with vegetable rather than milk fats. However, they may still contain up to 50% fat.

HALF-FAT CREAM This has about 13% fat—half that of full cream. However, if you use low-fat yoghurt as a substitute, you will reduce the fat level to just 1%.

	CARB g	FIBRE g	FAT g	ENERGY kcal	ENERGY kJ
COFFEE cont..					
decaffeinated, black,1 cup, 200ml	0	0	0	0	0
filtered, black, 1 cup, 200ml	Tr	0	0	7	30
ground, 1 cup + 25ml whole milk, 225ml	2.5	0	1	23	95
ground, 1 cup + 25ml skim milk, 225ml	2.5	0	0	18	75
iced, plain, 1 cup, 200ml	1.5	0	7	59	250
iced, with whole milk ice cream & cream, 325 ml	N	0	12	179	750
instant black, 1 cup, 200ml	0	0	0	2	8
instant, 1 cup + 25ml whole milk, 225ml	1.5	0	1	18	75
instant, 1 cup + 25ml skim milk, 225ml	1.5	0	0	13	55
Irish, 1 cup, 200ml	Tr	0	10	189	795
milk, 1tsp coffee + 1 cup whole milk, 200ml	12.5	0	10	173	725
mocha, 1 cup, 200ml	N	0	10	119	500
percolated, black, 1, cup, 200ml	Tr	0	0	0	0
whitener, 1tsp	2	0	1.5	21	90
CORDIAL (see also SOFT DRINKS)					
citrus, 25% juice, prepared, 1 glass, 250ml	17	0	0	65	275
citrus, 60% juice, prepared, 1 glass, 250ml	18	0	0	73	.305
citrus, reduced sugar					
lemon, prepared, 1 glass, 250ml	N	0	0	69	290
undiluted, 1tbsp	9	0	0	34	145
CORN					
baby, canned, 6, 100g	2	1.5	0.4	23	96
cob, 1, large, 100g	11.6	1.3	1.4	66	280
creamed, canned, 100g	20	+	1	81	340
kernels, canned, 30g	8	0.4	0.4	37	156
CORN CHIPS (see also SNACK FOOD)					
cheese, 40g	25.5	2	9.5	193	810
flavoured, 40g	20	2	12	198	830
toasted snacks, 40g	21.7	0.4	12.8	208	867
CORNMEAL					
dry, 40g	30	1	0.5	145	610
COUSCOUS					
cooked, 100g	23	+	0	112	470
CRABAPPLE					
raw, 60g	12	+	0	45	190
CRACKERS (see also CRISPBREAD)					
cheese flavour, 2	4	+	1	24	100
cream, 2	4.5	0.4	2	40	170
rye, 2	5.5	1.6	1.5	38	160
rice snacks, cheese, 30g	22	+	2	117	490
rice snacks, sesame, 30g	22	+	2	117	490
sesame, 2	3	+	1	20	85
water crackers, 2	4.5	0.4	0.5	25	105
CRANBERRY JUICE					
1 glass, 250ml	36.5	N	0	143	600
CREAM					
aerosol, whipped, 100ml	4	0	30.5	293	1230
clotted, 100ml	2	0	63	586	2413
crème fraîche, 100ml	2.5	0	48	440	1850
double thick, rich, 100ml	3	0	54.5	499	2095
light, 100ml	3.5	0	17.5	189	795

	CARB g	FIBRE g	FAT g	ENERGY kcal	ENERGY kJ
CREAM cont.					
regular, 100ml	3	0	35.5	333	1400
thickened, 100ml	3.5	0	36.5	345	1450
thickened, light, 100ml	6	0	19	211	885
CREAM, SOUR					
extra light, 100ml	7	0	12.5	158	665
light, 100ml	5	0	18	193	810
regular, dairy 100ml	4	0	19	199	835
CREPE					
plain, 20g	7.5	0.5	2.5	65	275
CRISPBREAD					
high fibre, 1, 5g	4	1	0	17	70
bran & malt, 1	3.5	0.5	0	19	80
plain, 1	4.5	0.5	1	27	115
rye, 1, 10g	7.1	1.2	0.2	32	137
fat-free, 1	7	+	0	34	145
original, low fat, 1	5	+	1	32	135
puffed, 1	4	N	0	19	80
wholemeal, 1	5	+	1	29	120
swiss type, 1	16	1.2	0.5	79	330
– with sesame whole rye, 1	15	1.2	1	81	340
– multigrain, 1	9	1.2	1.5	60	250
– wholemeal, 1	9	1	1	58	245
wheatgerm type, original, 1	4	1	0.5	23	95
CROISSANT					
plain, 60g	23	1	12.2	216	903
CROUTONS					
1 serving, 15g	11	1	1	61	255
CRUMPET					
regular, toasted, 40g	17.4	0.8	0.4	80	338
wholemeal, toasted, 45g	17	1.5	0.5	85	355
CUCUMBER					
lebanese, raw, unpeeled, 5 slices, 35g	1	0.5	0	4	15
raw, unpeeled, 5 slices, 45g	3	0.5	0	4	15
CUMQUAT (KUMQUAT)					
raw, peeled, 1, 20g	3	0.8	0	12	50
CURRANTS					
dried, 75g	50.9	1.4	0.3	200	854
CURRY PASTE					
curry paste, 1tbsp	1.5	N	2	24	100
curry powder 1tbsp	3	2.8	1.5	30	125
hot curry paste, 1tbsp	1.5	N	2	26	110
Indian, 1tbsp	5	0	9	98	410
tandoori, 1tbsp	2	0	0	49	205
CUSTARD					
baked, egg, 100ml	9	0	4.5	95	400
bread & butter custard, 100ml	15.5	0.5	5.5	132	555
custard & fruit, 100ml	16	+	1.5	86	360
powder, prepared with whole milk, 100ml	12.5	0	4	96	405
powder, prepared with reduced-fat milk 100ml	13.5	0	1.5	82	345
pouring, regular, 100ml	16	0	1.5	88	370
DANISH PASTRY					
almond, 100g	46	2	25	428	1800

For a delicious low-fat alternative to cream, try combining low-fat ricotta with a little low-fat vanilla yoghurt.

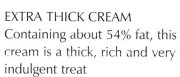

EXTRA THICK CREAM Containing about 54% fat, this cream is a thick, rich and very indulgent treat

BACK TO BASICS Home-made rice custard or bread-and-butter pudding made with skimmed milk are great reduced-fat desserts.

DESSERT A sweet treat is a perfect way to end a meal, and it doesn't have to be high in fat. A fruit sorbet is a delicious dessert with no fat at all, while pancakes or puddings made with low-fat dairy products are full of energy-giving carbohydrates. Fruit, eaten on its own or with some low-fat yoghurt, is one of the tastiest and healthiest desserts of all.

PIES AND TARTS The pastry in these tends to make them a high-fat option. Save them for occasional treats and choose fruit-based ones where possible.

CANNED FRUITS Fruits cooked in their own juice rather than in a sugar syrup are lower in calories.

	CARB g	FIBRE g	FAT g	ENERGY kcal	ENERGY kJ
DANISH PASTRY cont.					
apple, 100g	43.5	N	12	298	1250
apricot, 100g	38	N	12	270	1135
blueberry, 100g	40	N	12	286	1200
chocolate, 100g	24	N	19.5	280	1175
continental,100g	37.5	N	17	325	1365
custard, 100g	34.5	N	17	307	1290
pecan, 100g	52	N	20.5	417	1750
DATES					
dried, 6, 50g	28.5	2	0	113	485
fresh, seeded, chopped, 50g	14.5	0.9	0	54	228
DESSERT					
apple pie, bakery, 100g	28	+	8.5	198	830
apple pie, manufatured, 100g	38.5	1.7	12.5	279	1170
apple pie, reduced fat, 100g	32.5	+	7	199	835
apple & blackberry pie, 100g	42.5	+	17	336	1410
apple & rhubarb crumble, 120g	44	2	8	250	1050
apple strudel, 100g	41	+	11	273	1145
apricot pie, 100g	33	+	10	232	975
apricot pie, bought, 100g	38.5	+	14	293	1230
banana split with 3 scoops ice cream	55	1.1	10.5	325	1365
chocolate mocha, 100g	32.5	N	23.5	349	1465
bavarian, chocolate swirl, 100g	30.5	0	19.5	306	1285
blackberry & apple pie, 100g	35	+	10	232	975
chocolate mousse, 100g	28	0	13	232	975
chocolate mousse, dessert, 100g	23	0	9	201	845
chocolate mousse, light, 100g	19	0	4	136	570
Christmas pudding, 1 piece, 50g	29	1	6	167	700
custard tart 1, 135g	41	1.5	17.5	350	1470
junket (blancmange), 100g	48	0	3.5	114	480
lemon meringue pie, 1 piece, 75g	28.5	0.5	12.5	238	1000
pecan pie, 1 piece, 115g	64.5	+	21	450	1890
profiteroles, 1, 55g	N	+	9	130	545
pudding, blackberry sponge, 100g	59.9	+	5	299	1255
pudding, bread & butter, 100g	N	0.3	10	299	1255
pudding, chocolate mousse, 100g	32	N	6	209	880
pudding, chocolate sponge, 100g	41.5	+	4	217	910
pudding, creme caramel, 100g	20	N	3	119	500
pudding, lemon sponge, 100g	41	+	3	204	855
pudding, plum, 60g	30	+	4.5	164	690
pudding, rice, banana, canned, 125g	N	+	13	244	1025
pudding, rice, canned, 150g	22.5	0.3	3.75	135	562
pudding, rice, chocolate, canned, 125g	N	+	6.5	209	880
souffle, 100g	10.5	N	14.5	200	840
tiramisu, 100g	N	N	20	328	1380
trifle, bought, 120g	33	0.5	7	209	880
DEVON					
split, 50g	3	+	9	117	490
DIPS					
barbecue, 1tbsp	2.5	0	4.5	51	215
chicken & asparagus, 1tbsp	2	0	3	40	170
chilli, chip & dip type, 1tbsp	1.5	N	0	8	35
chive & onion, 1tbsp	1	0	6.5	65	275

	CARB g	FIBRE g	FAT g	ENERGY kcal	kJ
DIPS CONT.					
chunky bean, 1tbsp	2.5	+	0	11	45
corn & bacon, 1tbsp	2	+	1	20	85
corn relish, 1tbsp	2	0	3	37	155
cucumber & yoghurt, 1tbsp	0	+	2	26	110
French onion, reduced fat, 1tbsp	1	0	3.5	43	180
French onion, average, 1tbsp	0	0	5	61	255
French onion, low-fat, 1tbsp	3	0	2.5	42	175
gherkin dip, 1tbsp	3	+	4	49	205
herb & garlic, 1tbsp	2	+	4	45	190
hot & spicy, 1tbsp	2	0	3.5	44	185
hummus, 1tbsp	2	0.6	3.5	45	190
taramasalata, 1tbsp	2	+	4	46	195
DOLMADES					
60g	14.5	+	4	101	425
DOUGHNUT					
cinnamon sugar, 1 large, 75g	36.6	+	10.9	252	1061
cream-filled, 1, 70g	21	+	17	251	1055
iced, 1, 80g	38.5	+	19.5	339	1425
DRESSINGS (see also MAYONNAISE)					
caesar, 1tbsp	3	0	7	76	320
caesar, creamy, 1tbsp	2	0	7	70	295
coleslaw, average, 1tbsp	7	0	7	88	370
coleslaw, reduced fat, 1tbsp	5	0	7	82	345
coleslaw, light, 1tbsp	5.5	0	3.5	57	240
French, 1tbsp	2.5	0	4.5	49	205
French, olive oil, 1tbsp	3	0	3.5	43	180
French, low-fat, 1tbsp	3.5	0	0	14	60
Italian, 1tbsp	1.5	0	6	59	250
Italian, light, 1tbsp	2	0	3.5	40	170
Italian, low fat, 1tbsp	3.1	0	0	12	50
lemon pepper, reduced fat, 1tbsp	5	0	2	37	155
potato salad, 1tbsp	2.5	0	7	76	320
thousand island, 1tbsp	3.5	0	7	76	320
thousand island, light, 1tbsp	3.5	0	4	51	215
DRINKING POWDER					
barley type milk drink, 1tbsp	6	N	0	31	130
bournvita, 1tbsp	1.5	N	0	24	100
cocoa, 1tbsp	1.5	1.2	1	21	90
diet hot chocolate mix, 1 sachet	7	N	1	44	185
malted milk drink, 1tbsp	8	Tr	0	38	160
milk, 1tbsp	5.5	0	0.5	32	135
milkshake, strawberry, 1tbsp	12	0	0	50	210
Swiss style diet hot chocolate mix, 1 sachet	4	N	0	20	85
DUCK					
roast, no skin, 100g	0	0	9.5	182	765
roast, skin, 100g	0	0	26	307	1290
EGG					
1 small, 45g	0	0	4.5	64	270
1 medium, 55g	0	0	5.5	77	325
1 large, 60g	0	0	6	84	355
boiled 1, 53g	0	0	5.5	80	335
duck, boiled, 1, 65g	Tr	0	9	114	480

DRESSINGS A green salad is packed with fibre, vitamins and minerals, but a heavy hand with the dressing can add lots of unwanted calories. However, the vegetable oils in most dressings contain the more healthy monounsaturated or polyunsaturated fats, as well as vitamin E. Use more juice or vinegar to oil for a zesty dressing with less fat.

VINAIGRETTE All oils have the same fat content, but extra virgin olive oil has more taste, so a little in a vinaigrette goes a long way

CREAMY DRESSING This can add lots of saturated fat to your salad. For a healthy alternative, combine low-fat yoghurt with orange juice, mustard and herbs.

EGG A good source of protein, vitamins and minerals, eggs have had a hard time because of fears about their high cholesterol level. In fact, to keep your blood cholesterol low, it is more important to avoid saturated fat in your diet. So providing they are eaten in moderation, eggs can form part of a nutritious diet.

EGG YOLK Very nutritious, but also the source of cholesterol and fat in an egg.

EGG WHITE Contains no fat, so where possible, use an egg white rather than the whole egg.

SATURATED FAT Eggs contains about 10% fat, of which under half is saturated. The healthiest way to cook an egg is by boiling or poaching it.

	CARB g	FIBRE g	FAT g	ENERGY kcal	ENERGY kJ
EGG cont.					
eggs benedict, 2 eggs	0	N	52	690	2900
fried, 1, 60g	0	0	8	98	410
fried, 2 x 60g, with 1 lean grilled bacon rasher	Tr	0	19	251	1055
omelette, plain or herb, 2 x 60g eggs	0	0	17	214	900
poached, 1, 60g	0	0	6	76	320
poached, 2 x 60g, with lean grilled bacon rasher	Tr	0	16	236	990
quail, raw, 1, 10g	0	0	1	15	65
replacer, 1tsp	1.5	0	1	31	130
scrambled, 2 x 60g	Tr	0	16	195	820
turkey, raw, 1, 80g	Tr	0	9.5	134	565
white only, 1, 31g	0	0	0	14	60
yolk only, 1	0	0	5	54	225
EGGPLANT (see also AUBERGINE)					
baby, 4, 65g	1.5	1.5	0	11	45
fried in oil, 100g	2.8	2.3	32	302	1262
grilled, 3 slices, 90g	2.5	2	0	18	75
raw, 100g	2.2	2	0.4	15	64
ELDERBERRIES					
raw, 145g	10.5	++	0.5	51	215
ENDIVE					
Belgian, raw, 60g	0	1.2	0	6	25
curly, 80g	0	1.6	0	6	25
FALAFEL					
commercial, 2, 60g	10	+	9	140	590
FAST FOOD (shop bought)					
apple pie, 1, 80g	30.5	1.3	13	239	1005
bacon & cheese chicken fillet burger, 190g	34.5	+	22.2	460	1930
bacon & cheese burger, 1, 213g	52	+	18.3	487	2045
big burger, 1, 345g	55	+	32	646	2715
chips, regular, 117g	33	2.2	20	327	1375
chips, thick cut, 95g	25	2	13	233	980
chips, thin, 110g	37.4	2.3	17	308	1291
chicken nuggets, 7, 133g	17.5	+	29.5	411	1725
chicken nuggets, 4, 76g	10	+	17	236	990
chicken fillet burger, 1, 160g	28	+	16.5	282	1185
coleslaw, small tub, 116g	16	+	7	129	540
corn, 1 cobette, 78g	17	1.1	1	89	375
cornish pastie, 1, 155g	48	1.4	31.6	515	2151
fish, battered & deep-fried, 1 fillet, 145g	20	0.6	23	365	1535
fish stick, crab-flavoured, fried, 1, 27g	3.5	0	1.5	38	160
frankfurters, boiled, 2, 100g	3.5	+	20	247	1040
french fries, small, 76g	28.5	1.5	12	226	950
french fries, regular, 114g	42.5	2.3	18	337	1415
french fries, large, 159g	59	3	25	470	1975
fried chicken, coated, 2 pieces, 154g	8.5	+	29	413	1735
grilled chicken burger, 1, 180g	43.5	+	20	484	2035
hamburger, plain, 1, 170g	38	+	17.5	379	1590
hamburger, with bacon, 1, 185g	40.5	+	24	467	1960
hamburger, with cheese, 1, 195g	41.5	+	26	501	2105
hamburger, with egg, 1, 220g	44	+	26	517	2170
hot dog, 1, 100g	18.5	+	15	246	1035
individual cheesecake, 75g	25	0.3	7	175	735

	CARB g	FIBRE g	FAT g	ENERGY kcal	kJ
FAST FOOD (shop bought) cont.					
individual chocolate mousse, 75g	17	N	5.5	132	555
mashed potato & gravy, small tub, 120g	12.5	+	2	80	335
nuggets, 6 pieces, 106g	18.5	+	16.5	276	1160
sundae, caramel/chocolate, 1, 141g	36	0	9	240	1010
sundae, strawberry, 1, 141g	36	0	6.5	218	915
thickshake, average, all flavours, 1, 240g	48.5	0	8	299	1255
FAST FOOD (take-away)					
apple pie, 1, individual, 100g	56.7	1.7	15.5	369	1554
bacon and egg muffin, 1, 145g	32.5	+	19.5	377	1585
big breakfast, 1, 250g	475	+	31	568	2385
big burger in bun, 1, 205g	40	+	30	562	2360
cheeseburger, 1, 122g	33	+	12.5	300	1260
chicken nuggets, 9 pieces, 171g	26	+	26.5	212	890
cookies, 1 box	47	+	8.5	274	1150
fillet-of-fish, 1, 146g	40	N	16	351	1475
french fries, small	37.4	2.3	17	308	1291
french fries, medium	52	3.2	22.5	414	1740
french fries, large	65	4	30	527	2215
fried chicken, 1, 184g	46	0	20.5	424	1780
hash browns, 1, 54g	15	1.5	7	124	520
hot cakes, with butter & syrup, 1 serving	85	N	15	479	2010
junior burger, 1, 100g	30	N	10	267	1120
pan pizza, cheese, 1 slice, 105g	24.8	1.5	11.8	235	984
pan pizza, hawaiian, 1 slice, 125g	35	2	11	292	1225
pan pizza, premium range, 1 slice, 143g	35.5	2.5	15	339	1425
pan pizza, extra topping, 1 slice, 136g	32	2	16	342	1435
pizza thin crispy base, cheese, 1 slice, 79g	21.5	1.5	9	217	910
pizza thin crispy base, hawaiian, 1 slice, 99g	26	2	9.5	242	1015
pizza thin crispy base, premium type, 1 slice, 114g	25.5	2	14	289	1215
pizza thin, crispy base, extra topping, 1 slice, 114g	27	2.5	12.5	286	1200
quarter pounder burger, no cheese, 1, 176g	36	+	19.5	417	1750
sausage & egg muffin, 1, 162g	32	+	22	412	1730
sundae, hot caramel, 1, 175g	56.5	0	8	311	1305
sundae, hot fudge, 1, 175g	50	0	11	319	1340
sundae, strawberry, 1, 171g	47	Tr	6	255	1070
sundae, without topping, 1, 134g	29	0	6	183	770
samosa, meat, commercial, heated, 3, 45g	14	1	9	145	610
sausage roll, 1, 130g	31.5	1.5	23	371	1560
spring roll, deep-fried, 1 large, 175g	48	2	17	398	1670
thickshake, chocolate, regular, 1, 305g	60	+	9.5	360	1510
thickshake, strawberry, large, 1, 419g	81	0	12.5	480	2015
FAT (see also BUTTER)					
cocoa butter, 1tbsp	0	0	20	176	740
dripping, 1tbsp	0	0	20	176	740
lard, 1tbsp	0	0	20	176	740
replacer, 1tbsp	0	0	0	75	315
shortening, 1tbsp	0	0	16	143	600
suet, 1tbsp	Tr	0	17.5	162	680
FENNEL					
raw, 1 bulb, 150g	5	3.6	0	18	75

FAST FOOD Today, more and more people are taking advantage of take-away food. It can be high in fat but, if you look carefully, you'll find there are healthy options. A side dish of vegetables or a salad will fill you up and should be low in fat, providing it doesn't come with lashings of dressing. Choose chunky bread for sandwiches with low-fat fillings.

HAMBURGER This can be nutritious if home- made with lean mince, lettuce and tomato. If you're getting a take-away, skipping the cheese can cut the fat intake by about a third.

PIES These are generally very high in fat, especially saturated fat – even if the filling isn't meat. Try to keep your consumption of pies and pastries to a minimum.

FLOUR Made into breads, cakes, biscuits and pasta, flour is a good source of carbohydrate. Wholemeal flour is made from the whole grain, while white flour is made after the husk of the grain has been removed and, though still nutritious, does have less fibre, vitamins and minerals. Self-raising flour has more sodium than plain flour.

WHITE FLOUR For those who really don't like wholemeal flour, white flour can still be nutritious and is a good protein source.

SOYA A strong, gluten-free flour that is a richer source of protein than most flours. It can be combined with other flours to make batters and breads.

	CARB g	FIBRE g	FAT g	ENERGY kcal	ENERGY kJ
FENNEL cont.					
steamed, 1 bulb, 150g	5.5	3.4	0	16	70
FIGS					
dried, 5, 75g	40	5.6	1.2	40	168
ready to eat, 30g	14	2	0.5	63	267
raw, 1, 40g	4	0.6	0	17	74
stewed, sweetened, 100g	34	3.9	0.8	143	612
FISH (see SEAFOOD)					
FLOUR					
arrowroot, 100g	94	0.1	0.1	355	1515
barley, 100g	74.5	+	1.5	344	1445
besan, chickpea, 100g	49.6	10.7	5.4	313	1328
buckwheat, 100g	76.3	2.1	1.5	364	1522
corn, 100g	92	0.1	0.7	354	1508
maize, 100g	76	+	4	363	1525
millet, 100g	75.4	N	1.7	354	1481
potato, 100g	80	5.7	0.5	329	1380
rice, 100g	80.1	2	0.8	366	1531
rye, wholemeal, 100g	75.9	11.7	2	335	1428
semolina, raw, 100g	77.5	1.2	1.8	350	1489
soya, full-fat, 100g	23.5	11.2	23.5	447	1871
soya, low-fat 100g	28.2	13.5	7.2	352	1488
wheat, white, plain, 100g	77.7	3.1	1.3	341	1450
wheat, white, self-raising, 100g	75.6	3.1	1.2	330	1407
wheat, wholemeal, plain, 100g	63.9	9	2.2	310	1318
FRANKFURTER					
canned, drained, cooked, 175g	1.5	N	13	155	650
cocktail, canned. cooked, 1, 30g	0.5	0	5	62	260
cocktail, fresh, cooked, 1, 30g	1	N	6	74	310
fresh, cooked, 1, 75g	2.5	N	15	186	780
FRITTATA					
courgette & spinach, 1 slice, 250g	2	+	38.5	434	1825
Spanish (potato), 1 slice, 250g	13.5	+	27.5	369	1550
FROGS LEGS					
2 fried	0	0	10	178	750
FROMAGE FRAIS					
apricot, honey & vanilla, 130g	20	0	0.5	118	495
orange tangerine, 130g	20	0	0.5	120	505
peach & mango, 130g	14.5	0	5	113	475
strawberry, 130g	15	0	5	115	485
strawberry, light, 130g	18	0	0.5	111	465
vanilla, 130g	15	0	5	115	485
vanilla, light 130g	29	0	6	230	965
petit pot, 60g	10	0	5	87	365
FROZEN DINNERS					
beef goulash, 400g	57	N	10	409	1720
beef hot-pot, 400g	39	N	11	356	1495
beef, healthy eating type, 310g	37	+	8	277	1165
bubble & squeak, 1 serving	8.5	0	2	51	215
chicken carbonara, low fat, 400g	76	N	11.5	424	1780
chicken chasseur, healthy eating type, 310g	34	+	3.5	251	1055
chicken tikka, healthy eating type, 400g	56	N	11	390	1640
curried prawns, 350g	53	N	4.6	299	1255

	CARB g	FIBRE g	FAT g	ENERGY kcal	kJ
FROZEN DINNERS cont.					
fettucine carbonara, 375g	49	N	30.8	552	2320
fettucine mediterranean, healthy eating type, 400g	58	N	11	395	1660
fillet of lamb, healthy eating type, 310g	9	+	8	236	990
fish fingers, grilled, 375g	15	0.5	7.5	155	650
French style chicken, low fat variety, 400g	72	N	11.5	486	2040
fried rice, 350g	20	N	7.5	390	1640
Indian style chicken, low fat, 400g	64	N	11	448	1880
roast pork, healthy eating type, 320g	34	N	5.5	277	1165
lamb, low fat, 400g	64	N	10	419	1760
shepherd's pie, 170g	13.5	1.5	8	177	745
Thai style chicken curry, low fat, 400g	64	N	12	438	1840
veal cordon bleu, healthy eating type, 320g	47	N	29	515	2165
FRUIT (see INDIVIDUAL FRUITS)					
FRUIT BAR					
fruit fingers, apricot/strawberry/ tropical, 1, 22g	15	1	0.5	74	310
fruit fingers, raspberry, 1 bar, 15.6g	13	+	0.5	58	245
fruit roll, 1 bar, 37.5g	23	+	2	162	680
FRUIT, DRIED (see INDIVIDUAL FRUITS)					
FRUIT SALAD (see also INDIVIDUAL FRUITS)					
canned in pear juice, drained, 1 bowl, 220g	20.5	3.5	0	92	385
canned in syrup, drained, 1 bowl, 220g	25.5	2.5	0	106	445
fresh, 1 bowl, 140g	19.3	2.1	0.1	77	332
GARLIC					
fresh, 2 peeled cloves, 6g	0.5	+	0	6	25
powder, 1tbsp	7.5	0	0	13	55
puree, 1tbsp, 15g	2.5	N	5	57	236
GELATINE					
1tbsp	0	0	0	42	175
GHERKINS					
drained, 36g	9	0.4	0	38	160
GINGER					
beer, dry, 1 cup, 250ml	22	0	0	82	345
gingerbread biscuit, large, figure type, 70g	34.5	1	11.5	249	1045
ground, 1tbsp	4	+	0.5	19	80
raw, peeled, grated, 1tbsp	0.5	N	0	4	15
GNOCCHI					
potato/pumpkin, average serving, 150g	13	N	12	213	895
GOLDEN SYRUP					
1tbsp	21.5	0	0	83	350
GOOSE					
lean, roast, 100g	0	0	23	315	1325
GOOSEBERRIES					
canned, in syrup, 100g	18.5	1.7	0.2	73	310
raw, 100g	3	2.4	0	19	81
GOURD					
bottle, raw, peeled, 75g	0.6	1.9	0	8	35
ridge, raw, peeled, 75g	N	1.5	0	13	55
wax, raw, peeled, 75g	1	1	0	4	15

FRUIT Packed with vitamins and fibre, fruit is also low in fat and calories. According to healthy guidelines, we should all aim to eat at least five portions of fruit and vegetables every day. Choose from a variety of fresh, dried, canned (in natural juice rather than syrup) and frozen. Fruits are also rich in antioxidants.

DRIED FRUITS A rich source of dietary fibre, potassium and some iron, dried fruits don't contain much vitamin C. They can also be high in 'natural' fruit sugar—fructose, which causes tooth decay in the same way as sugar.

APPLE A good source of Vitamin C and fibre, apples make a cheap, convenient, healthy snack for between meals.

HERBS Adding herbs to your food is a healthy way to enhance the flavour of dishes without loading on the fat and salt. Many people also claim that herbs have medicinal properties and many of today's medical drugs do indeed come from plants. If you are interested in herbal medicine, try some herbal teas, which are now widely available.

RECIPE Make a healthy fresh salsa from some ginger, pawpaw, chilli, red onion and coriander leaves. Serve with chicken or fish.

PARSLEY High in vitamins A and C, it is delicious with egg and seafood dishes. Also a great sugarless breath freshener.

	CARB g	FIBRE g	FAT g	ENERGY kcal	ENERGY kJ
GRAPEFRUIT					
canned in juice, 125g	19	0.5	0	78	330
juice, sweetened, 1 glass, 200ml	19	0	0	87	365
juice, unsweetened, 1 glass, 200ml	16	0	0	71	300
raw, peeled, 1/2 whole, 110g	5	1	0	27	115
GRAPES					
black, 100g	15	0.7	0	63	265
black, muscatel, 100g	19	0.7	0	78	330
green, 100g	12.5	0.7	0	56	235
green, sultana, 100g	15	0.7	0	61	255
juice, sweetened, 1 glass, 200ml	N	0	1	84	355
juice, unsweetened, 1 glass, 200ml	N	0	1	84	355
GRAVY POWDER					
dry, 1tbsp	8	0	0.5	39	165
prepared, 225g	3	0	0	14	60
GUAVA					
canned in juice, 100g	15.7	3	0	60	258
raw, 1 medium, 100g	5	3.7	0.5	26	112
HAGGIS					
boiled, 100g	19.2	N	21.7	310	1292
HALVA					
30g	14.5	+	5	102	430
HAM					
& chicken luncheon meat, 2 slices, 23g	1	N	4	53	225
leg, canned, 2 slices, 35g	0	0	1.5	39	165
leg, fresh, lean, 2 slices, 46g	0	0	1.5	50	210
leg, fresh, untrimmed, 2. slices, 50g	0	0	4	70	295
light, 90% fat-free, 2 slices, 50g	0	0	2.5	36	150
shoulder, 2 slices, 50g	0	0	3	55	230
shoulder, canned, 2 slices, 35g	0	0	2	42	175
steak, grilled, 1, 115g	0	0	9	186	780
HAMBURGER (see FAST FOOD)					
HERBS					
average all varieties, dried, 1tbsp	Tr	N	0	19	80
average all varieties, fresh, chopped, 1tbsp	Tr	N	0	17	70
HONEY					
1tbsp	22	0	0	84	355
HONEYCOMB					
1 piece, 30g	22.2	0	1.5	86	360
HORSERADISH					
cream, 1tbsp	2.5	0.2	2	32	135
fresh, 5g	0.5	0.3	0.5	8	35
HUMMUS					
average serving, 100g	11.6	2.4	12.6	187	781
ICE CREAM BLOCK					
chocolate, 1, 158ml	36.5	0	0	150	630
neopolitan, 100ml	20	0	0	88	370
fruit-flavoured, 100ml	12.5	0	1	67	280
ICE CREAM					
caramel, 1	18	0	6	133	560
chocolate bar type, 1	21	0	19	260	1090
chocolate, 100ml	23	0	11.5	208	875
cone, large, vanilla, 1, 70g	24	0	12.5	220	925

	CARB g	FIBRE g	FAT g	ENERGY kcal	kJ
ICE CREAM cont.					
cone, chocolate, 1, 70g	23	0	13.5	226	950
cone, single, plain wafer type, 1, 15g	4	0	0	19	80
cone, sugar, 1, 10g	8.5	0	0.5	40	170
cone, waffle, 1, 18g	3.5	0	0	15	65
cone with 1 small scoop ice cream	8.5	0	3	64	270
cone with 1 small scoop reduced-fat ice cream	8.5	0	1.5	54	225
fruits of the forest, 1, 86ml	20	0	6	142	595
lemon, 86ml	18.5	0	6	137	575
mango, 100ml	21	0	8	168	705
raspberry, 1, 90ml	17.5	0	3.5	107	450
soft-serve, 1, 100ml	21.5	0	4.5	137	575
stick, chocolate flavoured, 1, 90ml	19	0	3.5	126	530
stick, vanilla, chocolate coated, 1, 93ml	20.5	0	17.5	248	1040
stick, Belgian chocolate coated ice cream 1, 120ml	43	0	27	432	1815
tub, fruit cream, 100ml	10	+	5	94	395
tub, chocolate, 100ml	9.5	0	5.5	92	385
tub, cookies & fudge,100ml	14.5	0	16	215	905
tub, light & creamy vanilla, 100ml	15	0	1.5	77	325
tub, natural vanilla, 100ml	10	0	6	101	425
tub, original vanilla, 100ml	10	0	4.8	89	375
tub, original extra creamy vanilla, 100ml	10.5	0	5.5	99	415
tub, strawberries & cream, 100ml	22.5	0	10.5	198	830
tub, double choc, 100ml	21	0	13.5	218	915
tub, vanilla choc-chip, 100ml	N	0	6	106	445
tub, vanilla light, 100ml	12	0	3	83	350
vanilla, 100ml	21	0	10	187	785
viennetta style, chocolate, 100ml	13	0	9	133	559
viennetta style, toffee, 100ml	13	0	10	129	540
viennetta style, vanilla, 100ml	13	0	10	124	520
JAM					
apricot, reduced sugar, 1tbsp	4	+	0	17	70
average, all types, 1tbsp	17	+	0	67	280
berry, 1tbsp	17.5	+	0	68	285
fruits of the forest, reduced sugar, 1tbsp	4	+	0	17	70
marmalade, orange, 1tbsp	17	+	0	65	275
marmalade, reduced sugar, 1tbsp	4	+	0	17	70
JELLY					
jelly, low-sugar, prepared, 1 bowl, 270ml	0	0	0	24	100
jelly, prepared, 1 bowl, 280ml	45.5	0	0	188	790
JUICE (see INDIVIDUAL FRUITS)					
KALE					
cooked, 65g	3.5	1.5	0.5	18	75
raw, 35g	3.5	1	0	18	75
KIWI FRUIT					
raw, peeled, 1 small, 75g	7.5	1.5	0	36	150
KOHL RABI					
peeled, boiled, 50g	2.5	1	0	18	75
LAMB					
chump chop, lean, grilled, 1, 55g	0	0	4.5	111	465
chump chop, untrimmed, grilled, 1, 65g	0	0	12	182	765
cutlet lean, grilled or baked, 1, 30g	0	0	4	70	295
cutlet, untrimmed, grilled or baked, 1, 40g	0	0	10.5	131	550

ICE CREAM As a general rule, the creamier the ice cream is, the higher the fat content. Ice cream is a good source of vitamins and calcium, but the milk or cream does add saturated fat. There are now many alternatives to ice cream in our supermarkets, including frozen fruit, tofu or yoghurt desserts – look out for the low-fat varieties.

SORBET With no fat, this is a refreshing, but sweet, alternative to ice cream. Usually made with fruit, so it can be high in vitamin C.

LOW-FAT FROZEN FRUIT DESSERTS Sometimes with less than 2g fat per serving, these desserts are guilt-free and come in a variety of flavours.

LAMB Although lamb was once considered to be a very fatty meat, changes in farming and breeding techniques have produced much leaner lamb that is widely available. Average, well-trimmed lamb can contain less than 8% fat, which is no more than many cuts of beef or pork. It's also worth trying out healthier methods of cooking, such as grilling, rather than just roasting.

TRIM LAMB For a very lean cut of lamb, try eye of loin or backstrap. Avoid overcooking as lean cuts tend to dry out. Add to a stir-fry or try searing under the grill.

RECIPE For no-fuss, low-fat lamb, marinate trimmed lamb cutlets in tandoori paste, lemon juice and plain low-fat yoghurt overnight. Grill until tender.

	CARB g	FIBRE g	FAT g	ENERGY kcal	kJ
LAMB cont.					
heart, baked, 70g	0	0	5.5	129	540
kidney, simmered, 150g	0	0	6.5	218	915
leg, lean, baked, 2 slices, 80g	0	0	5	158	665
leg, untrimmed, baked, 2 slices, 90g	0	0	10.5	201	845
liver, fried, 40g	0	0	5.5	96	405
loin chop, lean, grilled, 1, 35g	0	0	2.5	62	260
loin chop, untrimmed, grilled, 1, 50g	0	0	15.5	182	765
neck chop, lean, stewed, 1, 40g	0	0	5.5	101	425
neck chop, untrimmed, stewed, 1, 50g	0	0	14	176	740
shank, lean, cooked, 1, 130g	0	0	4.5	180	755
shank, untrimmed, cooked, 1, 100g	0	0	10.5	223	935
shoulder, lean, baked, 1 slice, 25g	0	0	2	46	195
shoulder, untrimmed, baked, 1 slice, 30g	0	0	6	87	365
trim, butterfly steak, grilled, 100g	0	0	4.5	125	525
trim, fillet, grilled, 100g	0	0	4	115	485.
trim, roast loin, baked, 100g	0	0	4	119	500
trim, schnitzel steak, grilled, 100g	0	0	3.5	111	465
strips, grilled, 100g	0	0	3.5	114	480
LASAGNE (see also PASTA)					
beef, commercial, 400g	62.8	2.8	24	572	2412
bolognaise, 400g	67.5	+	11.5	481	2020
lean beef lasagne, 400g	64	+	8.5	440	1850
LEEK					
sliced, boiled, l serving, 45g	1.2	0.8	0.3	9	39
LEMON					
curd, 1tbsp	10.5	0	3.5	76	320
juice, 100 ml	2.5	0	0	26	110
flavoured-spread, 1tbsp	13	0	1	60	250
raw, whole, 1, 65g	2.1	+	0	12	51
LENTILS					
burger, 1, 70g	15.5	2	1.5	213	895
dhal, 125g	14	2.5	9	177	745
dried, boiled, 200g	35	3.8	0.8	200	848
LETTUCE					
cos, 1 serving, 35g	0.6	0.3	0	6	25
iceberg, 35g	0.6	0.3	0	2	10
average, 35g	0.6	0.3	0	5	21
LIME					
juice, 1tbsp	2	0	0	6	25
raw, peeled, whole, 1, 45g	0.5	+	0	9	40
LINSEEDS (FLAXSEEDS)					
1tbsp	4	+	4	58	245
LIQUORICE					
allsorts, 6, 56g	43	1	1.2	195	821
pieces, 5, 65g	42	1	1	181	759
LIVERWURST					
60g	0.5	+	17.5	198	830
LOGANBERRIES					
raw, 100g	13	2.4	0.5	55	230
LOQUATS					
6 medium, 78g	4	+	0	20	85

	CARB g	FIBRE g	FAT g	ENERGY kcal	kJ
LOTUS ROOT					
canned, cooked, 100g	16	+	0	65	275
raw, peeled, 100g	17	+	0	74	310
LYCHEES					
canned in syrup, drained, 100g	17.7	0.5	0	68	290
raw, peeled, 100g	14.3	0.7	0.1	58	248
MACARONI					
cheese, home-made, 1 serving, 150g	20.4	0.8	16.2	267	1115
cheese, bought, 1 serving, 243g	49	1	15.5	405	1700
cheese, traditional, canned, 1 serving, 335g	71	1	21	557	2340
cheese & bacon, 1 serving, 293g	58	1	21	476	2000
cheesy fun shapes, 1 serving, 335g	71	1	21	557	2340
plain, boiled, 1 serving, 100g	18.5	0.9	0.5	86	365
MANDARIN					
canned in juice, drained, 1 serving, 100g	7.7	0.3	0	32	135
peeled, whole, 1, 60g	5	1	0	24	100
MANGO					
canned in syrup, 200g	40.6	1.4	0	144	660
chutney, 1tbsp	8.5	0.5	0	34	145
green, 150g	25	3	0	50	245
ripe, raw, peeled, whole, 1, 150g	21.2	3.9	0.3	86	368
MARGARINE					
average, 1 portion, 11g	0.1	0	9	81	334
light, salt-reduced, 11g	0	0	4	36	150
lite, 1tsp, 5g	0	0	3	26	110
sunflower spread, 11g	0.1	0	7.3	67	274
dairy blend, extra-soft, 1tsp, 5g	0	0	3	26	110
blended, 1tsp, 5g	0	0	3.5	31	130
butter type, 1tsp, 5g	0	0	4	36	150
high polyunsaturated spread, 1tsp	0	0	4	33	140
olive oil, type, 1tsp, 5g	0	0	4	33	140
sunflower spread, fat-reduced, 1 tsp, 5g	0	0	2.5	21	90
MARROW					
peeled, boiled, 100g	4	0.5	0	19	80
raw, peeled, 100g	3.5	0.5	0	17	70
MARZIPAN					
20g	11	0.6	3.5	80	335
MATZO					
meal, 50g	40	+	0	171	720
plain cracker, 30g	25	1	0.5	118	495
MAYONNAISE					
97% fat free, 1tbsp	9	0	20	45	190
cholesterol free, 1tbsp	7.5	0	3.5	63	265
sunflower type, 1tbsp	7.5	0	7.5	107	450
light, 1tbsp	8	0	7	63	265
olive oil type, 1tbsp	5	0	8.5	97	410
premium type, 1tbsp	7	0	3	58	245
traditional, 1tbsp	3	0	21.5	201	845
reduced calorie, 1tbsp	7	0	3	55	230
MEAT SUBSTITUTES					
micro protein, 100g	2	4.8	3.5	86	360
vegetarian mince, 100g	22	1.4	2.5	304	1280

DICED LAMB To make sure your diced lamb is lean, purchase lean cuts such as fillet or eye of loin and dice your own.

CUTTING FAT OFF LAMB When buying lamb, check how much fat you can see and whether it can be removed—a lamb cutlet that has been trimmed will have a lot less saturated fat. The leanest cuts are the leg and shank, the fattiest are the shoulder and rack.

MILK Is an excellent source of calcium and protein and also contains vitamins and minerals. It is an essential part of many people's diet, and is particularly important for infants and young children.

BUTTERMILK A low-fat alternative to milk, buttermilk has a slightly sour taste and can be used in cooking to replace whole milk.

SOYA MILK As it is not a natural source of calcium, many varieties have calcium added. However, they may also be sweetened so avoid frequent consumption.

	CARB g	FIBRE g	FAT g	ENERGY kcal	kJ
MELON					
casaba, raw, peeled, 100g	6	0.4	0	32	135
honeydew, raw, peeled, 160g	10.5	0.6	0.5	50	210
rock, raw, peeled, 250g	12	1	0	55	230
water, raw, peeled, 100g	5	0.2	0	23	95
MERINGUE					
25g	22.5	0	0	92	385
MILK					
buttermilk, cultured, dairy, 1 carton, 250ml	4	0	5.5	132	555
calcium enriched, 1 cup, 250ml	12.5	0	2.5	119	500
condensed, sweetened, 1 tin, 250ml	180	0	30	1060	4455
condensed, sweetened, skim, 250ml	199	0	1	901	3785
cultured, reduced-fat, 250ml	12	0	5	134	565
cultured, skim, 250ml	14.5	0	0.5	108	455
evaporated, reduced-fat, canned, 250ml	28.5	0	5.5	241	1015
evaporated, skim, canned, 250ml	28.5	0	1	200	840
evaporated, whole-fat, canned, 250ml	27	0	21.5	373	1565
fat-reduced, protein-increased, 250ml	14	0	3.5	126	530
flavoured, chocolate, 250ml	23	0	9.5	204	855
flavoured, chocolate, reduced-fat, 1 cup, 250ml	21.5	0	4.5	156	655
flavoured, malt & honey, 250ml	27	0	2.5	170	715
flavoured, strawberry, 250ml	23	0	9	201	845
flavoured, strawberry, reduced-fat, 250ml	24	0	4	158	665
full-cream, 250ml	12	0	10	167	700
goat's, 1 cup, 250ml	9.5	0	6.5	127	535
lite, 250ml	14.5	0	3.5	133	558
low-fat, high-calcium, 250ml	17	0	0.5	120	505
milkshake, 275ml	47	0	12	349	1465
milkshake, thick, 300ml	60	0	10	355	1490
powder, malted, 1tbsp	5.5	0	0.5	32	135
powdered, full-cream, 1tbsp	3	0	2	39	165
powdered, skim, 1tbsp	4	0	0	29	120
rice, 250ml	N	0	2.5	157	660
sheep's, 250ml	13.5	0	17.5	268	1125
skimmed, 250ml	12.5	0	0.5	88	370
soya, natural, 250ml	18.5	+	7	158	665
soya, low-fat, 250ml	12	N	1.8	91	382
soya, lite, 250ml	15	N	1.5	107	450
soya, flavoured, banana, 250ml	23	+	2	138	580
soya, flavoured, chocolate hazelnut, 250ml	18.5	5	7	158	665
MILLET					
cooked, 174g	41	+	1.5	206	865
MISO (SOYA BEAN PASTE)					
1tbsp	6	+	1	40	170
MIXED PEEL					
100g	59	4.8	1	231	984
MIXED VEGETABLES					
frozen, boiled, 1 serving 100g	6.6	+	0.5	42	180
MOLASSES					
1tbsp	14	0	0	54	225
MUESLI (see CEREAL)					
MUESLI BAR (see also CEREAL BAR)					
apricot & coconut, 1 bar, 31g	19.5	N	7.5	149	625

	CARB g	FIBRE g	FAT g	ENERGY kcal	kJ
MUESLI BAR (see also CEREAL BAR) cont.					
apricot & fibre, yoghurt-coated bar,					
1 bar, 50g	28	+	9.5	202	850
brown rice, macadamia & ginger, 1 bar, 50g	26	+	14	234	985
chewy fruit, 1 bar, 31g	21	1	5	131	550
crunchy fruit, 1 bar, 31g	17.5	1.2	7	146	615
crunchy original, yoghurt, 1 bar, 31g	22	+	4	126	530
fruit, apricot, 1 bar, 32g	22.5	+	4.5	137	575
nut crumble, 1 bar, 31g	20	+	6	143	600
nut & muesli, carob-coated, 1 bar, 50g	28	+	11	218	915
peach & pear, 100% fruit, 1 bar, 25g	15	N	8.6	131	550
yoghurt, apricot, 1 bar, 31g	20.5	+	5.5	138	580
yoghurt tops, fruit salad, 1 bar, 31g	21.5	+	5	136	570
MUFFIN					
1 medium, plain, 60g	29	1.5	8	169	710
1 large, 100g	48	2	13	279	1170
1 extra large, 150g	72	3	19.5	418	1755
blueberry, 1 , 150g	56	+	13	352	1480
bran, 1, 190g	67	15	27.5	550	2310
calorie-reduced, 1, 152g	47.5	+	18	370	1555
high-fibre, 1, 63g	27.5	+	2	152	640
fruit, 1, 60g	27	+	1.5	151	635
soya & linseed, 1, 67g	N	++	6.5	180	755
spicy fruit topped, 1, 67g	30	+	2	168	705
white, bread type, 1, 67g	28.5	2	1	151	635
wholemeal, bread type, 1, 67g	N	+	2	156	655
low-fat, 1, 152g	57.5	+	2.5	283	1190
mixed berry, 1, 60g	38	+	5	207	870
muffin mix, apple & sultana, prepared, 1, 60g	33	+	7	202	850
muffin mix, blueberry & apricot,					
prepared, 1, 60g	32	+	6.7	202	850
muffin mix, choc-chip, prepared, 1, 60g	32	N	7	213	895
MULBERRIES					
raw, 100g	4.5	++	0	29	120
MUSHROOMS					
button, raw, 100g	1.5	1.1	0.5	24	100
canned, 100g	1.5	1.3	0.5	15	65
canned in butter sauce, 100g	3.5	1	1	27	115
champignon, canned, 100g	1	1	0	13	55
chinese, dried & rehydrated, 25g	4	N	0	14	60
enoki, raw, 100g	7	N	0.5	35	145
oyster, raw, 100g	6	+	0.5	37	155
shiitake, dried, 4, 15g	11	+	0	44	185
straw, canned, drained, 100g	4.5	+	0.5	32	135
swiss brown, 100g	N	+	0	23	95
MUSTARD					
American, 1tbsp	1	0	0	15	65
English, 1tbsp	1	0	0	15	65
French, 1tbsp	1	0	0	15	65
powder, wholegrain, 1tsp, 5g	0.5	1	1	18	75
seeded, 1tbsp	1	+	0	15	65
NASHI PEAR					
raw, unpeeled, 1, 130g	9.2	2	0	38	158

MUESLI & CEREAL BARS Often eaten as a quick snack, muesli bars can be a good source of dietary fibre and may be a healthier snack option than a packet of crisps or a chocolate bar. However, they are not always as healthy as they seem and can contain up to 17g of fat and lots of sugar per bar. Check the label carefully.

CAROB-COATED BARS An alternative to chocolate, carob has the same amount of fat but is free of caffeine.

MUESLI BARS Some varieties are high in sugar and provide a great energy boost when eaten before or after exercise. If you are not that active, they may provide more energy than you need.

OIL All oils contain roughly the same amount of fat, but the important issue is the type of fat. Palm and coconut oils, often used for frying, are high in saturated fat and should be avoided, while the other oils have more monounsaturated and polyunsaturated fats, both of which have health benefits.

MONOUNSATURATED OILS
These oils, such as olive, canola or peanut, are thought to lower blood cholesterol when they replace saturated fat in the diet.

POLYUNSATURATED OILS
These oils, such as sunflower or corn oil, contain essential fatty acids that the body cannot produce itself. They may also lower blood cholesterol when they replace saturated fats in the diet.

	CARB g	FIBRE g	FAT g	ENERGY kcal	kJ
NECTARINE					
raw, unpeeled, 1, 75g	6.75	1	0	30	126
NOODLES					
egg, boiled, 1 portion, 100g	13	0.6	0.5	62	264
instant, boiled, 1 portion, 100g	N	+	5	367	1540
rice, boiled, 1 portion, 100g	21.5	0.5	0.5	99	415
rice, fried, 1 portion, 150g	16.8	0.8	17.2	230	964
rice, vermicelli, boiled, 30g	N	+	0.5	110	460
buckwheat, boiled, 100g	21.5	+	0	99	415
quick-cook noodles, all flavours, 1 packet, 85g	54	+	16	390	1640
noodles, rice, dry, 100g	81.5	+	0.1	360	1506
wheat, fried, 80g	50	+	17	374	1570
wheat, steamed, 80g	60	+	2	283	1190
NUTMEAT					
canned, 100g	6	+	8.5	195	820
NUTS					
almond, blanched, 85g	5.8	6.3	47.5	520	2185
almond, chocolate-coated, 75g	49.5	4.5	33.5	517	2170
almond, raw, 4	0.5	1.5	8	87	365
almond, raw & unpeeled, 85g	2	2.3	17.5	195	817
almond, smoked, 30g	1.5	N	15	194	815
almond, sugar-coated, 30g	N	N	12	130	545
brazil, raw, 80g	2.5	3.4	54.5	546	2291
cashew, raw, 75g	13.6	2.4	36	430	1805
cashew, roasted, 75g	14	2.4	38	458	1925
chestnut, raw, 72g	26	3	2	122	514
hazelnut, raw, 70g	4.2	4.5	44.4	455	1911
macadamia, salted, 73g	3.5	3.8	56.6	546	2293
mixed, 78g	6	4.7	42	473	1988
mixed nuts & raisins, 100g	31.5	4.5	34	481	2004
peanut, raw, 78g	9.75	4.8	35.9	440	1848
peanut, roasted, 78g	8	5	38.8	459	1930
pecan, raw, 55g	3.2	2.6	38.5	379	1592
pinenut, raw, 1tbsp, 15g	0.6	0.3	10.2	103	433
pistachio, raw, 63g	5	3.8	35	379	1590
walnut chopped, raw, 55g	1.8	2	38	378	1589
OATMEAL					
40g	29	2.7	3.5	160	674
OIL					
blended, 1tbsp	0	0	20	176	740
cod liver, 1tbsp	0	0	20	176	740
olive oil, 1tbsp	0	0	19	167	703
OKRA					
boiled, 6 pods, 65g	1	2.3	0	13	55
OLIVES					
black, 6 medium, 40g	N	N	7	39	165
green, 6 medium, 50g	Tr	1.5	5.5	56	211
stuffed, 5 olives, 20g	0.5	1.5	1.5	18	75
ONION					
brown, raw, peeled, 1 medium, 100g	4.5	1.4	0	24	100
pickled, drained, 2, 36g	4.5	0.4	0	21	90
red, raw, peeled, 1 small, 100g	4.5	1.4	0	25	105
spring, raw, whole, 1, 14g	0.5	0.2	0	3	14

	CARB g	FIBRE g	FAT g	ENERGY kcal	kJ
ONION cont.					
white, raw, peeled, 1 medium, 100g	4.5	1.4	0	26	110
ORANGE					
all varieties, raw, peeled, 120g	10.2	2	0	44	186
juice, freshly squeezed, 100ml	8.1	0.1	0	33	140
juice, commercial, unsweetened, 100ml	8.8	0.1	0	36	153
PANCAKE					
average, homemade, 1, 16 cm, 50g	14	0.5	1	75	315
PAPADUM					
fried, 3 small, 10g	3.9	N	1.7	37	155
grilled or microwaved, 3 small	N	N	0	17	70
PAPAYA (PAWPAW)					
raw, peeled, 100g	8.8	2.2	0	36	153
canned in juice, 100g	17	0.7	0	65	275
PARSNIP					
raw, peeled, boiled, 100g	12.9	4.7	1.2	66	278
PASSIONFRUIT					
1 average, 40g	2.5	1.5	0	19	80
PASTA (see also LASAGNE AND SPAGHETTI)					
egg, cooked, 1 serving, 200g	51	?	1	261	1095
plain, all shapes, cooked, 1 serving, 180g	44.5	1.8	0.5	213	895
ravioli, cheese & spinach, cooked, 1 serving, 265g	88	+	16.5	640	2690
ravioli, meat, cooked, 1 serving, 265g	82.5	+	17.5	602	2530
spinach, cooked, 1 serving, 200g	54.5	+	1	258	1085
tomato & herb fettucine, cooked, 200g	39	+	1.5	186	780
tortellini, cheese & spinach, cooked, 1 serving, 265g	88	+	16.5	640	2690
tortellini, meat, 1 serving	N	N	5	379	1590
wholemeal, cooked, 1 serving, 180g	42	6.3	1.6	203	854
PASTA SAUCE					
carbonara, jar, 1 serving, 125g	21.5	+	6.5	158	665
creamy mushroom, 1 serving, 280g	25	+	0.5	119	500
spicy tomato, 1 serving, 125g	20.5	+	5	140	589
tomato, bottled, 1 serving, 280g	26.5	+	2	134	565
PASTRY					
choux, cooked, 30g	9	0.4	7	108	454
filo, 2 sheets	15	N	0.5	77	325
flaky, average portion, cooked, 50g	23	0.9	20.3	280	1176
hot-water, 50g	27	N	10	213	895
puff, 1 sheet, 170g	63	N	42.3	671	2820
shortcrust, cooked, 100g	54.2	2.2	32.3	521	2174
strudel, 50g	23	N	20	267	1120
suet crust, 50g	27	N	10	213	895
wholemeal, cooked, 100g	44.6	6.3	32.9	499	2080
PATE					
chicken liver, 1tbsp	N	0	2.5	27	112
country, 1tbsp	0.5	0.5	5	59	250
PAVLOVA					
pavlova shell mix, prepared, 1 serving, 60g	4	0	0	173	725
shell, with cream & passion fruit, 1 serving	N	+	11	315	1325
PAWPAW whole, raw, 100g	7	2	0	30	125
PEACH					
canned in jelly, snack pack	N	N	0	95	400
canned in juice, drained, 140g	12.5	1.2	0	56	235

PASTA & PASTA SAUCE
High in starchy carbohydrates and low in fat, pasta is a healthy way to fill up. However, it's the pasta sauce that can pile on the fat and calories. Always serve plenty of pasta with only a relatively small amount of topping, and opt for a homemade tomato sauce, rather than high-fat creamy or cheesy sauces.

WHOLEMEAL PASTA With over twice the dietary fibre of plain pasta, wholemeal is particularly good in pasta bakes and salads.

PLAIN PASTA Though the flour used to make plain pasta has had the wheatgerm and bran removed, it still contains plenty of fibre and starch.

PORK Thought of as a fatty meat, pork is now bred to be leaner. In fact, lean cuts of pork often have less fat than beef, lamb and chicken. However, other pork products, such as salami, sausages, spare ribs and bacon, have a much higher fat content in general, and are also quite high in saturated fat.

BACON The fat content of bacon can be reduced by up to 50%, simply by trimming off all visible fat and grilling rather than frying.

LEAN STEAK Lean pork steaks are ideal for grilling or pan-frying with little or no added fat. Always remove visible fat before cooking.

	CARB g	FIBRE g	FAT g	ENERGY kcal	ENERGY kJ
PEACH cont.					
canned in syrup, 250g	14	2.2	0	61	255
dried, 25g	13	1.8	0	61	255
raw, 1 medium, 140g	9	2	0	44	185
stewed, with sugar, 100g	25.5	2.9	0.5	106	445
stewed, without sugar, 100g	21.5	3	0.5	92	385
PEAR					
canned, snack pack 140g	N	2	0	82	345
canned in pear juice, drained, 250g	25.5	3.5	0	106	445
canned in syrup, drained, 250g	37	2.75	0	148	620
canned in water, drained, 250g	16	3.5	0	64	270
dried, 2, 87g	60.5	7.2	0.5	227	955
juice, canned, 200ml	27.5	0	0	112	470
raw, unpeeled, 185g	18.5	4	0	74	311
PEAS					
green, cooked, 1 serving, 165g	10.5	7.4	0.5	80	335
peas, raw, 170g	10	8	1	98	410
split, dried, cooked, 1 serving, 180g	12	4.9	1	104	435
sugar snap, 170g	10	2.2	1	98	410
PHEASANT					
raw, meat only, 125g	0	0	4.5	165	695
PIGEON					
breast, lean, roasted, 125g	0	0	14.5	263	1105
PINEAPPLE					
canned in juice, drained, 1 bowl, 250ml	25.5	1.25	0	112	470
canned in syrup, drained, 1 slice, 40g	8	0.3	0	33	140
juice, unsweetened, canned, 250ml	27	0	0	111	465
raw, peeled, 1 slice, 110g	9	1.3	0	42	175
PIE meat, average,					
all types, 1, 190g	34	0.8	26	429	1800
PIZZA (see FAST FOOD)					
PLUM					
canned in syrup, drained, 1 serving, 225g	35	1.8	0.3	132	557
raw, 100g	8.8	1.6	0	36	155
stewed, without sugar, 1 serving, 250g	17	4	0	85	357
POLENTA					
dry, 60g	41	+	1	198	830.
POMEGRANATE					
raw, peeled, 100g	11.8	3.4	0.2	51	218
POPCORN					
caramel-coated, 100g	77.6	N	20	480	2018
plain, commercial, 2 scoops, 16g	8.5	N	4	75	315
PORK					
bacon, breakfast rasher, grilled, 1, 34g	0	0	1.5	48	200
barbecued, Chinese-style, 100g	3.5	N	15	233	980
belly, rasher, untrimmed, grilled, 100g	0	0	22	298	1250
crackling, 30g	0	0	9	142	610
fillet lean, baked, 1, 100g	0	0	5	169	710
forequarter chop, lean, grilled, 1, 95g	0	0	7.5	171	720
forequarter chop, untrimmed, grilled, 1, 100g	0	0	28.5	343	1440
leg roast, lean, 2 slices, 95g	0	0	4	163	685
leg roast with fat, 2 slices, 100g	0	0	26.5	338	1420
leg, lean, grilled, 1, 100g	0	0	3.5	156	655

	CARB g	FIBRE g	FAT g	ENERGY kcal	kJ
PORK cont.					
leg, untrimmed, grilled, 1, 100g	0	0	6	171	720
loin chop, lean, grilled. 1, 100g	0	0	5.5	174	730
loin chop, untrimmed, grilled, 1, 100g	0	0	30	362	1520
medallion steak, lean, grilled, 1 small, 100g	0	0	5.5	187	785
medallion steak, untrimmed, grilled, 1 small, 100g	0	0	22.5	307	1290
mince, 100g	0	0	30	75	315
pie, 1, 180g	46.5	1.8	53.5	763	3205
ribs, spare, 100g	0	0	10	114	480
steak, lean, grilled, 100g	0	0	4.5	161	675
steak untrimmed, grilled, 100g	0	0	17.5	259	1090
POTATO					
baked, jacket, no oil, 1 medium, 150g	21.5	2	1	109	460
boiled, peeled, 1 medium, 150g	19.5	1.5	0.5	96	405
boiled, unpeeled, 1 medium, 150g	20	2	0	98	410
chips, oven-cook, frozen, cooked, 100g	25	2	3	131	550
fries (thin-cut), medium serving	43	1	18	338	1420
oven-fried, 100g	29	6	13	245	1030
hash brown, 1 average, 55g	15	1	12	171	720
mashed with milk & butter, 1 serving, 120g	N	2.5	1	77	325
mashed with skim milk, 120g	N	2.5	0	71	300
new, peeled, boiled, 3, 165g	21	3	0	103	435
roast, no skin, 150g	26	2.5	4	159	670
roast, with skin. 150g	25	2	4	159	670
steamed, new, peeled, 165g	20	3	0	102	430
wedges, crunchy, 100g	26	4.5	6	165	695
POTATO CRISPS					
(see CORN CHIPS and SNACK FOOD)					
PRICKLY PEAR					
raw, peeled, 86g	7.5	N	0	34	145
PRUNES					
dried, 5, 38g	16.5	2.2	0	70	295
juice, 250ml	44.5	Tr	0	181	760.
stewed, with sugar, 150g	29.5	4.6	0	119	500
stewed, without sugar, 150g	18.5	4.8	0	78	330
PUMPKIN					
peeled, boiled, 85g	6	1	0.5	36	150
pie, 1 slice, 109g	29.5	3	10.5	229	960
roasted in oil with 1/2tbsp oil, 85g	8	1.5	8	125	525
seeds, dry roasted, 1tbsp	4.5	1	11.5	134	565
PURSLANE					
boiled, 1 cup, 115g	4	N	0	20	85
QUAIL					
roasted, with skin, 180g	0	0	6	180	755
roasted, without skin, 125g	0	0	20	349	1465
QUICHE					
cheese & egg, average homemade, slice, 125g	21.5	1	27.5	390	1640
lorraine, average, 100g	18	N	22	293	1230
mushroom, average homemade, 1 slice, 125g	23	1.5	24.5	352	1480
vegetable, average, 100g	20	N	18	259	1090

POTATO High in carbohydrate, potassium and vitamin C, potatoes are a great staple food – it's just the way they're cooked, and their affinity with butter and salt, that can make them unhealthy. Baking is a healthy way to cook potatoes. Boiled potatoes are also low in fat, but some of the vitamin C may be lost in the cooking water.

MASH You can make delicious mashed potatoes without too much butter. Use skimmed milk or stock, or try adding a little olive oil instead of the butter.

FRIES Fried potatoes are all fatty, but the thicker the chip, the less fat is absorbed during cooking. If you love fries, choose wedges.

RICE The main staple of half the people in the world and an excellent source of energy, rice makes the perfect accompaniment to any meal as it gives a feeling of fullness without adding fat. When mixed with legumes, rice forms a complete protein, which is particularly important for vegetarians. It is also a gluten-free alternative to bread.

WILD RICE Not a true rice, but a grass native to North America. It can be blended with brown or white rice to add a delicious nutty flavour to dishes

WHOLEGRAIN RICE This contains more fibre than white varieties. Although it can take longer to cook, it has a delicious, nutty flavour.

	CARB g	FIBRE g	FAT g	ENERGY kcal	ENERGY kJ
QUINCE					
raw, 100g	11	++	0	48	200
stewed, with added sugar, 100g	21	+	0	83	350
RABBIT					
meat only, baked, 100g	0	0	5.5	169	710
RADISH					
red, raw, 3, 45g	1	0.5	0	0.6	2.5
white, raw, peeled, sliced, 90g	2.5	1.5	0.5	15	65
RAISINS					
100g	69.3	2	0.4	272	1159
RASPBERRIES					
canned in syrup, drained, 100g	22.5	1.5	0	88	374
raw, 65g	3	1.6	0.2	16	71
REDCURRANTS					
raw, 100g	14	3.4	0	56	235
RELISH					
corn, 1tbsp	4.5	0.2	0	20	85
mustard, 1tbsp	4.5	N	0	20	85
tomato, 1tbsp	4.5	0.2	0	19	80
RHUBARB					
raw, 100g	0.8	1.4	0	7	32
stewed with sugar, 125g	14.5	1.5	0	60	252
RICE					
average, cooked, 100g	33.4	0.1	1.1	157	660
basmati, cooked, 1 serving	42	+	0.3	177	742
brown, cooked, 1 serving, 180g	57	1.5	2	270	1135
extra-long grain, cooked, 70g	54.5	0.5	0.5	232	973
fragrant, cooked, 100g	34.6	0.5	0.4	155	651
fried, 190g	56	1.1	16	413	1735
long grain, cooked, 100g	34.6	+	0.4	155	651
white, cooked, 1 serving, 190g	53	0.2	0.5	237	995
wild, cooked, 1 serving, 164g	35	+	N	165	695
RICE CAKES					
corn & buckwheat, 1, 12g	10	+	0	49	205
corn cakes, natural, 2, 10g	9	+	0	36	150
natural brown, 2, 10g	8	+	0.5	14	60
rice & rye, 2, 10g	8	+	0.5	39	165
SAFFRON					
1tbsp	1.5	0	0	6	25
SALADS					
bean salad, commercial, 1 serving, 210g	27	6.3	18	309	1298
coleslaw, commercial, 1 carton, 200g	8.4	2.8	52.8	516	1872
potato salad, 1 carton, 180g	20.5	1.4	47	517	1913
SALAMI					
average, all varieties, 50g	0.5	0	19	214	900
Danish, 4 slices, 20g	0.5	N	8	88	370
pepperoni, 4 slices, 20g	0.5	0	7	80	335
SAUCES					
mayonnaise, 1tbsp	0.1	0	13	118	495
apricot chicken, 1 serving, 118g	15	0	1	69	290
apricot chicken, jar, 1 serving, 115g	16	0	10.5	67	280
barbecue, 1 tbsp	10	0	0	40	170
beef & black bean, 115g	11	0	1.5	58	245

	CARB g	FIBRE g	FAT g	ENERGY kcal	kJ
SAUCES cont.					
bolognaise, 160g	3.5	N	14	192	805
butterscotch, 45g	15	0	17	214	900
chilli, 20g	10.5	0	0	9	40
country French chicken, 118g	5	0	11.5	126	530
creamy lemon chicken, 118g	15	0	0.7	69	290
creamy mushroom, 1 serving, 120g	6.5	0	1.5	133	560
golden honey mustard, 118g	12	0	13	170	715
gravy, commercial, 60g	5.5	0	5.5	81	340
gravy, made from powder, prepared, 60g	2.5	0	0	14	60
herbed chicken & wine, 1 serving, 115g	7.5	0	6.5	14	60
honey & sesame, 1 serving, 120g	23	0	1	108	455
honey, sesame & garlic, 1 serving, 115g	23	0	0.5	85	400
Hungarian goulash, 1 serving, 125g	7.5	0	3.5	105	440
Malaysian satay, 1tbsp	5	+	5	67	280
mild Indian, 1 serving, 115g	8	0	7	93	390
mint homemade, 1 tbsp	0	0	0	9	40
mornay, bought, 1 serving, 120g	5	0	14	161	675
onion, made from powdered mix, prepared, 125g	8.5	0	7	110	460
oyster, 1 tbsp	5	0	0	29	120
packet, average all types, 1 serving, 125g	10	0	20	263	1105
pesto, 1 tbsp	9	+	5	90	380
soya, 1 tbsp	0.5	0	0	9	40
spicy plum, 1 serving, 115g	21	N	0.5	86	360
sweet & sour, 1 serving, 115g	30.5	N	0	120	505
sweet & sour, lite, 1 serving, 115g	20.5	N	0	80	335
sweet Thai chilli, 115g	52.5	N	0.5	204	855
toffee, 1, 20g	15	0	2	80	335
tomato, 1tbsp	5.5	+	0	23	95
white, homemade, 1tbsp	2.5	+	5	27	115
worcestershire, 1tbsp	4	0	0	17	70
SAUSAGE					
beef, fried, homemade, 1, 50g	2	0.3	9	117	490
beef, grilled, homemade, 1, 50g	3	0.3	9	127	535
Bierschinken, 1, 30g	0	0	5	309	1300
black pudding, grilled, 1, 90g	6.5	+	21	281	1180
bratwurst, 100g	0	0	30	362	1520
cabanossi, 1, 30g	0	N	10	109	460
chicken, thin, 2, 50g	0	0	6	89	375
chicken, thin, low-fat, 2, 40g	0	0	3	70	295
chipolates (skinless), 2, 25g	0	0	5	55	230
Italian, cooked, 100g	0	0	30	362	1520
Chinese sausage, 100g	3	0	40	429	1800
low-fat, 1, 50g	0	0	5	75	315
pork, thick, grilled, 2, 150g	9	1	33	425	1785
pork, thin, grilled, 2, 100g	6	0.7	21.5	283	1190
Schinkenwurst, 30g	0	0	15	154	645
vegetarian, 1, 60g	4	1	4	98	410
SCONE					
fruit, 1, 50g	20	+	3	118	495
plain, average, 1, 50g	23	1	5	154	645
SEAFOOD					
baked, 85g	0	0	1	95	400

SAUCES If you are using a small quantity of a sauce like tomato ketchup, you don't need to worry too much about its nutritional value. However, some sauces, especially cheesy or creamy sauces, can be high in fat. Ready-made commercial sauces tend also to be high in salt. Where possible, make your own, healthy varieties.

COOK-IN SAUCES Can be high in fat and additives, so check the labels. Next time you make a tomato sauce, freeze half so you can add to meat or pasta for an instant dinner.

WHITE SAUCE For a low-fat alternative to this creamy sauce, use skimmed milk and replace the flour and butter with cornflour.

SEAFOOD—FRESH FISH

Nutritionists recommend eating at least two portions of fish, one of which should be an oily fish, each week. Fish is an excellent, low-fat source of vitamins, minerals and protein. Oily fish, such as salmon and mackerel, also contain omega-3 fatty acids, which may help to reduce the risk of arteries clotting.

TUNA An oily fish, tuna is a good source of vitamin D and omega-3 fatty acids. Sushi and sashimi are a delicious, low-fat way to consume very fresh fish.

TROUT An oily fish that contains omega-3 fatty acids. It is delicious baked or cooked under the grill.

SEAFOOD cont.	CARB g	FIBRE g	FAT g	ENERGY kcal	ENERGY kJ
anchovies, canned in oil, drained, 5, 18g	0	0	1.5	33	140
bass, 100g	0	0	1	93	390
blackfish, 100g	0	0	2	93	390
blue grenadier, 100g	0	0	2	93	390
blue threadfin, 100g	0	0	2	93	390
boarfish, 100g	0	0	2	93	390
bream, steamed, 1 fillet, 149g	0	0	8	206	865
calamari tubes, raw, 100g	0	0	0	69	290
calamari tubes, fried, 100g	12	N	17.5	276	1160
caviar, black, 1tbsp, 16g	0.5	0	3	40	170
caviar, red, 1tbsp, 16g	0.5	0	3	40	170
clams, 100g	0	N	2	81	340
cockles, raw, 100g	0	0	0	48	200
cod, baked, 100g	0	0	1	76	320
cod, grilled, 100g	0	0	2	95	400
cod, poached, 100g	0	0	2	95	400
cod, smoked, simmered, 1 fillet, 195g	0	0	1.5	89	375
crab, all varieties, 90g	0	0	0.5	54	230
crab, canned in brine, 145g	2	0	1	88	370
eel, 85g	0	0	12.5	190	800
eel, smoked, 100g	10	0	13	167	700
fish ball, boiled, 1, 50g	2	0	0.5	37	155
fish paste, 1tbsp, 20g	2	0	1.5	31	130
fish roe, black, 1tbsp, 20g	0	0	1	18	75
fish roe, red, 1tbsp, 20g	0	0	1.5	30	125
fish, steamed, 1 small fillet, 85g	0	0	2.5	105	440
flake, crumbed & fried, 1 fillet, 165g	10.5	+	8.5	293	1230
flake, steamed, 1 fillet, 150g	0	0	0	187	785
flathead, fried, 1 fillet, 104g	3.5	0	7	183	770
flathead, steamed, 1 fillet, 85g	0	0	1	96	405
flounder, 100g	0	0	1	67	280
garfish, 100g	0	0	2	93	390
gernfish, 1 fillet, 175g	0	0	27	393	1650
groper, 100g	0	0	1	86	360
gumard, 100g	0	0	2	86	390
haddock, smoked, 1 small fillet, 85g	0	0	1	8	35
herring, canned, drained, 125g	10	0	22.5	315	1325
jewfish (mulloway), steamed, 1 fillet, 145g	0	0	4	128	540
kamaboko, 100g	0	0	1	52	220
kingfish, 100g	0	0	3	105	440
leatherjacket, 100g	0	0	2	93	390
lemon sole, 1 small fillet, 85g	0	0	2	79	330
ling, 100g	0	0	2	93	390
lobster, boiled, 165g	0	0	1.5	159	670
lumpfish roe, 10g	0	0	1	12	50
mackerel, 100g	0	0	16	221	930
mullet, steamed, 1 fillet, 74g	0	0	3.5	99	415
mussels, 100g	0	0	2	87	365
mullet, steamed, 1 fillet, 74g	0	0	3.5	99	415
mussels, 100g	0	0	2	87	365
mussels, smoked, canned in oil, drained, 100g	4.5	0	10.5	193	810

	CARB g	FIBRE g	FAT g	ENERGY kcal	ENERGY kJ
SEAFOOD cont.					
ocean perch, 1 fillet, 120g	0	0	2.5	112	470
octopus, 100g	0	0	1	69	290
oysters, raw, 10, 60g	0.5	0	2.5	72	305
oysters, smoked, canned in oil, drained, 10, 60g	0.5	0	7	124	520
parrot fish, 100g	0	0	2	93	390
perch, 100g	0	0	1	86	360
pike, 100g	0	0	1	88	370
pilchards, 150g	0	0	3.5	157	660
pilchards, canned in tomato sauce, 225g	2	+	29	430	1805
prawn (shrimp) cutlets, fried, 3, 75g	15	+	12	218	915
prawns (shrimps), garlic, 100g	2.5	+	7.5	121	510
prawns (shrimps),, king, cooked, 100g	0	0	1	104	435
prawns (shrimps), school, steamed, 150g	0	0	1.5	114	480
redfish, 100g	0	0	2	93	390
salmon, canned in brine, drained, 100g	0	0	9.5	171	720
salmon, patty mix, 100g	0	0	7.5	202	850
salmon, pink, canned in brine, drained, 100g	0	0	6.5	146	615
salmon, raw, 100g	0	0	12	181	760
salmon, red, canned in brine, drained, 100g	0	0	12	194	815
salmon, roe, 1tbsp, 10g	0	0	1	12	50
salmon, smoked, 50g	0	0	2.5	67	280
sardines, fresh, 100g	0	0	2	67	280
sardines, canned in oil, drained, 100g	0	0	15.5	226	950
sardines, canned in tomato sauce, 100g	1	Tr	13	190	800
scallops, steamed, 160g	1	0	2.5	168	705
scampi, 100g	0	0	2	107	450
scampi, crumbed, fried, 2, 100g	0	1	17.5	314	1320
sea bream, 100g	0	0	5.5	138	580
sea perch, 100g	0	0	1	86	360
sea trout, 100g	0	0	2	93	390
shark, 100g	0	0	1	100	420
snapper, steamed, 100g	0	0	2.5	121	510
sole, 100g	0	0	1	81	340
squid, boiled, steamed, 100g	0	0	1	79	330
squid rings, fried, 125g	8.5	0	12	257	1080
trout, coral, grilled, 100g	0	0	2	93	390
trout, rainbow, steamed, 100g	0	0	6	155	650
trout, smoked, 100g	0	0	5	136	570
tuna, canned in brine/water, drained, 190g	0	0	5	234	985
tuna, canned in oil, drained, 250g	0	0	28	450	1890
tuna, steamed, 100g	0	0	3	119	500
whiting, all varieties, 100g	0	0	1	93	390
SEAWEED					
raw, average all types, 10g	Tr	1.2	0	1	4
SEEDS					
poppy, 1tbsp	2	+	4	46	195
pumpkin, 50g	5	2.6	7	155	650
sesame, 1tbsp	0	0.8	7	76	320
sunflower, 1tbsp	0.5	0.9	8	88	370
SEMOLINA					
cooked, 1 bowl, 245g	15.5	+	0	75	315

SEAFOOD—SHELLFISH
Although high in nutrients, shellfish also have a reputation for being high in cholesterol. However, cholesterol is present in all animals, and though some shellfish can have a high level, the fact that they are so low in fat, (on average less than 2%), means that they are one of the healthiest forms of protein.

OYSTERS Their reputed aphrodisiac quality can be attributed to the fact that oysters have the highest zinc content of any food, a mineral needed for growth and sexual development.

SELENIUM Shellfish contain the trace mineral selenium, a powerful antioxidant that may protect against disease, and have anti-ageing properties.

SOFT DRINKS These tend to be high in sugar and low in nutrients, and should therefore not be consumed on a regular basis. Their high sugar content also means high consumption can lead to dental caries. Small bottles of mineral water are equally easy to carry around, as are 'diet' soft drinks – although these do contain artificial sweeteners such as saccharin.

COLA With 8–10 teaspoons of sugar per can, these drinks are high in calories. Cola also contains significant quantities of caffeine.

DIET SOFT DRINKS Sweetened with artificial sweeteners, such as saccharin, these drinks may be suitable for people watching their weight or suffering from diabetes. However, mineral water is a healthier option.

	CARB g	FIBRE g	FAT g	ENERGY kcal	kJ
SHALLOT					
25g	N	0.3	0	6	25
SNACK FOOD (see also CORN CHIPS)					
bacon rings, 1 packet, 25g	N	0	6,5	124	520
burger rings,1 packet, 50g	0	1	13	249	1045
cheese & bacon balls, 1 packet, 50g	N	N	17	265	1115
cheese twists, 1 packet, 50g	30	0.5	13	249	1045
cheese potato puff type, 1 packet, 50g	30	0.5	15	258	1085
popcorn, microwave, l pack, 100g	4	1	2	32	135
potato crisps, plain, 1 large packet, 50g	25	2.6	15	249	1045
potato crisps, 1 large packet, 50g	N	2.6	16	250	1050
potato crisps, lite, 1 packet, 50g	30	3	15	258	1085
potato crisps, average all flavours, 50g	N	2.6	18	282	1185
potato twists, plain, 1 packet, 50g	N	1.3	17	258	1085
pork rind, crackling, 1 packet, 30g	N	0.1	8.5	145	610
prawn crackers, 5, 30g	N	0	2	45	190
pretzels-type, 10g	6.5	+	0.5	37	155
sesame seed bar, 1, 45g	20	+	12	167	700
SNAIL cooked, 2, 30g	N	0	0.5	29	120
SOFT DRINKS – carbonated					
(see also CORDIAL, SPORTS DRINKS AND WATER)					
cola, 375ml	39	0	0	150	630
diet cola, 375ml	1	0	0	1	5
dry ginger ale, 375ml	28	0	0	124	520
dry ginger ale, diet, 375ml	1	0	0	4	15
orangeade, 275ml	48	0	0	194	815
orangeade, diet, 375ml	1	0	0	2	10
lemonade, 375ml	40	0	0	159	670
lemonade, diet, 375ml	1	0	0	4	15
pineapple & grapefruit flavoured, 375ml	45	0	0	161	675
diet, 375ml	1	0	0	6	25
lemon & lime flavoured, 375ml	40	0	0	179	750
lime flavoured, 375ml	40	0	0	150	630
diet, 375ml	1	0	0	4	15
tonic water, 250ml	0	0	0	82	345
SORBET					
lemon, 50g	7	0	0	62	260
SOUP					
chicken, low calorie, 220ml	8	N	1	50	210
condensed, beef broth, 220ml	12.5	N	2.5	81	340
condensed, creamy chicken, 220ml	12	N	6	120	505
condensed, creamy chicken & corn, 220ml	14.5	N	7	131	550
condensed, creamy chicken & mushroom, 220ml	15	N	0	70	295
condensed, creamy chicken & vegetable, natural, 215ml	10.5	N	8	139	585
condensed, creamy mushroom, 1 serving, 215ml	7	N	8	139	585
condensed, pumpkin, 1 serving, 215ml	13	N	4	96	403
condensed, creamy minestrone, 1 serving, 215ml	15	N	0.5	74	310
condensed, creamy potato & leek, 215ml	12	N	13	180	755
condensed, minestrone, 220ml	15	+	0	70	295

	CARB g	FIBRE g	FAT g	ENERGY kcal	kJ
SOUP cont.					
condensed, mushroom, 220ml	13	N	6.5	126	530
condensed, pea & ham, 220ml	15	+	0.5	94	395
condensed, tomato, 1 serving, 220ml	12	+	0.5	57	240
instant, chicken noodle, lite, 1 mug, 200ml	5	N	0.5	29	120
instant, chicken & vegetable, 1 mug, 200ml	14	N	0	60	250
instant, chunky chicken, 1 serving, 1 mug, 250ml,	31	N	3	167	700
instant, creamy cauliflower & cheese, 1 mug, lite, 200ml	9	N	1	45	190
instant, mushroom & chives, 1 mug, lite, 200ml	5.5	N	1.5	38	160
instant, pea & ham supreme, 1 mug, lite, 200ml	9.5	N	1	55	230
instant pumpkin & vegetable, 1 mug, lite, 200ml	9	N	0.5	40	170
minestrone, reduced calorie, 220ml	10	+	0	50	210
tomato, reduced calorie, 220ml	11	1.5	0	50	210
vegetable, reduced calorie, 220ml	9	1.5	0.5	48	200
SPAGHETTI (see also PASTA)					
canned, bolognaise, 130g	12.5	1.3	0.5	68	285
canned, tomato sauce, 130g	16.5	1	1.3	87	365
canned, tomato sauce & cheese, 130g	16.5	+	1	82	345
SPICES					
average all types, 1tsp	0	N	0	9	40
SPINACH					
cooked, 35g	0.3	0.7	0	7	28
frozen, cooked, 35g	0.2	0.7	0	7	28
raw, 35g	0.5	0.7	0	9	37
SPORTS DRINKS					
isotonic type, 500ml	36	0	0	150	630
isotonic type, lite, 500ml	N	0	0	144	605
glucose type, 300ml	58	0	0	151	635
glucose type, lite, 500ml	N	0	0	100	420
SPREADS (see also HONEY and JAM)					
almond spread, 100g	19	+	54	571	2400
cheddar cheese, 1tbsp	0	0	5	60	250
cheddar cheese, light, 1tbsp	1.5	0	3.5	48	200
gherkin, 1tbsp	9.5	+	0	57	240
lemon-flavoured, 1tbsp	13	0	1	59	250
marmalade, orange, 1tbsp	9	0	0	34	145
nut and chocolate, 1tbsp	N	0	6	105	440
peanut butter, crunchy, 1tbsp	3.5	1.2	10.5	125	525
peanut butter, crunchy lite, 1tbsp	6	+	7.5	112	470
peanut butter, smooth, 1tbsp	2.6	1	10.5	125	525
peanut butter, smooth lite, 1tbsp	6	+	7.5	112	470
pickles, low-calorie, 1tbsp	N	0	0	8	35
sandwich spread, 1tbsp	6	0.2	2.5	47	195
vegemite, 1tsp	0.5	0	0	8	35
yeast extract, 1tsp	Tr	0	0	8	35
SPRING ONION					
raw, 12g	0.5	0	0	2	10
SPROUTS					
alfalfa seeds, sprouted, raw, 100g	4	+	0.5	29	120

SPICES Just like herbs, spices are used in such small quantities that they usually add little nutritional value to our diet. However, adding flavourful and fragrant spices to your food can allow you to use a lighter hand with the salt and cooking oil. Spices have also been renowned for their medicinal properties for centuries.

GARLIC This contains a compound called allinin, thought to help reduce blood cholesterol levels. Its pungent taste and smell make it a great flavouring to add to low-fat dishes.

SWEET SPICE Cinnamon, star anise and cardamom are spices that can be used to add flavour to sweet dishes. Infuse in milk, or in a syrup.

SUGAR Most healthy eating advice today focuses on eating less fat and saturated fat. However, consuming too many sugary foods and drinks can lead to both tooth decay and weight gain. Sugar is sometimes associated with 'empty calories' as it provides only energy and has no nutritional benefit.

HIDDEN SUGAR Most of the sugar in our diet comes from the sugar in confectionery, cakes, biscuits, soft drinks and other processed foods.

SOFT BROWN SUGAR This is in fact white sugar that has been coloured and flavoured with sugar cane molasses. It has no nutritional benefits over white sugar.

	CARB g	FIBRE g	FAT g	ENERGY kcal	kJ
SPROUTS cont.					
lentils, sprouted, raw, 100g	22	+	0.5	106	445
mung beans, sprouted, raw, 100g	4	1.5	0.5	31	131
radish seeds, sprouted, raw, 100g	3.5	+	2.5	43	180
soya beans, sprouted, raw, 100g	9.5	+	6.5	121	510
wheat seeds, sprouted, raw, 100g	42.5	+	1.5	198	830
SQUASH					
acorn, baked, 70g	9	2.2	0	39	165
butternut, baked, 70g	5	1	0	22	94
STAR FRUIT (CARAMBOLA)					
raw, 100g	7.3	1.3	0	32	136
STOCK CUBES					
all varieties, 1, 5g	1	0	0,5	11	45
STOCK POWDER					
all varieties, 1tbsp	2	0	0.5	19	80
STRAWBERRIES					
canned in syrup, 100g	17	0.7	0	65	279
raw, 100g	6	1.1	0	27	113
STUFFING					
average, small serving, 30g	6.5	0.5	2.5	56	235
SUET MIX					
100g	10	0	90	807	3390
SUGAR					
average, 1tsp	5	0	0	19	80
any type, 1tbsp	17	0	0	64	270
icing, 1tbsp	20	0	0	76	320
SULTANAS dried,					
1tbsp	13.5	0.5	0	55	230
SUSHI					
Californian roll, 5 pieces	N	N	2	139	585
inari (bean curd pouch with rice), 85g	N	N	2	130	545
nigiri, 30g	N	N	0.5	30	125
SWEDE					
peeled, boiled, 150g	3	1	0	16	69
SWEET POTATO					
peeled, boiled, l00g	20.5	2.3	0	84	358
raw, 1, 235g	50	5.6	0	56	237
SWEETS (see also CHOCOLATE)					
boiled, 1	5	0	0	15	65
butterscotch, 1	5.5	0	0	24	100
caramels, 1	4	0	0	24	100
fruit gums, 30g	27	0	0	8	35
fudge, 2 pieces, 35g	28.5	0	4.5	155	650
jaffas, 55g	N	0	18	245	1030
jelly babies, 1	3.5	0	0	15	65
jellybeans, 1	3	0	0	11	45
liquorice allsorts, 100g	77	2	5.2	349	1483
liquorice pieces, 100g	65	1.9	1.4	278	1185
peppermints, 1 packet	N	0	0	84	355
marshmallows, 1 packet, 85g	68	0	0	283	1190
sesame seed bar, 45g	N	+	12	167	700
sherbet lemons, 1	N	0	0	20	85
toffees, 1	3.5	0	0.5	20	85

	CARB g	FIBRE g	FAT g	ENERGY kcal	ENERGY kJ
SWISS CHARD					
raw, 30g	1	N	0	6	25
TACO					
with meat & bean sauce,					
1 serving, 180g	N	+	14	231	970
TAHINI					
paste, 1tbsp	0.2	1.6	11.8	121	510
TAMARILLO (TREE TOMATO)					
raw, peeled, 90g	4	+	0	24	100
TANGERINE					
raw, peeled, 100g	8	1.3	0	35	147
TAPIOCA					
cooked, 1 bowl, 265g	18.5	0.3	0	75	315
TEA					
for each teaspoon of sugar in tea, add ...	5	0	0	19	80
black, no sugar, 1 cup, 250 ml	Tr	0	0	Tr	Tr
with whole milk, I cup, 250ml	1	0	1	18	75
with skim milk, 1 cup, 250ml	1.5	0	0	13	55
TINNED FRUITS (see also FRUIT SALAD)					
peach & mango in syrup, 133g	12	1	0	56	235
sliced peaches in syrup, 133g	18	1.2	0	71	300
fruit salad in syrup, 125g	15	1.5	0	59	250
TOFU					
dessert, fruit-flavoured, 100g	12.5	N	1	67	280
firm, 100g	0.7	N	4.2	73	304
fried, 100g	2	N	17.7	261	1086
silken, 100g	3	0	2.5	55	230
tofu burgers, 100g	N	N	9.5	174	730
tofu veggie burgers, 100g	N	N	9.5	174	730
soya burger mix, 30g	26	+	1.3	168	704
TOMATO					
canned in juice, 250g	7.5	1.7	0.2	40	172
juice, 250g	7.5	1.5	0	35	155
purée, 1tbsp	2	0.6	0	13	55
cherry, 100g	3	1	0.4	18	76
raw, 1 large, 100g	3.1	1	0	17	73
sundried, natural, 5 pieces, 10g	5.5	+	0.5	26	110
sundried, in oil, drained, 3 pieces, 10g	2.5	+	1.5	21	90
TOPPING					
caramel, 1tbsp	11	0	0	45	190
chocolate, 1tbsp	12.5	0	0	54	225
strawberry, 1tbsp	9	0	0	39	165
TORTILLA					
corn, 1, 50g	24.5	N	4.5	152	640
wheat flour, 1, 50g	30	1.2	0.5	131	557
TRIFLE					
commercial, made with cream, 1 serving, 120g	23	0.6	11	199	837
TURKEY					
baked, lean. 120g	0	0	5	186	780
breast, no skin, 80g	0	0	3.5	20	83
breast, with skin, basted, 100g	0	0	8	145	610
1 slice	0	0	4	149	625
cooked meat, 100g	0	0	11.5	167	700

TOFU Made from soya beans, these are low in fat, high in calcium and excellent sources of protein for vegetarians. All soya products contain phytoestrogens, which are hormone-like substances in plants. Although opinion is divided, some studies suggest that these substances may help to protect women from breast cancer and symptoms of the menopause.

TEMPEH A fermented soya bean cake, this Indonesian food has a nutty taste and can be thinly sliced and grilled, or used in stir-fries.

FIRM TOFU This holds its shape well when cooked. It can be marinated and then fried or grilled, or cut into pieces and added to curries. Store in water in the refrigerator.

VEGETABLES Try to eat at least five portions of vegetables and fruit each day. Vegetables are high in fibre and are packed with vitamins and minerals. Choose from fresh, frozen, raw and canned varieties, but bear in mind that vegetables lose vitamin C if stored for a long time or are cooked for too long in a lot of water.

CARROTS Rich in beta-carotene, an antioxidant that may help prevent chronic diseases such as heart disease. Carrots are the best source as there is no evidence that beta carotene supplements have any benefit.

BROCCOLI A rich source of vitamin C and folic acid, broccoli is also associated with antioxidant properties.

	CARB g	FIBRE g	FAT g	ENERGY kcal	kJ
TURKEY cont.					
roast, dark meat, 100g	0	0	4	133	560
roast, light meat, 100g	0	0	1.5	133	560
roast, with skin, 100g	0	0	6.5	170	715
salami, 100g	0	0	4	149	625
smoked, 75g	0	0	1	80	335
TURNIP					
peeled, boiled, 240g	4.8	4.5	0	29	121
VEAL					
boneless, unspecified cut, lean, 1, 190g	0	0	5	282	1185
boneless, unspecified cut, untrimmed, 1, 200g	0	0	8	319	1340
cutlet crumbed & fried, 1	0	0	5	174	730
forequarter steak lean, 119g	0	0	6	329	1380
forequarter steak, untrimmed, 1, 200g	0	0	10.5	373	1565
heart, baked, 100g	0	0	6	181	760
kidney, grilled, 100g	0	0	5.51	167	700
leg, lean, baked, 2 slices, 44g	0	0	0.5	54	225
leg, untrimmed, baked, 2 slices, 45g	0	0	0.5	64	270
leg, steak, lean, fried, 1, 85g	0	0	2.5	131	550
leg steak, untrimmed, fried, 1, 100g	0	0	4	159	670
liver, grilled, 85g	1.5	0	7	159	670
loin chop, lean, baked or grilled, 1, 50g	0	0	1.5	73	305
loin chop, untrimmed, baked or grilled, 1, 55g	0	0	2.5	88	370
schnitzel, fried, 1, 85g	8.5	N	23	287	1205
shank, lean, simmered, 1, 80g	0	0	2	117	490
shank, untrimmed, simmered, 1, 90g	0	0	6	160	670
shoulder steak, lean, grilled, 1 small, 50g	0	0	1.5	73	305
shoulder steak, untrimmed, grilled, 1 small, 55g	0	0	2.5	84	355
VEGETABLE JUICE					
average, 250ml	11	0	0.5	51	215
VEGETABLES (see INDIVIDUAL VEGETABLES)					
VENISON					
roast, 100g	0	0	5.5	157	660
VINEGAR					
apple cider, 100ml	6	0	0	14	60
unspecified, 100ml	15.5	0	0	21	90
white, 1tbsp	0	0	0	4	15
WAFFLES					
frozen, 1 square, 35g	13.5	1	2.5	88	370
homemade, 1 round, 75g	24.5	2	10.5	218	915
WATER (see also SOFT DRNKS)					
plain mineral, soda, tap, 1 glass, 250g	0	0	0	0	0
bottled, average, all varieties, 1 glass, 250g	0	0	0	0	0
WATER CHESTNUTS					
canned, drained, 40g	3.5	+	0.5	19	80
raw, 5, 50g	12	+	0	49	205
WATERCRESS					
raw, 32g	0.5	0.5	0	6	25
WHEATGERM					
1tbsp	1.5	0.8	0.5	17	70
YEAST					
dried, bakers, compressed, 1 sachet, 7g	0.5	N	0	8	35
dried, brewers, 1 sachet, 7g	0.5	N	0.5	19	80

	CARB g	FIBRE g	FAT g	ENERGY kcal	kJ
YOGHURT					
acidophilus, live, low-fat, 100ml	11	0	0	56	235
acidophilus, plain, 100ml	8	0	3.3	24	100
bio type, acidophilus, low-fat, honey & strawberry, 100ml	13	0	3	100	420
black cherry, with live cultures, 100ml	17	0	4	104	435
drinking, apricot, 250ml	31	N	5	190	800
drinking, 100ml	13	0	1	81	340
drinking, swiss type, vanilla, 250ml	31.5	N	5	184	775
drinking, vitamin-enriched, 250ml	24	N	5	139	585
drinking, fruit, 250ml	31.8	N	5	190	800
frozen, fruit, 100ml	20	0	5	132	555
frozen, fruit yoghurt stick, raspberry, strawberry, 85ml	20	0	5	132	555
frozen, low-fat, 100ml	N	0	3	114	480
frozen, low-fat, flavoured, 100ml	22	0	0	83	350
frozen, low-fat, low sugar, 1 cone	N	0	0	45	190
frozen, fat-free, honey, 1 cone	N	0	0	109	460
frozen, reduced-fat honey, 1 cone	N	0	0	90	380
frozen, strawberry, 85ml	N	0	4	127	535
fruit cocktail, diet lite, 100ml	13	0	0.2	92	385
honey, dairy style, 100ml	11.5	0	7	132	555
kiwifruit & mango, diet lite, 100ml	13.6	0	0.2	94	395
lemon, cultured, 100ml	15	0	0	82	345
low-fat, berry, diet lite, 100ml	15	0	1	87	365
low-fat, berry fruits, live, diet lite, 100ml	7	0	0	43	180
low-fat, blueberry, diet lite, bio type, 100ml	7	0	0	43	180
low-fat, passionfruit, 100ml	16	0	0	89	375
low-fat peach, diet lite, bio type, 100ml	6.5	0	0	42	175
low-fat, peach & mango, diet lite, 100ml	15	0	2	194	815
low-fat, plain. dairy type, 100ml	6	0	0	51	215
low-fat, strawberry, diet lite, bio type, 100ml	6.5	0	0	42	175
low-fat, summer fruits, diet lite, 100ml	16	0	1	93	390
low-fat, vanilla, diet lite, bio type, 100ml	6	0	0	40	170
low-fat, vanilla, fruit & nut, diet lite, 100ml	16	0	1	40	170
plain, bio type, 100ml	5	0	4.5	95	400
plain, dairy type, 100ml	6	0	8	120	505
plain, skim milk natural, 100ml	7	0	0.1	51	215
plain, swiss style, creamy custard, 100ml	1	0	4.5	107	450
plain, traditional, dairy type, 100ml	6.5	0	35	77	325
soft serve, 100ml	16.5	0	0	80	335
soft serve, low-fat, average	N	0	0	80	335
soft serve, natural, 100ml	24	0	2	142	595
soft serve, fat-free, 100ml	4.5	0	0	21	90
strawberry delight, 125ml	20	0	4	136	570
vanilla, cultured, 100ml	19	0	4	114	480
yoghurt, cultured, 65ml	11	0	0	46	195
yoghurt, baby type, banana/vanilla, 100ml	N	0	4	107	450
yogurt, average, all flavours, 150ml	N	0	5	167	700
YORKSHIRE PUDDING					
small serve, 50g	12.3	0.5	5	104	437
ZUCCHINI					
green, boiled, 90g	1.5	1	0.5	13	55
yellow, boiled, 90g	1	1	0.5	17	70

YOGHURT The fat content of yoghurt will largely depend on whether it is made from whole or skimmed milk. It is always an excellent source of calcium and B-group vitamins. Although low-fat varieties make a healthy dessert, they may still be quite high in calories, as they often contain added sugars.

ACIDOPHILUS A live culture that can be added to yoghurt. There is evidence that it may help to restore levels of healthy bacteria in the gut after an infection or antibiotics.

DIET YOGHURT These are usually made with low-fat yoghurt sweetened artificially so that they are also low in sugar. These tend to be the lowest in calories of all the yoghurts.

The nutritional information given for each recipe does not include any garnishes or accompaniments, such as rice or pasta, unless they are included in specific quantities in the ingredients list. The nutritional values are approximations and can be affected by biological and seasonal variations in foods, the unknown composition of some manufactured foods and uncertainty in the dietary database. Nutrient data given are derived primarily from the NUTTAB95 database produced by the Australian and New Zealand Food Authority.

OVEN TEMPERATURES
You may find cooking times vary depending on the oven you are using. For fan-forced ovens, as a general rule, set oven temperature to 20°C (35°F) lower than indicated in the recipe.

NOTE: Those who might be at risk from the effects of salmonella food poisoning (the elderly, pregnant women, young children and those suffering from immune deficiency diseases) should consult their GP with any concerns about eating raw eggs.

Concept: James Mills-Hicks Designer: Peta Nugent
ISBN 978 1 74196 341 0
Printed by C&C Printing Company Ltd. PRINTED IN CHINA.